EEC
ENVIRONMENTAL POLICY
AND BRITAIN

An Essay and a Handbook

Nigel Haigh

1984

Environmental Data Services Ltd

ISBN 0-905347-50-1

Published in Great Britain 1984 by
Environmental Data Services Ltd
40 Bowling Green Lane
London EC1R 0NE

To Carola, Emily and Anna

Contents

PART THREE

* Recommended for a first reading (see Preface)

Preface

Considerable interest has been expressed in Britain in the environmental policy of the European Community. This can largely be explained by the "germ of controversy and difference about it", to use words applied to a proposed item of Community legislation by the Chairman of a parliamentary committee. British environmental policy is old and measured; Community environmental policy is young and expressed in ways only just becoming familiar in Britain. It was to explore the nature of this controversy that Konrad von Moltke, Director of the Institute for European Environmental Policy (IEEP), suggested an extended essay. The European Cultural Foundation made this possible by contributing a grant.

At that time, in 1980, I shared a view widely held - and certainly held within the Department of the Environment - that Community environmental policy had had little or no effect on Britain. As work proceeded I began finding larger effects than I had expected, and it became apparent that if the essay was to take a new line much more evidence was needed than originally I had planned to gather. A grant from the Nuffield Foundation enabled Gertrud Weber to help me for a year to assemble and analyse much of the material that forms the handbook contained in Part Two of this book. To her I am most grateful. The result is that the intended 'essay' has changed its shape and now surrounds the 'handbook'. My hope is that readers who cannot share the opinions in Parts One and Three may nonetheless find value in the information laid out in the much longer Part Two. Those wanting to skim Part Two may find most rewarding the ten sections marked by an asterisk on the Contents page.

This book would have been less useful and more difficult to write without the decision taken by the Rt Hon Tom King, when Minister for Environmental Services at the Department of the Environment, to make available the so-called 'compliance notices' by which a Member State informs the European Commission of the steps taken to comply with Community legislation. Mr Michel Carpentier, then head of the Commission's Environment and Consumer Protection Service (later to become the Directorate-General for the Environment) made available on a personal basis some of the correspondence from the Commission to the British government and enabled me to form a fuller view of certain issues.

So many people have helped with their time, with documents and with information that it would be impossible to thank them all by name. The majority, being officials, might prefer not to be identified. Collectively, therefore, I extend my thanks to many officials from central government departments (Department of the Environment particularly, but also of Transport and of Trade); from the Health and Safety Executive and the Nature Conservancy Council; from the Commission of the European Community in Brussels and its London office; from local authorities and water authorities; from the House of Commons and House of Lords; and from the London office of the European Parliament. One official I would nevertheless like to thank by name. Eric Lummis was from 1974 to his retirement in 1982 responsible at the Department of the Environment for co-ordinating the Department's dealings with the Community. He read nearly every section of Part Two in draft either while still at the Department or subsequently and, while being as discreet as British civil servants must be, pointed me in certain directions and saved me from several errors. Many other officials in Britain and at the Commission have also read and commented on drafts but any opinions, omissions and just plain mistakes remain my responsibility.

Many industrialists, representatives from trade associations, the Confederation of British Industry and the Chemical Industries Association were helpful in answering questions. Three British companies - BP International Ltd, Esso UK plc, and Johnson Matthey Chemicals Ltd - generously contributed towards the costs of publication.

Legal questions were discussed with lawyers from the Commission, from the Department of the Environment, from water authorities (conveniently assembled at a seminar by the now defunct National Water Council), with Richard Macrory, barrister, and with my colleague Pascale Kromarek, a French lawyer at the Bonn office of IEEP. The opinions expressed on compliance with Directives nevertheless remain my own, as do the views on legal matters set out in Appendix 3 and elsewhere.

The following helped with various subjects: Konrad von Moltke and Cynthia Whitehead with that most complicated but fascinating of all Directives, the 'Sixth Amendment'; Hubert Meiners with some air Directives; John Parslow, Alistair Gammell and Stuart Housden with the birds Directive; David Gilbert with pesticides; David Baldock with the less favoured areas Directive; and Annie Roncerel with documentation. Marek Mayer helped with several Directives, particularly the 'Seveso' Directive, and has given considerably more encouragement and support than an author expects of his publisher.

I wish to thank Dr M W Holdgate and the Cambridge University Press for permission to quote and to reproduce a figure from 'A Perspective of Environmental Pollution'.

Many ideas in this book have developed in discussions with colleagues at the Bonn and Paris offices of IEEP and in particular with Konrad von Moltke. Some I know I have taken wholesale and others my colleagues may not share. Our small Institute remains that rare thing in Europe, an organisation where developments in European policy are followed closely but from the point of view neither of a Member State and the interest groups within it nor yet one of the Community institutions.

Finally, I wish to thank Kate Partridge for typing everything. Our colleagues at the International Institute for Environment and Development (IIED) have provided a congenial home and have helped in various ways. It may sound confusing, but the London office of IEEP is housed in the London office of IIED and this study has been a project of both bodies.

Percy Street   Nigel Haigh
December 1983

PART ONE

PART ONE

CHAPTER 1

Two Movements Combine

British environmental policy is a deeply rooted plant which over the last ten years has shown fresh growth under a new stimulus. The year 1972 was intended by the United Nations as a turning point for environmental policy worldwide - and so it was for Britain. But what marks it as such is not so much the UN conference on the human environment held in Stockholm that year but something very different - the outcome of a movement of thought unconnected with environmental matters which by chance reached the point of decision that same year. With the benefit of hindsight it can now be seen that the passing by the British Parliament of the European Communities Act 1972 was the significant step that has changed the way an important part of British environmental policy is now thought about, is enunciated and ultimately is even put into practice.

The Stockholm conference was one of those rare official events that caught the tide of a world movement of thought. It stimulated many governments to take seriously certain ideas then gaining currency and to give attention to a subject that previously they may have neglected or not even thought about. For Britain, which can claim industrial pollution and degradation as among its inventions, the position has been different. Over a long period Britain had been legislating to protect and improve the environment, and although it is conceivable that the Stockholm conference would of itself have advanced environmental policy in Britain, it is harder to point to internal changes resulting from Stockholm than to changes resulting from membership of the European Community.

The national movement of thought that enabled the British Parliament to pass the European Communities Act 1972 did not carry all before it and the Opposition reflected this uncertainty by voting against the Bill. But whatever the doubts, the passing of the Act symbolised a shift in national posture. Formally it made effective a Treaty, signed earlier in the year, and thus enabled Britain to accede to the Treaty of Rome and to join the six original Member States and the other applicants within the European Community[*].

An event that year links these otherwise separate movements of thought. In Paris on 20 October 1972 the Heads of State or Government of the European Community made a declaration that the Community should adopt an environmental policy. The declaration would have had no significance for Britain without the almost simultaneous passage of the Act and, in anticipation of accession, the British Prime Minister attended the Paris meeting and was a party to the declaration. But equally the dec-

---

[*] The original Members were Belgium, the Federal Republic of Germany, France, Italy, Luxembourg, Netherlands. The other applicants who acceded in 1973 were Denmark and Ireland. Norway was also an applicant but rejected membership in a referendum. Greece acceded in 1981. Spain and Portugal are now applicants.

laration would never have been made without the international upsurge of concern for the environment that found expression in the Stockholm conference.

The Act was the culmination of a long and sometimes painful process of reassessment of Britain's diminished role in the world that followed the victory of the Allied Powers in 1945. Comforted by a special relationship, denied to others, with one of the two super-powers; having a permanent seat on the United Nations' Security Council; and preoccupied with transforming an Empire into a Commonwealth which many believed would continue to give it a special world role, Britain had distanced itself from the deliberations of its then much weaker continental neighbours that led to the formation of the European Community in 1957. When eventually in 1961 Britain applied for membership, the French President expressed his conviction that the British were not yet ready for entry and effectively vetoed negotiations. A second attempt in 1967 met much the same response and it was not till de Gaulle's resignation in 1969 that the Community agreed that negotiations could be opened. These were successfully concluded in 1971 and the Treaty of Accession signed and ratified the next year. On 1st January 1973 Britain thus became a member of an international body, hard to define, and possessing powers to be found nowhere else in the world. It had become part of an extraordinary development in international relations - an attempt by sovereign states to create the machinery necessary for dealing continuously with issues beyond the range of each one of them individually - machinery that has now, as a result of changing preoccupations, come to be applied in the environmental field.

As a matter of fact Britain had played a leading role after the war in the formation of various intergovernmental organisations concerned with European co-operation. Among these were the Organisation for European Economic Co-operation in 1947 (later to become OECD and originally created to administer Marshall aid), the Brussels Treaty Organisation in 1948 (concerned largely with defence), the Council of Europe in 1949 (whose hallmarks have been the fostering of Parliamentary democracy and human rights), and Western European Union in 1954 (which paved the way for German rearmament). Britain was in those years ready enough to initiate and play a part in intergovernmental organisations but had always shied away from any form of co-operation that involved a loss of sovereignty, that is to say, that had institutions able to legislate or otherwise take decisions directly affecting internal matters.

Whether because they shared the experience of discontinuity in government caused by defeat or foreign occupation; or because of a clearer assessment of the weakness of their individual roles in the world; or because the pressure of the Eastern bloc is just that much more keenly felt by some of them; or again because of a belief that only some kind of supra-nationalism could prevent another war, the six original Member States of the European Community felt no such inhibition. They had in 1951 first created the European Coal and Steel Community with supranational authority in a limited field. Then, following the collapse of the attempt to form a European Defence Community in 1954, they set about establishing closer economic integration as a way of approaching political integration. The unique character of the Community that they invented, and that Britain subsequently accepted, was its possession of institutions able to create legislation binding upon the Member States without further review or ratification and capable of being applied by a court established under the Treaty of Rome. The fields of activity of the Community are certainly circumscribed by the Treaty, but for those subjects falling within it the Member States have effectively transferred some of their own national powers to Community institutions.

When the Community* was established nobody thought that these powers should extend to the environment - since nobody thought of the environment as a subject requiring systematic international collaboration. And, it must be said, in the totality of the Community's activities, environmental policy remains a small, albeit growing, field. Nevertheless, at a time when other policies are in difficulties, the steady success of environmental policy gives it significance beyond its subject matter.

The change of heart in both Britain and abroad that led to British membership of the Community can be traced in parliamentary records. From the beginning the issue has been a matter for statesmen, and membership of the Community has been high on the political agenda and has continued to remain there since accession. By contrast, 'the environment' as a major subject, and one of international importance, has never been in issue between the major political parties, certainly in Britain, and partly for that reason has had to be forced onto the political agenda by the combined activity of writers and pressure groups working on public opinion over a period of years.

Although the word has only recently acquired its present broad meaning, the environment must always have been a human concern**. At the most basic level primitive man must have avoided fouling his own nest, and even if nature and wildlife were then more threatening than threatened, man took delight in it, as the paintings of Lascaux show us - whatever may be their intended purpose. When man began to build and his buildings became architecture, its purpose has always included 'commodity, firmness and delight', to use Sir Henry Wotton's seventeenth century aphorism. It is indeed the relegation of 'delight' to the exigencies of 'commodity' with quite such twentieth century thoroughness that has fuelled one particular strand of what we now call the environmental movement.

At its simplest the environment is what surrounds one and is firstly and foremost a local matter. So it is no surprise that the vast majority of

---

* Although it is now common to refer in the singular to the European Community there are in law three separate Communities: the European Economic Community (EEC) and the European Atomic Energy Community (EURATOM) established by two different Treaties, both signed in Rome in 1957, and the European Coal and Steel Community (ECSC) established by a Treaty signed in Paris in 1951. The institutions of these three Communities are now combined so that to refer to the Community, in the singular, reflects practical reality. Of these three Communities, it is the Economic Community that is the most important and when reference is made in this book to the Treaty of Rome it is to the Treaty establishing that Community.

** A definition used by the Commission of the European Communities is "those elements which in their complex inter-relationships form the framework, setting and living conditions for mankind, by their very existence or by virtue of their impact".

environmental issues remain ones to be handled by individuals or appropriate bodies locally. The development of local issues into national issues in Britain and elsewhere followed the industrial revolution and the growth in the population. It became evident that the resulting conflicts could not be resolved except by national legislation or by national institutions, and by the end of the nineteenth century we find many laws already in place in Britain and several of today's most important national voluntary bodies already concerning themselves with themes of today: air pollution, countryside and nature protection, open spaces, the planning of land and the protection of antiquities and historic buildings. It is doubtful whether at that time these organisations would have seen themselves as connected.and forming part of a single movement.

It is the evolution of environmental issues into international ones that concerns us here, and this came surprisingly suddenly. Although international conventions relating to such matters as bird protection had been entered into as long ago as the early years of this century, new ideas grew in the 1960s about the finite nature of the environment and the inter-connectedness of the assaults upon it. The striking image of the planet as a "little spaceship on which we travel together dependent on its vulnerable supplies of air and soil" used by former US Secretary of State Adlai Stevenson in a speech in 1965 was widely adopted as a means of emphasising that not only the conditions of life were in issue but possibly its very survival. The variant 'Only One Earth' even became the conference slogan at Stockholm in 1972 and was the title chosen for a book officially commissioned for it from Barbara Ward and René Dubos.

The origins of widespread public concern about the global implications of man's activities are often traced to the publication in 1962 of Rachel Carson's 'Silent Spring' which drew attention to the threats of worldwide pollution from the use of chemicals such as DDT. Despite the many criticisms of the book, its message that what is done locally may damage nature in distant places struck a deep chord and the book became a best seller. Concern about the finite nature of the earth's resources was also much discussed (e.g., 'The Economics of the Coming Spaceship Earth' by Kenneth Boulding, 1966) as were the misapplications of science and technology (e.g., 'Science and Survival' by Barry Commoner, 1966). The Malthusian theory of population pressing on food supply began to look as if its time had finally come, even if overpopulation was initially seen as primarily a problem of the third world. Nevertheless, pressure for population policies in developed countries also grew on the grounds that their inhabitants consumed far more energy and resources than their share (e.g., 'The Population Bomb' by Paul Ehrlich, 1968 - also a best seller).

In Europe these concerns were unexpectedly given a focus by a campaign for nature conservation organised by the Council of Europe which had designated 1970 as 'European Conservation Year'. Conferences were organised in Britain linked to the campaign and created the opportunity for the dissemination of ideas. Thus by accident a wider and more conservative audience was provided for the radical questioning of the adequacy of man's custody of natural resources and the benefits of science and technology. This questioning was one element of student unrest which marked much of the western world in the late sixties and that erupted often violently in 1968.

The theoretical message was underpinned by a number of dramatic incidents. The wreck of the oil tanker Torrey Canyon in 1967; the death of over a hundred children under a slag heap at Aberfan in 1966; the Santa Barbara oil well blow-out in 1969; mercury poisoning at Minamata throughout the 1960s; the death attributed to polychlorinated biphenyls (PCBs) of thousands of birds in the Irish Sea in 1969: all these were interpreted not just as isolated accidents but as signs of technology out of control.

Simultaneously public participation in planning was being officially encouraged in Britain (The Skeffington Report, 1969) as enough people began to doubt the unaided judgement of the 'experts' responsible for planning and development. Local groups defending familiar and well loved neighbourhoods and countryside grew in number in the face of pressures for building developments and the roads necessary for an increasingly mobile society. These many and varied local concerns began to be linked with global ones. What would be the environmental consequences of every family in Britain having a car? And if the resources were available for this, could the same possibly apply throughout the world?

A marked change in Britain can be plotted from two official documents. In 1965 the government published a White Paper (Cmnd 2764) on a 'National Plan' for Britain. It was a document running to nearly 500 pages and claiming to deal comprehensively with future development and what was needed to facilitate this process. It never mentioned the environment or the need to protect it or suggested there might be environmental or resource constraints on the developments foreseen. The word 'resources' was used extensively but only in the sense of money and manpower. By 1970 the government had published a White Paper (Cmnd 4373) called 'The Protection of the Environment: The Fight Against Pollution', and in the same year a great department of State was renamed the Department of the Environment. That year a standing Royal Commission on Environmental Pollution was also formed.

The 1970 White Paper shared a distinguishing feature of much environmental literature in setting today's activities against a broad framework of space and time:

"Profound changes in ecological systems have occurred in the hundreds of millions of years which make up geological time. But the changes were slow, and even after man's emergence about a million years ago, change continued to be very slow. Human beings were few in number and scattered, and they did not do much to their surroundings. With the explosive population growth and industrialisation of the last hundred years, all this has changed. Vastly increasing numbers of people, on a vastly increasing scale, now dig the earth to take and make what they want; they cut down forests, breed animals, grow crops, and fish the seas; and from everything that is made or eaten, pollution is generated".

It was in this climate that the United Nations developed the idea of a conference, and that Sweden volunteered to be the host country. Sweden's offer was partly self-interested because of the acidification of its lakes which it claimed was aggravated by air pollution from other countries. Despite many difficulties, the greatest being that many third world countries were not ready to accept the environment as their concern, the conference is

5

judged to have been a success. It was attended by 113 nations. Certainly the environment is now established as a major subject for attention in international organisations, and nearly all governments now recognise its importance. The right to a decent environment is now even enshrined in the constitutions of a growing number of countries as a direct result of the conference 'Declaration on the Human Environment'.

The European Community was not immune from this movement of thought and had to take the decision whether to ignore the subject, to seek an amendment to the Treaty of Rome explicitly to include environmental policy, or to give a gloss to the words of the Treaty and assume that environmental policy was implicit. The last course was chosen and in 1971 the Commission made a first communication (SEC(71)2616) about the Community's policy on the environment. One year later, as we have seen, the Heads of State and Government declared that the Community should have an environmental policy.

In making that declaration a still unresolved issue had to be faced. The Treaty of Rome calls for 'a harmonious development of economic activity' and a 'continuous and balanced expansion', while one of the arguments then being advanced (e.g., 'The Limits to Growth' by Meadows et al, 1972) was that in a finite world expansion cannot be continuous. The declaration dealt with the problem by what can, according to taste, be regarded either as a redefinition or a denial of the issue. The declaration asserted that:

"...economic expansion is not an end in itself: its first aim should be to enable disparities in living conditions to be reduced...It should result in an improvement in the quality of life as well as in standards of living. As befits the genius of Europe, particular attention will be given to intangible values and to protecting the environment so that progress may really be put at the service of mankind".

Although one impetus for the Stockholm conference had been the universal or at least international nature of environmental problems, the conference had great difficulties in handling that issue. In the 'Declaration on the Human Environment' the conference insisted on the sovereign right of nation states "to exploit their own resources pursuant to their own environmental policies" - though qualified by the responsibility not to cause damage to others.

The manner by which nation states place obligations upon one another is by the creation of international law embodied in treaties or conventions. These may have a more or less binding character but they are essentially without enforcement provisions. The actors can only be the governents of nation states and enforcement is left to them individually. Following the conference a number of conventions on environmental issues have been agreed, some of which can be attributed directly to it. The London Convention on the Prevention of Marine Pollution by Dumping of Wastes (1972) is one, and the Washington Convention on International Trade in Endangered Species (1973) is another. The Stockholm conference accelerated the creation of international law but its Declaration and its Plan of Action are largely in the nature of exhortation.

6

Given the coincidence of dates and their common origins it might be tempting to measure the Community's environmental policy against the products of the Stockholm conference, or more generally against the strands of thought that led to it. To do so would certainly disappoint many who feel the urgency of environmental problems. The sense of pressure to be found in the Stockholm Declaration is not to be found in the manner in which Community policy is proposed, agreed, and implemented. In contrast with the sometimes inspirational exhortations of Stockholm, Community policy may well appear mundane and the wheels to grind excessively small. Some of the subjects of Stockholm have hardly been touched on, and pollution, which is perhaps the easiest, has absorbed the greatest attention. Nevertheless, what the Community is now doing represents a real attempt by a limited number of nation states to deal systematically with environmental problems and is producing results with tangible effects. It is an attempt to apply one of the messages of Stockholm, that not all environmental problems can be handled by nation states alone.

As we have seen, the distinguishing feature of the Community is its possession of institutions able not only to bind the Member States to achieve certain ends, but also to ensure that the legislation doing so is enforced. What is agreed as Community policy has therefore to pass the acid test of being made to work, and this knowledge gives a sharpness of edge to discussion and sets the Community apart from all other intergovernmental bodies. If the European Community, possessed of such institutions, and composed of Member States that are so tied by links of history and culture as well as by those of trade, cannot deal with problems that transcend their boundaries, the prospect for other countries doing so cannot be encouraging. For the Community to ensure some consistency in environmental policy within its Member States and to bring the weaker up to the standards of the stronger would certainly be an achievement, but altogether a smaller one than enabling the Member States to achieve what is beyond the range of each individually. It is therefore by the test of its ability to handle issues of more than national significance, and the contribution that such a process will in turn make to the handling of global issues, that Community environmental policy will ultimately have to be judged.

To apply that test and to make that judgment now would be premature. This book provides merely a beginning by showing Community policy stretching national policy in just one country. In order to do so it is necessary first to consider what is meant by national policy and then what is meant by Community policy.

References

Boulding, Kenneth, **The Economics of the Coming Spaceship Earth**, from H Jarrett (ed), **Environmental Quality in a Growing Economy**, John Hopkins Press, 1966.

Carson, Rachel, **Silent Spring**, Hamish Hamilton, 1963 (published in USA 1962)

Commoner, Barry, **Science and Survival**, Gollancz, 1966

Ehrlich, Paul, **The Population Bomb,** Ballantine, New York 1968

Haigh, Anthony, **Congress of Vienna to Common Market – British Foreign Policy 1815–1972,** Harrap, 1973

Lodge, Juliet, **The European Community – Bibliographical Excursions,** Francis Pinter (Publishers) Ltd, 1983

Lowe, Philip, and Jane Goyder, **Environmental Groups in Politics,** Allen and Unwin, 1983

Meadows, Dennis, et al, **The Limits to Growth,** Pan Books, 1974 (first published 1972)

Nicholson, Max, **The Environmental Revolution – A Guide for the New Masters of the World,** Hodder and Stoughton, 1970

Stone, Peter, **Did We Save the Earth at Stockholm?,** Earth Island, 1973 (the complete UN conference Declaration and Plan of Action are reproduced in an annex)

Ward, Barbara, and René Dubos, **Only One Earth – The Care and Maintenance of a Small Planet,** Penguin, 1972

CHAPTER 2

What is National Policy?

"Over the last half-century or more Parliament has
passed an increasing volume of legislation, extending the
activities of government into a great number of fields,
and often involving provisions of considerable complexity.
At the same time, it has become more important to lighten
the load borne by the legislative machine".

Erskine May, **Parliamentary Practice**, 19th Edition, 1976

The growing involvement of government in the affairs of the individual
is a matter of constant comment.   The reasons are many and none is easily
reversible despite long standing calls for less legislation and now for
'deregulation'.   Among the varied reasons that have conspired since the
early years of this century to produce this result may be counted the
applications of science and technology, the acceptance by governments of all
political persuasions of the need to manage the economy and to provide for
social welfare, and the regimentation to which people grew accustomed in
two world wars.   With easier means of transport, and the increasing scale of
economic activities, larger problems - often extending far beyond national
boundaries - have demanded attention.   As government touches a topic
there must be a policy for it, and as public policies expand it becomes ever
more important to know what they are.   Although it is not the purpose of
this book to add to the discussion of what is meant by public policy, it is
necessary to establish in what way national policy is different from
Community policy if the effect of one upon the other is to be examined.
It is the purpose of this and the following Chapter to show that
national policy and Community policy are different in character: that
national policy can take forms which are varied and do not always obtrude
themselves, while Community policy has of necessity to be explicit.   It may
be objected that what is here described as national policy is not always
'national' at all, so a point must here be made that will recur in this book.
This is that, seen in a European Community context, things appear 'national'
which would not necessarily appear so when seen from within the nation
itself.   The European Community, it must be remembered, is still a
community of nation states in the sense that Community obligations
ultimately fall upon the Member States who then have to implement them.
When negotiating in the Community a government is forced to consider as
'national' what is done back home, when at home it may never have appeared
before as 'national' in the sense of being done by the national government.
It is precisely the point that national policy may be elusive, while Community
policy is not, that these two Chapters seek to make.
A recent study of the implementation of public policy, which happens
to take pollution control by way of example, defines public policy as "the
scope of activity associated with government and its agents" (1).   The

9

scope of activity associated with central government must in Britain include such matters as Bills presented to Parliament, White Papers, departmental circulars and reports, and Ministerial speeches and decisions. But in the pollution field such activity is only part of the story, since a whole range of bodies that are effectively agents of government also contribute to policy by their actions. These include the Alkali Inspectorate which has a certain measure of autonomy*, local authorities when carrying out their pollution control functions, the regional water authorities, and the various comparable bodies in Scotland and Northern Ireland. Once outside the pollution field the list can be extended.

Pollution policy in Britain has to be deduced from the intentions and activities of all these bodies. This proves in practice not always to be easy because of their independence and - finances apart - the limited extent of central government interference in their affairs. In the absence of a dispute (or a quasi-judicial appeal), central government does not always know what these bodies do in detail and would regard this, not as a criticism, but as a vindication of the principle of devolved responsibility.

This principle of devolved responsibility is not so much well understood in Britain but quite simply taken for granted. It is as well, therefore, to emphasise the principle and its practice, because they may appear quite differently in other countries and indeed have caused problems when Community environmental legislation has come to be implemented, as will emerge in Chapters that follow. Since a Community Directive places obligations on Member States and since its implementation may fall within the existing powers of a particular authority which can put the Directive into practical effect without central government compulsion, the Commission of the European Community has sometimes needed convincing that the United Kingdom was indeed implementing the Directive when the line of communication between the government and the authority has not involved a visible legal document instructing the authority to do what the Directive requires.

The principle of this independence extends in particular to local government and the arguments for it were concisely stated more than a hundred years ago by the Royal Commission on Sanitation of 1869 in words which, if one forgives their confident tone, would probably still find general acceptance today:

> "The principle of local government has been recognised as the essence of our national vigour. Local administration under central superintendence is the distinguishing feature of our Government. The theory is that all that can be done by local authorities should be done by them, and that public expenditure should be chiefly controlled by those who contribute to it. Whatever concerns the whole nation must be dealt with nationally while whatever concerns the district must be dealt with by the district."

---

*   The word 'Alkali' was, after 120 years dropped from the title of the Inspectorate in December 1982. It is now the Industrial Air Pollution Inspectorate and is formally part of the Health and Safety Executive which is a corporate body established under the Health and Safety at Work etc Act 1974.

Since much emphasis has been placed on this principle in relation to pollution control by the British government in its dealings with the Community, it is worth giving examples of the principle at work.

Devolved Responsibility – Water

The first example concerns the responsibilities of the river basin based regional water authorities in England and Wales which were established by the Water Act 1973. The Act gave them various duties, including the controlling of pollution, but simultaneously placed duties on the Secretary of State to promote a water policy for England and Wales and to secure the execution of a policy for the treatment of effluents and the 'restoration and maintenance of the wholesomeness of rivers and other inland waters'. The Secretary of State appoints the Chairmen and members of the water authorities and has the power to give them general directions as to how they are to carry out their functions. There can therefore be no doubt that, should he wish to do so, a Secretary of State could in the extreme insist on his will being carried out by a recalcitrant authority. More generally, the government can lay down policy guidelines in accordance with or even contrary to the wishes of authorities, and the example that follows shows it preferring not to do so. The story is told at length because of its importance when discussing Community water pollution policy in Chapter 7.

The novel and most significant feature of the Rivers (Prevention of Pollution) Act 1951 was that it gave water authorities (or rather their predecessors) powers to grant consent to the discharge of effluent from a new outlet to a river and to attach conditions to that consent. An Act of 1961[*] extended those powers to pre-1951 discharges, but neither Act laid down criteria for the setting of discharge consents. Quite how to maintain or restore the wholesomeness of rivers and other inland or coastal waters, which was the stated purpose of the Acts, was not explained. Not only were no specific objectives for the quality of rivers or stretches of rivers laid down in the Acts, they were not set out in the form of guidelines by central government either. It was left to the authorities concerned to work out for themselves how the obligations placed upon them were to be carried out.

As recently as 1973 it was thus possible for Mr Hugh Fish, then the Chief Purification Officer of the Thames Conservancy (now Chief Executive of the Thames Water Authority) to say:

> "It is perhaps surprising, but true, that the nation has been struggling towards cleaner rivers for twenty years without any precise instructions having been given as to the why and wherefore of the struggle. The preambles of the Pollution Prevention Acts indicate that the aim of these is to make provisions "for maintaining or restoring the wholesomeness of rivers and other inland and coastal waters". This is perhaps a clear enough statement of a

---

[*] The particular powers of the 1951 and 1961 Acts discussed here are repeated in the Control of Pollution Act 1974 and will not be affected when Part II of that Act is eventually implemented and the 1951 to 1961 Acts repealed.

vague intention. If we could establish what 'wholesomeness' really meant then we should know better what
has to be done.

"As to why the wholesomeness of waters is to be restored,
the 1951 Act gives clues in Section 5, now repealed.
Here it was stated that if river boards made byelaws for
the setting of general standards of effluent quality
(which none ever did), regard was to be paid to the uses
to which streams were put, or likely to be put, in the
future. The Water Act 1963 gives further indirect clues
on what targets for river quality should be set and
why".(2)

Chapter 7 (Section 7.8) will describe how Britain alone among the
Member States of the Community had in 1975 resisted proposed legislation -
eventually modified to become Directive 76/464 - which would have
predetermined the conditions that could be attached to discharge consents
irrespective of the quality or use of the receiving waters. The Directive
would have established the principle of having centrally fixed limit values
which discharge consent conditions (in the language of the Acts) or emission
standards (in the language of the Directive) were not to exceed for certain
dangerous substances. While it is perfectly clear that British legislation set
no such limit values and that to have adopted the principle would indeed have
been a departure from existing practice, there was nothing in British
legislation which compelled the use of the alternative tool of pollution
control that Britain finally accepted in the Directive. This alternative
involved specifying environmental quality objectives by reference to which
emission standards were to be set. But apart from the generalised duty to
maintain and restore the wholesomeness of rivers, there were no quality
objectives for rivers either laid down nationally or agreed among the various
authorities. Some authorities did have specific objectives for specific
stretches of water, such as those for the Thames Estuary, but these were not
widespread enough for Hugh Fish to feel able to say in 1973 that a national
policy existed embracing quality objectives for each stretch of river.
Chapter 5 will describe how the idea of tailoring discharges to the
capacity of the receiving water was thoroughly studied as long ago as 1912
by the Royal Commission on Sewage Disposal (3), and how the additional idea
of specifying different objectives for river quality according to their
intended use had been discussed in official reports in 1949 and again in 1970.
A Government White Paper (4) of 1970 had even promised a 'Clean Rivers'
Programme' with policies developed for each length of river throughout the
country - whatever that might mean. Nevertheless, before 1977 the
concept had neither been articulated nor elaborated to the point where
Britain could fairly have argued that it already possessed a tool for pollution
control similar to the environmental quality objectives agreed in the
Directive - although that claim is sometimes made*.
Thus it was that following agreement on the Directive a new policy had

---

* For example: "...thereby enabling Britain to continue with her present
policy of defining water quality objectives..." Foreword to the Water
Research Centre Technical Report TR17 1976 (5).

to be elaborated in Britain if the obligation laid upon the government by the Directive was to be honoured and if there was to be consistency between what was done in practice and what was said in Brussels. One way in which this could have been achieved would have been for central government to have enunciated the new policy, and even for officials to have worked it out in detail, and then for the government to have instructed the water authorities to carry it out. The policy which subsequently developed did so in quite a different way.

In 1976, the National Water Council (NWC)[*], a statutory body consisting mainly of the chairmen of the water authorities and charged with the duty to advise the government on national policy for water, invited a working party of scientific officers from the water authorities to consider the basis for existing consents for the discharge of effluents and how these should be reviewed. The following year the working party issued a consultation paper (6) recommending first a classification of the quality of surface waters in relation to the uses of those waters, and then that River Quality Objectives (RQOs) should be specified. The permissible maximum loads of pollutants in effluent discharges required to achieve the RQOs were then to be assessed and, from a knowledge of these loads, the maximum permissible concentration of pollutants in individual discharges were then to be determined as fixed figures and used in setting discharge consent conditions.

Many bodies replied to the consultation document - some highly critical of the proposal to review consents - and in April 1978 the NWC, having made minor modifications in the light of those comments, issued a policy statement (7) recommending that water authorities should set RQOs for each stretch of river. This statement was accompanied by an introduction by Lord Nugent, then Chairman of the NWC, in which he emphasised the novelty of the policy:

> "This is a major policy statement affecting the maintenance and improvement of water quality in our rivers. Taken in conjunction with the Control of Pollution Act 1974 this approach will mean that for the first time there will be published quality objectives for all our rivers and publicly available registers of the consent conditions for discharges and the results actually achieved..."[**]

In this introduction Lord Nugent also explained that Denis Howell, the Minister responsible, had endorsed the NWC's statement and had agreed to a statement of his own views being published together with that of NWC. The Minister's statement ended with these words:

---

[*]   The NWC was abolished in 1983.

[**]   Lord Nugent subsequently confirmed the novelty of the policy in a House of Lords' debate (17th April 1980 col 498): "It was my responsibility to introduce the policy of river board quality improvement in 1978, when I was Chairman of the National Water Council, and to introduce the concept to the regional water authorities of water quality objectives. We did that after very long and careful studies and discussion. There was a good deal of resistance to it..."

13

"To sum up, I see the Council's proposal, if implemented in the spirit of the document and the points made in (my) statement as being consistent with our declared aim of working for a steady improvement in the quality of our rivers."

So here we have a new national policy being made explicit in some detail, not by instructions sent down from the government to the water authorities, but by the water authorities themselves first proposing the new policy and then, after giving the interested public an opportunity to comment, publicly promulgating it. The fact that the Minister endorsed the policy served presumably to give it added authority but had he remained silent, there would be little doubt that so long as the water authorities actually did what was set out in the statement, a national policy could be said to exist. The Minister rubbed home the point: the policy would only really exist if it were implemented. It is what is done and not merely the statement of what ought to be done that constitutes national policy. (Since all the water authorities have now published RQOs for their non-tidal rivers the policy can truly be said to exist.)

Devolved Responsibility – Air

Air pollution from processes that are technically difficult to control is the responsibility of the Industrial Air Pollution Inspectorate (in Scotland the Industrial Pollution Inspectorate). A duty is placed on persons operating these processes and on the Inspectorate[*] to ensure that the processes use the best practicable means to prevent the escape of noxious or offensive gases into the atmosphere and for rendering such gases harmless and inoffensive. The phrase 'best practicable means' (BPM) has over the years acquired a particular significance, and reliance on BPM rather than fixed figures set down in statutory form has given British air pollution policy one of its special characteristics.(8) BPM has never been more concisely defended than by an assistant Alkali Inspector in 1876:

"Some persons have expressed a fear that this (BPM) is not sufficiently definite and binding on the manufacturer. For my part I feel it to be more binding than a definite figure, even if that could be given, for it is an elastic band, and may be kept always tight as the knowledge of the methods of suppressing the evils complained of increases" (quoted in (8)).

The way the elastic band is kept tight is by the Inspectorate from time to time redefining what they mean by BPM. BPM is now expressed in the form of 'Notes on BPM' published by the Inspectorate after consulting the industry affected, and these lay down numerical emission standards for pollutants from chimney stacks as well as various operating conditions for the plants in question. As technology advances the 'Notes on BPM' are

---

[*] Under the Alkali etc Works Registration Act 1906 and the Health and Safety at Work etc Act 1974.

revised and the emission standards, which are applied consistently throughout the country, are tightened.

Thus it is the Inspectorate who interpret BPM, and although it is possible for a manufacturer to challenge the Inspectorate's view in the courts, the Inspectorate have few other constraints in the exercise of their judgement and are not bound to consult the government. Once the Inspectorate satisfy themselves that some new process is practicable - that in their view it is technically feasible and affordable - they can require it to be used by new plant and can set emission standards accordingly. In other countries emission standards are often set by Statute or in Regulations made by Ministers.

The Chief Inspector's annual report for 1981 (9) gave an example of the elastic band being tightened. The Chief Inspector discussed the question of pollution by sulphur dioxide, in particular from power stations, in the context of the growing concern about transfrontier pollution and acid rain. He explained that two former power stations in London had had means - in fact the first in the world - to 'scrub' the gases with water from the Thames to remove most of the sulphur dioxide, but that the reasons for doing so had been exceptional and entailed difficulties, and that in the Inspectorate's view a general requirement to prevent SO_2 emissions would not then have been practicable. No power station in Britain has since been equipped with means for flue-gas desulphurisation (FGD) but, as the Chief Inspector explained, in the last few years FGD had been fitted to a number of plants in Japan and USA and the technical difficulties overcome. The Chief Inspector concluded his discussion with a scarcely veiled warning to the electricity generating industry that FGD was likely to be regarded as practicable for any new fossil fuelled power station to be built in Britain - and thus required by law.

Here we have a decision with considerable public expenditure implications, and dealing with arguably the most important environmental issue confronting Europe today, being taken without the involvement of Ministers but by an Inspectorate, on whom duties have been placed by law, exercising their judgement. This redefinition of what is to be regarded as 'practicable' will be regarded by some as the simple unfolding of the existing national policy that such technical matters are best left to a skilled Inspectorate. It can alternatively be seen as a major new 'national' policy initiative, and that is how it is likely to be seen from abroad. The fact that the 'government' has not been involved - and that Ministers have no powers to change the decision - is not always easy to explain.

Devolved Responsibility and National Policy

How the principle of devolved responsibility is put into practice in Britain is therefore as follows: Parliament, in deciding that a certain function needs to be performed, may place the statutory duty to carry out that function (e.g., to prevent pollution) on local authorities or other specialised agencies (which may be legal entities formally separate from the central government) and it is those authorities or agencies which will be given corresponding powers. Simultaneously a Minister may, or may not, be given reserve powers to perform that function and to adjudicate in the case of disputes, as well as the power to give guidance. Central government may, therefore, be involved but the extent of the involvement tends to be a matter of tradition bearing in mind that the statutory duty with the concomitant right to exercise discretion will lie elsewhere.

Such devolution of powers is not always practised in Britain even in the environmental field. Some subjects are clearly best handled by central government and, in those cases, national policy will be both formulated and sometimes executed by central government. An example is the decision taken in May 1981 to reduce the maximum lead content of petrol from 0.40 to 0.15 grams per litre, which is being implemented centrally by Regulations made under the Control of Pollution Act (see Section 9.3). The more recent policy of having unleaded petrol is also being pursued centrally by government. In some fields powers are divided between central and local government. Thus in the field of building conservation it is the Minister who adds buildings to the statutory list of buildings of architectural or historic interest and thereby gives them a measure of protection against alteration and demolition, but it is the district councils which designate 'conservation areas' which also give a measure of protection to the buildings within them. National policy on the conservation of buildings is therefore created partly by central government but is also moulded by the countless decisions of local authorities. Similarly, town and country planning is a function principally carried out by local government, but the Secretary of State may at any time call in a planning application for his own decision, and also has the power to amend structure plans. The government can lay down a policy framework and can try to steer the planning decisions of local authorities, but it cannot wholly control the multitude of local decisions, both because to do so would destroy the principle of devolved responsibility and because it would frankly involve too much work. Whatever policy framework is laid down by central government can to a large extent be modified by the day to day decisions of the authorities. No neat line distinguishes policy formulation from its implementation. It follows that national policy has to be pieced together like a mosaic, and depending on the subject the pieces may well be in different places. National policy is very much more than what Ministers, with the help of their advisers, decide upon.

Devolved Responsibility and the Community

The principle of devolved responsibility is to be found in all Member States of the Community, although the formal separation between central government and other authorities may well be different. In relation to pollution control, local discretion is also stated as a principle of the Community's environmental policy* and is implicit in the Community concept of 'competent authority' that we will come across in later chapters. There is, therefore, no fundamental difference of principle between Britain and other States in the Community. Differences arise, here as elsewhere, in the traditional practice in implementing this universally recognised principle, and here the degree of variation can be very substantial: it concerns essen-

---

* "In each different category of pollution, it is necessary to establish the level of action (local, regional, national, Community, international) that befits the type of pollution and the geographical zone to be protected."

16

tially the degree to which central government defines and circumscribes the scope of activity of local and other authorities by legislation or other prescriptive means; it concerns the degree of financial autonomy of those bodies; and it concerns the degree and methods of surveillance over implementation of decision-making in practice. The existence of a federal structure or other intermediate, regional bodies in some Member States adds further complexity. So do general principles of law which may exist in different countries, for example the principle of 'Rechtssichereit' found in Germany, which implies that persons affected by a legal provision or by administrative action must know in advance what to expect and must be secure in their rights for a reasonable period of time. The need for certainty and the freedom of officials to exercise their discretion will often pull in different directions. It is quite apparent that there is no ideal arrangement and that the crucial issue is whether the desired results can be achieved with reasonable effort.

In considering the consequences of Community environmental policy, it is not enough to consider effects on the environment (assuming these to be measurable), on legislation, and on the activity of various affected parties. Since Community legislation places obligations on central governments who in turn have to ensure that they are fulfilled, the process is likely to affect traditional relationships between central government and local and other authorities - an issue of considerable significance.

A point much commented upon is that the Community involves some loss of sovereignty for Member States - in practice loss of freedom for national parliaments and governments. What is less frequently noticed is that simultaneously it can also centralise into the government's hands some powers that had previously been devolved to local and other authorities. As a result of the very structure of the Community, what had previously been local government functions have to become national government functions the moment they fall within a Community policy, since the Community cannot deal with local government or other agencies. There can certainly be no question of a Community composed of nation states leading to the withering away of the nation state, but it can well modify traditional relationships within the nation state. If this process is not to be resented it must be justified on the grounds that some larger purpose is being served - in our case that a Community policy for the environment is not merely worthwhile but is necessary.

References

(1) Ruth Levitt, **Implementing Public Policy,** Croom Helm Ltd, 1980

(2) John Pickford (ed), **British and Continental Progress in Water Pollution Control,** Sixth Public Health Engineering Conference, Department of Civil Engineering, Loughborough University of Technology, January 1973.

(3) Royal Commission on Sewage Disposal, Eighth Report, HMSO, 1912.

(4) **The Protection of the Environment: the Fight Against Pollution,** Cmnd 4373, HMSO, 1970.

(5) Water Research Centre, **Technical Report TR17: Emission Standards in Relation to Water Quality Objectives,** June 1976.

(6) National Water Council, **Review of Discharge Consent Conditions: Consultation Paper,** February 1977.

(7) National Water Council, **River Water Quality, the Next Stage: Review of Discharge Consent Conditions,** April 1978.

(8) Eric Ashby and Mary Anderson, **The Politics of Clean Air,** Clarendon Press, Oxford, 1981.

(9) Health and Safety Executive, **Industrial Air Pollution 1981,** HMSO, 1982.

CHAPTER 3
What is Community Policy?

If national environmental policy is sometimes difficult to identify because it can include the intentions and actions of various agents of government, Community policy should be easier to grasp for the reason that, in the environmental field at least, the Community has no agents.

It is beyond the scope of this book to discuss what kind of agents the Community could have. In some fields it is quite possible that agents do exist, such as the Intervention Boards which carry out functions under the Community's Common Agricultural Policy and national customs officials who effectively operate the Customs Union affecting trade with other countries. But so far as concerns environmental policy, no executive agency of any kind can really yet be said to exist: there is, for example, no Community pollution inspectorate, and although an embryonic Community fund from which grants can be allocated specifically for environmental purposes exists, the sums involved have up till now been so small that the disbursement of the grants has not involved the creation of an executive agency.

Anything that is agreed as part of the Community's environmental policy is agreed by the Council of Ministers in a written text following a written proposal from the Commission. Constitutionally the Council consists of the foreign minister from each Member State, though in practice a minister with environmental responsibilities will represent him when environmental matters are under discussion. When the Council agrees to a Commission proposal the Member States take upon themselves an obligation to put the Community agreement into effect nationally. To suggest that in so doing a Member State is acting as the 'agent' of the Community would be to tread on dangerous ground, but there is no need to do so since the carrying out of a Community obligation arising out of a Community policy must be part of that Community policy. Actions taken by Member States which are not explicitly agreed as Community policy cannot be regarded as Community policy: even the most committed 'European' would be unlikely to regard Community policy as being the sum of national policies. No-one, for example, would regard the policies of 'smoke control areas' and 'best practicable means', which play such an important part in British air pollution policy, as in any sense a part of Community policy merely because Britain is one of its Member States. This would be so even if all Member States had 'smoke control areas' and pursued a policy of 'best practicable means', which they do not.

National policy and Community policy must therefore be regarded as distinct, whatever arguments there may be in favour of greater conformity. Community policy is not, as may be the case with national policy, what the Member States do but is limited to what is agreed as Community policy by the Member States and what the Member States then do to implement that policy. Community policy must therefore always be explicit.

The Council sometimes agrees that the Commission should act in international discussions and when the Commission does so it is executing –

and possibly even creating - Community policy. Matters of a technical nature are also sometimes delegated to a committee of national representatives chaired by a Commission official and empowered to make limited decisions - which are then published. Even in these instances there is always an explicit authority from the Council that the Commission should act in this way so the same conclusion holds.

From this it follows that what is not explicitly stated as part of the Community's environmental policy forms no part of that policy even if it is stated as part of some other policy of the Community. The Common Agricultural Policy and Common Transport Policy, for example, have effects, some of which impinge on the environment adversely and some beneficially. These are not considered in this book, which is confined to the effect on Britain of the Community's environmental policy as here defined.

A broad framework for the Community's environmental policy has been set out in three Programmes of Action (1,2,3) drafted by the Commission and approved by the Council of Ministers respectively in 1973, 1977 and 1982, although surrounded by a certain ambiguity. This ambiguity is to be found even in the heading to the Resolutions by which the Programmes were approved. These record them as being Resolutions not just of the Council but also of the 'Representatives of the Governments of the Member States meeting within the Council'. A clue to the meaning of this formulation is to be found in the Resolutions themselves, which note that the projects to which the programmes will give rise "should in some cases be carried out at Community level, and in others be carried out by the Member States". In other words it has not been agreed that all the items in the Programmes are to be regarded as appropriate for Community policy, but only that some may be and some may not. The Programmes can therefore only be regarded as indications of subject matter suitable for consideration as Community policy, each item of which will be decided on its merits once it has been elaborated by the Commission and transmitted to the Council for a decision. There is, however, a novel development in the Resolution on the third Action Programme (3). As well as approving the 'general approach' of the Programme, this Resolution sets out eleven priority areas for Community actions, and these eleven areas must now therefore be regarded as broad indications of Community policy.

The first two Action Programmes started off with a general statement of the objectives and principles of a Community environmental policy and then went on between them to spell out action that the Commission would propose in the following four broad fields:

- reduction of pollution and nuisances;
- non-damaging use and rational management of land, the environment and natural resources;
- general action to protect and improve the environment;
- action at international level.

The third Action Programme adds the new general heading of 'developing an overall strategy'.

The Programmes of Action are indeed very comprehensive but the instruments for putting them into effect are few. The Community can enunciate principles; it can commission studies and research; it can make grants from the small experimental fund for environmental purposes; it can set up advisory committees and otherwise exhort Member States and people within them by promoting meetings, conferences and publications; above all, it can legislate. What it cannot do itself, or through an agency, is directly to administer its environmental policies: that must be done by the Member States.

Research may be an essential preliminary but is a weak instrument of policy since its outcome is uncertain and the time between the commissioning of the research and useful conclusions is often long. A statement of principles, or any other form of exhortation, cannot be guaranteed to result in action, though it may be a necessary preliminary to it. Money is a powerful instrument of policy – and in other fields such as agriculture is of the greatest importance – but since only a tiny experimental environment fund presently exists it is not surprising that legislation is the instrument most often resorted to by the Community in the environmental field: in this field it is the most powerful. This bears repeating as the criticism is often made, at least in Britain, that there is too much Community legislation. The reason is not far to seek. Whereas the British government, once resolved to pursue a certain policy, will use administrative means and financial measures to put it into effect, and will only turn to legislation if existing legislation is inadequate, the Commission turns instinctively to legislation as the one tool that it knows will bite. British ministers and civil servants, conscious of the constraints of the parliamentary timetable, will only introduce a Bill before Parliament if circumstances make it essential, or to launch a political initiative, but if they do they will then endeavour to make it general enough to last for many years. New legislation will occupy only a small proportion of their time. Commission officials in the Directorate-General concerned with the environment, on the other hand, devote a large proportion of their time to the drafting of proposals for legislation of a quite specific character, and the agenda of Council meetings is largely taken up with these proposals. Thus it is no surprise to find that the most comprehensive report on progress made in connection with the Environmental Action Programmes and submitted by the Commission to the Council (4) is in large measure a catalogue, with commentary, of the legislative texts adopted under the Action Programmes. At times it is almost as if progress is measured by the number of items of legislation adopted, and a President of the Council – the Presidency passes from Member State to Member State every six months – will congratulate himself if he has succeeded in having a number of items adopted during his Presidency.

The legislative means available to the Community are set out in Article 189 of the Treaty of Rome and comprise: Regulations, Directives, Decisions, Recommendations and Opinions. The last two have no binding force. A Regulation is directly applicable law in the Member States and is mostly used for rather precise purposes such as the day to day management of the Common Agricultural Policy. It has so far only rarely been used for environmental purposes (see Sections 11.2 and 11.3). A Directive is binding as to the result to be achieved, but leaves to the Member States the choice of form and methods. It is therefore the most appropriate instrument for more general purposes where a certain flexibility is required to accommodate existing national procedures. A Decision is binding in its entirety upon those to whom it is addressed. In carrying out the Environmental Action Programmes the tool of the Directive has been used more extensively than any other, and therefore a study of the effect of Community environmental policy in Britain finds itself largely concentrating on them and the effect that they have had. The array of environmental Directives together with the few Regulations and Decisions effectively embody the Community's environmental policy.

Not everyone will agree with the restricted definition of Community environmental policy adopted here, but for the purposes of this book it has a very practical advantage: to assess the effect of precise legislative measures in a particular country is a task that can be undertaken with some precision, and such an assessment for Britain forms Part Two of this book. To evaluate the effect of certain broad principles and loose promises for the future contained in the Action Programmes is neither easy nor particularly fruitful. They may nevertheless exert an influence – as may any published literature - whatever views are held about their formal status. The possibility of adopting a broader definition of what should be regarded as Community environmental policy cannot be dismissed out of hand, but anyone doing so will either have to accept the limitations of a loose definition or will have the difficult task of drawing the line elsewhere.

The different meanings given to the words common (or Community) policy were discussed by the House of Lords' Select Committee on the European Communities in the context of a review of the Community's transport policy (5):

> "The Common Policy for Transport is one of four common policies explicitly provided for in the EEC Treaty of Rome* but there is no one clearly defined meaning that can be ascribed in all contexts to the words 'common policy'.
>
> Indeed, during the last decade it has become established usage in the Community Institutions to use the terms 'common policy' even with reference to sectors for which no such policy is provided for explicitly by the Treaty. For the purposes of discussion, however, it is convenient to distinguish three levels of meaning. First, the term 'common transport policy' can be regarded as meaning the overall Community jurisdiction and the right to legislate in this field. Secondly, the term can be taken to mean the objectives to be achieved. Thirdly, the term can be used to refer to the measures, such as Regulations, Directives and Decisions, which constitute the means by which the objectives are achieved. All three levels of meaning are found in discussions in the Community Institutions."

These three levels of meaning can be applied to environmental policy. Since there is no explicit provision for Community environmental policy in the Treaty of Rome, the first level of meaning mentioned in the Lords' report remains an area of some uncertainty and is a major exception to the proposition above that Community policy must be explicit. The subject has

---

*   The other three are common policies with respect to agriculture, commerce (Article 3) and vocational training (Article 128).

been discussed elsewhere (6,7,8) and will not be touched on in this book.

The second level, consisting of the objectives to be achieved, can be regarded as effectively provided by the Action Programmes on the Environment. A discussion of the third level and how it is implemented in practice constitutes Part Two of this book.

Implementation

The importance of implementation was emphasised in the Lords' report in the rather portentous sentence following the passage quoted above:

> "Unfortunately, there can be no assurance that the spokesmen of other Member States will necessarily share the British view that policies are not being 'implemented' in any real sense of that word unless the measures introduced to attain the objectives are being effectively enforced."

This suspicion that other Member States do not adequately enforce Community legislation is by no means confined to Britain, but since this book is concerned with Britain only incidental comments can be made about implementation elsewhere. A particular justification for studying implementation of Community legislation is that the chain between the legislator and action on the ground is one link longer than is the case with national legislation. This is because Community Directives can only become effective after first passing through the step of national legislation. One result is that Community legislation is not drafted by the body that will ultimately be responsible for implementing it.

In the national context it is parliaments which usually pass legislation, but that legislation is in practice often drafted by the government department that will have to implement it. On the other hand, although in the Community context it is the Council that formally agrees the legislation, and although it is the Commission that proposes the draft, it is not the Commission that will be responsible for actually implementing it: that is a matter for the Member States. The draftsman is therefore likely to feel less responsible for the consequences of his draft. In fact, the process of discussion of proposed legislation in the Council and in the working groups of officials who prepare material for decision by the Council - meeting behind closed doors of course - is to a large extent a struggle by national representatives to ensure that Community legislation is compatible with their own national legislative and administrative practices. In other words it is an attempt to ensure that Community legislation can be made to work or be enforced. Inevitably compromises have to be made and countries may well find themselves accepting commitments before their internal institutions are ready. Implementation is therefore likely to be uneven, and it is no surprise to find that many countries have been late in implementing environmental Directives. Britain has been no exception.

Linkages between National and Community Policy

In the discussion above a distinction has been drawn between Community policy and national policy. They have been shown to be different in character but they are very far from being totally separate - so much so that it becomes increasingly difficult to discuss one without discussing the other. When the Council adopts a Directive it becomes Community policy and simultaneously the Member States undertake to make it part of their national policies. What is agreed as Community policy inevitably becomes part of national policy. On the other hand the converse holds true only to a limited extent. What is national policy in one Member State may remain just that, but it may initiate and ripen into Community policy which will in turn become national policy in the other Member States. Although national and Community policies are distinct, there is nevertheless a continuous interplay between them.

Community policy is not therefore something that always flows first from the fountain-head of the Commission, notwithstanding the power of initiative that it holds by virtue of the Treaty. Discussion on policy has a way of leaping between the States and the Community institutions so that a matter which starts as a national issue may become 'Europeanised' and so in turn becomes an issue in other Member States. A topical example is provided by the question of lead in petrol (see Section 9.3), which first became a European issue as long ago as in 1971 as a result of proposed German legislation severely restricting its use. After many years' discussion in the Community institutions, which inevitably involved discussion in national institutions too, the matter eventually became the subject of a Community Directive in 1978. It subsequently became a national issue again, this time in Britain. National manoeuvres involving a public campaign and a report from the Royal Commission on Environmental Pollution eventually resulted in a request from the British government in 1983 to amend the Directive, so that the issue is once again on the European agenda. In many other fields national policies and Community policies are similarly intertwined.

This interplay between the Member States via the medium of the Community is by no means easy to follow and probably for that reason is still poorly understood even by those involved in making policy or trying to influence it. Partly this is because of the unjustifiable secrecy that so much surrounds Community policy making, and partly because of the natural reluctance of governments to admit that they have been influenced by other governments despite their readiness to claim influence the other way round. There is neither an easily accessible public record which can make manifest this interplay nor are there entirely reliable witnesses to it.

The difficulty in following this process could to some extent be eased by a greater knowledge of the two formalised linkages that exist between national and Community environmental policy. These linkages are provided by the so-called 'information agreement' under which Member States alert the Commission to proposals for national legislation, and the so-called 'compliance notices' which the Member States must send to the Commission explaining the steps taken formally to comply with a Directive.

The 'information agreement' was made even before the First Action Programme on the Environment[*] and requires Member States to transmit relevant proposals for legislation and administrative measures to the Commission, whereupon the Commission may within two months decide that the matter is appropriate for action at Community level. The Member State

---

[*] See OJ C9 15.3.73 and OJ C86 20.7.74.

24

must then suspend its own proposal for five months while the Commission drafts Community legislation. If the system works effectively the Commission should always be aware of developments in national environmental policy, and simultaneously the Member States are provided with a mechanism for initiating Community policy. Unfortunately only the Commission benefits from the information provided, since no reports analysing the information or even describing it have ever been published. The most that has ever been revealed is the numbers of notifications[*].

The 'compliance notices', by contrast, come after Community legislation has been agreed, and their purpose is to provide the evidence to enable the Commission to decide whether or not the Member States have taken all the formal steps necessary to comply with a Directive. (These steps may involve introducing new legislation or regulations or adopting administrative measures). Again only the Commission benefits from these 'compliance notices', since the Commission does not make them public nor, in general, do the Member States. The general availability of 'compliance notices' would go some way to removing an unnecessary element of secrecy in Community policy and would also provide the raw material to enable any Member State to check any accusation that another Member State is not complying with a Directive. It cannot, however, demonstrate that the national legislation is being enforced.

To its credit the Department of the Environment of the British government made available 'compliance notices' for the purposes of this book and simultaneously decided that anyone with an interest could have access to them. Part Two of this book would not have been the same without this decision. It now seems possible that other Member States may do likewise, in which case the character of explicitness which marks Community policy will extend as well to the links which bind it to national policy.

References

(1) **First Programme of Action on the Environment,** Official Journal of the European Communities, Vol 16, No C112, 20.12.73.

(2) **Second Programme of Action on the Environment,** Official Journal of the European Communities, Vol 20, No C134, 13.6.77.

(3) **Third Programme of Action on the Environment** (1982-1986), Official Journal of the European Communities, Vol 26, No C46, 17.2.83.

(4) **Progress made in Connection with the Environment Action Programme and Assessment of the Work Done to Implement It,** Communication from the Commission to the Council, COM(80)222, 7.5.80.

(5) House of Lords, Select Commitee on the European Communities, **EEC Transport Policy,** 43rd Report, Session 1977-78.

(6) Konrad von Moltke: **European Communities: the Legal Basis for Environmental Policy,** Environmental Policy and Law (3), 1977.

---

[*] See Introduction (para 7) to the Second Action Programme (2) and reply to European Parliamentary Question OJ C86 8.4.80.

(7) House of Lords, Select Committee on the European Communities, **Approximation of Laws under Article 100 of the EEC Treaty,** 22nd Report, Session 1977-78.

(8) House of Lords, Select Committee on the European Communities, **Environmental Problems and the Treaty of Rome,** Session 1979-80.

CHAPTER 4
Tools for Pollution Control

The tools for pollution control that we have encountered in Chapter 2 - namely emission standards and environmental quality objectives - are only two of those available and several others have also been used in Community legislation.

As a result of the dispute between Britain and the other Member States concerning the best means for controlling pollution of water by dangerous substances, a misconception has developed in Britain. The idea has gained currency that the Commission and other Member States have a particular preference for uniform emission standards as the principal tool for pollution control, while only Britain has insisted on setting emission standards individually by reference to environmental quality objectives. While this may fairly describe the positions adopted by the various parties over the disputed part of Directive 76/464 (see Section 7.8) it does not fairly describe the positions taken over the rest of the Directive, and it becomes an oversimplification and positively misleading once it is extended to pollution generally or even generally to water pollution. To argue that there are two paths which are in some sense opposed, and that Britain has long been committed to one and the other Member States to another, is both to misrepresent British practice - as will emerge in Chapter 5 - as well as to misrepresent the complexity and variety of Community pollution legislation that has been agreed by all Member States. This chapter therefore outlines the range of pollution control tools that have been used in Community legislation so as to provide a context for the discussion of the Directives that follows in Part Two of this book.

Pollutants have been defined by Holdgate (1) as substances causing damage to targets in the environment. The pollutant may be emitted from a source into the environment, through which it travels along a pathway till it reaches a target. The target may be man, or animal or plant life, or an inanimate structure (e.g., the stonework of a cathedral). It follows from this definition that if the pollutant reaches no target in damaging quantities because it has been rendered harmless either by being transformed into another substance or into a form where it cannot affect the target or because it has been diluted to harmless levels, then there has been no pollution.

It also follows that the mere emission of a potential pollutant to the environment does not necessarily constitute pollution and that to eliminate pollution one does not have to restrict emissions to zero.

Figure 1 illustrates the journey of a pollutant from source to target diagrammatically. To quote Holdgate:

"...the concentration a pollutant attains at a point is the resultant of the quantity of the input to the environment (from whatever pattern of sources, at whatever distance), the dispersion characteristics determined by

27

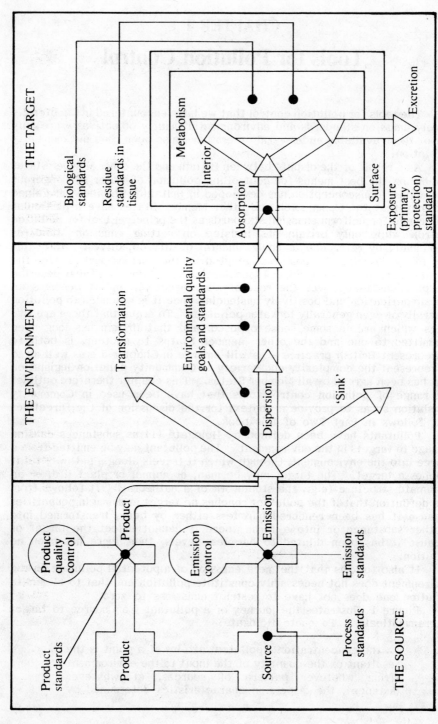

Figure 1: Possible points on the pollutant pathway at which standards or objectives may be set (Reproduced, with permission, from M W Holdgate, 'A Perspective of Environmental Pollution', CUP 1979)

the properties of the pollutant (density, solubility, diffusion co-efficient) and those of the medium (current direction, rate of flow, rate of inter-mingling, absorption properties) and the rate of removal from the environment at all points along the pathway, whether caused by physical or biological agencies...Where emissions of a substance to the environment are tolerated, controls need to be adjusted so that targets are not unduly hazarded (just what constitutes undue hazard depends on the nature of the target and the value set upon it)".

Figure 1 shows possible points along the pollutant pathway at which standards or objectives may be set as tools for control. The points may be at the source, in the environment, or at or in the target itself. For the purposes of the present discussion it is immaterial whether the standards are set with legally binding force or are merely guidelines, and the words 'standards' and 'objectives' are used in this Chapter rather loosely and interchangeably. When it comes to controlling pollution in the real world there is a vast difference between what is legally enforceable and what is only a guide, but these differences need not concern us in this chapter. (Fuller definitions are given in Appendix I which discusses the terminology used in the Directives.)

Let us take by way of example a fairly common pollutant which is known to present a hazard to human health and examine the possible tools for controlling it.

Lead can reach human beings from a number of sources. Lead occurs naturally in soil and is taken up by food plants; lead is washed from the soil into river water, from where it enters into water supply and so reaches the household tap; lead is discharged to rivers from sewage works and factories; some houses have lead plumbing which may dissolve if the water has certain properties; lead is found in paint which can be chewed by children or can flake and be picked up and swallowed; lead is emitted into the air from lead works and can be inhaled or it can settle as dust on food or on the soil where it is taken up in food plants; lead is put into petrol and is dispersed with vehicle exhausts throughout centres of population.

Some of these sources are natural and so difficult or impossible to do anything about, while others are clearly within the power of man to control. The pathways from the sources to the target include air, water, and soil, sometimes in combination.

As part of its environmental policy the Community has agreed Directives which seek to control lead at a number of points along its pathways to man or other targets. Let us consider these under the headings of the different tools for control shown in Figure 1 starting at the target and working backwards along the pathways:

1 Biological Standards

The Commission in 1975 proposed a Directive setting lead levels not to be exceeded in the human bloodstream. In the event this proposal was modified into a Directive designed to gather information about blood lead levels in the population at large and in critical groups (see Section 9.4). The Directive no longer sets a biological standard in a legally binding way but does set certain reference levels which indicate that too much lead is present.

The advantage of a biological standard as a tool for control is that it covers the combined effect from all sources at the point where it matters, that is at the target to be protected, but it suffers from the difficulty that it provides a signal only when the pollutant has already reached the target – possibly in excessive amounts. The Directive deals with this problem in these words:

> "When the results of the analyses indicate that the reference levels have been exceeded in one or more cases, Member States shall take action to trace the exposure sources responsible for the levels being exceeded (and shall) take all appropriate measures..."

Whatever remedial measures are appropriate must be taken somewhere further back along the pathway, since it is not possible to take any control measures at the target itself except by removing the target from the pathway – such as by moving children away from homes near lead smelters.

2 Exposure Standards

One control point further back along the pathway is the point of entry to the target. The standard here is called an 'exposure standard' or, in some circumstances, a 'primary protection standard'. By agreeing a Directive setting standards for the quality of drinking water (see Section 7.4), including the maximum concentration of lead permitted, the Community has sought to ensure that the amount of lead swallowed with water is limited. Water supply can be tested and the water treatment or supply system adjusted to ensure that the standard is met. A standard where the exposure is by breathing is set in a Directive on air quality standards for lead (see Section 9.5). Yet another Directive limits the quantity of lead, among other substances, in animal feedingstuffs (Directive 74/63 OJ L38 11.2.74).

3 Environmental Quality Standards

Going yet further back, standards can be set at a number of points in the pathway through the environment. One Directive sets a quality standard for surface water from which drinking water is to be abstracted (see Section 7.2). If the constituents of river water, including lead, exceed a given concentration, then that point in the river must either not be used at all for abstracting drinking water or, in other cases, the treatment given to it must be of a specified kind. Other environmental quality standards for water have been set by Directives, including ones for bathing water (Section 7.7), and water supporting freshwater fish and shellfish (Sections 7.5 and 7.6) and although these could have included standards for lead they have not done so. In the case of the freshwater fish and shellfish Directives, the targets could have been regarded as either the fish and shellfish themselves or the humans that consume them, although it emerges that the Directives are not intended primarily to protect man. The Directive on air quality standards for lead (Section 9.5), classed above as an exposure standard, can also be classed as an environmental quality standard.

30

As with biological and exposure standards, the breaching of an environmental quality standard does not provide an immediate indication of the action to be taken, but serves only as a signal that the pathway to the target contains too much of the pollutant.

Environmental quality standards may be expressed numerically as concentrations of substances, e.g., in water or sediments, or in air, but it is also possible to have generalised quality objectives expressed in words relating to the use of the environment, e.g., suitable for the passage of migratory fish at all times, or suitable for the abstraction of drinking water. Different usages of the terms 'quality objectives' and 'quality standards' are described in Appendix 1. Chapter 5 describes the evolution of quality objectives for water in Britain.

4 Emission Standards

A pollutant may be emitted to the environment at point sources as from an outlet pipe to a river or from a chimney stack to air, or alternatively in a diffused way, e.g., through the ventilation system of a factory, or from the exhausts of innumerable motor cars, or again by the diffused application of a herbicide or fertiliser to land. Only where the pollutant comes from a point source is it possible to set an emission standard at that point.

Emission standards may be set individually for each discharge, or uniform standards for a particular class of discharge may be applied across a whole area or country or even the Community. Directive 76/464 (see Section 7.8) requires all discharges to water of certain listed dangerous substances to be subject to emission standards but does not specify numerically what the emission standards are to be. Instead, limit values (i.e., upper limits) for these emission standards are to be laid down in subsequent (or daughter) Directives for certain particularly dangerous substances set out in a List I, but for possibly less dangerous substances, set out in a List II, emission standards are the responsibility of the Member States. Since lead appears on List II and not on List I, the Community has no plans for setting emission standards for lead discharged to water, but this does not mean that Member States are not circumscribed by Community legislation. As we have seen, the Community has already laid down an environmental quality standard for surface water that is to be abstracted for drinking, and any emission standards laid down in Member States must be such that those quality standards are met at the abstraction points.

It is only for the List I substances that the Commission is to propose limit values which emission standards are not to exceed, but even here the Directive allows Member States the alternative of setting emission standards locally so long as environmental quality standards set by the Community are met, and it is this alternative that Britain has chosen. By following this alternative the emission standard will depend on a number of factors including the capacity of the receiving environment, the environmental quality that will have been prescribed for it, and the quantity and quality of other emissions to it.

Emission standards may be set numerically (either in legislation or administratively) as so many parts of a substance per million of effluent or per unit of productive output. Alternatively an obligation may be placed on the discharger to use the 'best practicable means' or 'best technical means available' for reducing emissions (see Section 9.0 for a discussion of these terms).   As we have seen in Chapter 2, this approach is used in Britain for air pollution, and as technology improves the emission standard will be progressively tightened.   To make this system workable the Industrial Air Pollution Inspectorate sets numerical emission standards (called 'presumptive limits') which certain emissions to air are not to exceed, and these are revised from time to time.

5 Process or Operating Standards

Within a factory emitting a pollutant to the environment standards may be set relating to production methods, either to protect workers or to ensure that the minimum amount of pollutant is eventually discharged to the environment.   In Britain, the Industrial Air Pollution Inspectorate prescribes methods of operating plants to minimise emissions.   Such standards have so far not formed part of the Community's environmental policy, though Directive 82/605 has been agreed as part of the Action Programme on safety and health at work to protect workers from lead (OJ L 247 23.8.82).

6 Product Standards

The product of a manufacturing process may itself give rise to pollution when in use, or upon disposal, in addition to any pollution that may have been caused during its manufacture.   Accordingly product standards may be set to control the composition or construction of the product.   One example is the Directive setting standards for the lead content of petrol (Section 9.3).   Other examples are the Directives concerned with the composition of detergents (Section 7.1) and with emissions from motor vehicles (Section 9.6).   If drinking water is regarded as a product then the Directive on the quality of drinking water (Section 7.4) – classed above as an exposure standard – could also be regarded as a product standard.

A special case of a product standard is a total prohibition on the use of a substance for specified purposes such as that contained in the Directive restricting the use of polychlorinated biphenyls (see Section 10.2) to closed circuit electrical systems and some other limited applications.   The use of lead has not been banned in this way.

Although not strictly setting product standards, a number of Directives require certain products to be packaged and labelled in specified ways so as to minimise risks to the environment (see Section 10.1 and 10.5).   One such Directive requires paints containing more than a certain quantity of lead to be appropriately labelled (Directive 77/728 OJ L303 28.11.77).

In addition to the six standards applied at the control points shown in Figure 1, other forms of control are also possible such as the two described below.

7 Standards for Total Emissions or the 'Bubble'

Rather than setting emission standards for each source of pollutant from a plant it is possible to set an upper limit for all emissions irrespective of origin.   In the USA this is known as the 'bubble' concept: a notional bubble is drawn around a plant or area and an upper limit is put on the total amount of a pollutant allowed to pass into the bubble. Thus if a manufacturer succeeds in reducing his diffuse discharges he may emit more through a chimney stack and vice versa. The concept can be extended to an area covering several manufacturers in which case market forces may lead them to sell and buy among themselves the right to emit pollutants so long as the total does not exceed that prescribed. Thus a new manufacturer may have to pay existing polluters to reduce their emissions in order to create the 'space' for himself. This is also known as the 'emission offset policy'. The concept can be extended to a whole country or even to the whole Community or indeed globally. The Netherlands, for example, has set a target upper limit for the emission of sulphur dioxide and the Community has set an upper limit on the total production, and thus effectively the emission, of chlorofluorocarbons (see Section 10.4). A total emission limit for such a useful and versatile material as lead is obviously inappropriate.

8 Preventative Controls

The controls described above are all tools for limiting existing pollution rather than trying to anticipate and so prevent it. Community preventative controls include one Directive, known as the 'Sixth Amendment' (see Section 10.1), which requires the potentially toxic effect of chemicals to be identified before they are marketed. Another, known as the 'Seveso' Directive (see Section 10.3), requires manufacturers to identify and take steps to forestall the risks to the environment from a major accident. A proposed Directive on the environmental assessment of development projects (OJ C169 9.7.80) requires systematic identification of the threat of pollution from a planned development and consideration of alternative sites where the polluting impact might be less.

* * * * * *

This catalogue of available tools for controlling pollution shows that the Community has used them all - though not necessarily all of them for the example of lead that we have chosen. The use of one tool does not exclude the use of others and they are usually used in combination with one another to provide a network of protection.

In particular, this catalogue shows that several environmental quality standards have been set at Community level and that the Community has agreed that all Member States should set emission standards for discharges to water of the dangerous substances listed in Directive 76/464 (section 7.8). The essential point of the dispute between Britain and the other Member States that arose during negotiations on Directive 76/464 concerned the proposal that for certain particularly dangerous substances limit values for emission standards should be set centrally at Community level rather than allowing emission standards to be set nationally or locally to take account of local circumstances. So far only two emission standards have been set for use throughout the Community (concerned with mercury - see Section 7.10 - and cadmium) and a concession was made for Britain so that these do not have to be observed so long as specified environmental quality objectives are met.

The dispute is usually and rightly seen as concerned with the most practical and economic means to achieve an end on which all are agreed, but underlying it there are also differences in pollution theory. For those who believe that the purpose of pollution control is to prevent targets from being unduly put at risk, then the best points for controls are those nearest to the target. The reasons for exercising controls further back along the pathway are then practical: it simply may not be possible to exercise controls anywhere else. Viewed in this way emission standards are merely a means to achieve quality objectives which in turn are set to protect identified targets, and these emission standards need be no more stringent than required to meet those quality objectives. The emission standards will therefore quite logically vary from place to place.

For those who believe that man should emit the least possible quantity of pollutant, even if it is having no known effect[*], then the point of emission is the logical point to set the controls and they should be as stringent as technology permits: controls further down the pathway then serve only as checks that pollutants are not in fact reaching vulnerable targets, possibly from diffuse sources that are not controlled by emission standards. According to this view of pollution control there is no objection to uniformly fixed emission standards - although there may well be objections in economic theory since 'as stringent as technology permits' begs a number of questions and uniform standards may not result in the best use of financial resources.

These alternative views are not always made explicit and are not always held consistently even in one country. In Britain, air pollution control has if anything been founded on the second view, since there is a duty to use the best practicable means (BPM) to prevent the escape of 'noxious or offensive gases' whether damage is being done or not, and the emission standards that form part of BPM are set nationally and applied with some consistency throughout the country (see Section 9.0). In contrast, water pollution control in Britain has evolved so that it is now firmly founded on the first view with an emphasis on achieving quality objectives by setting emission standards locally - though Chapter 5 will show that this has not always been the case.

Although differences in pollution theory are important, the dispute between Britain and the other Member States over water pollution has in practice been much more concerned with administrative convenience and economic competition, both of which need a word of explanation.

The administration of centrally fixed limit values may well be easier than emission standards set by reference to quality objectives, firstly when granting authorisations and, secondly, when monitoring to ensure compliance. When authorising a discharge to water using the limit value approach the presumption will be that the emission standard will equal the limit value - unless there is an obvious reason for it to be more stringent - and so the authority is spared the difficulty of calculating the emission standard by first defining a quality objective (if none already exists) and

---

[*] An extreme statement of this view is that by J Davis quoted in Holdgate (1): "When damaging pollutants are identified, they must be stopped ...No longer are we going to depend on nature's assimilative capacity to take care of the problem. Even in remote areas where discharges have been allowed, we will no longer allow it...We simply do not know enough about the science of ecology to predict the results and we must be sure. The only way to be sure is to stop the pollutants at source - to keep them inside the factory fence".

then taking into account the existing quality of the river, volume of flow, and the number, quantity and quality of other discharges. Indeed, one of the arguments against variable emission standards is that quality objectives do not provide a complete guide for allocating the permitted pollutant load between dischargers. When a river crosses a frontier between authorities – which may be within a Member State or may be a national frontier – the administrative advantages of uniform emission standards become greater since the tricky problem of allocating the permitted pollutant load is eliminated. When monitoring to ensure compliance it may also be easier simply to sample the actual discharge to ensure that the emission standard has not been exceeded than to sample the receiving waters at a number of points to ensure that quality objectives have not been exceeded and, if they have been exceeded, then to try to determine which of a number of discharges was responsible. Furthermore, the concentration of the pollutant will be higher in the discharge than in the environment and so easier to measure – indeed in the environment it may be below the limit of detection.

These are the practical advantages of limit values. The economic arguments in favour are not that the approach results in the best use of economic resources but that all manufacturers are treated equally. In relation to air pollution, this has been stated in Britain by a former Chief Alkali Inspector:

> "It is to the trade's advantage to have uniformity of
> application of control measures and it would be unjust to
> give one works a commercial advantage over another."(2)

The advantages of setting emission standards individually by reference to quality objectives are threefold. First, controls will be most stringent where the environment is most vulnerable. This not only ensures protection of the environment but also provides economic incentives to industrialists to locate where the environment is best able to cope with the discharge. In theory industrialists will consequently choose of their own volition, other things being equal, to locate on a large river or an estuary rather than a small tributary. (If the limit value approach is pursued single-mindedly without regard for the receiving environment it would be possible to discharge into a small stream and to destroy all life in it while remaining within the limit value.) Secondly, the monitoring of the river which is essential to ensure that the quality objectives are being maintained, ensures that non-point source discharges are taken into account and not just direct discharges. Thirdly, abatement will not be more burdensome than is necessary and limited financial resources can then be applied where they produce the maximum benefit.

Since Britain has short fast rivers and is washed by a turbulent and tidal sea, there has been an obvious argument of economic self-interest for Britain not to accept emission standards set by reference to what is necessary to protect, say, the Rhine, which drains many industrial areas and which is used as an important source of drinking water by Germans and Dutch. Since many of Britain's most polluting industries have chosen to locate on estuaries and drinking water is abstracted upstream, it can plausibly be argued that to set emission standards as stringent as those needed for a river that is to be used for drinking water is to fly in the face of the economic principle of comparative advantage: Britain for pollution purposes, it can be argued, is well favoured by geography just as for transport purposes or, more facetiously, for the purposes of growing lemons, it is disadvantaged by geography. Since Italian lemon growers take advantage of the sun that geography brings them, and grow lemons rather than engage in some other activity for that very reason, and since German industrialists benefit from proximity to continental markets as a result of geography, so also it is argued that Britain should quite properly profit from the ability to locate industries on estuaries or on the coast where acute pollution problems are less likely to arise and where the sea water can assimilate or destroy the pollutants.

The opposing arguments for limit values and for quality objectives that came to a head with Directive 76/464 have had the effect of forcing Member States into camps, with Britain often alone in one. But it would be a mistake to suppose that the two approaches are totally incompatible and that Britain and the other Member States have pursued one to the exclusion of the other. In Britain, as in other countries, policy has not always been single-minded, and elements of both approaches have been used for both water and air pollution. In developing national positions for the purposes of the debate in the Community there has been a tendency - not entirely excusable, it must be said - to play down the elements that do not fit the negotiating position adopted so that a distorted picture emerges. Nationalism, even of a benign kind, and regard for the facts have never been easy bedfellows.

In the next Chapter we take up the story partly told in Chapter 2 and describe how both fixed emission standards and quality objectives were considered in Britain for water pollution control, and how under the stimulus of Community legislation Britain felt its way towards a more coherent policy of river quality objectives.

References

(1) M W Holdgate: **A Perspective of Environmental Pollution**, Cambridge University Press, 1979

(2) F E Ireland: **Control of Special Industrial Emissions in Britain**, Proceedings of the Second International Clean Air Congress, Academic Press, 1971.

CHAPTER 5

River Quality Objectives in Britain

The dispute between Britain and the other Member States on the relative merits of centrally fixed limit values for emission standards as against setting them locally by reference to quality objectives has many aspects: it concerns pollution control theory; it concerns administrative tradition; it concerns economic theory; and it concerns economic self-interest. In Chapter 2 we saw the adoption by the water authorities of River Quality Objectives in 1978 as an example of the extensive discretion granted to administrative agencies in Britain, and in Chapter 4 we touched on aspects of pollution control theory and the related economic arguments. The way these aspects link together only serves to emphasise the difficulty underlying this important dispute over water pollution policy. Water pollution is of course only a part of the Community's environmental policy, but in no other field have quite the same difficulties arisen nor have the government's views been raised in quite the same way to the status of dogma. Since there are those who have argued that environmental quality objectives have long been British policy and practice for water pollution[*], it is necessary to examine that policy rather more fully than in Chapter 2 to see in what way that is so and what effect if any Community policy has had upon it. That is the purpose of this Chapter.

How to maintain water quality and how to control emissions to it are problems which have exercised British policy makers for over a hundred years, and some of the arguments used today in Community discussions turn out to have been rehearsed many times before. The major landmarks in the evolution of this policy are set out below, and, since the courts had been struggling with the problem long before legislators and administrators intervened, we begin with the role of the common law.

The Common Law

The English common law, that is to say the legal principles developed by the courts through case law, and not expressed in a code or in statutes, is today still very much relied upon to protect water against pollution, despite extensive legislation. The owner of a river bank can bring an action in the civil courts, technically for nuisance, and claim damages and an injunction if there is an infringement of his right to have the water of the river reach him unaltered from its accustomed quality and quantity. The statement of the

---

[*] E.g., a leading article in The Times which claimed that "The preferred British method of statutory pollution control, most recently embodied in the Control of Pollution Act which was passed last year, is to set quality objectives for the environment.." (15th October 1975). Also the foreword to the 1976 Water Research Centre Report TR17 referred to in Chapter 2.

law regarded as definitive (1) is that of Lord Macnaghten in the case of **Young v Bankier Distillery Co** (1893):

> "A riparian proprietor is entitled to have the water of the stream, on the banks of which his property lies, flow down as it has been accustomed to flow down to his property, subject to the ordinary use of the flowing water by the upper proprietors and to such further use, if any, on their part in connexion with their property as may be reasonable under the circumstances. Every riparian proprietor is thus entitled to the water of his stream in its natural flow, without sensible dimunition or increase and without sensible alteration in its character or quality. Any invasion of this right causing actual damage or calculated to found a claim which may ripen into an adverse right entitles the party injured to the intervention of the court."

The common law is therefore primarily concerned with the quantity and quality of the river water rather than of the discharge into it, and if the riparian owner can show that there has been sensible alteration in the river quality he may bring a case against the discharger. The composition of the discharge is relevant only as evidence of a causal connection between the discharge and the interference with his rights.

It can therefore be argued that the English common law has from time immemorial provided an environmental quality objective for all stretches of river water: there is to be no sensible alteration from 'its natural flow'. The right has not degenerated as a result of modern legislation into a matter to be found only in text books because, following a successful common law action in 1948 by a landowner against Luton Corporation for polluting the River Lea, the Anglers' Cooperative Association was formed with the sole purpose of fighting pollution by making use of the common law and thus keeping it alive. The Association encourages angling clubs to become leaseholders and thus to acquire riparian rights. As a result anglers bring a number of cases before the courts each year[*]. The fact that riparian owners have not always defended their rights is easy to show since the ideal quality objective of a 'natural flow' has not everywhere been maintained in England. Indeed, as the right is a private one and the riparian owner can be bought off by the discharger, it has provided no basis for public policy. The common law does however embody the idea that it is the quality of the river itself that matters more than that of any discharge.

The Rivers Pollution Prevention Act 1876

The first statute making it a criminal offence to pollute any British river was the Rivers Pollution Prevention Act 1876, although local Acts had existed earlier. This Act dealt with sewage and industrial effluents sepa-

---

[*] Anglers are ever watchful that legislation does not take away their common law rights and their vigilance should extend to Community legislation too.

rately and did not prescribe emission standards, although an earlier Royal Commission on River Pollution had recommended them (2).

Sewage could only be discharged if the 'best practicable and available means to render harmless the sewage matter' had been used. Industrial effluents, however, were virtually prohibited: it became an offence to allow to flow into any stream 'any poisonous, noxious or polluting liquid proceeding from any factory or manufacturing process'. Quite what constituted a polluting effluent was left to the courts to decide. Since enforcement would have led to the closure of many industries, the Act limited the circumstances under which the law could be enforced and made it virtually unenforceable in districts which were the 'seat of any manufacturing industry'. The effect of this must have been to create two regimes: non-industrial areas where the law was enforced, and industrial areas where it was not*. This fortuitously provided a rather crude manner of setting environmental quality objectives according to the use to which water was put: a river in an industrial area where the water was already polluted and clearly unsuitable for use as drinking water or fish life would remain polluted and be used for drainage and navigation, whereas upstream where the river was clean it could have been protected for other uses.

In addition to the 1876 Act, a number of local Acts protected specific rivers. The non-tidal parts of the rivers Thames and Lea, for example, were from the nineteenth century positively protected as sources for London's drinking water. Again this can be regarded as a rather generalised environmental quality objective.

The Royal Commission on Sewage Disposal 1896-1915

This Royal Commission carried out many original investigations, published a total of ten reports, and is now chiefly remembered for its Eighth Report of 1912 which set standards for discharge of sewage to rivers which are still in use today**.

The Royal Commission showed that "the nuisance-producing power of a normal sewage or effluent is broadly proportional to its power of deoxygenating the water" and proposed as a test of the quality of rivers and sewage effluent the amount of dissolved oxygen taken up in five days (now called the Biochemical Oxygen Demand and abbreviated as BOD_5). This test is now widely used throughout the world and appears as a standard in Community Directives***.

---

*   This is speculative but plausible. There appears to be no full history of British water pollution control, though there is a brief historical introduction in Louis Klein's three volume work on River Pollution (Butterworth 1962). The 1876 Act remained in force until 1951 and there must still be people who remember how it operated.

**   The complete text of the Eighth Report is reprinted in Newsome and Sherratt (1)

***   This is despite the reason the Royal Commission is believed to have chosen five days: they thought it the longest residence time of any particle of water in a British river.

A number of rivers were classified by the Royal Commission according to the appearance which they presented to observers and corresponding BOD_5 values of the river water were then measured and averaged to produce the following table:

Quality	BOD_5 values (mg/l)[*]
Very clean	1.0
Clean	2.0
Fairly clean	3.0
Doubtful	5.0
Bad	10.0

A BOD_5 of 4.0 was regarded as being just free of signs of pollution, and the Royal Commission accordingly concluded that sewage discharged to any river should always be treated sufficiently to ensure that the river quality did not fall below this limiting figure of 4.0.

The Commission then considered the relative merits of setting environmental (or river) quality standards and emission standards (although they did not use these terms):

> "A chemical standard can be applied in any one of two ways - either to the contaminating discharge by itself or to the stream which has received the discharge. Since our main objective is primarily the improvement of rivers, and only secondarily the improvement of effluents, it would seem logical that standards should be applied not to sewage liquors or effluents alone but to such discharges under ordinary conditions, i.e. when mixed with the river water.

> "On this principle it would be sufficient to apply the dissolved oxygen test to the river water at a point where it has received and mingled with the polluting discharge. The standard would be fixed at 4.0 and if the mixture should yield a figure exceeding the standard, then the sewage liquor or effluent would have to be improved."

The Commission set out a method for making the calculation to achieve the standard of 4.0 in the river and gave some worked examples: if the river was itself of quality 1.0 and provided a tenfold dilution of the effluent, then the quality of the effluent would have to be no worse than 34; if the river was itself of quality 2.0 and provided an eightfold dilution, then the quality of the effluent would have to be no worse than 20.

So here we have a concise exposition of the procedure for setting emission standards by reference to a river quality objective. The Commission went on:

---

[*]   The units used by the Commission were grams of dissolved oxygen per 100,000 cubic centimetres of water. These are here translated into the units commonly used today: milligrams per litre.

"A system of standards framed on these lines would at first sight seem to effect by the simplest means the object which we have in view, viz. that a local authority should not be required to incur further expenditure on sewage disposal than the circumstances of the area require".

Having argued for emission standards set locally in accordance with a river quality objective, the Royal Commission then recoiled from their own suggestion using arguments that are familiar to anyone involved in today's debate in the Community in respect of dangerous substances:

"...such a system generally applied would be open to three serious objections:

(a) It would be very difficult to administer
(b) It would distribute the burden of purification un-
    equally as between different authorities in the same
    watershed
(c) It would go further in the direction of differentation
    than is necessary to ensure economy."

The second of these objections was expanded as follows:

"(b) In the ordinary case of a river receiving successive pollutions at intervals along its course, the quality of the water would tend to deteriorate from source to tideway, unless the intervals should be so wide or the influx of clean tributary water so great, as to permit the river to recover naturally from the effects of one pollution before it received the next. To comply with a standard applied to the mixture of sewage liquor and river water the quality of the discharge would have, broadly speaking, to vary inversely with the quality of the river water. Thus more purification would be required of the lower of the two towns because less was required of the higher. The rigid enforcement of such a standard might cause hardship to the communities lower down the stream, while those higher up were treated with needless leniency."

It is precisely this argument that is used today in countries bordering the Rhine with respect to industrial discharges. (They can point to a major weakness of relying on quality objectives in that it provides no complete guide on how to allocate the permitted pollutant load between various dischargers.)
Having now recommended against:

"...a system by which a degree of purification required of each separate discharge is determined automatically by the quality and the relative quantity of the waters receiving it",

the Commission resolved its dilemma with a magnificent compromise:

41

"...one normal standard should be fixed which would be suitable for the majority of places, and provisions should be made for fixing one or two higher or lower standards to meet cases in which a different standard could be justified."

The normal standard[*] the Commission recommended for an effluent was a BOD_5 of 20 which mixed with eight times its volume of river water of a BOD_5 of 2.0 just met the limiting river quality of 4.0. This standard was chosen pragmatically: it could be achieved by existing techniques; it did not assume too clean a river to start with; and most discharges were diluted more than eight times anyway. The standard was to be set by Statute or by Order and was to apply to all sewage discharges except where a 'Central Authority' could be satisfied that local circumstances justified a special standard.

Perhaps because of the difficulties in creating a mechanism for making exceptions, this recommendation was never enacted as law. The Royal Commission is now remembered for the technical standard it proposed, but the arguments leading up to the standards are often forgotten so that its report is now called upon both in support of a uniform emission standard and in support of emission standards locally determined by reference to the receiving waters. In truth it supports both to some extent and in doing so provides a cautionary tale for the advocates of a single path in today's debate in a European context: it may be that water pollution control is just too complicated a subject for one system to be applied in too inflexible a manner and to the exclusion of others.

Despite never being given legally binding force, the Royal Commission standard nevertheless proved extraordinarily effective. Most sewage works were built to comply with it, though exceptionally more stringent standards were required, such as at the Luton sewage works following the successful common law action in 1948 mentioned above.

However relevant the Royal Commission's deliberations may still appear today, one element was certainly missing. There was no suggestion that different stretches of river should have different quality objectives prescribed for them according to the use to which they were put. The Royal Commission effectively considered only one quality objective (i.e., that the river was to be just free of signs of pollution) and therefore did not describe the system as it is understood today, involving specified quality objectives for a number of different uses. Nor did the Eighth Report deal with anything other than biodegradable sewage. It was the Ninth Report of 1915 which dealt with industrial effluents and that firmly recommended uniform emission standards, though with the possibilities of more stringent standards in special circumstances:

"We think it generally desirable to aim at securing uniformity of treatment for those engaged in any given branch of industry rather than at providing for preferential treatment in those cases where merely local conditions would seem to warrant a relaxation of the ordinary requirements."

---

[*] The Royal Commission also recommended a standard for suspended solids of 30mg per litre. The two standards are often referred to together as the 30/20 standard.

This conclusion is the very opposite to the position now adopted by the British government in its dealings with its Community partners, and British officials, if they know of it, presumably think it just as well that the Ninth Report has been quite forgotten.

The Hobday Report 1949 and the Rivers (Pollution Prevention) Act 1951

It was to be another twenty years before the problem of setting emission standards was taken up again by an official committee, this one appointed specifically to consider strengthening the 1876 Act. The resulting Hobday Report (3) discussed the need for some uniformity for standards for industrial discharges; the need for industrialists to know where they stood; the difficulty of setting standards nationally; and the need for different qualities to be achieved in rivers according to their uses which the report specified: domestic supplies, industrial use, fisheries, agricultural use, navigation, or for general amenities. In attempting to reconcile these conflicting requirements, the report recommended that River Boards should be able to make bye-laws prescribing emission standards which must be complied with either for the whole river or for stretches of it; i.e., uniform emission standards for the stretch of river in question. The bye-laws would have to be confirmed by the Minister of Health who would provide a national overview. This was enacted in Section 5 of the Rivers (Pollution Prevention) Act 1951 but as only two bye-laws were ever proposed and these were not confirmed, this provision of the 1951 Act was repealed ten years later. Paradoxically, Section 5 also required River Boards to consider the uses to which the river was put, and this requirement thus also disappeared with the repeal of the Section.

Nevertheless, Britain can fairly argue that the idea of emission standards laid down and applied uniformly over stretches of river, or whole rivers, was put to the practical test of being allowed for in legislation for ten years, and failed that test. The legislation was complicated so whether that test was a fair one is difficult to say.

The more enduring part of the 1951 Act was the ability to grant discharge consents subject to conditions*. Hugh Fish in 1973 described this as 'the mainspring of the success of the Act' and as being 'substantially unique to this country' (4). This was the essential tool for a policy of setting emission standards individually.

The 1951 Act also introduced the general duty to maintain or restore the wholesomeness of rivers which can be regarded as a very generalised quality objective.

The Jeger Report 1970 and the 1970 White Paper

River quality was looked at again by an official working party which published its report (the Jeger Report) (5) in 1970. It stated what it understood policy and practice then to be:

---

* This provision of the 1951 Act was inspired by a similar provision in the Lee Conservancy Act 1928.

"The river authorities have the general duty of maintaining or restoring the wholesomeness of rivers, but there is no common standard which they have to require for the effluent discharged to rivers. No standard has been fixed by statute because the character and use of rivers vary so greatly. The river authorities are expected to impose consent conditions with the particular conditions and uses of each river in mind. For example, rivers used for public water supply will in general require effluents of a higher quality than those not so used. We agree that it is not desirable, nor indeed practicable, to have a uniform standard for effluents in this country, and favour the system adopted of relating consent conditions of individual effluents to the particular receiving water".

The lesson of the failure of Section 5 of the 1951 Act had been learnt but the idea of explicitly specifying environmental quality objectives for stretches of river as a guide to the setting of emission standards was not yet the practice. The originality of the Jeger Report for our purposes is that it recommended just that. It wanted a more positive national policy to ensure freshwater **quality** integrated with the forward planning for water **quantity** (the Report's emphases). This was to be achieved by placing a statutory duty on the authorities to assess the quality of the waters in their rivers, **and the standards of quality required related to the uses** of the rivers (our emphasis). Although the Jeger Report did not use the phrase 'river quality objectives' or 'river quality standards', the concept was there.

A White Paper (6) in 1970 said that the Jeger Report together with a survey of river conditions would "enable the Government and the River Authorities to develop policies for each length of river throughout the country", and that the government would also be in a position to undertake a 'Clean Rivers Programme'. These rather cryptic statements confirm that in 1970 it was still a novelty to introduce river quality objectives. The 'Clean Rivers Programme' was either forgotten or the name abandoned and, as we have seen in Chapter 2, it was not till 1978 that a national policy was established of having river quality objectives laid down for each stretch of river.

The Water Act 1973 and the Control of Pollution Act 1974

The opportunity to implement the recommendation of the Jeger Report that there should be a statutory duty to prepare river quality objectives came with the Water Act 1973 and the Control of Pollution Act 1974. Although the 1973 Act hints at the idea rather vaguely[*], the Control of Pollution Act, where this idea should properly have found a place, is wholly silent.

The result is that there is today no British legislation authorising or

---

[*] Section 24 requires Water Authorities to prepare "a plan of action...for the purpose of securing more efficient management of water...including the meeting of future demands for water and the use of water and restoring or maintaining the wholesomeness of rivers..."

requiring quality objectives comparable to the French Water Law of 1964 and the subsequent French Ministerial circular of 29th July 1971, where the phrase 'objectifs de qualité' appears and is precisely explained. Had there been such legislation, Britain would have been in a rather stronger negotiating position when the Commission made the proposal in 1974 that became Directive 76/464. The state of official thinking on the subject of river quality objectives at the time can be judged from the report of a DOE Committee (7) dated February 1973 and publicised by means of a circular two years later. This committee had considered water quality criteria for different uses (potable water supplies, agriculture, amenity and recreation, fishery and wildlife, and industrial requirements), but took the matter no further than saying that:

> "as so many parties are interested in water quality for
> different purposes, for example as abstractors, as
> dischargers, as being involved in river basin management,
> occasionally with conflicting interests among them, there
> is a need for publication of guidelines on water quality
> applicable to conditions in the United Kingdom..."

This amounts to a statement that the environmental quality objective idea was desirable and confirms that it was not yet formalised in Britain at the time that Directive 76/464 was being proposed. The concept certainly existed but it had been enunciated only in a vague form and certainly without effective statutory backing. On the other hand, the idea of uniform emission standards certainly had no support.

The Commission in proposing what became Directive 76/464 was responding to pressures (see Section 7.8), and no careful evaluation of the difficulties of establishing limit values for emission standards throughout Europe seems to have been made in advance. Equally, the British government was in a curious position in opposing the limit value part of the proposal. Its own policy was in a state of evolution: uniformly fixed emission standards had earlier been considered but never adopted, but quality objectives had not been explicitly laid down by reference to which emission standards could be individually tailored. The individual tailoring had been done in an ad hoc way, perhaps often with success, but nevertheless in a manner rather difficult to explain. It would be difficult to find a better example of the stereotype of British pragmatism (a succession of actions without guiding principle that somehow seems to work) offending the susceptibility of those from countries with tidier habits of thought. No wonder there was so much irritation.

The historical outline above shows that the idea of tailoring discharges to the quality of the river was clearly understood by 1912, and that the further idea of river quality objectives for rivers had existed in a vague form and had permeated British thinking at least since the Hobday Report of 1949. The Jeger Report and the 1970 White Paper suggested that the idea might be formalised more precisely, but the opportunity to enshrine it in national legislation - which would have been one way of overcoming the inertia created by the difficulties in being explicit - was not taken when it presented itself in 1974. Lord Nugent, then the Chairman of the National Water Council, explained the difficulties encountered in introducing river quality objectives in 1978:

"We did that after very long and careful studies and discussion. There was a good deal of resistance to it, because of course, among other things, it has committed all of the regional water authorities to define precisely what the objectives are for the different length of river for which they are responsible..." (House of Lords, 17th April 1980, col 498)

Whether it was the legal obligation of the Directive that provided the stimulus to overcome the difficulties that Lord Nugent described, or whether it was some other reason, cannot be proved. Arguably, explicit river quality objectives would have been forced on Britain by the provisions of the Control of Pollution Act 1974 requiring public registers of consent conditions for discharges in order to justify how these were set. But the very slowness of the evolution of the quality objective idea, the resistance created by the practical difficulties, the lost opportunity of the 1974 Act, and the fact that in 1983 the registers are still not open, all taken together with the British reluctance to set principles down on paper, may lead one to doubt it. It is also possible to imagine the Control of Pollution Act being fully implemented without quality objectives. Certainly the dates fit the hypothesis that water authorities were encouraged by central government to adopt explicit quality objectives in order to comply with Community legislation and in order for there to be consistency with the British government's posture in negotiating that legislation, and in particular in resisting the limit values of Directive 76/464. This at least is the opinion of two senior British officials (now both retired):

"Whatever one's views of the desirability or otherwise of the Directives, they are undoubtedly resulting in a fresh look at the whole water cycle. In particular they have shown a need in the UK to define and refine more clearly the concept of environmental quality objectives for fresh, estuarial and coastal waters."[8]

"It was, I believe, the uniform emission standards' policy of the EEC which provoked us into formulating a coherent system for controlling emissions by reference to their effect upon the receiving water and its required use."[9]

For one Directive to have provoked Britain into formulating a 'coherent system for controlling emissions' is, given the difficulty of the subject and the slowness with which policy has otherwise evolved in Britain, a significant effect indeed.

Although Directive 76/464 has probably caused more controversy in Britain than any other environmental Directive and has therefore deserved special attention in these introductory chapters, it is not the only one to have had an effect in Britain. Of course many will have had only little effect, but there are others that have also had major effects. This will emerge from a consideration of each item of environmental legislation that follows in Part Two of this book. In Part Three we draw general conclusions.

References

(1) George Newson, QC and J G Sherratt, **Water Pollution,** John Sherratt and Son Ltd, 1972.

(2) G M Richardson and A I Ogus: **The Regulatory Approach to Environmental Control,** Urban Law and Policy 2 (1979), pp 337-357.

(3) **Prevention of River Pollution,** Report of the Rivers' Pollution Prevention Sub-Committee of the Central Advisory Water Committee (the Hobday Report), HMSO, 1949.

(4) John Pickford (ed): **British and Continental Progress in Water Pollution Control,** Sixth Public Health Engineering Conference, Department of Civil Engineering, Loughborough University of Technology, January 1973.

(5) **Taken for Granted,** Report of the Working Party on Sewage Disposal (the Jeger Report), HMSO, 1970.

(6) **The Protection of the Environment: the Fight Against Pollution,** Cmnd 4373, HMSO 1970.

(7) **Second Report of the Steering Committee on Water Quality,** H.S.Tricker (Chairman). Issued with Department of the Environment Circular 20/75, HMSO.

(8) T A Dick, **EEC Directives and the Aquatic Environment – Setting the Scene,** Institute of Water Pollution Control, Scottish Branch Symposium, 15th March 1978.

(9) D H A Price, **The Changing Scene: the Twelfth J B Croll Memorial Lecture,** Journal of the Institute of Water Pollution Control Vol 79 (1980) No 2.

References

(1) Department of the Environment, Water Pollution Control Engineering, HMSO, 1970.

(2) Klein, L., River Pollution 2: Causes and Prevention, Butterworths, 1962.

(3) Prevention of River Pollution, Report of the River Pollution Survey sub-committee, HMSO, 1949.

48

PART TWO

HANDBOOK

CHAPTER 6
Scope of the Handbook

The conclusion reached in Chapter 3 that the Community's environmental policy is effectively embodied in items of Community legislation leads to the framework adopted in Part II of this book. Its purpose is to set out these items in such a way that their effect on Britain can be assessed. Accordingly, all Directives, Regulations and Decisions which can reasonably be described as forming part of the Community's environmental policy and are capable of having an effect on Britain have been listed and analysed. The result is a handbook. A list of legislation relating to the environment but which has been excluded for reasons outlined below is contained in Appendix 2.

Matter Included

To be useful a handbook should be complete, but there are always difficulties in deciding what constitutes completeness. The guiding principle adopted here has been to include everything listed by the Commission as part of its environmental policy as well as other items that are clearly environmental in their purpose and which can have affected British environmental policy. The comprehensive report that the Commission communicated to the Council in 1980 on progress made in connection with the Environmental Action Programme - COM(80)222 - did not, for example, list the Directives concerned with the composition of detergents (presumably because they originated before the Action Programme) but they are nevertheless included here (Section 7.1) as their purpose is certainly connected with water pollution and they have affected water pollution policy in Britain. A marginal case is the Directive on hill farming which is not strictly a part of the Community's environmental policy but of its agricultural policy, and for that reason can only be analysed in the context of an assessment of the Common Agricultural Policy which forms no part of this book. It has nevertheless been included for reference (Section 11.4) since it includes countryside protection as one of its objectives.

It must be emphasised that the material here presented is designed to enable an assessment to be made of the effect on Britain of the Community's environmental policy, and not of the effect on the British environment of the Community's policies generally. That would be an altogether different and larger task - if indeed it is possible at all.

Nearly all the items of legislation included are Directives, but in addition there are a few Regulations and Decisions. A number of Decisions that appear in the Commission's lists (e.g., in COM(80)222 and in lists subsequently made available) have not been included either because they are of an essentially administrative nature, e.g., Decisions 75/441 and 77/795 requiring the supply of information respectively about air and water quality, or because they deal with accession to international Conventions. Some of these Conventions cannot directly affect Britain (e.g., the Barcelona Convention which relates to the Mediterranean) but others which could do so turn out already to include Britain among the signatories. The accession by the Community to a Convention to which Britain is already a party is unlikely to affect Britain's obligations under the Convention, although it may well affect Britain's powers to develop policies in the field covered by the Convention and to negotiate developments to the Convention. The Decisions by which the Community accedes to Conventions therefore raise legal and even constitutional issues of some importance but which are outside the scope of this book. It would be a mistake to say that these Decisions have no effect on the future of Britain's environmental policy, but the nature of the effect, if any, is oblique and is not one that can easily or even very fruitfully be assessed. Some Conventions dealing with wildlife protection with which the Community is involved are included for reference in Section 11.3.

The Commission also includes a number of non-binding instruments in its lists of environmental measures (e.g., the Recommendations on recycling paper, and on protection of the architectural heritage), but since no effect of these can be observed they too have been excluded. Two Recommendations relating to the important Polluter Pays Principle have been excluded because Britain already subscribed to the principle in a general way, as has been discussed in a House of Lords report (1).

The exclusion of certain items that appear in the Commission's list is therefore a matter of judgment with which not everyone will agree. However, in the three years that this study has taken the Community's environmental policy has been discussed with a very many people, none of whom referred to the excluded matter as having been influential in Britain.

Timing

All subject matter not published in the Official Journal by 31st December 1982 has in general been excluded. However, where a Directive that is here described has subsequently been amended by a Directive published during 1983 before the end of October, the amendment is noted. Other relevant items published in 1983 before the end of October are listed in Appendix 2.

Setting the cut-off date at the end of 1982 has meant that some important Directives such as that on cadmium discharges to water (Directive 83/513 OJ L291 24.10.83) have been excluded. A related and equally important Directive on mercury discharges which was published in 1982 has however only been summarised and not analysed (Section 7.10). This is because it forms part of a group of Directives which need to be considered together.

Structure of Handbook

The handbook is divided into six Chapters each dealing with one of the subject matter areas into which Community environmental policy can conveniently be divided. Each Chapter is in turn divided into sections dealing with each item of Community legislation or group of items, and is preceded by a section outlining the relevant British legislation. The section on British legislation is not intended to be complete but only to cover the same ground covered by the Community legislation, its purpose being to position the Community legislation in a British context and to enable an assessment to be made of the extent to which the British legislation already implements the requirements of the Community legislation.

(a) Summary of Directives

Each section starts with a summary of the Community legislation. Ease of comprehensibility has sometimes had to be sacrificed for completeness where a particular Article proves to be contentious or particularly significant for the subsequent discussion. As any summary of legislation is bound to do some violence to its intended meaning, the reader should always refer to the Official Journal for a definite statement of the law.

(b) Development of Directives

The development of each Directive is then described to the extent that this is possible. This has been done by reference to the public record, including:

(1) the original typescript proposal from the Commission accompanied by an explanatory memorandum and bearing a 'COM' number, e.g. COM(79)834. The same proposal is subsequently published in the Official Journal but without the benefit of the important explanatory memorandum;

(2) the report of the relevant Committee of the European Parliament;

(3) the debate in the European Parliament and its formal opinion;

(4) the opinion of the Economic and Social Committee;

(5) the report of the House of Commons' Select Committee and debate in the House (if any);

(6) the report of the House of Lords' Select Committee and debate in the House (if any).

The elaboration by the Commission of its original proposal is likely to have been known only to a limited circle, and the subsequent negotiations in the Council, and in the Council working groups that prepare material for decision by the Council, are confidential. Parliamentary discussion may nevertheless provide some reflection of the discussions taking place in the Council machinery and of the amendments being made, and may also point to difficulties that are being foreseen for the future. The Minister, for example, in reply to a debate in Parliament will often describe the current position on a proposed Directive including the amendments already agreed. Particularly useful is the evidence that is usually published with the House of Lords' reports recording the views of the major interested parties at a particular date, including that of government officials. The government also makes a practice of submitting explanatory memoranda to Parliament, and these too shed light on the process and the government's opinion at a particular time.

The Parliamentary record in other countries has not been examined as part of this study, and such an examination could well yet reveal more about the development of various Directives than is recorded here. The Federal Republic of Germany and Denmark have parliamentary procedures for the systematic review of Community proposals, but it is widely recognised that in no other country are such proposals so systematically scrutinised publicly in Parliament as in Britain, so that the material examined for the purposes of this study is likely to have covered a considerable portion of the material publicly available.

Many officials have been consulted and occasionally reliance has been placed on information supplied by them which appears nowhere in the public record. In general, however, this approach has been avoided. Where the point is of importance, information given by a national official which cannot be confirmed from the public record has been checked with an official in another country or in the Commission.

It sometimes happens that points of difficulty in negotiating a Directive are resolved by the Council inserting general wording in the Directive and a statement in the minutes of the Council meeting by way of elaboration. These statements are sometimes published with the Directive, are sometimes made public in other ways, but are otherise confidential. For example, as appears in Section 7.8, some statements have become known by appearing in a book published by a former Commission official (2). To the extent that these statements affect the interpretation of a Directive and are not made public they amount to secret legislation and so cannot have been noted here.*

(c) Formal Compliance with Directives

Directives usually require the Member States to transmit to the Commission within a given period a statement of the national legislation, regulations or administrative measures that give formal effect to the Directive. These 'compliance letters', as they are referred to, together with departmental circulars to the relevant administrative bodies (e.g., local authorities, water authorities) provide the basic raw material for an assessment of the effect of the Directives on British legislation. An additional source of information are 'Reasoned Opinions' sent by the Commission to the government when it believes that particular Directives are not being fully complied with. Whereas the Department of the Environment made compliance letters available for the purposes of this study and went further by saying that they would in future be available to those needing to see them, the 'Reasoned Opinions' from the Commission are not generally available, although access to some was arranged for the purposes of this study on the authority of the then head of the Commission's Environment and Consumer Protection Service.

In some cases secondary legislation has had to be introduced in Britain

---

* The Institute for European Environmental Policy, while recognising the right of the Council to conduct its business in confidence, has called for any minutes which can affect the meaning of legislation to be published with that legislation (3).

to comply with certain Directives.   In other cases the government has relied on existing primary and/or secondary legislation and has achieved compliance by taking certain administrative steps.   The adequacy of these measures has been critically assessed and the conclusions reached do not always coincide with those of the government.   Appendix 3 discusses implementation by administrative means.

(d) Effect on Practice

A Directive is binding as to certain ends to be achieved, e.g., that certain standards are to be met by certain dates, while leaving to the Member State the choice of methods for doing so.   For a Directive to be fully implemented, not only must the Member State have introduced the necessary laws, regulations or administrative provisions to enable these ends to be achieved,   but it must also ensure that the ends specified in the Directive are also achieved in practice.   A distinction may therefore in theory be drawn between **formal** and **practical** compliance, although the two will sometimes overlap.

Thus the designation of an existing body such as a water authority as the 'competent authority' for fulfilling certain functions under a Directive can be regarded as a mere **formal** step, but if a new body has had to be specifically created and given staff and money its creation would be a **practical** step as well.

It is in fact possible to have **formal** compliance without **practical** compliance and vice versa.   Thus Luxembourg has ensured that there is **formal** compliance with a Directive concerned with titanium dioxide wastes (see Section 7.11) by issuing a Decree largely repeating the Directive, but there can be no **practical** compliance in Luxembourg since there is no titanium dioxide production there.   Conversely there was for a time a failure of **formal** compliance by Britain of Directives concerned with the composition of detergents (Section 7.1) and the sulphur content of fuels (Section 9.1) since the necessary British Regulations were late in being made, but the British government argued that the failure was only one of form since in both cases the relevant industries had voluntarily taken the required **practical** steps to achieve the standards before the regulations came into force.

Although the Member States are usually obliged by Directives to inform the Commission by means of the 'compliance letters' of the steps they have taken for **formal** compliance, and the Commission has a duty to see that the measures adopted are adequate, there is usually no obligation to inform the Commission of the **practical** steps taken, nor does the Commission have an inspectorate able to monitor what happens.   The Community's interest must, however, extend beyond formal compliance alone.   Sometimes Directives require 'situation reports' to be submitted to the Commission, and examination of these will disclose some practical effects of a Directive. Otherwise the principal way of finding out the effects of a Directive is to consult people on whom duties are placed or whose behaviour may have been influenced.   This was done largely by interviews or by correspondence.

In the case of the water Directives described in Chapter 7, a questionnaire was sent to the ten water authorities in England and Wales, and in the case of nine of them, was followed by visits during 1981.   In the case of Northern Ireland, questions were put in correspondence with the Department of the Environment of the Northern Ireland Office. Questions were also put in correspondence with the Scottish Development Department and selected Scottish River Purification Boards. Interviews were also held with officials at the Confederation of British Industry, the Chemical Industries Association and from selected industrial companies. In the case of the other Directives the appropriate officials and industrialists were approached. Interviews were held with officials from the Commission's Environment and Consumer Protection Service which turned into the Directorate-General for the Environment, Consumer Protection and Nuclear Safety during the course of the study.

The ultimate purpose of Community environmental legislation is of course to protect or improve the environment and not just to affect the behaviour of officials and industrialists. It is however notoriously difficult quantitatively to attribute an environmental effect to a particular item of legislation even when intended to produce such an effect. For example, the smoke control orders made in Britain under the Clean Air Act 1956 will certainly have discouraged some people from burning raw coal in open fires, but since the public were anyway switching to other forms of heating it remains uncertain what proportion of the reduction in smoke is attributable to the Act. The same general point applies to Community legislation and the assessment is even harder given that the legislation is so new. The fact that there must be an effect on the environment is noted where it is possible to be confident of the fact, but no quantitative assessment of the extent of those effects has been attempted. Similarly, financial effects are sometimes noted, but no systematic attempt has been made to assess the cost of the Community's environmental policy either to the nation as a whole or to individual authorities or enterprises.

References

(1)   House of Lords Select Committee on the European Communities, **The Polluter Pays Principle,** 10th Report, Session 1982-83.

(2)   Stanley P Johnson, **The Pollution Control Policy of the European Community,** Graham and Trotman Ltd, 1979.

(3)   Institute for European Environmental Policy, Annual Report 1982.

CHAPTER 7
Water

7.0   Relevant British Legislation

The Water Act 1973 resulted in a complete reorganisation of the water industry in England and Wales. Ten river basin-based water authorities were created and took over the responsibilities previously exercised by over 1,600 separate local authorities, water undertakings and river authorities. These responsibilities include water supply, sewerage, sewage treatment, and the management of rivers and aquifers including pollution control, land drainage, flood prevention and fisheries. In Scotland it is the River Purification Boards that are responsible for controlling the quality of rivers.

The evolution of aspects of British policy on water quality has already been described in Chapter 5. The Control of Pollution Act 1974 (COPA), which covers Scotland too, will become the principle Act concerned with water pollution when it is brought fully into force. The government hopes to achieve this in large measure by 1986. Until then powers concerning water pollution are still largely contained in the Rivers (Prevention of Pollution) Acts 1951 and 1961 and the Clean Rivers (Estuaries and Tidal Waters) Act 1960. Unlike Part I of the Control of Pollution Act, which introduced entirely new changes to British legislation, Part II dealing with water is a logical extension of existing powers and its only really original feature is the provision for public access to information about discharges. Otherwise it effectively consolidates the matter in the earlier Acts and extends it to cover discharges to waters not previously controlled.

Consents for Discharges

COPA will require discharges to rivers, the sea, specified underground waters or land to have the consent of the water authority, which may be given subject to conditions. Until Part II is in force, discharges to coastal waters are not controlled, nor are all discharges to estuaries and groundwater. There is no power in the Act for the Secretary of State to set emission standards to be applied uniformly throughout the country.

Quality Objectives

As has already been described in Chapters 2 and 5, neither the water authorities nor the Secretary of State have any duty to set water quality standards or objectives, although these have been set administratively and without legally binding force. Once quality objectives have been set, the authorities can endeavour to achieve them by controlling the discharges from their own sewage works and by setting appropriate conditions on the consents they grant to discharges from trade premises. The only statutory obligations as to river quality are, perhaps surprisingly, not to be found in COPA but in the Water Act 1973, which places a general duty on the Secretary of State to secure the execution of a national policy for water including the restoration and maintenance of the wholesomeness of rivers and other inland waters (Section 1), and the duty on water authorities (Section 24) to prepare plans for "the meeting of future demands for water and the use of water and restoring or maintaining the wholesomeness of rivers and other inland or coastal waters in their area".

To implement the various Directives that set quality standards or objectives for certain waters, reliance has had to be placed almost exclusively on the powers to set conditions on discharge consents, coupled with the powers of authorities to make plans for the management of rivers.

Groundwater

Comprehensive powers to control most discharges to groundwater are contained in Sections of COPA yet to be brought into force, but some powers exist in other legislation mentioned in connection with the groundwater Directive 80/68 (Section 7.9). The legislation concerning waste disposal, which is a potential major source of groundwater pollution, is described in Section 8.0.

Drinking Water

The Water Act 1973 places a duty on the water authorities to supply drinking water and a duty on the local authority to ensure that it is wholesome. Any dispute between water authorities and local authorities is determined by the Secretary of State. Before the drinking water Directive 80/778 came into force (Section 7.4) there were no mandatory standards in Britain defining what was to be regarded as wholesome, although the World Health Organisation's European Standards were generally used as guidelines.

Detergents

There is no primary legislation controlling the composition or biodegradability of detergents for the purpose of preventing water pollution, and for many years standards were agreed voluntarily between government and the manufacturers. Standards for detergents are now laid down in Regulations made under the European Communities Act 1972 in order to implement various Directives (see Section 7.1).

Further Developments

Attention is now being concentrated on a programme to bring Part II of COPA into force. The most important new powers should be available to water authorities by mid-1984 and by July 1986 the programme should be virtually complete. However, by virtue of the Control of Pollution (Exemption of Certain Discharges from Control) Order 1983 (SI 1983 No 1182) a large number of discharges are being exempted but not those discharges that need to be controlled for the purposes of implementing a number of Directives.

7.1   Detergents

1) 73/404/EEC (L347 17.12.73)
   proposed 16.6.71 - COM(71)655

   Directive on detergents

2) 73/405/EEC (L347 17.12.73)
   proposed 16.6.71 - COM(71)655

   Directive relating to methods of testing the biodegradability of non-ionic surfactants

3) 82/242/EEC (L109 22.4.82)
   proposed 8.2.80 - COM(80)40

   Directive relating to methods of testing the biodegradability of non-ionic surfactants and amending Directive 73/404/EEC

4) 82/243/EEC (L109 22.4.82)
   proposed 24.3.81 - COM(81)128

   Directive amending Directive 73/405/EEC relating to the methods of testing the biodegradability of anionic surfactants

Binding dates (73/404 and 73/405)
Notification date[*]:   27 November 1973
Formal compliance: 27 May 1975
Exemptions possible: until 31 March 1986

Binding dates (82/242 and 82/243)
Notification date: 8 April 1982
Formal compliance: 8 October 1983

Purpose of the Directives

In the 1950s widespread foaming of rivers resulted from the growing domestic use of 'hard' detergents which were not broken down by sewage treatment. This foam is unpleasant to look at, impairs photosynthesis and oxygenation of water, and interferes with the sewage treatment process. 'Soft' or more biodegradable detergents were subsequently developed, and one purpose of the Directives is to prevent the sale of 'hard' detergents. The other purpose is to ensure free trade in detergents within the Community.

---

[*]   The notification date is the date when the Member States are notified of the existence of the Directive. Time limits normally run from the notification date which is usually a few days after the date of the Directive, i.e., the date when it was signed by the President of the Council. The notification date used not to be printed in the Official Journal and had to be obtained from a computer in Brussels but there has been a recent and welcome change in practice.

Summary of the Directives

Directive 73/404 covers many types of detergent: anionic, cationic, non-ionic and ampholytic. It prohibits the marketing of any of these detergents where the average level of biodegradability of the surfactants is less than 90 per cent. ('Surfactants' or 'surface active agents' are the essential constituents of detergents to which other constituents may be added. The Directive is not concerned with the biodegradability of any other constituents). The Directive can be called a 'framework' Directive because by itself it is largely unenforceable since it specifies no methods by which testing is to be carried out. These, being specific to the different types of detergents, are promised in subsequent 'daughter' Directives.

If a Member State decides that an imported detergent does not comply with the requirements of the Directive it can prohibit the marketing and use of the detergent and must inform the country of origin and the Commission accordingly. If the exporting country objects and agreement cannot be reached the Commission must obtain an opinion from an authorised laboratory in another Member State using the reference methods laid down in daughter Directives.

Directive 73/404 has been amended by Directive 82/242 to provide for exemptions for certain types of detergent and for certain uses until 31st March 1986, and thereafter only if they have a higher level of biodegradability than existing products for those uses. Another amendment is made by Directive 82/242 under which a committee is established for adapting the detergent Directives to technical progress.

Directive 73/405, the first of the 'daughter' Directives, is concerned only with anionic detergents - the kind most commonly used. It originally laid down three methods of testing: a French method, a German method, and an OECD method, but an amendment made by Directive 82/243 has added a British method called the 'porous pot test'. The biodegradability is to be no less than 80 per cent, the assumption apparently being that if this level is obtained on every test then the average level of 90 per cent required by 73/404 would also be obtained. This point is not made clear but compatability between the two Directives must presumably be assumed[*].

Directive 82/242 is concerned with non-ionic detergents and lays down four methods of testing - an OECD method, a German method, a French method, and a British method called the 'porous pot test'. The biodegradability is to be no less than 80%. The Directive also amends Directive 73/404 - see above.

Directive 82/243 amends Directive 73/405 by updating the approved testing methods and - as described above - by including the British 'porous pot test' as one of the methods. It also amends 73/405 by laying down in an Annex a reference testing method which is to be used during the procedure set out in Directive 73/404 in the event of a dispute between Member States.

Formal Compliance in the UK

Directives 73/404 and 73/405, although formally adopted in November

---

[*] The British government pointed out to the Commission the apparent inconsistency between the 90% of 73/404 and the 80% of 73/405 without apparently ever receiving a satisfactory reply.

1973, had been agreed in principle one year earlier, before Britain joined the Community. They therefore formed part of the 'acquis communautaire' - a phrase for which there is no real English equivalent but which means those duties, powers and obligations that the Community has acquired and by inference will not lightly give up or change[*]. The lack of British influence may have been the cause of subsequent difficulties: although the Member States were to have put into force the legal and administrative measures necessary to comply with the two earlier Directives in May 1975, it was not until 1st January 1979 that Regulations made under the European Communities Act 1972 came into force in Britain. These are the Detergents (Composition) Regulations 1978 (SI 1978 No 564) (amended by SI 1978 No 1546) and they apply to Scotland and Northern Ireland as well as to England and Wales. In December 1977 the Commission had issued a 'Reasoned Opinion' to the effect that the UK was not complying with the Directives. The delay in compliance seems to have been caused at least in part by the difficulties in establishing laboratory facilities able to test by the methods specified in Directive 73/405 which did not include the method traditionally used in Britain.

Even now compliance is not strictly complete, though this may be as much a criticism of the framework Directive as of the Regulations. Although the Regulations claim, in their explanatory note, to give effect to both Directives, the only detergents which will contravene the Regulations are those which are anionic and have a level of biodegradability less than 80 per cent. The other types of detergent are not mentioned nor is there mention of 90 per cent average biodegradability. Directive 73/404 has therefore not been complied with in UK law insofar as it relates to detergents other than anionic ones, and the Commission in not following up their Reasoned Opinion by initiating proceedings before the European Court has presumably accepted that 73/404 is effectively not capable of being complied with where it deals with detergents not separately covered by a daughter Directive. The confusion concerning the 90% requirement of 73/404 and the 80% of 73/405 and the failure of the Commission to explain this seems to have been another reason for the delay over compliance.

The two later Directives will require further Regulations.

Effect on UK Practice

The official response in Britain to the foaming of rivers had been the appointment of a committee in 1953, by the Minister of Housing and Local Government, to examine the effects of the increasing use of synthetic detergents.

The committee published a report in 1956 (the Jephcott Report) (1) which, among other matters, recommended the Government to consider introducing legislation to be held in reserve to control detergents. This was never done so that the present Detergents (Composition) Regulations have had to be made under the broad powers provided by the European Communities Act 1972 which enable the Government to implement any Community obligation.

---

[*]   'What we have we hold' may be too strong but conveys the flavour of the phrase.

The main recommendations of the Jephcott Report were that sewage authorities and detergent manufacturers should co-operate closely and find technical solutions to the problems of foaming and that a central co-ordinating body, to include government representatives, should keep progress under review. This resulted in the setting up of the Standing Technical Committee on Synthetic Detergents. The Committee issued a total of 20 annual reports before being wound up in 1980, and these tell a story of voluntary agreement and gradual technical progress. By 1964 the Confederation of British Industry felt able to give an undertaking to the Minister that after the end of 1964 no detergents based on propylene tetramer, i.e., the old 'hard' material, would be supplied to the British domestic market. This agreement specified no set standards of 'hardness'. The Standing Committee continued to stress the need for improvement and by the time of the first two Directives British detergents already met the standards specified: indeed the Directives were criticised in Britain for being too lax. However, there is no intention to reduce standards because it is now as cheap or cheaper to manufacture the softer detergents.

The Directives have therefore had no practical effect upon the quality of detergents manufactured in Britain. This does not mean that the Directives are useless as far as Britain is concerned since, without them, there would have been no Detergents (Composition) Regulations 1978 and without these Regulations, imports in the UK of 'hard' detergents could not be controlled without going through the rather elaborate procedure of Section 100 of the Control of Pollution Act 1974. The Standing Committee was abolished in 1980 in the Government purge of 'quangos', and without anyone to monitor the voluntary undertakings given by industry it is now the Regulations and the Directives that prevent backsliding.

References

(1) Sir Henry Jephcott (Chairman), **Report of the Committee on Synthetic Detergents**, HMSO, 1956.

7.2   Surface Water for Drinking

75/440/EEC (OJ L194 25.7.75)
proposed 15.1.74 - COM(74)11

Directive concerning the quality
required of surface water intended
for the abstraction of drinking
water in the Member States

Binding dates

Notification date: 18 June 1975
Formal compliance: 18 June 1977
Standards to be set   No set date, therefore presumably
  and met: by 18 June 1977
Improvements to be   'Over the next 10 years', i.e., by
  achieved   18 June 1985

Purpose of the Directive

The Directive has two purposes: to ensure that surface water
abstracted for use as drinking water reaches certain standards and is given
adequate treatment before being put into public supply, and thereby to
improve rivers or other surface waters used as sources of drinking water.

Summary of the Directive

Sources of surface water for the abstraction of drinking water
(referred to as 'surface water') are to be classified by their existing quality
into three categories: A1, A2 and A3 corresponding to the three standard
methods of treatment required to transform the 'surface water' into drinking
water.   Annex I defines the three methods of treatment that must be used
for A1, A2 and A3 waters respectively.   In summary, A1 water requires only
simple physical treatment (filtration) and disinfection, A2 requires normal
physical treatment, chemical treatment and disinfection, while A3 water
requires intensive physical and chemical treatment and disinfection.

The physical, chemical and micro-biological characteristics which
define the quality of A1, A2 and A3 water are set out in Annex II.   Forty six
'parameters' are listed against which numerical values are given under six
columns: an I (or imperative) value and a G (or guide) value for each
category A1, A2, A3.   The parameters include temperature, BOD_5, nitrates,
lead and faecal coliforms.   For some parameters no I or G values are yet
given, but the Directive provides for these to be added later.

The Member States are required to lay down values for sampling points
where water is abstracted whenever an I or G value is given.   The values set
must be no less stringent than the I values and the G values are to be
respected as guidelines.   Sometimes no I value is given in Annex II and the
G value then provides guidance.   Once values are set, Member States must
then ensure that 95 per cent of the samples of 'surface water' meet the
values laid down for the I values and that 90 per cent of the samples do so for

the other values laid down.

Article 8 provides for waivers in the case of floods or natural disasters and in the case of certain parameters because of exceptional conditions. The Commission must be notified of these.

Article 4 prohibits the use of 'surface water' worse than A3 from being used for the abstraction of drinking water. In exceptional circumstances, such water may be used provided suitable processes such as blending raise the quality, but the Commission must be notified of the exceptions - in advance in the case of new installations.

Article 4 also requires a plan of action, including a timetable, for the improvement of 'surface water' and especially A3 water. This timetable is to be drawn up in the light of the need to improve the surface water and of economic and technical constraints. Considerable improvements of low quality sources are to be achieved within 10 years. The Commission is to examine the plans and timetables and will, if necessary, submit appropriate proposals to the Council. There is no obligation on the Commission to publish a report comparing these plans. There is also no obligation on Member States to send a report to the Commission on the improvements achieved within the 10 year period.

Development of the Directive

This was the first proposal for a Directive concerning water following adoption of the First Action Programme on the Environment of November 1973, and was inspired by a draft French decree setting out a legally binding technical specification for 'surface water'. Discussion on the proposal had in fact started before Britain joined the Community on 1st January 1973.

The Environment Committee of the European Parliament wanted the proposed Directive strengthened by prohibiting absolutely - without any temporary derogation - the use of surface water falling below a minimum standard, but the Commissioner, Mr Scarascia Mugnozza, replying to the debate in the European Parliament (13th May 1974) discussed the conflict - which was to occur with subsequent Directives - between perfection and practicality:

> "We believe that if this reservation were omitted, we should encounter difficulties in implementation, in that where there were no alternative water resources, use of this type of water would of necessity become unavoidable; it is better, therefore, to provide in advance for possible exceptions (though only on a temporary basis), but have at our disposal a generally applicable piece of legislation, than to lay down a restriction which we know cannot be observed."

Since the House of Commons and the House of Lords had not yet established Scrutiny Committees when the Directive was proposed, it escaped parliamentary discussion in Britain. British officials, despite feeling disadvantaged by their unfamiliarity with the procedures for influence and negotiation, have nevertheless claimed responsibility for several practical provisions now in the Directive (1). Notable among these is the provision that only 95 per cent of the samples need comply with the values set, and the vague description of 'sampling point' which enables it to mean the point at which water leaves a reservoir for treatment rather than the point in the river from which it is abstracted to be stored in a reservoir.

Formal Compliance in the UK

There is no legislation setting standards for 'surface water' in Britain but the water authorities in England and Wales and other authorities in Scotland and Northern Ireland have a statutory duty to supply 'wholesome' water and have the powers to do so. They also have powers to control discharges to rivers and will gain powers to control discharges to lakes when the Control of Pollution Act 1974 is fully implemented. The Directive has therefore not been implemented by any new legislation or regulations made under existing legislation, but by administrative action, that is to say by the central government informing the authorities of the Directive and advising them of the steps that they should take. The assumption is that the authorities responsible will interpret their statutory duties in the light of the Directive. The existing legislation enabling this to be done is as follows:

England and Wales

Water Acts 1945 and 1973
Rivers (Prevention of Pollution) Act 1951 to 1961 (these
    will be superseded by Part II of the Control of Pollution
    Act 1974 when it is brought into force)

Scotland

The Local Government (Scotland) Act 1973
The Water (Scotland) Act 1980 (which superseded Acts of
    1946 and 1967)
The Rivers (Prevention of Pollution) Scotland Act 1951
    and 1965 (these will be superseded by Part II of the
    Control of Pollution Act 1974 when it is brought into
    force)

Northern Ireland

The Water Act (Northern Ireland) 1972
The Pollution Control and Local Government (Northern
    Ireland) Order 1978
The Water and Sewage Services Order 1973

On 17th June 1977, i.e., one day before the date for complying with the Directive, the Department of the Environment (DOE) wrote formally to all the water authorities in England sending them a copy of the Directive and advising them of the steps they had to take. This followed discussion with water authorities over the previous year. A copy of the letter was sent to the Commission as evidence of this administrative action.

The Commission was not convinced that this constituted compliance and after letters and a meeting, the DOE on 19th October 1979 sent a memorandum to the Commission explaining the relationship between the DOE and the water authorities and the comparable arrangements in Scotland and Northern Ireland. The memorandum stated that:

> "...obligations which are clear from the Directive itself are not the subject of 'instructions' from the government to the water authorities. As with domestic legislation, the authorities apply the Directive using their own resources and legal advice. The government is responsible to the Community for seeing that the aims of the Directive are met, and in the event of a water authority's failing to ensure that a Directive was implemented the government could take action to ensure that it did so. However this is a 'safety net' procedure which is not likely to be required in practice."

Notwithstanding this memorandum, the Commission issued a 'Reasoned Opinion' on 18th July 1980 to the effect that the UK had not adopted all the necessary provisions for compliance with the Directive and published this fact in the Bulletin of the European Communities. The 'Reasoned Opinion' mentioned in particular that the measures for implementing the Directive in Scotland and Northern Ireland had not been communicated to the Commission.

The government replied to the 'Reasoned Opinion' by letter dated 18th September 1980 and referred to further existing legislation covering Scotland and Northern Ireland. It expressed the view that the Directive had indeed been properly complied with all along and, in effect, asked the Commission to withdraw its 'Reasoned Opinion'. Since this has neither happened nor has the Commission pursued the matter in the Court, it still remains unclear, over two years later, whether or not the Commission is satisfied that the Directive is being properly complied with. The issue of compliance by administrative action which so troubles the Commission is discussed further in Appendix 3.

The Effect on UK Practice

Fears expressed when the Directive was initially proposed that many drinking water sources might have to be abandoned and large sums of money spent on improvement schemes have not turned out to be justified (1). Lists of 'surface waters' submitted to the Commission by the DOE in September 1981 covering England and Wales and in February 1982 covering Scotland included no source worse than A3 and no such British sources have otherwise been notified to the Commission under Article 4*. Of the 679 sources listed in England and Wales, 207 are A1, 408 are A2 and 10 are A3: 54 sources are not classified but are understood to be A1 or A2. Of the 29 sources listed in

---

* One source is on a river which receives an intermittent discharge from a mine. During discharge the river is below A3 quality but the rest of the time it is A2 quality with a waiver. Abstraction only takes place when the river is of A2 quality.

Northern Ireland, one is A1 and 28 are A2. All sources in Scotland are unpolluted upland rivers of A1 or A2 quality. Some of the A3 sources have only achieved their A3 status by virtue of waivers under Article 8. The fact that a particular source has received a waiver for a particular parameter has been notified to the Commission but the exact extent of the waivers has not been made public. The waivers usually concern colour and NO_3, Fe, NH_4, and SO_4. Waivers for lead have been given in three instances when the sources are in areas where lead exists in the soil and lead compounds are found in surface waters after heavy rainfall. The DOE has said that public health is not at risk in these cases because the lead is removed during treatment processes. In four cases the treatment given to the 'surface water' is lower than specified in the Directive. Since there is no specific provision in British law that treatment must match the quality of the source - though clearly this is normal practice - the Directive may well have highlighted these deficiencies.

When interviewed all water authorities in England and Wales had set values for the sampling points. All had followed DOE advice and set values equal to the I values in the Directive.

Where G values only appear in the Directive, the practices differed and five water authorities have used their own initiative in setting G values - sometimes more stringent than the G values in the Directive. The rest of the water authorities have set G values given in the Directive. The actual values set have not been transmitted to the Commission, nor are they necessarily to be published.

The plans, with timetable, for improving 'surface waters' required under Article 4 will, in England and Wales, form part of the plans for 'the use of water and restoring or maintaining the wholesomeness of rivers' that water authorities have a duty to prepare under Section 24 of the Water Act 1973. All water authorities have already prepared one such plan since 1974 and they amend the plan from time to time. It is expected that in the future these Section 24 plans will specifically include reference to action to be taken to implement the Directive. It would be easy to say that all upgrading of treatment plants to match the quality of the source was a result of the Directive, but many of these improvements would have been programmed anyway. The most that can be said is that the Directive has drawn attention to some deficiencies and may have hastened improvements.

Sampling and analysis of the parameters are the subject of a separate Directive 79/869 described next (section 7.3) and during a debate in the House of Commons (18th June 1979) on the proposal for that Directive the Minister, Marcus Fox, referred to the surface water Directive and summed up the official view:

> "Its application in the United Kingdom has caused no concern or difficulty, since the standards of water that we abstract for drinking are at least as good as and often better than those laid down".

References

(1) A H Goodman, **EEC Directive on the Quality of Surface Water Intended for the Abstraction of Drinking Water,** Journal of the Institute of Water Pollution Control, Vol 78, 1979, No 2.

7.3   Sampling Surface Water for Drinking

79/869/EEC (OJ L271 29.10.79)
proposed 26.7.78 - COM(78)363

Directive concerning the methods of measurement and frequency of sampling and analysis of surface water intended for the abstraction of drinking water in the Member States

Binding dates
　Notification date:
　Formal compliance:

11 October 1979
11 October 1981

Purpose of the Directive

The Directive supplements Directive 75/440 (Section 7.2) by recommending methods of measuring the parameters for surface water quality and setting the frequencies for such measurements.

Summary of the Directive

The parameters listed in Directive 75/440 must be measured with the 'precision' and 'accuracy' (as defined) set out in Annex I. The 'reference methods' of measurement also set out in Annex I must be used 'as far as possible' but are not mandatory. The frequency of sampling is to be set by Member States and is to be no less than the frequencies set out in Annex II. These frequencies increase as the quality category of 'surface water' decreases and as the population served increases, i.e., A3 water has to be sampled more frequently than A2 water, and an A2 source for a population over 100,000 has to be sampled more frequently than for a smaller population. The Member States may reduce the frequency of sampling for certain parameters if a survey shows that the values obtained are much better than the values set. If the water is of better than A1 quality no regular analysis may be necessary. Member States may also determine the frequencies themselves for 'surface water' serving very small populations.
　Member States are to provide the Commission, at its request, with information on the frequency and methods of analysis used. The Commission is at regular intervals to draw up a consolidated report but does not have to publish it.

Development of the Directive

The government submitted two memoranda on this Directive to the House of Commons, one in January 1979 and one in June 1979. Between these dates the proposal for the Directive was substantially modified and the government's attitude changed. The first memorandum listed a number of unsatisfactory features and said:

> "It is difficult to see what justification there is for using
> a Directive to impose a Community policy on such highly
> complex, detailed and technical matters."

The second memorandum explained that the analytical methods were no longer to be mandatory but were now merely 'reference methods' and that the provision for reducing the sampling frequencies could be used without having to seek the consent of the Commission. Accordingly the Minister, Marcus Fox, said in the House of Commons' debate (18th June 1979) that the proposed Directive was now more like a Recommendation and that:

> "It does not perhaps matter too much what title is given
> to a document which has so little effect on the United
> Kingdom."

The Minister also claimed that:

> "The United Kingdom managed to secure a number of
> major changes which meet some of the points of
> criticism....in its present form, the Directive would not
> hinder the continuation of present United Kingdom
> practices, and would not force additional burdens upon
> us."

Formal Compliance in the UK

The legal powers set out in the previous section (7.2) describing Directive 75/440 also provide for monitoring water quality so no new legislation has been required. As with that parent Directive, implementation has been by administrative action. A circular letter from the DOE, with the Directive reproduced as an Appendix, was sent to the water authorities on 31st March 1982 (i.e., nearly six months after the due date) appointing them as competent authorities for the purposes of the Directive. An identical circular letter was sent by the Welsh Office to the Welsh Water Authority, and a generally similar letter was sent by the Scottish Development Department to the Scottish water supply authorities. The circulars explained the Directive. On 5th July 1982, in reply to a letter from the Commission pointing out that the date for formal compliance had passed, copies of these letters were sent as evidence of the administrative action taken to comply with the Directive.

The Effect on UK Practice

The statement by the Minister that the Directive would not force additional burdens on Britain was largely, but not entirely, confirmed by the responses received from questions put to the water authorities before the Directive had to be complied with.

The methods of measurement used were said already to conform with the 'precision' and 'accuracy' of the reference methods set out in the

70

Directive. Several water authorities said they were having to include more parameters in their analytical programme but the increases in expenditure due to more sophisticated analytical techniques were not expected in general to result in any overall increase in expenditure - other measurements would be cut back - and since the frequency of sampling has, in general, been much greater than is required by the Directive, no problems arise. Only two water authorities claimed that they might be short of staff at divisional level able to handle the extra measurements. In Scotland the requirements of the Directive were not expected to cause any difficulty, and in Northern Ireland the only changes expected were in the number of parameters which need to be examined.

The circular letters mentioned above and sent by central government departments to the water authorities (and water supply authorities in Scotland) asked the authorities to supply information in a prescribed form about frequency of sampling and the methods of analysis to enable the DOE to supply information to the Commission at its request. This information was to be supplied within a year (i.e., by end March 1983) and therefore one effect of the Directive is that central government will have more information than it would have had otherwise. Apart from the information aspect, the general effect of the Directive was summed up by the Head of the Analytical Division of the Water Research Centre in an otherwise fairly critical paper (1):

"In fact, the frequencies commonly applied at present for many waters are substantially greater than those in the Directive. The main impact on the UK seems, therefore, to be the need to obtain information on the concentrations of any parameters not previously measured. Depending on the extent of this need, a substantial amount of additional analysis may initially be involved but it will be of value to make good any gaps in knowledge of water quality."

A more jaundiced view of the Directive was expressed by a DOE official to the House of Lords in connection with their investigation into a rather similar proposed Directive (Section 7.11):

"In the end we dealt with the problem by negotiating in Brussels with our partners a directive which, whilst one may not think it is of any particular use, at least does not do any particular harm. It sits there, as it were, as a monument to precedent."(2)

References

(1) A L Wilson, **EEC Directives: Requirements for sampling and analysis,** Symposium on EEC Directives, The Institution of Water Engineers and Scientists, 1980.

(2) House of Lords, Select Committee on the European Communities, **Monitoring of Waste from the Titanium Dioxide Industry,** 40th Report, Session 1980-81, HMSO.

7.4   Drinking Water

80/778/EEC (OJ L229 30.8.80) proposed 22.7.75 - COM(75)394	Directive relating to the quality of water intended for human consumption

Binding dates
Notification date:	17 July 1980
Formal compliance:	17 July 1982
Standards to be met:	17 July 1985 (unless derogations made or delay granted)

Purpose of the Directive

Standards for the quality of water intended for drinking or for use in food and drink manufacture are laid down in order to protect human health. Although the Directive has formed part of the Action Programme on the Environment, it is concerned with consumer rather than environmental protection and is therefore not strictly relevant to this study. Since, however, the Directive links indirectly with Directives 75/440 and 79/869 (Sections 7.2 and 7.3) a summary is provided for completeness.

Summary of the Directive

The water covered by the Directive is defined to include all water intended for human consumption, whether in its original state or after treatment and whether supplied for consumption or used in food or drink manufacture. Some exceptions can be made for water used in food or drink manufacture (see below). Natural mineral waters (such waters are defined in Directive 80/777) and medicinal waters are excluded from the Directive, but other bottled waters for human consumption are included.

The Directive has three Annexes:

Annex I lists more than 60 parameters and a figure indicating a Guide Level (GL) and a less stringent Maximum Admissible Concentration (MAC) appears against many of the parameters. The Council may add figures where none now appears. When no figure appears the Annex may nevertheless include comments which have to be observed. The parameters are divided into six Tables:

- A   organoleptic parameters, e.g., colour, taste
- B   physico-chemical parameters e.g., conductivity, chlorides
- C   substances undesirable in excessive amounts, e.g., nitrates, phenols
- D   toxic substances, e.g., arsenic, mercury, lead

- E microbiological parameters, e.g., coliforms, streptococci
- F minimum required concentration (MRC) for softened water, e.g., hydrogen ion concentration, alkalinity (there are no MACs in this Table).

Annex II is concerned with monitoring and lists patterns and frequency of standard analyses. As the population served increases the frequency of monitoring also increases.

Annex III lists reference methods of analysis.

Member States are to fix values for the parameters in Annex I wherever a figure appears and are to ensure that water meets them. For the parameters in Tables A, B, C, D, and E the values fixed must be less than or equal to the MAC figures, and the GL figures are to provide a guide. The parameters in Table F do not apply to water used in food production.

Member States are to ensure that any substances used in the preparation of water for human consumption do not remain in concentrations higher than the MAC figure in water made available to the user and that they do not constitute a public health hazard.

Derogations may be made by Member States in two circumstances: in order to take account of situations arising from the nature and structure of the ground in the area from which the water comes, and of situations arising from exceptional meteorological conditions. (Derogations related to the nature of the ground may be permanent, the others only temporary.) The Commission is to be informed and given the reasons for derogations relating to a supply of more than $1,000m^3$ or to a population of at least 5,000. The derogations may not relate to toxic or microbiological factors, nor may they constitute a health hazard.

Under two circumstances the competent authorities may allow the MAC figures to be exceeded for a limited period and up to a given value provided that there is no unacceptable risk to human health and that water supply cannot be maintained in any other way. The Commission must be informed and given reasons. The circumstances are (a) in emergencies, and (b) when, as allowed by Article 4 of Directive 75/440 (see Section 7.2), a Member State is obliged to use surface water worse than A3 quality and when it cannot devise suitable treatment.

Member States must ensure that water complies with the Directive by 17th July 1985, but they may, in exceptional cases and for geographically defined population groups, ask the Commission for delay in complying with Annex I. This request must set out the difficulties experienced and must propose an improvement programme with a timetable. The Commission must examine these programmes and in the case of disagreement with the Member State must submit appropriate proposals to the Council.

Water used in food or drink manufacture need only meet the values if it affects the wholesomeness of the foodstuff in its finished form, and Member States are to send to the Commission information on food industries where the wholesomeness of the product is not believed to be affected by water quality. Water used in the food and drink industry must nevertheless meet the MAC values given in Table D (toxic substances) and Table E (microbiological parameters) and values set by the Member States for the other parameters which the competent national authorities consider are

73

likely to affect the wholesomeness of the foodstuff in its finished form. These national values must be sent to the Commission. The Commission is to examine the information supplied and is periodically to draw up a comprehensive report for the Member States (there is no obligation to publish this).

Member States may lay down more stringent provisions than those in the Directive, but may not prohibit the marketing of foodstuffs on grounds relating to the quality of water used where the quality meets the values in the Directive.

Member States may adopt special provisions regarding information (packaging, labels or advertising) concerning the suitability of water for feeding infants, but must first inform the other Member States and the Commission.

Regular monitoring is to be ensured by the Member States. Water is to be monitored at the point where it is made available to the user. The sampling points are to be determined by the competent national authorities. Monitoring is to conform with the patterns and frequency set out in Annex II, and as far as practicable Member States are to use the reference methods of analysis set out in Annex III. Where other methods are used they must be comparable.

7.5 Water Standards for Freshwater Fish

78/659/EEC (OJ L222 14.8.78)
proposed 26.7.76 - COM(76)401

Directive on the quality of
fresh waters needing protection
in order to support fish life

Binding dates

Notification date: 20 July 1978
Formal compliance: 20 July 1980
Designation of waters: 20 July 1980
Standards to be met: 20 July 1985
Report to Commission: 20 July 1985

Purpose of the Directive

In order to allow fish to live in favourable conditions, quality objectives are to be set for designated stretches of river or other fresh waters.

Summary of the Directive

The Member States are themselves to designate fresh waters needing protection or improvement in order to support fish life. Two categories of water are to be designated: suitable for salmonids (salmon, trout), and suitable for cyprinids (coarse fish). An Annex sets out 14 physical and chemical parameters against which are listed I (imperative) and G (guide) values for salmonid and cyprinid waters. Member States are to set values no less stringent than the I values and "shall endeavour to respect the values in column G".

Member States are to establish pollution reduction programmes and are to ensure that within five years of designation the waters conform to the values set. The Annex also sets out minimum sampling frequencies but where the water quality is high, sampling frequency may be reduced. Certain reference methods of analysis for the parameters are set out in the Annex but other methods may be used so long as comparable results are obtained. If sampling shows that a set value is not being met, appropriate measures are to be taken.

Derogations may be given by Member States for certain parameters because of exceptional weather or special geographical conditions or because of 'natural enrichment'. These are to be communicated to the Commission.

Member States are to supply the Commission with a list of designated waters and, five years later, with a detailed report on the designated waters. With the consent of the Member States the Commission is to publish this.

Development of the Directive

Two difficulties were posed by the Directive as proposed. Who was to be responsible for designation, and were the parameters realistic? Both difficulties were eventually resolved by amendment but not before a considerable amount of heat had been generated. The two difficulties seem to have been universally noted because they were discussed in the European Parliament's debate (14th January 1977), in the report of the Economic and Social Committee (23rd February 1977), in the House of Lords' debate (28th June 1977), and the House of Commons' debate (6th April 1978).

The first difficulty was created by ambiguous draftsmanship. Article 1 of the Directive as finally agreed is quite clear:

"This Directive concerns the quality of fresh waters and applies to those waters designated by the Member States as needing protection or improvement in order to support freshwater fish" (Article 1).

The proposed Directive on the other hand had Articles 1 and 4 as follows:

"This Directive concerns the quality requirements for waters capable of supporting freshwater fish" (Article 1).
"For the purposes of applying this Directive, the Member States shall specify those waters capable of supporting freshwater fish" (Article 4).

The difficulty posed by the original wording was explained in a memorandum submitted on 29th March 1978 by the Minister, Denis Howell, to the House of Commons before it debated the proposed Directive:

"...the extent of a Member State's obligation to designate waters under the Directive was obscure. The original text of Articles 1 and 4 might have implied designation of all rivers which supported fish life or which were potentially capable of doing so, whether or not the Member State was willing or able to provide the resources necessary to bring them up to prescribed standards within the five years allowed under Article 5."

Although the original Article 4 laid on Member States the administrative task of designation, the Article was not clear whether their discretion was unfettered. Would the Commission, for example, be able to question why a certain stretch of river had not been designated, and in the extreme could the Commission have taken the Member State to the Court for failure to designate a stretch of river 'capable of supporting freshwater fish'? The very use of the word 'capable' must also cause confusion since almost any waters are capable of supporting fish if given adequate treatment.

Not everyone could see the ambiguity. In the European Parliament's debate, the rapporteur, Mrs Kruchow, argued against an amendment by a

76

British MEP, James Spicer, which sought to draw attention to the ambiguity:

"...I cannot commend this proposed amendment. I fear it
is based on a misunderstanding. The Directive we are
dealing with today does not deal with the existence of
fish in freshwater areas capable of supporting them, but
with the freshwater areas in which the individual
governments have decided fish should be able to survive".

Lady White in the Lords' debate quoted Mrs Kruchow's words and commented that:

"This is an attitude of mind to which we...find it
extraordinarily hard to adapt ourselves".

Lady White pointed out that Mrs Kruchow's interpretation could mean that Member States need designate nothing at all and that the Directive would then be inoperative. The same point was made by the Economic and Social Committee:

"The Committee feels that leaving it (designation) up to
the Member State...could slow up or even rule out any
action to improve quality standards for water in a large
number of EEC rivers".

The then Director of the Commission's Environment and Consumer Protection Service (Mr Michel Carpentier) tried to answer these points in long letters to Lady White and Lord Ashby following the Lords' debate. Lord Ashby, having assumed little or no discretion on the part of Member States, had argued in the debate that if the Directive applied to all waters in Britain already supporting fish, then vast costs would be incurred. To Lord Ashby, Mr Carpentier wrote as follows, though without acknowledging that another interpretation was possible:

"It is quite inaccurate to say that the Directive will
apply...to all rivers in which fish are currently found.
This is not the case. It will apply to designated waters,
and it is, in your case, the United Kingdom which will
make the designation."

To Lady White, Mr Carpentier explained why the Directive would still be effective:

"I am shocked by your suggestion that Member States will
simply select a few areas of pure waters as the designated
area, and let the question rest there. I have more faith
in the seriousness and commitment to the improvement of
the environment of the government of our Member
States...What will be the reaction of public opinion if it
discovers that in the Member States where it resides, few
or no areas have been designated under the
Directives...there would be a clamorous protest."

77

In the event Lady White has been proved right and Mr Carpentier's faith is being put to the test. Some Member States have not designated any waters and in those countries the Directive is therefore effectively inoperative.

The misunderstandings described above led us to consider, as part of this study, whether the difference between English and continental traditions of drafting and interpreting legal documents could have led to different people giving a different meaning to the words of the Directive as proposed. This possibility has been discussed with a number of lawyers, but has had to be dismissed in the present instance. With the benefit of hindsight, one can see that had the Commission and its critics both realised that the original Articles 1 and 4 could be read in two ways, the ambiguity would have been resolved without acrimony. It would then not have been necessary for Mr Carpentier to say "Why did Lord Ashby presume that the Directive automatically applies to all fish-bearing waters in the UK?" and Lord Ashby would not have presumed that it did.

The second difficulty created by the Directive as proposed concerned the parameters. Lord Nugent, then the Chairman of the National Water Council, giving evidence to the Lords' Select Committee said:

"The fact is that the Commission are here proposing standards of perfection, which is what they have done before. I have had the pleasure of meeting the officials concerned and I know that this is their policy; they think that the right thing to do is to establish standards of perfection although, quite obviously, in practice it is simply impossible to conform to them. So we do make a stringent criticism of these standards as being higher than is normal in practice for rivers in which fish live and thrive".

In the event, a number of parameters originally proposed were altered including temperature, dissolved oxygen, phosphates and phenols. The nitrate parameter was completely deleted. In the Commons' debate the Minister, Kenneth Marks, commented:

"All the changes were towards the United Kingdom point of view, quite a few to meet specific United Kingdom problems and in response to pressure from us."

Linked to the realism of the parameters was the issue of the scientific basis for them. The Lords' report had said:

"The reason why the draft Directive's standards are so unrealistic may be explained, in part, by the failure of the Commission to accept some of the advice submitted by a group of experts set up by the Commission for that purpose."

Lord Ashby in the Lords' debate emphasised the point which continues to be a live one. He urged the government to persuade the Commission to set out clearly the scientific evidence upon which they base their proposals for Directives, and to state their reasons when Directives differ from that advice.

Formal Compliance in the UK

The water authorities in England and Wales and the appropriate bodies in Scotland and Northern Ireland already have the powers to control discharges to all rivers and to take samples. Control over discharges to lakes awaits the implementation of Part II of the Control of Pollution Act 1974. No new legislation was therefore necessary to implement the Directive. The existing legislation is:

Rivers (Prevention of Pollution) Acts 1951 and 1961
Salmon and Freshwater Fisheries Act 1975
Rivers (Prevention of Pollution) (Scotland) Acts 1951
   and 1965
Water Act (Northern Ireland) 1972
Pollution Control and Local Government (Northern Ireland)
   Order 1978

Implementation has accordingly been by the following administrative action. In October 1978 the DOE sent a copy of the Directive to the water authorities together with an eight-page circular letter explaining it and stating that many of the functions involved were being delegated to the water authorities. The Circular advised water authorities to consult local authorities and fishing and other environmental interests on the designation of waters and on other matters.

The Scottish Development Department sent a circular letter on 7th March 1979 to the Convention of Scottish Local Authorities, the Scottish River Purification Boards' Association and the Association of Scottish District Salmon Fishery Boards explaining the Directive and stating that the Secretary of State for Scotland would designate the waters although suggestions were invited.

The Department of the Enviroment for Northern Ireland is also the water authority and so no question of delegating the task of designation arose.

The Effect on UK Practice

The DOE Circular of October 1978 suggested the setting up of a working group with representatives of government departments and water authorities to prepare more detailed advice on the Directive. The result was an undated 18- page advice note issued in the second half of 1979. This note stated that the aim should be to designate as many waters as possible without affecting existing capital expenditure plans, in other words to designate intially only those waters which already met the standards or would do so by July 1985 after improvements which were already programmed.

In July 1980 the DOE sent to the Commission a list of waters designated in England, Wales, Scotland and Northern Ireland. The

79

government's advice seems to have been followed and in England and Wales only two water authorities designated waters which did not then already comply with the standards. Designations are nevertheless extensive and some water authorities have designated 50 per cent of their total length of rivers. In Scotland almost all the designated waters already met the standards and all did in Northern Ireland. Some water authorities issued consultation papers setting out their intended designations and made changes as a result of representations received from fishing interests. Only those authorities which designated waters not yet up to the required standards are required by the Directive to have programmes for river improvement and these are covered by existing forward plans.

The water authorities reported no increase in manpower to carry out the monitoring required, though several said that they had to redeploy staff. They had to monitor for substances which they had not monitored before. In Northern Ireland monitoring has involved some increase in expenditure. Most water authorities reported that their existing monitoring was more frequent than required by the Directive. One water authority hinted that the Directive had prevented a cutback in monitoring.

One water authority remarked that an indirect effect of the Directive had been a refinement of its water quality classification system.

The values set for the parameters have not been published and the Directive is silent on the need to do so. The DOE did, however, say in its circular of October 1978 that it would expect information about the application of the Directive to be available to the public.

Overall, it cannot be said that the Directive has yet had any significant effect on Britain. It does however provide a prop against backsliding which is particularly important at a time of financial cutbacks. The comment of one water authority that the Directive had prevented a cutback in monitoring is perhaps a pointer here. Unlike the bathing water Directive (see Section 7.7), the Directive allows more designations in the future and fishery interests can, therefore, use the Directive in arguments about raising the standards of stretches not yet designated.

7.6   Shellfish Waters

79/923/EEC (OJ L281 10.11.79)   Directive on the quality
proposed 3.11.76 - COM(76)570   required for shellfish waters

Binding dates
  Notification date: 5 November 1979
  Formal compliance: 5 November 1981
  Designation of waters: 5 November 1981
  Standards to be met: 5 November 1987
  Report to Commission: 5 November 1987

Purpose of the Directive

The Directive seeks to ensure a suitable environment for shellfish growth.   It is not intended by itself to protect the quality of shellfish for consumption, which in Britain is usually achieved by cleansing the shellfish after harvesting.

Summary of the Directive

The Member States are themselves to designate coastal and brackish waters which need protection or improvement so as to support shellfish. Initial designations were to be made by 5th November 1981 but additional designations can be made subsequently.   Member States are to establish pollution reduction programmes so that within six years of designation the waters conform with values set by Member States.   These values must be set for 12 physical, chemical or bacteriological parameters listed in an Annex. The Annex sometimes specifies I (imperative) values and sometimes G (guide) values and sometimes both.   The values set by the Member States must be at least as stringent as the I values.   The waters must be sampled at frequencies given in the Annex but sampling frequency may be reduced when the quality of the water is known to be high.

Member States must provide the Commission with a list of designations and, six years following designation, with a detailed report on the designated waters.   With the consent of the Member States the Commission is to publish this.

Development of the Directive

The European Parliament pointed out that the proposed Directive would require an increase in the number of personnel carrying out sampling, but otherwise welcomed the proposal.   The House of Lords' Scrutiny Committee expressed sharp criticisms but were not alone in doing so as is shown by the comment of the Minister, Kenneth Marks, in the House of Commons' debate (6th April 1978):

"The shellfish proposal has been so severely criticised on all sides in Brussels that if any new proposal does emerge it will have to be radically different from the original if it is to be acceptable either to the United Kingdom or to other Member States."

Replying to the debate in the House of Lords (28th June 1977) the Minister, Baroness Birk, agreed with the main criticisms of the Lords' report:

"...it is hard to see just what is the aim of the proposal. According to the Commission it is concerned with encouraging shellfish growth, not with protecting human health. But the bacterial levels proposed relate only to human health."

This point was obviously successfully pressed in negotiations because the faecal coliform count - an indicator of pollution by sewage - proposed initially as an I value appears only as a G value in the Directive. Thus if Member States want to use the Directive as a means of protecting human health they may do so but are not obliged to.

The proposal made in the Lords' report that the Commission should consider a strategy based on monitoring the shellfish directly rather than the water in which they grow was however not supported by the Government. Baroness Birk said:

"This is interesting but it does have limitations. Direct examination of shellfish can give us an immediate impression of their state of health. But I am told that shellfish are generally more sensitive to pollution in their early stages. While certain environmental conditions would allow the adults to survive and grow, they might not be good enough for the larvae. So, if the aim was to protect shellfish, we would set standards for the water quality and monitor that as well as the shellfish themselves."

The proposed Directive was also criticised on the same grounds as the freshwater fish Directive (Section 7.5): who was to be responsible for designating waters? When this point was clarified, the other criticisms had less force since Member States were then at liberty not to designate any waters where they felt the provisions of the Directive to be excessively burdensome. Indeed, by April 1982 only Denmark, Ireland and the United Kingdom had designated shellfish waters, and the Federal Republic of Germany has stated that it will not be making any designations for the time being (see European Parliamentary Question No 120/82 - OJ C132 24.5.82). In the event, substantial changes to the proposed Directive were made before it was adopted.

Formal Compliance in the UK

Control of pollution of tidal waters and the sea came later in Britain than control of inland waters and is still incomplete. When Part II of the

Control of Pollution Act eventually comes into force, there will be control of all discharges to estuaries and coastal waters up to the three mile limit, but in the meantime, compliance with the Directive in England and Wales has been based on the Clean Rivers (Estuaries and Tidal Waters) Act 1960 which only covers post-1961 discharges. So long as shellfish waters are not polluted by a discharge not controlled under that Act the existing legislation is held to be sufficient.

In Scotland, the Rivers (Prevention of Pollution) Scotland Act 1951 and 1965, and in Northern Ireland the Water Act (Northern Ireland) 1972, are being relied upon.

Accordingly, no new legislation has been introduced in Britain to comply with the Directive, nor have any Regulations been made under existing Acts. Compliance has been by the following administrative action. In January 1980 the DOE sent a copy of the Directive together with a seven page advice note to the water authorities. This note explained the Directive, explained that water authorities would be largely responsible for implementation, and concluded by suggesting the establishment of a Working Group with representatives of Government departments and water authorities to prepare further advice to ensure consistency of implementation. This further advice followed in a note dated November 1980.

In March 1981 the Scottish Development Department issued a circular letter with an advice note not dissimilar to the DOE note of November 1980, except that it announced that it was the Scottish Office that would be responsible for designations. This Scottish letter suggested certain designations but, in inviting suggestions for further designations, pointed out that only waters already controlled by the Rivers (Prevention of Pollution) Scotland Act should be included.

In November 1981 the DOE sent to the Commission a list of 27 shellfish waters which had been designated in England and Scotland totalling some 314 square kilometres in area. No waters in Northern Ireland or Wales were included in that list, but in January 1983 the DOE wrote to the Commission saying that Strangford Lough in Northern Ireland and Menai Strait in Wales had been designated.

It is at least questionable whether Britain is in full compliance with the Directive since the choice of waters for designation may have been distorted by the constraints that only waters protected by existing legislation could be considered for designation. Any doubt on this point will be resolved when Part II of the Control of Pollution Act is brought into force.

The Effect on UK Practice

The advice given by the DOE in its note of November 1980 was that the initial round of designations should not put an extra burden on capital expenditure in the current economic circumstances and that, consequently, only a fairly small number of waters should be designated. These were to be those which either already met the standards or which were capable of doing so by October 1987 after improvements which were already programmed. This advice seems to have been followed. The water authorities interviewed early in 1981, i.e., before designations had been made but while some of them were being considered, spoke of waters which were being considered for designation but which did not then meet the standards. These waters have not been designated in the first round but some are under consideration for designation later when water quality improves.

Some extra expenditure on sampling and monitoring will be incurred, but it is not possible to be precise about this because at the time that the water authorities in England and Wales were interviewed they did not yet know which waters would be designated. One Scottish River Purification Board said:

"It is anticipated that sampling and monitoring will be carried out within the Board's present programme of expenditure, by redistribution of effort and resources, if necessary."

Another Scottish Board said:

"Yes, implementation of the Directive is likely to cause changes in our practices, financial outlay and manpower. Because the designated waters will, for the most part, be of good quality the Board will have afforded them low priority for monitoring purposes in the past. Once they are designated, we are committed to providing a certain level of surveillance which means that, unless additional resources are granted to meet this, we will have to direct some of our existing resources away from investigations of areas which are more seriously polluted, and therefore of fundamentally greater concern to us."

The designation of waters in Northern Ireland must be resulting in a change in practice because no monitoring programme for shellfish waters was previously carried out.

The Directive must also provide additional pressure for bringing Part II of the Control of Pollution Act 1974 into force. When that happens, water authorities will concern themselves more with sea water than they have had to at present. The mere fact of having to consider shellfish waters for designation (and bathing waters - see Section 7.7) has forced the water authorities to involve themselves with sea water earlier than they would have otherwise.

7.7　Bathing Water

76/160/EEC (OJ L31 5.2.76)　　Directive concerning the
proposed 3.2.75 - COM(74)2255　quality of bathing water

Binding dates
　Notification date:　　　　　　10 December 1975
　Formal compliance:　　　　　　10 December 1977
　First regular report to be
　　submitted to Commission:　　10 December 1979
　Derogations to be communicated
　　to Commission:　　　　　　　10 December 1981
　Standards to be met:　　　　　10 December 1985 (unless
　　　　　　　　　　　　　　　　derogations given)

Purpose of the Directive

　　The quality of bathing water is to be raised over time, or maintained, not just to protect public health but also for reasons of amenity.　This is to be done largely by ensuring that sewage is not present or has been adequately diluted or destroyed.

Summary of the Directive

Bathing water is defined as fresh or sea water in which:

　- bathing is explicitly authorised, or
　- is not prohibited and is traditionally practised by a large number
　　of bathers.

　　An Annex lists 19 physical, chemical and microbiological parameters against 13 of which are indicated I (imperative) and/or G (guide) values. The most important of these values are the coliform counts.　The Member States must set values which bathing water must meet, the values being no less stringent than the I values, with the G values being observed as guidelines.　The values set have to be met by December 1985, but in exceptional circumstances, derogations from the time limit may be granted by the Member States.　Derogations have to be justified by reference to a management plan and must be communicated to the Commission by December 1981.
　　To conform with the Directive, 95 per cent of samples for parameters where an I value is given must meet the values set and 90 per cent of samples in other cases.
　　The Annex lays down minimum sampling frequencies (for several parameters this is fortnightly during the bathing season, i.e., about 10 to 12 times a year) and the Directive specifies where and how samples are to be taken, but it does not specify how samples are to be handled before analysis.

Some parameters, e.g., streptococci and salmonellae, only have to be checked when there is reason to suppose that the substance (sic) is present. The Directive does not specify methods of analysis but sets out 'reference methods' and any other methods used must be comparable.

Investigations have to be carried out "to determine the volume and nature of all polluting and potentially polluting discharges and their effects according to the distance from the bathing area".

Waivers may be granted for certain parameters because of exceptional weather or geographical conditions or because of 'natural enrichment'. Waivers must be notified to the Commission together with the reasons for them and the periods anticipated.

At regular intervals from December 1979 Member States are to submit a comprehensive report to the Commission on their bathing waters. The Commission may publish this information with the consent of the Member State concerned.

Development of the Directive

In addition to technical difficulties relating to the parameters and to the time allowed for meeting them, the main difficulty experienced during development of the Directive concerned the definition of bathing waters. A further difficulty was created by the European Parliament and exacerbated by a possibly inadvertent remark by a Commissioner.

In its formal opinion, the Parliament proposed that bathing should be prohibited in water that did not meet the values set in the Directive. During the debate preceeding the adoption of this opinion (13th May 1975) three British members objected to this proposal. Sir Derek Walker-Smith said prohibition would pose problems of acceptability by individual citizens; Lord Bethell said that large numbers of warning signs would have to be erected where water quality was not up to the standard required; and James Spicer said that prohibition would be bad law because it could not be enforced. James Spicer proposed an amendment to say that bathing should be discouraged rather than prohibited. In replying to the debate, Commissioner Scarascia Mugnozza could have said that the Commission's proposal did not contemplate any prohibition of bathing but, quite inexplicably, he spoke against James Spicer's amendment which was accordingly defeated. By doing so, the Commissioner created the idea that prohibition was to form a part of the Directive and thereby caused a needless reaction at least in Britain.

Six weeks later the House of Commons' scrutiny committee in taking evidence from the Minister, Denis Howell, asked as its first question whether bathing would be forbidden. Despite the Minister's reply that he thought the short answer was 'no', the Committee's interim report on 8th July said that further information was being sought. The House of Lords' scrutiny committee also allowed itself to be misled. Its report of 29th July pointed to the possibility either of widespread prohibition of bathing or of the United Kingdom being in default of the Directive. The committee added that prohibition would produce a very strong public reaction. Some assurance on this point must subsequently have been given because the Commons' scrutiny committee's final report on 16th September stated "there would be no question of any restriction or prohibition of bathing as a result of the

Directive". Such an assurance at second hand could not have satisfied one of the law lords, Lord Diplock, who felt moved to say in the House of Lords' debate (13th October 1975) that any subordinate legislation made in Britain under the European Communities Act prohibiting bathing could be questioned by a person prosecuted for unlawful bathing for being ultra vires the Treaty of Rome. The Minister, Lady Birk, attempted to still these fears:

> "The proposal at no point mentions prohibition of bathing...I can say quite categorically that the Government have no intention whatsoever of asking for powers to prohibit bathing in this country where the standards in the Directive cannot be met..."

Despite this firm assurance it took some time before the idea that the Community would prohibit bathing finally died in Britain.

The difficulty of finding a definition for bathing water arises from the fact that whereas many countries have a system for authorising bathing no such authorisation is known to take place in Britain. The Directive as proposed accordingly defined bathing waters as those where bathing was authorised **or tolerated**. Since bathing is tolerated almost everywhere in Britain, the whole of the British coastline, which was then the longest of any Member State*, would have to be monitored at great expense, despite the fact that very little bathing takes place along much of it. This problem was overcome in the Directive as agreed by omitting 'tolerated' and referring instead to water "in which bathing is not prohibited and is traditionally practised by a large number of bathers". The Directive is therefore different from the freshwater fish and shellfish Directives (Sections 7.5 and 7.6) in that bathing waters are not 'designated' by Member States. Waters either are, or are not, 'bathing waters' within the definition of the Directive though what constitutes a large number of bathers has created problems of its own.

Various other changes were made to the proposal before it was adopted, one being to give Member States the power to grant derogations from the 10 year time limit, a change which Britain had pressed for.

Technical Issues

The values set out in the Directive have been the subject of much discussion and criticism with scientific questions becoming intertwined with policy matters. Was the Directive intended as a public health measure, or was it also concerned with ensuring that bathing was pleasurable? The British government's recently reiterated view** based on a 1959 report from the Medical Research Council (1) is that for all practical purposes there is no risk to health from bathing in British coastal waters unless the pollution is so gross as to be aesthetically revolting. If correct, this view must lead to the conclusion that the Directive goes much further than protecting public health and is intended to ensure minimum standards of amenity. The ques-

---

* Greece was yet to join the Community.

** Reply to a Parliamentary Question, House of Commons, 28.7.81

tion then arises whether setting bacteriological values for sea water is a reasonable method of establishing amenity standards. The Chairman of the Committee that produced the Medical Research Council report believes it is not and has criticised the Directive for laying down limits for coliform organisms with no attempt to relate these to health or aesthetics, and contrasts this with the British approach which, he argues, has been to concentrate on practical measures to ensure aesthetically satisfactory conditions.(2) This view is not shared by all in Britain and many of the water authorities said they found it helpful to have the numerical values of the Directive as a yardstick. The Clyde River Purification Board found that waters which were visibly polluted and where noticeable amounts of sewage solids were present invariably had coliform concentrations greatly exceeding the values in the Directive while, conversely, waters which conformed to the values were almost invariably satisfactory from an aesthetic standpoint.(3)

Coliform counts have the merit of being easy to carry out. Coliforms grow in the human gut and, though they are not themselves all harmful to man, their presence in water indicates faecal contamination. A coliform count therefore provides a reasonable indicator of the extent to which sewage has been diluted or destroyed, but is not a good indicator of risk to health since the pathogens contained in the sewage depend on the health of the population giving rise to it. (Dilute sewage from a town infected by cholera is more dangerous than stronger sewage from a healthy town). This reinforces the view that the Directive is concerned more with amenity than with health, in which case the practice of chlorinating sewage to kill bacteria - a practice sometimes adopted to meet the values in the Directive - has little to commend it. If the Directive is concerned with health, then it has been argued that warm southern waters need a more stringent standard than do colder waters because the longer a bather stays in the water, the more water and pathogens will he swallow. In fact, the Directive as proposed made a distinction between waters warmer and colder than $20^{o}C$ but this disappeared before the Directive was agreed. A factor pulling in the opposite direction is that the stronger sunlight in the Mediterranean kills bacteria more quickly.

Technical questions such as whether salmonellae would provide a better indicator than coliforms (4) cannot be discussed here, but one further technical point must be mentioned since it affects the value of any comparative reports between countries. The Directive gives no guidance on the manner in which samples are to be handled before being analysed but since exposure to bright summer sunshine for half an hour may reduce the coliform count by 90%,(5) samples must be handled in similar ways by the different authorities if the results of analysis are to be comparable. It is all too easy to cheat since "by the judicious choice of sampling time and place, method of transport to the laboratory and analytical technique, doubtful beaches could appear to comply with the mandatory limits".(3) The comparative reports on water quality to be issued by the Commission will have to be treated with caution.

Formal Compliance in the UK

When the Directive was being negotiated, it was expected that Part II of the Control of Pollution Act 1974 would be in force by the date for formal

- 88

compliance in December 1977. In March 1977 the DOE sent a six-page advice note to the water authorities which described the Directive and said that there was doubt over how far compliance could be achieved without the Act being in force. Doubts concerned both the power to monitor coastal waters and the ability to control discharges.

Shortly after the date for formal compliance, the Government sent a letter to the Commission referring to the Control of Pollution Act as containing the necessary powers for compliance but omitting to say that the relevant sections of the Act were not yet in force. The letter also said that discussions were being held with the relevant authorities about identification of bathing waters. Curiously, in all the correspondence that was to follow between the Commission and the government, the Commission apparently never mentioned that the relevant sections of the Control of Pollution Act were not in force, although its officials were aware of this, nor did the government point out that it had subsequently satisfied itself that other powers existed which effectively enabled it to comply with the Directive without the benefit of the Control of Pollution Act. For England and Wales these powers are contained in the Water Resources Act 1963 and the Water Act 1973. Section 113(1)(b) of the 1963 Act provides water authorities with the power to take samples from the sea and tidal waters and the 1973 Act gives the water authorities control over their own sewage discharges. Some industrial discharges (which may include sewage) are not yet controlled but, in practice, none of the bathing waters identified are affected by these.

The Commission's disquiet about British compliance with the Directive - which ultimately led to a 'Reasoned Opinion' being issued in 1980 - first concerned the administrative steps taken by the government. This disquiet was expressed in a letter from the Commission of 3rd July 1979 and probably stemmed from the knowledge - the story is told by Ruth Levitt (6) - that the Secretary of State for the Environment, Peter Shore, had delayed advice from the Department to the water authorities while he considered the matter personally. But by the time the Commission had sent its letter, a new government was in power and the long awaited advice note to water authorities was ready to be issued and was simultaneously released to the press on 9th July 1979, i.e., only a few days after the Commission's letter. The advice note announced that the water authorities in England and Wales were being formally appointed as the competent authorities and then set out guidelines to enable them to identify bathing waters - only just in time for the bathing season.

On 19th October 1979 the government replied formally to the Commission's letter of 3rd July 1979. This reply summarised the action taken in England and Wales but explained that in Scotland the Scottish Development Department would be responsible for identifying bathing waters and in Northern Ireland responsibility would lie with the Department of the Environment for Northern Ireland. This letter had followed a meeting between Commission officials and DOE officials at which the administrative arrangements had been discussed and which had resulted in the DOE sending the Commission a memorandum[*] setting out the relationship between the various authorities in England, Wales, Scotland and Northern

---

[*]   This is the same memorandum referred to in connection with the surface water Directive (see Section 7.2).

Ireland.

Two months later, on 18th December 1979, thereby just missing the due date, the government sent a formal letter to the Commission enclosing a list of the waters which had been identified together with a technical report on their quality.

The list, no doubt inadvertently, failed to indicate positively that no waters had been identified in Scotland and Northern Ireland, so that it was left to the Commission to guess whether the process of identification had or had not taken place in those countries.

On 3rd July 1980 the Commission wrote enquiring, among other matters, why no waters had been identified in Scotland and Northern Ireland, but barely could a reply be sent before, on 16th July, the Commission issued a 'Reasoned Opinion' to the effect that the UK had failed to take all the necessary steps to comply with the Directive. The government replied on 18th September 1980 saying nothing that had not been said before except to confirm that no waters in Scotland or Northern Ireland had been identified as bathing waters. The letter effectively asked for the Reasoned Opinion to be withdrawn. Over two years later this has neither happened, nor has the Commission started proceedings before the Court. In October 1981 the Commission said in reply to a question in the European Parliament (OJ C303 23.11.81) that it was not satisfied that the United Kingdom was complying with the Directive, but the reply did not make it clear whether this dissatisfaction relates to the administrative arrangements for complying with the Directive or with the actual bathing waters identified.

Identifying Bathing Waters

In many European countries bathing is explicitly authorised from certain beaches, sometimes during a prescribed bathing season, and in such countries there can be no argument that those waters fall within the definition of the Directive. The British government has stated that it is not aware of any statutory provision enabling any public body explicitly to authorise bathing. The government's view is that to fall within this first limb of the definition of the Directive, there must be some authorisation made in an open and declaratory form, but that in Britain entitlement to bathe derives from custom or prescription which is the very antithesis of explicit authorisation, since one can only acquire something by custom or prescription if there has been no positive grant. The government argues that the making of by-laws under Section 231 of the Public Health Act 1936 regulating the areas in which public bathing is permitted merely allows local authorities to limit an existing entitlement and does not create one. Accordingly, Britain has relied entirely on the second limb of the definition of bathing waters, i.e., where it is traditionally practised by a large number of people.

In its first advice note of March 1977 the DOE suggested the setting of guidelines to ensure consistency by the various water authorities in identifying bathing waters. The advice note went on to point out that Mediterranean beaches would be used much more by bathers who actually entered the water than northern ones, and that on that basis there were likely to be rather few places in Britain that fell within the definition. The advice note also pointed out that the financial implications were potentially significant.

It seems from the beginning to have been the government's policy - a policy consistent with its stance on the shellfish and freshwater fish Directives (Sections 7.5 and 7.6) - that existing water authority priorities for spending money on water quality should not be excessively distorted by Community commitments and that, therefore, few waters should be identified. A DOE official has pointed out that "evidence collected by water authorities for the purpose of this Directive has shown a tendency for the British holiday-maker to sit on the beach, but not to venture into the water" (7), and it has even been suggested that, seen in a European context, there are no British bathing waters used by a 'large number' of bathers. It was also assumed that district councils covering seaside resorts would want to see their bathing waters identified for promotional reasons but that water authorities could not be expected to undertake excessive financial burdens. A draft DOE advice note apparently circulated among water authorities late in 1977 suggested a lower density of bathers as a guide to the meaning of 'large' than was finally decided upon. The final guidelines published in the advice note of 9th July 1979 were that bathing waters with fewer than 500 people in the water at any time should not be identified; that any stretch where the number of bathers was more than 1,500 per mile should be identified; while those with between 750 and 1,500 per mile were open to negotiation between water authority and district council.

The water authorities and district councils conducted an identification exercise in August 1979 and, as a result, 27 bathing waters* were communicated to the Commission in December 1979. This must be contrasted with over 600 beaches in England and Wales from which bathing regularly takes place (8).

There can be little doubt that the final choice of guidelines was influenced by the government's desire to do something to implement the Directive while not putting too great a financial burden on water authorities at a time of public expenditure restraint. Blackpool, assessed at between 750 and 1,500 bathers per mile, and which, by agreement between the water authority and district council, has not been identified, would probably have fallen within guidelines suggested at an early stage resulting in an expenditure of between £10 and £50 million to bring the water up to standard. Similarly, there are bathing waters in Scotland which could possibly have been identified if the earlier suggested guidelines had been followed. At Brighton the numbers fell just within the range for identification, and although the water conforms with the Directive it has not been identified despite the desire of the district council that it should be. The suspicion inevitably arises that it would have been difficult simultaneously to include Brighton but exclude Blackpool despite the fact that the formal decision to identify waters had been delegated to water authorities.

Whether the guidelines finally issued by the DOE as to what constitutes 'a large number' of bathers is reasonable in the circumstances as the DOE would argue, or whether they fall short of what is required by the Directive as the Commission perhaps may suspect, are questions which may

---

* The list originally sent to the Commission included 25 'bathing waters' but subsequently two of these (Sandown and Southend-on-Sea) have each been subdivided into two for monitoring purposes.

yet have to be answered by the Court if the Commission finally makes up its mind to continue along the path it has taken. In effect, the Court would have to decide how large is large and in doing so it would presumably have regard to what happens in other countries who may be having their own difficulties with the Directive.

It must be debatable, even with the little experience of the Directive that there has been so far, whether the definition of bathing water has proved satisfactory and whether the approach used in the shellfish and freshwater fish Directives would not have been more effective in achieving the aims of the Directive. Giving discretion to the Member States not only cuts out the friction between the Member State and the Commission but makes it easier to adopt a more dynamic approach, with additional waters being designated as standards improve. The bathing water Directive by using the words 'traditionally practised' is backward rather than forward looking and arguably allows no new bathing waters to be identified until a new tradition is established. There is also something unsatisfactory in the existence of so many bathing waters throughout Britain which are not recorded in the reports sent to the Commission. These reports, by listing only 27 bathing waters out of at least 600 regularly used for bathing, are inevitably partial and do not provide a useful picture of the state of British bathing waters.

The Effect on UK Practice

Even before the Directive came into force its existence stimulated some water authorities to monitor coastal waters. Water authorities were expecting to have to do this anyway in fulfilment of their forthcoming duties under the Control of Pollution Act but, as those duties have yet to materialise, it was the Directive that gave the sharper stimulus, particularly in providing a yardstick by which to measure water quality.

Despite the many criticisms that have been made of this Directive[*], several water authorities claim to have found it useful. Even for water authorities that have identified no bathing waters, the Directive provides a yardstick which can be used in the design and location of new sewage outfalls. A yardstick is also useful in taking emotion out of discussions between those responsible for water quality and those responsible for finance. The Directive has also resulted in research on water movement using modelling techniques and microbiological tracing methods.

Five water authorities have identified a total of 27 bathing waters and in all cases the values set have been the I values in the Directive:

South West WA   11   Meadford Beach, Oddicombe Beach, Torre Abbey Sands, Broadsands Beach, Goodrington Beach, Paignton Beach, Fistral Beach, Newquay Town Beach, Porthmear Beach, Porthminster Beach, Sennen Cove

---

[*]   The National Water Council has called it "..the least satisfactory EEC Directive on water quality to emerge up to now...It is not well judged scientifically and may well be costly to administer; it would also lead to a distortion of investment in environmental improvement" (Water Industry Review 1978).

Wessex WA	6	Christchurch, Bournemouth, Weston-super-Mare, Weymouth, Poole, Swanage
Yorkshire WA	4	Scarborough North Bay, Scarborough South Bay, Bridlington North Bay, Bridlington South Bay
Southern WA	4	Sandown Beach, Shanklin Beach, Ryde, Margate
Thames WA	2	Southend/Thorpe Bay, Southend/Westcliffe Beach

Annual reports on the quality of these bathing waters are now being submitted to the Commission by the DOE. In the 1980 report four of these waters clearly did not conform to the I values (Bridlington South, Goodrington, Ryde and Weston-super-Mare) while six were borderline (Bridlington North, Christchurch, Sennen Cove, Shanklin, Scarborough South, and Southend/Thorpe Bay). The others conformed to the standards.

In the 1981 report four of these waters clearly did not conform to the I values (Bridlington South, Ryde, Scarborough South and Weston-super-Mare) while three were borderline (Bridlington North, Scarborough North, Shanklin).

In December 1981 the DOE informed the Commission that it had granted derogations from the 10-year time limit in respect of four of the identified bathing waters on the assumption that compliance for these waters would not be guaranteed:

(i)   Scarborough North and South Bays
(ii)   Ryde
(iii)   Margate

As required by the Directive, these derogations were justified by management plans. At Scarborough the presence of three short outfalls makes it uncertain that compliance can be guaranteed and a new long outfall is planned to replace them at an estimated cost of £10m. Subject to financial constraints, work should start in 1984. At Ryde long sea outfalls costing £6m are being investigated but the earliest the works could start would be 1984. At Margate consideration is being given to a number of schemes ranging from those of local significance to major works to improve the whole of the Thanet coastline. Both an inland sewage works and new sea outfalls have been considered, both involving a major interceptor sewer. These schemes have been costed at £41m for an inland works and £32m for an outfall and would take many years to complete. These schemes were under discussion before the Directive so it will not be possible to attribute this expenditure, if it takes place, entirely to it, though the Directive provides considerable extra pressure.

The DOE assumes that the other waters will be able to reach the standards of the Directive by the due date in 1985. At Bridlington a 1,700m outfall pipe is being built at a cost of £4.5 million. It is due to be completed in 1983 but was planned before the Directive and cannot be attributed to it. Goodrington is affected by a storm sewage outfall and measures entailing alterations to the pumping regimes and pump improvement at a cost of £8,000 are being tried, but if found insufficient, will have to be replaced by a major scheme. Weston-super-Mare will, in the long term, require a new outfall system at considerable expense but, in the meanwhile, the sewage is being chlorinated at a capital cost of £100,000 with an annual running cost of £20,000.

All the water authorities reported some small expenditure on sampling and analysis. In one case the samples are taken by district councils at a cost of around £2,500 per annum. Another authority reported an annual sampling cost of around £15,000.

Even from these few examples, it can be seen that the costs of new long sea outfalls are large and that the benefits accrue to rather few people so that a difficult political decision has to be made. Given that the water authorities have other priorities for water quality improvement, quite apart from other calls on their funds which are locally raised, it becomes easy to see why the government has been at pains not to have its hands and those of the water authorities tied too tightly by identifying too many waters under the Directive. In Britain the political decision to spend money on outfalls has been a local one taken by self-financing water authorities, and an underlying political question raised by the Directive is the extent to which this local discretion should be constrained. If the Directive had provided for no derogations and had included all waters where bathing takes place, as originally proposed, it would quite probably have been unworkable and might well have encouraged the authorities to pretend that their waters were better than they were – we have already seen how easy it is to do this. Now that derogations are permitted and a very strict view has been taken of what constitutes 'a large number of bathers', the Directive can be made to work in Britain. In other countries constrained by 'explicit authorisations' the position may be different[*]. This point may be clarified if and when the Commission publishes a comparative report – though with the caveat already expressed about the value of comparisons.

Undoubtedly one effect of the Directive has been to promote a greater knowledge of bathing water among the appropriate authorities and to increase the DOE's involvement so that nationally more is now known about bathing water quality. This could now be capitalised upon by expanding the reports which are prepared for the Commission. If, instead of these being confined to only 27 identified bathing waters, they were extended to a much larger number, a better picture would emerge of the state of coastal waters. The DOE already publishes a River Quality Survey every five years, and when Part II of the Control of Pollution Act is in force it would be logical to publish a coastal water survey too. This survey could use the values of the Directive as a yardstick, as is already done by the Clyde River Purification Board in its annual reports despite there being no identified bathing waters in Scotland.

Although it is impossible to point with confidence to any one improvement scheme, beyond those involving chlorination, and say that it was initiated in response to the Directive, the Directive may well serve to

---

[*] Lord Nugent, former Chairman of the National Water Council, in a debate in the House of Lords (2nd March 1981), expressed the view that the work needed to bring certain Mediterranean waters up to standard would require a programme taking decades rather than years to complete and would cost billions of pounds. He criticised the absence of a survey which would have established this and which would have revealed that a Directive setting standards was premature.

speed the completion of some existing schemes.

The greatest effect of the Directive may, in the long run, turn out to be on waters which are not identified as bathing waters for the purposes of the Directive. For these waters the values in the Directive are not mandatory but provide guidelines when planning future investment. Britain, so chary of mandatory limits, has turned what was intended as such into working guidelines with which it feels much happier.

References

(1) Medical Research Council, **Sewage Contamination of Bathing Beaches in England and Wales**, Memorandum No 37, HMSO, London 1959.

(2) B Moore, **The EEC Bathing Water Directive**, Marine Pollution Bulletin, Vol 8, No 12, 1977.

(3) D Hammerton, **EEC Directives on the Quality of Bathing Water and on Water Pollution Caused by the Discharge of Dangerous Substances – The River Purification Board Viewpoint**, Institute of Water Pollution Control (Scottish Branch), Symposium on River Pollution Prevention, March 1978.

(4) H Fennell (Yorkshire Water Authority), **Standards Should be Practical and Scientific**, paper presented to Symposium on Sea Bathing, Genoa, April 1981.

(5) A L H Gameson, **EEC Directive on Quality of Bathing Water**, Journal of the Institute of Water Pollution Control, Vol 78, No 2, 1979.

(6) Ruth Levitt, **Implementing Public Policy**, Croom Helm, London, 1980 (Chapter 5 takes the Bathing Water Directive as a case study).

(7) D C Renshaw, **The EEC Directives and Water Quality**, The Institution of Water Engineers and Scientists, Symposium on EEC Directives, London 1980.

(8) **The Golden List of Clean Beaches in England and Wales**, The Coastal Anti-Pollution League Ltd.

7.8　Dangerous Substances in Water

76/464/EEC* (OJ L129 18.5.76)
proposed 21.10.74-COM(74)1706

Directive on pollution caused by
certain dangerous substances
discharged into the aquatic
environment of the Community

Binding dates
Notification date:　　　　　　　　5 May 1976

As no dates are set in the Directive, the Commission suggested the following
deadlines in a letter dated 3rd November 1976:

System of authorisations:　　　　15 September 1978
Pollution reduction programmes
　for List II substances:　　　　15 September 1981
Programmes to be implemented:　15 September 1986

Purpose of the Directive

　　The Directive sets a framework for the elimination or reduction of
pollution of inland, coastal and territorial waters by particularly dangerous
substances.　It seeks to establish the extent of such pollution by requiring
an inventory of discharges.　The Directive also has political and economic
purposes: to ensure consistency in implementing various international
Conventions and to reduce distortion to conditions of competition.

Summary of the Directive

　　An Annex has a List I and a List II of families and groups of dangerous
substances.　List I includes substances selected on the basis of their
toxicity, persistence and bioaccumulation, e.g., organohalogen and
organophosphorus compounds, carcinogenic substances, and mercury and
cadmium compounds.　List II includes possibly less dangerous substances
such as zinc, copper and lead compounds, cyanide and ammonia.　For the
purposes of the Directive any List I substance is to be treated as a List II
substance until a 'daughter' Directive sets limit values for it (see below).
　　Member States are to take appropriate steps to **eliminate** pollution by
List I substances and to **reduce** pollution by List II substances.
'Elimination' of pollution does not necessarily mean a zero-emission since
pollution is defined not by reference to the presence of a substance but to its
effects.
　　Discharges of both List I and List II substances are to be subject to

---

*　　This Directive is often incorrectly referred to as ENV 131, a design-
　　ation referring to an unpublished draft which differed substantially from
　　the Directive.

prior authorisation, but these authorisations are arrived at in different ways.

For controlling **List II** substances, Member States are to establish pollution reduction programmes with deadlines for implementation. All discharges liable to contain a List II substance require prior authorisation with emission standards being laid down. These emission standards are to be based on quality objectives. These quality objectives must be laid down in accordance with any existing Directives, i.e., it is foreseen that these may be laid down at Community level. Summaries of the programmes and the results of implementation are to be communicated to the Commission which is to arrange for regular comparisons.

For controlling **List I** substances, Member States may choose between two alternative regimes. The preferred regime entails limit values which emission standards are not to exceed[*]. These are to be fixed uniformly throughout the Community in 'daughter' Directives. The alternative regime entails emission standards set by reference to quality objectives. The quality objectives are also to be laid down in 'daughter' Directives. Use of the alternative regime is conditional on the Member State proving to the Commission in accordance with a monitoring procedure set up by the Council that the quality objectives are being met.

At the Council meeting of 4th May 1976 all Member States except Britain declared that they would adopt the preferred regime[**].

The limit values are to be laid down mainly on the basis of toxicity, persistence and bioaccumulation taking into account the best technical means available, though this latter point was qualified in a statement made at the Council meeting[**] of 4th May 1976 to the effect that 'best technical means available' is to take into account the economic availability of those means.

Member States are to draw up inventories of all discharges which may contain List I substances, and supply them to the Commission at its request. The Commission may also ask for information about authorisations and the results of monitoring.

Two points need to be emphasised. First, programmes for the reduction of pollution are required for List II but not for List I substances. But, secondly, since all substances are to be treated in law as List II substances until a 'daughter' Directive converts a substance into a List I substance, all substances, at least initially, are to be the subject of pollution reduction programmes, based on quality objectives. By the end of June 1983 only mercury discharged by the chlor-alkali electrolysis industry and cadmium had been put into List I (see 'Further Developments' below). Mercury from all other sources and all other potential List I substances remain, in law, List II substances.

---

[*]   It is often said in Britain that the Directive requires 'uniform emission standards' to be laid down. This is incorrect and the words uniform emission standards do not appear in the Directive. What the Directive requires is the laying down of **limit values** at Community level and the authorities in the Member States may impose emission standards more stringent than the limit values but not less stringent.

[**]   Council Minutes are usually kept confidential but these statements were published in a book (1) by a Commission official (now a Member of the European Parliament).

Development of the Directive

The day before the Council was due to consider this Directive on 16th October 1975 a leading article in The Times explained the differences between the British government and the Commission concerning this Directive in terms highly critical of the Commission. No other environmental Directive has been the focus of so much attention in Britain. As well as being the most contentious, it is also potentially one of the most important and certainly implies the largest programme of work for the future. It also has a number of other distinctive features: unlike all other water Directives, no date is set for compliance; the proposal submitted by the Commission to the Council was a proposal for a Decision and not a Directive; and there is no foundation for that part of the Directive dealing with limit values in the First Action Programme.

The preamble to the Directive explains its origins by referring to the need to co-ordinate the implementation of several international Conventions concerned with river pollution that were under discussion when the Directive was proposed in October 1974:

- the Paris Convention for the prevention of marine pollution from land based sources – adopted 4th June 1974
- the Convention for the Protection of the Rhine against chemical pollution – adopted 3rd December 1976
- the draft Strasbourg Convention for the protection of international watercourses against pollution – not yet adopted.

The three Conventions affect, or will affect, different Member States to different extents. The Paris Convention is concerned only with discharges, including those from rivers, into the North Sea and north east Atlantic. The parties to the Rhine Convention are its riparian states plus the European Community. The Strasbourg Convention, being drafted under the auspices of the Council of Europe, will deal only with rivers crossing national frontiers and so will not affect, for example, the Seine or the Thames. All three Conventions have two lists inspired by the generally similar lists in the Oslo and London Conventions concerned with dumping at sea.

The **Paris Convention** has two lists which are similar but not identical to the lists in the Directive. Unlike the Directive, pollution reduction programmes with time limits are to be implemented for both lists but for neither list, again unlike the Directive, do limit values have to be laid down.

The **Rhine Convention** similarly has two lists. An International Commission is to lay down limit values which discharges of List I substances are not to exceed, but List II substances are to be subject to emission standards set by national authorities by reference to quality objectives and national programmes. The Rhine Convention is therefore rather similar to the preferred regime of the Directive.

The **Strasbourg Convention** has not been agreed, and officially no draft is public, but the Commission's explanatory memorandum accompanying the proposal for the Directive (or Decision as it then was) – COM(74)1706 – suggested that the Convention might include quite stringent standards for the international rivers that would be covered by it.

The Belgian government is given the credit for initiating the Directive by the report of the Environment Committee of the European Parliament. The Belgian government appears to have believed that Antwerp, lying on the Scheldt, and hence subject to the possibly stringent standards of the Strasbourg Convention, would be at a disadvantage in comparison with, say, London or Le Havre which do not lie on international rivers. The Belgian government appears to have persuaded the Commission that there was a need to ensure that all Member States should be subject to similar provisions. Seen thus, the origin of the Directive was economic, and the economic self-interest of Britain with its short fast rivers lay in resisting centrally fixed limit values for emission standards. The discussions that followed were clearly coloured by this as emerges from the deliberations in Parliament.

The Directive/Decision as proposed involved limit values for both List I and List II substances set by a qualified majority vote in the Council. On 15th January 1975 DOE officials giving evidence to the House of Lords' Scrutiny Committee were asked whether this was something that appealed to the British government or whether it was something that had "at the very least, a germ of controversy and difference about it". They were also asked whether behind the technicalities "there might lurk a controversial political problem of inequality in competitive trading relations between ourselves and our continental partners?" The replies indicated clearly the government's concern but curiously the Scrutiny Committee's report did not make much of the issue - certainly in comparison to reports that were to follow. Indeed, the House of Lords never formally debated the proposal though they often referred to it in debates on other Directives.

Two months later when the Minister, Denis Howell, and DOE officials gave evidence before the House of Commons' Scrutiny Committee, the proposal had already been modified. An official explained that "there is general agreement among the delegations that the right approach for dealing with the substances in List II would be to set environmental quality objectives". The Rhine Convention, to which Britain is not a party, also shows that the use of variable emission standards set nationally according to quality objectives was a concept accepted by other countries even for dangerous substances. It was only over the List I substances that Britain was eventually to differ from the other Member States.

The Chairman of the Commons' Scrutiny Committee asked whether the government would be pressing strongly for the retention of the delegated authority to set emission standards in accordance with current British practice "or whether you will be tending to assent to a more centralised Directive of the kind which the instrument predicts". The official's reply was ambivalent implying that Britain might be prepared to accept centrally fixed limit values for List I substances:

"I think it worth stressing that List I substances are, in fact, a very small and special group, and there are reasons why a particular approach might be appropriate for them."

When pressed further, he explained that List I substances were already closely controlled in Britain and said:

"...these are, of course, very toxic substances, and the differences would not be great between a uniform

99

emission standards' approach and a flexible approach such as we adopt in this country."

In the event, as is well known, the British government finally decided to resist centrally fixed limit values for emission standards for List I substances and no agreement was reached at the Council meeting of 16 October 1975. A compromise allowing two regimes for List I was then agreed in principle at the Council meeting in December.

The replies by DOE officials to the Commons' Scrutiny Committee show that there was the possibility of Britain agreeing to centrally fixed limit values for List I substances, a possibility known to Commission officials. The confusion that finally culminated in the failure of the 16th October Council meeting, and the subsequent recriminations were exacerbated by the difficulty that British officials had in obtaining a decision from Ministers at a time when a referendum was being held in Britain on the question of Britain's continuing membership of the Community. British industry was strongly opposed to centrally fixed limit values for reasons of self interest and this view finally prevailed in the government. The fullest statement of the British government's position is the 3,700 word speech made by the Minister, Denis Howell, at the October Council Meeting. The Minister emphasised the environmental, administrative and economic soundness of the British government's traditionally decentralised approach, and while accepting that other reasons applied in other countries, ignored the counter arguments that had been rehearsed even in the British context (see Chapter 5). The Commission and the other Member States for their part emphasised the competition argument and the administrative convenience of fixed limit values, while overlooking the lack of logic inherent in holding such a position for List I but not List II substances. Whatever arguments about competition and administrative convenience apply to List I must also apply to List II, and everyone had agreed that List II substances should not be subject to limit values. The protagonists thus found themselves in curious positions: the British who so frequently like to describe themselves as being pragmatic found themselves wedded to a doctrine, and other countries who pride themselves on being logical found themslves advocating a Directive with a fundamental illogicality which can only be justified on grounds of convenience. The British insistence on the doctrine of environmental quality objectives is all the more curious given that it was not a doctrine that had been practised in Britain in the explicit way required by the Directive (see Chapters 2 and 5).

In addition to the major changes concerning Lists I and II, the proposal was also changed in a way which renders the inventory of much less value. Whereas the proposal required an inventory for discharges of both List I and List II substances, the Directive only requires an inventory of List I substances. Since all substances are to be treated in law as List II until effectively put into List I by a 'daughter' Directive and since only two daughter Directives had been agreed by October 1983, the inventory is of very limited value.

Formal Compliance in the UK

Being a framework Directive few obligations are immediately placed on Member States, and since the Directive differs from most in not specifying dates by which Member States are to bring in the laws, regulations and administrative provisions necessary for compliance, the government has never formally written to the Commission about them nor has the Commission asked for details. Why no dates were set remains a mystery. The Commission realised, after the Directive was adopted, that dates were desirable and accordingly wrote to Member States on 3rd November 1976 suggesting that a system for the authorisation of List I and List II substances should be introduced by 15th September 1978, and that programmes for reducing pollution by List II substances should be introduced by 15th September 1981 and implemented by 15th September 1986.

When Part II of the Control of Pollution Act is brought into force, it will be possible to authorise all discharges of List I and List II substances except those produced by the Crown including the Royal Naval Dockyards. Until then some discharges to estuaries and coastal waters cannot be subject to authorisations and legal compliance is therefore incomplete. Most discharges can however be controlled under the existing legislation which has been listed in connection with the surface water Directive (see Section 7.2) and the shellfish Directive (see Section 7.6). The Royal Naval Dockyards pose a problem: although significant sources of pollution, they are not covered by existing legislation nor does the Directive provide exemption for them, although they could possibly be exempted by the provisions of Article 223 of the Treaty of Rome dealing with security matters.

The requirement for Member States to establish programmes with deadlines for the reduction of pollution is covered by existing legislation. The DOE can ask water authorities to include these in their plans prepared under Section 24(1)(c) of the Water Act 1973:

"It shall be the duty of each Water Authority...to prepare a plan as to action to be taken during the period...for the purpose of...restoring or maintaining the wholesomeness of rivers and other inland or coastal waters..."

There is however no legislation requiring the authorities to lay down environmental quality objectives by reference to which the Directive says that emission standards must be set, although they are free to do so.

The Effect on UK Practice

The major effect of this Directive has already been described in Chapters 2 and 5 and so far this has been less of a change in practice than a refinement of thought: the British have been stimulated into developing their previously imprecise ideas on the use of environmental quality objectives since the Directive makes these mandatory for the first time. The River Quality Objectives (RQOs) that Water Authorities have laid down for each stretch of inland river can therefore be attributed to the Directive even though the Directive does not require RQOs in quite that form. Having said this, it must be emphasised that some people in the water industry do not attribute the introduction of RQOs to the Directive but to the impending introduction of Part II of the Control of Pollution Act which would have resulted in publication of authorisations and the possibility of prosecution if discharges did not comply with them. According to this account, the introduction of RQOs was to enable a logical revision of emission standards before their publication. It is perfectly possible that both explanations are correct and simply happened to coincide. Whatever explanation is given by the water authorities for the introduction of RQOs, government officials were aware that the Directive made quality objectives mandatory and would therefore have encouraged their introduction.

The precise requirement of the Directive is that quality objectives should be laid down specifically for the purposes of programmes for the reduction of pollution by List II substances. This specific requirement has not yet been fully implemented, since unlike the generalised RQOs these quality objectives will, in practice, have to specify concentrations of each List II substance for different stretches of rivers, estuaries and coastal waters according to their uses. The response of the DOE to this requirement has been the placing of a research contract with the Water Research Centre to propose appropriate quality objectives for different waters initially for six non-ferrous metals: copper, lead, nickel, zinc, chromium and arsenic. This research and the greater emphasis on toxic substances that it implies can be attributed directly to the Directive. A report of this research is complete (2) but not yet published so it is likely that water authorities will not establish the programmes required under the Directive for some time. Other Member States are not thought to be any further advanced, and the 1981 deadline suggested by the Commission has proved to be unrealistic. Even the requirement for authorisation for List I and List II substances has yet to be fully implemented in practice since not all List I and List II substances have been individually authorised. For example, every sewage works discharges zinc, but it is very unusual for a specific authorisation for zinc to be given to a sewage works' discharge. The form of the authorisation - the Rivers (Prevention of Pollution) Act 1951 uses the word 'consent' - has usually been for consent to be given in a generalised form to all effluent from a sewage works subject to Biochemical Oxygen Demand (BOD_5) not exceeding X and Suspended Solids (SS) not exceeding Y. Zinc, being a constituent of sewage works' effluent, is therefore 'consented' or 'authorised' but not with a specific emission standard laid down for it as required by the Directive. Even when a sewage works is receiving industrial discharges it is quite usual for toxic metals not to be individually authorised. Major industrial dischargers of toxic substances may also well have emission standards laid down for a group of toxic substances taken together. One water authority said it would be changing its manner of drafting consent conditions as a result of the Directive but this process would take time. Full implementation of the Directive is therefore still some way away.

The inventory of List I substances is also something for the future. Since only mercury and cadmium have so far been effectively put into List I, the Commission can only formally ask for an inventory of mercury and cadmium discharges. Nevertheless, the requirements for an inventory have stimulated the DOE and the water authorities to consider how this information could be gathered and some extra monitoring work can be attributed to the Directive. In no case did any water authority claim that this had resulted in an increase of staff.

One other effect of this Directive mentioned by some water authorities was that they have had to provide information to the DOE about List I substances in order to help the DOE in its negotiations over the various 'daughter' Directives, e.g., mercury and cadmium. Despite complaints about the time involved, this process has also concentrated thinking on the control of toxic substances.

Further Developments

(a) List I Substances

In June 1982 the Commission submitted a Communication to the Council (OJ C176 14.7.82) concerning List I substances. This explained that studies had identified 1,500 substances used for technical purposes belonging to the families and groups of List I and that of these 1,000 are produced or used in quantities of less than 100 tonnes per year, 186 more than 1,000t/yr, 44 more than 10,000t/yr and only 25 in excess of 100,000t/yr.

Five hundred of the substances had been examined to evaluate risks to water and pared down to a priority list of 108 substances for further study. Fifteen were selected to be studied first. In addition to these 108 substances, 21 substances had already been studied, making a total of 129 substances. They are listed in the Communication with the caveat that the list is not final.

The list includes the following for which proposals have already been made or a decision taken not to make one:

(1) Mercury and its compounds: The subject of one daughter Directive 82/176 (see Section 7.10) and the subject of another proposed Directive (OJ C20 25.1.83 - COM(82)838)

(2) Cadmium and its compounds: The subject of daughter Directive 83/513 (OJ L291 24.10.83)

(3) Aldrin, dieldrin and endrin: The subject of a proposed Directive (OJ C146 12.6.79 - COM(79)243)

(4) Chlordane and heptachlor: No Directive to be proposed - use already restricted by Directive 79/117 (see Section 10.5)

(5) Hexachlorocyclohexane and in particular lindane: The subject of a proposed Directive (OJ C215 11.8.83 - COM(83)422)

In February 1983 the Council adopted a Resolution (OJ C46 17.2.83) noting the Commission's Communication described above and stating that the list of 129 substances would serve as a basis for further work. Member States were to provide the Commission within three years with all readily available data concerning the list including data on:

- production, use and discharges by industries;
- diffuse sources;
- concentration in water, sediments and organisms;
- remedial measures taken or envisaged and their effect.

Initial attention was to be focussed on 11 listed substances. This Resolution in effect supersedes the ineffective provision for an inventory in Directive 76/464.

(b) List II Substances

The Commission called a meeting of experts from Member States in 1981 (see European Parliamentary Question C305 22.11.82) at which priorities were set for comparing national programmes for List II substances. Six substances have been selected for priority attention: chromium, lead, zinc, copper, nickel and arsenic (the same list that has been studied by the Water Research Centre (2) - see above) and Member States have been asked about their programmes for chromium. The possibility of treating arsenic as a List I substance has been considered, but the Commission has concluded that it should be subject to the provisions applicable to List II substances (COM(83)306).

References

(1) Stanley P Johnson, **The Pollution Control Policy of the European Communities,** Graham & Trotman Ltd, London, 1979.

(2) J Gardiner and J Mance, **Environmental Standards for List II Substances,** Water Research Centre, 1982.

7.9   Groundwater

80/68/EEC (OJ L20 26.1.80)
proposed 24.1.78 - COM(78)3

Directive on the protection of
groundwater against pollution
caused by certain dangerous
substances

Binding dates
  Notification date   19 December 1979
  Formal compliance: 19 December 1981
  New discharges to be
    controlled: 19 December 1981
  Existing discharges to
    be controlled: 19 December 1985

Purpose of the Directive

Seventy per cent of the Community's drinking water and 25-30 per cent of the United Kingdom's is extracted from underground sources. In order to protect exploitable underground sources, which are very difficult to restore once polluted, both direct and indirect discharges of dangerous substances are to be prohibited or regulated.

Summary of the Directive

A List I and List II of families and groups of dangerous substances are given in an Annex, those on List I being generally more dangerous than those on List II.   The Annex makes it clear that only those substances within the limited groups and families which exhibit certain characteristics are to be classed in the appropriate list.   (The lists are not quite identical to Lists I and II of Directive 76/464 - Section 7.8).

Member States are to 'prevent' the introduction into groundwater of List I substances and to 'limit' the introduction of List II substances so as to avoid pollution. 'Pollution' is defined by reference to the effect of a substance rather than by its presence. 'Groundwater' is also defined.

The Directive does not apply to radioactive substances or to discharges of domestic effluents from isolated dwellings situated outside areas protected for the abstraction of drinking water. Nor does it apply to discharges containing List I or List II substances in a quantity and concentration so small as to obviate any present or future danger.

All direct discharges (i.e., without percolation through the ground) of **List I** substances are to be prohibited (except in trace quantities), though if after investigation the groundwater is found unsuitable for other uses such discharges may be authorised. Reinjection into the same aquifer of water used for geothermal purposes, water pumped out of mines or quarries, or water pumped out for civil engineering works, may be authorised after investigation.

All direct discharges of **List II** substances are to be subjected to investigation before being authorised.

Any disposal on land of either **List I** or **List II** substances which might lead to indirect discharges is to be subject to investigation before being authorised. (Authorisations are also required under the waste Directives - see Sections 8.1 and 8.2). Any other activity likely to lead to indirect discharges of List I substances is also to be controlled, and the control measures in respect of List I substances are to be notified to the Commission.

Artificial discharges for the purpose of groundwater management are to be specially authorised on a case by case basis, and only when there is no risk of polluting the groundwater.

All the authorisations mentioned above may only be issued if the groundwater quality is undergoing the requisite surveillance.

The nature of the above mentioned prior investigations is explained, and the particulars of the above mentioned authorisations are set out. All authorisations may only be granted for a limited period and must be reviewed every four years. The competent authorities are to monitor compliance with authorisations and the effects of discharges on groundwater.

Existing discharges of List I and List II substances must be brought within the provisions of the Directive by 19th December 1985.

An inventory of authorisations is to be kept. The Commission may ask for information, on a case by case basis, about: authorisations, the inventory, the prior investigations mentioned above, and the results of monitoring. The information acquired by the Commission must only be used for the purpose for which it was requested. This is not to prevent publication of general information or surveys which do not contain information relating to particular undertakings.

Where transfrontier groundwater is concerned, the competent authority of a Member State which intends to grant authorisation for a discharge must first inform other Member States concerned. At the request of one of the Member States, consultation must be held before an authorisation is issued, and the Commission may participate.

Development of the Directive

Although the Directive was agreed within two years of being proposed - which is quite rapid for Community legislation - it underwent quite significant modification in the process. The European Parliament's Environment Committee proposed many amendments in some respects making the Directive more stringent. The most important of these was that List I substances should not be indirectly discharged to groundwater even when subject to authorisation, and a ban on all direct and indirect discharges in areas where the groundwater is used, or could be used, for drinking. In the debate in the European Parliament (14th November 1978) the Commissioner, Mr Natali, welcomed the amendments but noted that the Commission "must expect serious objections from some Member States during the discussion at the Council of Ministers". He was probably right, because on the very same day the House of Commons debated the proposal and amended the Government's motion for a resolution to read "this House...cannot accept proposals that require a ban on all types of direct discharge, particularly those found acceptable in the United Kingdom". This resolution, although apparently tying the Government's hands by forcing it to resist the proposed Directive as amended by the European Parliament, in practice did not really do so since the European Parliament had already proposed significant exceptions to allow traces of List I substances and to allow the practice of recharging aquifers from rivers which inevitably contain some List I substances. The Minister, Ken Marks, expressed the Government's preference for the freedom to examine each case on its merits, and opposition to the idea of generalised bans:

> "...this kind of case by case approach which we have
> adopted is a very different matter from an extended ban
> plus exemptions. It is more flexible...."

In the event, the European Parliament's proposed amendments were substantially modified, and the Directive as agreed is in effect an 'extended ban' with enough exemptions to overcome what the British Minister called 'our basic dislike of outright banning'.

Formal Compliance in the UK

The government's formal 'compliance letter' sent to the Commission in December 1981 stated that the statutory powers necessary to secure compliance were contained primarily in the Control of Pollution Act 1974, and referred to the powers of the water authorities and waste disposal authorities to grant or withhold authorisations for the discharge of effluent and the disposal of waste respectively. (See Section 8.0 for a description of legislation on waste).

The letter went on to explain that for the disposal of wastes from mines and quarries the necessary powers were available to planning authorities under the Town and Country Planning Act 1971 and the Town and Country Planning (General Development) Order 1977 and, in addition, that Section 18 of the Control of Pollution Act 1974 enabled regulations to be made to bring these wastes under the licensing controls in that Act, should it prove expedient to do so.

The letter also listed the extra legislation covering Scotland and Northern Ireland.

In March 1982 the DOE published Circular 4/82 explaining the provisions of the Directive to the water authorities, waste disposal authorities, and mineral planning authorities and appointing them the competent authorities for the discharges under their control. A similar circular was issued in Scotland. A copy of the circulars was sent to the Commission.

The 'compliance letter' did not, however, say that the relevant parts of Part II of the Control of Pollution Act dealing with water were not yet in force, nor did the Circular do so explicitly (although the fact could be deduced by the careful reader noting the choice of tense, e.g., "the necessary authorisation of discharges or discharge producing activities **will** be provided under the consent procedures in sections 34 et seq...").

Even though existing discharges do not have to be brought within the provisions of the Directive until December 1985 there must be a formal failure to comply with the Directive, since it requires the Member States to have brought into force the 'laws, regulations and administrative provisions necessary to comply with this Directive within two years of its notification' (i.e., by December 1981). For existing discharges this failure may be merely one of form which will have little significance so long as the relevant parts of the Act are indeed brought into force, as planned, before December 1985. However, the Directive applied to new discharges from December 1981 and, to the extent that there have been such discharges that cannot have been controlled by existing legislation, the failure will have been more than merely a matter of form.

In addition to the existing powers to control waste disposal in Part I of the Control of Pollution Act, there are some other controls over groundwater pollution even without Part II being in force. These include powers under the Water Act 1945 for water authorities to make byelaws preventing discharges where water supplies might be contaminated whether on the surface or underground, and powers under the Water Resources Act 1963 to prevent pollution of underground water by discharges into wells, boreholes and pipes. However, these provisions are not adequate for complete compliance and were not mentioned in the compliance letter presumably because they will effectively be superseded when Part II of the Control of Pollution Act is in force. Under the Control of Pollution (Exemption of Certain Discharges from Control) Order 1983 (SI 1983 No 1182) certain discharges which would otherwise be controlled when Part II of the Control of Pollution Act is brought into force will be exempted but not those discharges which need to be controlled in order to comply with the Directive. This shows that the Directive has exerted pressure on the government to bring Part II of the Control of Pollution Act into force, since if the existing legislation was adequate exceptions would not have had to be made from the exemptions.

Since the Directive requires direct discharges to **any** groundwater of both List I and List II substances to be controlled, and since Sections 31 and 56 of the Control of Pollution Act only give powers of control to 'specified' underground waters, the circular explained that it would be necessary for water authorities to 'specify' **all** underground waters. Interestingly, the Act only empowers underground waters to be 'specified' if they are capable of being used for any purpose, but the DOE's advice is that all groundwaters must be capable of some use and can therefore be 'specified'.

Effect on UK Practice

Circular 4/82 asserted that the Directive "will serve in the main to underline and reinforce, rather than alter, current policy and procedures on (the protection of groundwater against pollution by certain substances) insofar as the United Kingdom is concerned", and this is a fair summary of the attitude of the water authorities expressed in reply to the questionnaire put to them in 1981. However, the water authorities gave their answers before the circular was issued and before the date for formal compliance, and the replies now would doubtless be more precise in recognising more clearly the extent of the extra work involved.

The major advance in control of groundwater in Britain came with the establishment of the water authorities in 1974 and, given that waste disposal is a potential major source of groundwater pollution, with the bringing into force in 1976 of Part I of the Control of Pollution Act which placed an

108

obligation on waste disposal authorities to refer any applications for a site licence for the disposal of waste to the water authority (see Section 8.0). Any unresolved dispute between the authorities has to be referred to the Secretary of State. Partly in order to provide guidance to the waste disposal authorities, some water authorities have drawn up aquifer protection policies (1) which among other matters have indicated zones where waste disposal is not acceptable, and this policy development cannot be attributed to the Directive. By and large, a good working relationship has developed between water authorities and waste disposal authorities with rather few disputes being referred to the Secretary of State - although a survey of waste disposal authorities in 1980 showed that there are some exceptions to this (2).

What the Directive should do is to concentrate attention on the possibility of the listed substances reaching groundwater both when consenting direct discharges, either from waste disposal sites or elsewhere, and when authorising indirect discharges from waste disposal sites under the site licensing provisions of Part I of the Control of Pollution Act. Circular 4/82 explained, however, (paraphrasing the Directive) that "waste disposal operations will not come within the terms of the Directive unless they might result in listed substances reaching groundwater, and in a quantity and concentration likely to cause deterioration in the quality of usable groundwater...This will limit the number of sites likely to be affected". It is too soon to know how many sites are indeed affected.

One consequence of the Directive is that DOE Circular 39/76 which gave advice on the balancing of interests between water protection and waste disposal has had to be modified. The volume of an aquifer is no longer to be a factor for consideration in reaching a decision since the Directive requires **all** usable groundwater to be protected.

The discharges from the disposal of mining and quarrying waste can also give rise to groundwater pollution, although Circular 4/82 claimed that the number of cases where discharges would come within the terms of the Directive is likely to be minimal. The circular nevertheless advised the mineral planning authorities, in consultation with the water authorities, to consider whether conditions imposed on existing permissions at sites in active use are sufficient to ensure the protection of groundwater, and this must result in extra work. The circular explained that changes are envisaged in the legislation (The Town and Country Planning General Development Order 1977) requiring water authorities to be consulted on all applications for the winning and working of minerals, and requiring the submission for approval of schemes for tipping on an existing tip on which water authorities will also have to be consulted.

References

1.   K H Selby and A C Skinner, **Aquifer Protection in the Severn-Trent Region: Policy and Practice,** Journal of the Institute of Water Pollution Control, Vol 78, 1979, No 22.

2.   J M Nash and A Q Kahn (South Yorkshire County Council), **Waste Disposal by Landfill and Groundwater Pollution: A Survey of Waste Disposal Authorities in England by Questionnaire,** 1980 (typescript provided by authors).

7.10   Mercury from the Chlor-Alkali Industry

82/176/EEC (OJ L81 27.3.82)
proposed 14.6.79 - COM(79)296

Directive on limit values and
quality objectives for mercury
discharges by the chlor-alkali
electrolysis industry

Binding dates
Notification date: 25 March 1982
Formal compliance: 1 July 1983
Standards to be met: 1 July 1983 and 1 July 1986
Commission to send
  comparative assessment
  to Council: Every five years, i.e., first report
                                  presumably due 25 March 1987

Purpose of the Directive

This is the first of the 'daughter' Directives flowing from Directive
76/464 which dealt with pollution of water by particularly dangerous
substances (see Section 7.8).   The present Directive is concerned with only
one substance - mercury - discharged by only one manufacturing process.
The production of chlorine by plants in which alkali chlorides are
electrolysed by means of mercury cells (known as chlor-alkali electrolysis)
was selected for early attention because of the large quantity of mercury
discharged.   A proposal for a Directive (OJ C20 25.1.83 - COM(82)838)
covers mercury discharged from other sources.

Summary of the Directive

In accordance with the compromise enshrined in the parent Directive
76/464 (Section 7.8) Member States may authorise discharges of mercury and
its compounds from chlor-alkali electrolysis plants following any of the two
regimes described in Directive 76/464, i.e., authorisations are to conform
either to limit values or to quality objectives specified below (although a
special provision not foreshadowed in the parent Directive has been
introduced for new plants):

1. Limit Values

The limit values are summarised in the table below. The
authorisations issued by the Member States must be at least as stringent as
these limit values and must be reviewed at least every four years.
Different limit values are laid down for plants using the 'lost brine' and
'recycled brine' processes.   The limit values are expressed in two ways: (a)
in terms of concentration, i.e., micrograms of mercury per litre discharged
and (b) in terms of quantity in relation to capacity, i.e., grams of mercury

110

per tonne of installed chlorine production capacity. The limit values in terms of quantity **must** be observed, while those given in terms of concentration should **in principle** not be exceeded.

The limit values set out in the table below are monthly average limit values, and daily average limit values are four times these. Sampling is to be done daily.

	1 July 1983	1 July 1986
1. **In terms of Concentration** (micrograms per litre of all mercury containing water discharged)	75	50
2. **In terms of Quantity** (grams per tonne installed chlorine capacity):		
Recycled brine (mercury in discharges from chlorine production unit)	0.5	0.5
Recycled brine (total mercury in all mercury-containing waters discharged from site)	1.5	1.0
Lost brine (total mercury in all mercury-containing waters discharged from site)	8.0	5.0

2. Quality Objectives

The following four quality objectives for mercury concentrations are laid down and in addition the quality objective laid down in any other Directive must also be observed. The concentrations in affected areas of water (the arithmetic mean of the results obtained over a year) may be multiplied by 1.5 until 30th June 1986 provided the Commission is notified beforehand.

1.	Fish flesh:	0.3 mg/kg wet flesh
2.	Inland surface waters:	1.0 µg/l
3.	Estuary waters:	0.5 µg/l
4.	Sea and coastal waters:	0.3 µg/l

It is for the competent authority to determine the area affected by discharges in each case and to select from among the above quality objectives those that it deems appropriate having regard to the intended use of the area affected and that the purpose of the Directive is to eliminate all pollution. Emission standards are to be set by the Member States so that the appropriate quality objective(s) is or are complied with in the area affected.

111

In addition, the concentration of mercury in sediments or in shellfish must not increase significantly with time.

3. New Plant

Member States may grant authorisations for new plant only if such authorisations **contain a reference** to the standards corresponding to the best technical means available for preventing discharges of mercury. In a Statement printed with the Directive but not legally forming part of it, the Council and Commission stated that:

> "...the application of the best technical means available makes it possible to limit discharges of mercury from the site of a new industrial plant using the recycled brine process to less than 0.5g/tonne of installed chlorine production capacity".

A Member State wishing to grant an authorisation for a new plant when for technical reasons the best technical means available are not to be used, must first justify this to the Commission. Within three months the Commission is to send a report to the Member States with its opinion on the proposed derogation.

(The purpose of this provision is apparently to shame any Member State into insisting on the best technical means available for new plant even if the limit values or the quality objectives would be met by cheaper but less than the best technically available means. However, in this connection it is necessary to bear in mind that when Directive 76/464 was agreed a Statement was recorded in the Council minutes to the effect that 'best technical means available' is to take into account the economic availability of those means - see Section 7.8.)

4. Monitoring and Analysis

A reference method of analysis for determining the presence of mercury is given, but other methods may be used provided the limits of detection, precision and accuracy are as good. Member States are to be responsible for monitoring waters affected. When the waters of several Member States are affected, the Member States are to co-operate with a view to harmonising monitoring procedures.

5. Comparative Assessments

The Member States are to supply the Commission at its request with details of authorisations and the results of monitoring to determine mercury concentrations. The Commission is to prepare a comparative assessment of the implementation of the Directive by the Member States and every five years forward it to the Council. (As it does not have to be sent to the Parliament it need not be published).

7.11 Titanium Dioxide

1) 78/176/EEC (OJ L54 25.2.78)   Directive on waste from the
   proposed 14.7.75 - COM(75)339   titanium dioxide industry

2) 83/29/EEC (OJ L32 3.2.83)   (Amendment)
   proposed 8.7.82 - COM(82)430

3) 82/883/EEC (OJ L378 31.12.82)   Directive on procedures for
   proposed 17.12.80 - COM(82)831   the surveillance and monitoring
                                     of environments concerned by waste
                                     from the titanium dioxide industry

Binding dates (78/176):
Notification date: 22 February 1978
Formal compliance: 22 February 1979
Pollution reduction programmes
  submitted to Commission: 1 July 1980
Programmes to be introduced: 1 January 1982
Programme targets to be met: 1 July 1987
First three yearly report to
  be submitted to Commission: 22 February 1981

Purpose of Directive 78/176

The main aim of the Directive is the prevention and progressive reduction of pollution caused by waste from the titanium dioxide (TiO_2) industry. Eventually all pollution is to be eliminated. TiO_2 is a white pigment used in paints and for other purposes. Its manufacture may result in a much larger quantity of waste than product and this has frequently been dumped at sea or discharged into estuaries. 'Red mud' in the Mediterranean resulting from discharges from an Italian TiO_2 plant drew strong protests from Corsica in 1972 resulting in a Court case and restrictions on the plant. Another aim of the Directive is to reduce the distortion to conditions of competition resulting from different controls.

Summary of Directive 78/176

General duties are placed on Member States to ensure that TiO_2 waste is disposed of without endangering human health or harming the environment and to encourage recycling.

All discharge, dumping, storage and injection of waste must be subjected to prior authorisation by the competent authority. Authorisation may be granted for a limited period only and may be renewed. Authorisation may only be given if the waste cannot be disposed of by more appropriate means, and an assessment shows that no deleterious effects will result. An Annex I lists the particulars of the waste, the site and the methods of disposal that must be supplied in order to obtain an authorisation.

Disposal must be accompanied by monitoring of the waste and of the environment in accordance with particulars laid down in an Annex II. The Commission was to propose more precise monitoring procedures (this has resulted in Directive 82/883 - see below).

Member States must take steps to remedy unsatisfactory situations that may arise (five such are listed) if necessary by suspending disposal.

Member States must send to the Commission programmes for the progressive reduction and eventual elimination of pollution. The programmes must be introduced by 1st January 1982 and must include targets to be achieved by 1st July 1987.

Within six months of receiving all the national programmes, the Commission may submit proposals to the Council for harmonising them, both as regards pollution reduction and the conditions of competition (the word 'may' was amended to 'shall' by Directive 83/29 and the period for submitting proposals extended to 15th March 1983. However, the Commission, having placed an obligation on itself, then failed to meet the amended deadline - see below).

Where a Member State considered that in the case of an individual establishment no additional measures were necessary to fulfil the requirements of the Directive, it had to provide the Commission with the evidence leading to that conclusion by 20th August 1979. The Commission could indicate its agreement, but if it did not agree, additional measures had to be included in the programme (Article 10).

Prior authorisation is required before any new industrial establishment can be built and an environmental impact survey (sic) must be conducted. Authorisation may only be granted to firms giving an undertaking to use only such materials, processes and techniques available on the market as are least damaging to the environment.

Member States must supply the Commission with information relating to authorisations, the results of monitoring and any remedial measures taken.

Every three years, Member States must submit a report to the Commission on the progressive reduction of pollution. The Commission must communicate this report to the other Member States. The Commission must in turn report every three years to the Council and Parliament.

Development of Directive 78/176

One of the wastes from TiO_2 production is ferrous sulphate and there seems little doubt that it was the conflict between France and Italy in the early 1970s over the dumping at sea of this waste from the Montedison factory at Scarlino that gave rise to the Directive. The waste became known as 'red mud'. Speaking in the European Parliament's debate on the Directive on 13th January 1976, Mr della Briotta described how in Corsica there had been something like an insurrection over the issue. He went on:

"...in the Scarlino case we find all the aspects of the problem: the movement among the population protesting against the pollution, the involvement of the press, the action by the authorities which, following judgment by the courts, ordered the company to stop the pollution and seized some ships, the consequent reprisals on the part of

114

the company which first threatened to close its factory
and finally actually did so, putting the workers on the
dole".

Mr della Briotta explained how the measures eventually taken in Italy –
thought to involve a purer ore and dumping deeper in the sea – had increased
costs and resulted in a distortion to competition, and he went on to
congratulate the Commission for tackling the problem since an effective
solution could not be achieved by national action alone. Mr Premoli,
speaking in the same debate, expressed approval of the Commission for not
making a distinction between inland seas like the Mediterranean and open
seas like the Atlantic but appeared not to notice that he was thereby
contradicting the motion that he, as the rapporteur of the Environment
Committee, was presenting to the Parliament. This motion regretted the
absence of quality objectives in the Directive, and such objectives would
inevitably have led to different disposal practices in the Atlantic with its
larger tidal excursions than those needed in the Mediterranean.

The original proposal was much more stringent than the Directive as
eventually agreed. As well as requiring authorisation and monitoring, it
also specified a phased reduction of emissions so that by 1985 only five per
cent of the total untreated emissions would be allowed to be dumped at sea
or in estuaries. The Minister, Denis Howell, declared in the Council on 16th
October 1975 that Britain could not accept the proposal in that form since it
embodied uniform standards for controlling discharges of waste, regardless
of environmental circumstances. In the House of Lords' debate (1st April
1976) the Minister, Baroness Stedman, explained why:

"Discharges are said to present a problem in the
Mediterranean, but we have no significant problems from
our industry which discharges into the North Sea".

The argument of the government has been all along that since the
British factories discharge continuously to estuaries with large tidal
excursions and high flow rates, the acid in the waste is rapidly neutralised on
mixing with sea water and the resulting precipitates, as well as the iron,
titanium and other trace metals, are quickly dispersed. The British sites
were in fact chosen so that discharges were to estuaries already high in
suspended solids. The lack of tide in the Mediterranean, on the other hand,
makes dispersion difficult and intermittent dumping of concentrated acids
from ships – the acid is concentrated to reduce shipping costs – produces
stronger concentrations in the sea water instantaneously than a continuous
discharge of dilute acid from a pipeline.

The view widely held in Britain was that there was no reason why the
well sited British TiO_2 industry, producing 40 per cent of European output,
should be made to suffer economically in an attempt to solve a problem of
bad planning in Italy, especially when the loss making Montedison factory
was responsible for only six per cent of European production.

The TiO_2 proposal was used in Britain to emphasise the disadvantages
of the limit value approach embodied in part of Directive 76/464 (see Section
7.8). The further point was made that waste from TiO_2 production did not
include substances in List I of that Directive (except in trace amounts) and
that all Member States had agreed that emissions of other substances were to

115

be controlled by reference to environmental quality objectives. Commissioner Scarascia Mugnozza, speaking in the European Parliament's debate only a few weeks after the compromise decision reached by the Council on Directive 76/464, conceded that the compromise decision was a relevant factor in discussing the TiO_2 proposal.

The solution eventually agreed for TiO_2, which a memorandum from the DOE to Parliament (14th November 1977) said had emerged under the British Presidency of the Council, was that Member States would draw up and submit to the Commission their own programmes for progressive reduction of pollution. There can be little doubt that Britain was the principle opponent of uniform controls, but the danger of excessively stringent standards was also very much in the minds of others. The Economic and Social Committee, for instance, in their report of 25th February 1976 pointed to the danger of the TiO_2 industry moving to countries outside the Community, with an associated loss of jobs, if the financial consequences of complying with the Directive were too high.

Britain was also responsible for the abortive Article 10 which allowed Member States to submit to the Commission, in respect of a particular factory, that no pollution reduction programme was necessary if no pollution was being caused. This provision, introduced under pressure from the British industry, resulted in the first environmental case being brought before the European Court (see below). The Minister, Denis Howell, possibly had this in mind when he publicly quoted the TiO_2 Directive as an example of how closely the government sometimes works with industry in defending their interests:

> "As an environmental Minister I go to Brussels to meet my ministerial colleagues in the Common Market. In the three years since I have had those responsibilities there has been an increasing number of occasions when I have had to take up cudgels particularly on behalf of British industries in an attempt to demonstrate that the issues being discussed by the Environmental Committee (sic) in Brussels, in which I try to protect the interests of British industry, are in no way in conflict with the philosophy and develoment of an environmental policy. I found myself splendidly isolated and one against eight on the subject of the paper pulp industry; I was in a similar position over titanium dioxide..."(1)

The TiO_2 Directive is an example of the 'sectoral approach' envisaged in the First Action Programme of 1973 which grouped the TiO_2 industry together with the paper pulp industry and the iron and steel industry for early attention. The 'sectoral approach' is shorthand for dealing with a particular industry rather than with a particular pollutant or a particular environment. With the failure to agree a proposed Directive on paper pulp (OJ C99 2.5.75 - COM(74)2256), the sectoral approach now seems to have been abandoned*. The TiO_2 Directive may therefore prove to have been an

---

* The 'daughter' Directives of 76/464 (Section 7.8) may however follow the sectoral approach, e.g., mercury from the chlor-alkali industry (Section 7.10).

exception to be explained as the product of exceptional circumstances: an acute local problem resulting in a dispute between two Member States.

The development of the Directive was influenced not only by arguments about competition but also by doubts about the technical report on which it was based.

Technical Issues

The Commission proposal for the Directive was published not just with the usual explanatory memorandum but also with a 77 page technical report – COM(75)339. This report described the preparation and uses of TiO_2, the market situation, the processes for TiO_2 production, the raw materials, the kinds of waste that arise, the methods of treatment, and both long term and short term environmental effects. The section on environmental effects quoted extensively from the French Government's report published in connection with the Montedison case. It did not say, though in fairness it could have done, that the growth of the TiO_2 industry has enabled the use of toxic substances such as lead and zinc to be reduced in paints. TiO_2 is itself believed to be harmless and has largely replaced the toxic pigments though mainly because it is a better pigment.

TiO_2 is extracted from ore by one of two processes: the sulphate and chloride, the more recent chloride process generating less waste by allowing the use of a purer ore. This ore is scarce and expensive and in 1975 only 12 per cent of the EEC industry used the chloride process. The sulphate process gives rise to ferrous sulphate, acids and traces of some heavy metals. The technical report said that in the immediate vicinity of discharge of these wastes there was reduced oxygenation and increased acidity resulting in a local reduction of zooplankton biomass and departure of fish, but that evidence of actual damage to fish was inconclusive. The House of Lords' Scrutiny Committee in their report said that members of the Committee had examined biological studies carried out under the auspices of a manufacturer (BTP, now Tioxide) in the estuary of the Humber and near French discharges at Calais which indicated that effluent from TiO_2 works did not appear to have any detrimental effect on the ecology of these two areas. The Committee remained "in no doubt that the best way to get rid of titanium dioxide waste is in the sea. If this is done under the right conditions, no significant environmental damage need result". The government's view was the same. A memorandum to Parliament dated 14th November 1977 said:

"...all the scientific evidence indicates that TiO_2 waste can be disposed of to the sea without harming the environment; as the only feasible alternative would be neutralisation using lime and dumping of the resultant solid waste on land, the net effect of the Commission's proposals would have been to increase pollution and impose unnecessary costs on the UK industry".

The Commission proposal that only five per cent of the untreated wastes was to be discharged to sea was based on the assertion that several feasible treatment processes existed to reduce pollution. The Lords' Scrutiny Committee commented tartly that the methods of treatment listed did not appear to justify this statement, and went on to point out that none of these methods had yet been put into commercial use.

Notwithstanding the arguments that disposal from British plants was not creating environmental problems, representatives of the two British producers of TiO_2 in giving evidence before the Lords' Scrutiny Committee implied that any new plants would use the chloride process rather than the sulphate process, partly because of the environmental problems associated with the sulphate process. Since then the switch from the sulphate to the chloride process has accelerated in Britain, while in Germany, Bayer AG, which still uses the sulphate process, has announced that it will soon stop discharging or dumping at sea altogether, thus suggesting that a technical breakthrough has been made. It is thought that this involves using the acid wastes in other processes in the same complex rather than recycling them in the TiO_2 operation.

Formal Compliance in the UK - Directive 78/176

In February 1979, when the Directive had formally to be complied with, there were four dischargers of TiO_2 waste in Britain, two into the Humber estuary and two into the estuary of the River Tees:

Teeside (Northumbrian Water Authority) Approx capacity in 1976 (tons per annum)[*]

1) Tioxide Ltd	Billingham	sulphate	27,000	**closed**
2) Tioxide Ltd	Seal Sands, Hartlepool	chloride	60,000	

Humberside (Anglian Water Authority)

3) Tioxide Ltd	Grimsby	sulphate	90,000	
4) Laporte Industries Ltd	Stalling-borough (Immingham)	a)sulphate	55,000	**curtailed**
		b)chloride	60,000	

The Laporte plant included both a sulphate and a chloride process. In March 1981 the Tioxide plant at Billingham was closed and in the same year output from the Laporte sulphate process was curtailed by 80 per cent.

The government wrote to the Commission on 14th February 1979 saying that it was satisfied that the Control of Pollution Act 1974 provided adequate powers to meet the objectives of the Directive, but omitted to say that the relevant part of the Act was not then in force and that one plant was sufficiently old not to be covered by a consent and was therefore not 'authorised'. This can be rectified when Part II of the Control of Pollution Act is brought into force, but meanwhile there is a formal failure to comply with the Directive. The Commission has either not noticed this or is turning a blind eye, because in reply to a European Parliamentary question in June 1982 (OJ C167 5.7.82) it said that the Directive had been incorporated into

---

[*] These capacity figures were given by the manufacturers in evidence to the House of Lords except for that from Tioxide's Hartlepool plant.

national law in all Member States except Belgium.

The government's letter of 14th February 1979 also said that the Control of Pollution Act 1974 allowed the preparation of the programmes for reduction of pollution. This seems to be a mistake since there is nothing in that Act which provides for plans or programmes, although provision for these is made in Section 24 of the Water Act 1973.

There is no dumping of British TiO_2 waste at sea from ships at present, but should any such plans be put forward they could be controlled by the Dumping at Sea Act 1974. Some neutralised solid wastes from TiO_2 production at Tioxide's Hartlepool plant is dumped on land in Britain and this is covered by Part I of the Control of Pollution Act 1974. The Directive has therefore required no new primary legislation but requires Part II of the Control of Pollution Act to be brought into force by secondary legislation.

The discharges to the Humber fall within the area of the Anglian Water Authority and the discharges to the Tees within the area of the Northumbrian Water Authority. Letters from the DOE formally appointed these two authorities as 'competent authorities' for the purposes of the Directive and explained that programmes would have to be drawn up for the reduction of pollution.

The Court Case

The first official action taken in Britain following the notification of the Directive was a request from the government to the Commission for exemptions, under Article 10, from the need to prepare pollution reduction programmes in respect of the two establishments discharging into the Humber. This request was presumably made at the instigation of the two companies concerned. A similar request was also made by the West German Government in respect of dumping in the North Sea*.

The Commission did not accept the British government's argument and, in a letter of 19th February 1979, refused to grant exemptions to the two establishments. Since the Directive provides no appeal against the Commission's decision, the government could only accept the Commission's opinion that programmes were necessary and informed the relevant water authority accordingly. The two companies were less easily satisfied and on 17th May 1979 they simultaneously brought an action in the European Court against the Commission seeking annulment of the Commission's opinion that programmes were necessary. The Bulletin of the European Communities (No 5, 1979, p 118) asserted that this was the first action brought to the Court relating directly to environmental matters. The British government for its part has made it clear that it is not associated in any way with the action.

All that is publicly known of this action is contained in the brief statement of case published in the Official Journal (OJ C153 20.6.79). The statement claims that the Court should not only annul the opinion contained in the Commission's letter of 19th February 1979 but should also declare the Directive illegal. The second point is thought to turn on the extent to which a draft Directive can be modified by the Council before being agreed

---

* A proposal for a Directive, which has not been agreed, would ban the dumping at sea of acids from the titanium dioxide industry (OJ C40/3, 20.2.76)

without having to be resubmitted to the Parliament for an opinion. It is a point of the greatest importance and goes well beyond environmental policy.

The action has now been suspended and neither party (the companies and the Commission) is seeking to activate it. Possibly the companies are waiting to see what happens to the Commission's proposal for harmonising the pollution reduction programmes (see below) before deciding whether to proceed or not.

The Effect on UK Practice

A pollution reduction programme was submitted by the government to the Commission in respect of the Tees on 3rd July 1980 and in respect of the Humber on 6th January 1981. These two programmes also constituted the first three- yearly report. The Humber programme was six months late but in this Britain was not alone - Commissioner Narjes, replying to a question in the European Parliament (OJ C87/21 16.4.81), said that all Member States had been late.

The programme in respect of the Humber argues that near neither discharge has any accumulation of heavy metal been found nor is there any significant effect on the estuary as a whole, so that the only cause for concern is the local reduction of pH around the outfalls. The objective of the programme is therefore to effect a better dispersion of the effluent so that the area of low pH is significantly reduced. The first step in the programme is therefore research, to be completed by the end of 1982, to see which of three options, or a combination of them, is the most effective:

(1) storage facilities on land so that no discharge (which is presently continuous) takes place during periods of slack water;
(2) the fitting of diffusers to the effluent pipeline;
(3) alterations to the position of the pipeline outlet.

When the results of the research are available, works are to be put in hand to be completed during 1986. Some ferrous sulphate is already removed from the effluent and the programme says that research will continue into possible further uses for this by-product. Although not specifically mentioned as part of point 3 of the programme, a £15 million sewage outfall is being constructed and has been designed in such a way that it could receive at least a part of the effluent from the Tioxide factory, and thus discharge it further out to sea.

Although the research stage of the programme should now be complete, it is not yet known which option has been chosen and it is even possible that the choice of options will be delayed until the outcome of the proposed 'harmonising' Directive is known (see below). It is thus not possible to be precise about the effect of the Directive on capital costs, but it is unlikely that any of the three options in the programme would readily have been undertaken in the absence of the Directive. The Directive will have strengthened the hand of the authorities in negotiating with the companies.

In 1980/81 Laporte's sulphate plant was curtailed by 80 per cent resulting in 1,000 redundancies, the reason given being over-capacity in the industry and reduced profitability. This cannot be regarded as part of a pollution reduction programme. However, later in 1981 plans were announced for an expansion of the chloride process. The existence of the Directive is likely to have been one factor in the decision to expand the chloride rather than the sulphate process.

The programme for Teeside has not been made available but the view of the Northumbrian Water Authority is that the one remaining factory does not create any significant problems. Since it uses the relatively clean chloride process, there is no red or brown discharge and the only cause for concern is said to be the discharge of TiO_2 pigment creating a whitish plume. To reduce this the company, in 1980 and 1981, improved filtration within the factory to reduce pigment being discharged and improved the settlement/storage capacity. It is arguable that these improvements would have been carried out anyway without the Directive.

The full impact of the Directive on the companies is therefore at present hard to assess, though Tioxide claim that the £100,000 per annum that they spend on monitoring is double what they used to spend before. Both water authorities agree that the Directive has involved them in increased monitoring. The Anglian Water Authority also believes the Directive has acted as a stimulus to thought about the Humber estuary generally.

What must be an unanticipated side effect of the Directive has been a drawing together of the DOE, water authorities and the industry; a closing of ranks, as it were, when confronted with an outside stimulus. In the normal way there would be no reason for the DOE to be involved with the discharge of one industry among many, particularly if it has not caused any noticeable public controversy in this country[*], but since it is the DOE that is responsible for submitting the pollution reduction programmes to the Commission, the DOE has had to be involved in the work of the water authorities. For their part, the water authorities have been provided with extra leverage when dealing with the industrialists since formally it is the water authorities who have had to prepare the pollution reduction programmes, and the industrialists have an interest in ensuring that these programmes satisfy the Commission in order to head off what they might regard as draconian proposals from the Commission harmonising the various national programmes. More is now known about the problems by all three parties and more information on the monitoring programmes carried out by the industry has been made available to the authorities. However, the full effect of the Directive can only be assessed when the outcome of the proposed 'harmonising' Directive is known (see below).

The Monitoring Directive 82/883

This Directive fulfils the obligation placed on the Commission by Directive 78/176 to propose procedures for surveillance and monitoring (the parent Directive required a proposal within one year but the Commission overran the date by nearly two years).

The Directive lays down in five Annexes the steps to be taken in

---

[*] In mid-1983, after this was written, a campaign was launched against British discharges of TiO_2 waste by the environmental organisation Greenpeace (UK).

monitoring air, salt water, fresh water, storage and dumping on land, and injection into soil. The Directive will not affect the industries but only the competent authorities. The Anglian Water Authority in written evidence to the House of Lords Scrutiny Committee expressed concern about the potential cost (£50,000 per annum) if a Directive was agreed as proposed, but the Directive was amended so the costs are now probably reduced. In particular it was amended so that Member States may, without consulting the Commission, allow less frequent sampling once the behaviour, fate and effects of the wastes are known. In addition, the requirement to monitor SO_2 has been significantly modified so that an existing SO_2 monitoring station will suffice. Precisely what procedures the two water authorities will adopt has yet to be worked out in detail between them and DOE.

Full compliance with the Directive – required by December 1984 – can be assured with existing legislation.

Harmonising National Programmes

Member States were to submit national programmes for reducing and eliminating pollution to the Commission by 1st July 1980, and six months after receipt of all these national programmes the Commission was to make proposals for harmonising them. In fact the Commission did not receive all the national programmes until 15th October 1981 and found that they were neither comparable nor provided adequate information. The Commission therefore had to ask for extra information and proposed a Directive extending the time period (see European Parliamentary Question OJ C93 7.4.83). This proposal was agreed as Directive 83/29 which set a new deadline of 15th March 1983 (although the Commission had first proposed October 1982 and then December). There was some suggestion that a Directive harmonising the national programmes could have been agreed by majority voting in the Council if it was made under the authority of the parent Directive 78/76, but that possibility – even if legally sustainable – disappeared when the Commission failed to produce a proposal by the revised deadline of 15th March 1982.

A proposed 'harmonising' Directive eventually emerged on 14th April 1983 – COM(83)189. It proposes uniform reductions in discharges largely irrespective of the environments into which the discharges are being made. As we have seen this was a course rejected when the parent Directive was being negotiated. It is therefore likely to reopen the original conflict and quite possibly Britain will find itself alone again.

References

(1) Seminar on Industry and the Environment, Royal Society of Arts, London, 31st May 1977

CHAPTER 8
Waste

8.0   Relevant British Legislation

1.   Origins of Current Legislation

Before 1972 there was no legislation concerned primarily with the broad problems of waste disposal but local authorities have long had powers to control waste as an aspect of public health.   The Public Health Act 1936, which consolidated much earlier legislation, empowers them to remove house and trade refuse and to require removal of 'any accumulation of noxious matter'. It also places on them a duty to inspect their areas to detect 'statutory nuisances' including 'any accumulation or deposit which is prejudicial to health or a nuisance' and gives them the concomitant power to serve abatement notices and prosecute offenders*.   These powers and duties could not prevent a nuisance arising, but at least they should have ensured that there are no unknown major toxic waste deposits in Britain similar to the dramatic discoveries made elsewhere.   Indeed, the very idea of voluntary bodies organising themselves with official encouragement to 'hunt the dump' as happens elsewhere rings strangely in British ears, since local authority environmental health officers (or 'inspectors of nuisances', 'sanitary inspectors', 'public health inspectors' - their names have changed over time) have been doing this as part of their normal duties for over a century.

The first preventive legislation was contained in the Town and Country Planning Act 1947 which required any new development, including waste disposal sites or plants, to have planning permission.   However, growing concern in the 1960s about the environmental effects of waste led the government to set up two Working Groups, one on toxic waste in 1964 and the other on refuse disposal in 1967.   The resulting reports (1,2), though largely technical, paved the way for Part I of the Control of Pollution Act 1974 which now deals comprehensively with both household and toxic waste.   But before the 1974 Act was even drafted a well publicised scare about the dumping of toxic waste - the story is told by Lord Ashby (3) - forced the government to rush the Deposit of Poisonous Waste Act 1972 onto the statute book.   It was always the intention that the 1972 Act would be repealed when the more comprehensive system embodied in the Control of Pollution Act 1974 was fully in operation and this happened in 1981.

2.   Waste Disposal Plans

The Control of Pollution Act 1974 requires each waste disposal authority (County Councils in England, District Councils in Wales, and Scotland) to prepare a plan for the disposal of all household, commercial and industrial waste (including toxic waste) likely to be situated in its area and to review the plan and modify it where appropriate.   In preparing the plan the authority must consult water authorities, other levels of local government, and other relevant bodies, and must give adequate publicity to

---

*   The **power** to inspect first appears in the Public Health Act 1848 and the **duty** to do so in the Sanitary Act 1866.

the draft plan and provide opportunities for the public to make representations. The plan must include information about:

- the kinds and quantities of waste which will arise in the area, or be brought into it, during the period of the plan;
- what waste the authority expects to dispose of itself;
- what waste others are expected to dispose of;
- the methods of disposal, e.g. reclamation, incineration, landfill;
- the sites and equipment being provided, and
- the cost.

The Act requires disposal authorities to consider what arrangements can reasonably be made for reclaiming waste materials. The plan does not require the approval of central government but a copy must be sent to DOE; very few plans have yet been completed (see Section 8.1).

3. Site Licensing

The Act also introduced a comprehensive licensing system for the disposal of wastes over and above existing planning controls. It makes it an offence to deposit household, commercial or industrial waste on land or to use waste disposal plant unless the land in question is licensed by the waste disposal authority. The authority must maintain a public register with particulars of all disposal licences - sometimes also known as site licences. A site licence, with any conditions, can only be issued by the authority if any required planning permission for the site is in force. An application for a licence must be referred to the water authority and any unresolved dispute between the water authority and the waste disposal authority is referred to the Secretary of State.

Site licences can be made subject to such conditions as the waste disposal authority sees fit and may relate, inter alia, to:

- duration of the licence;
- supervision by the licence holder of licensed activities;
- the kinds and quantities of waste, the methods of dealing with them, and the recording of information;
- precautions to be taken;
- the hours when waste may be dealt with;
- the works to be carried out before licensed activities begin or while they continue.

4. Toxic Waste

The Deposit of Poisonous Waste Act 1972 made it an offence to deposit on land poisonous, noxious or polluting waste in circumstances in which it can give rise to an environmental hazard. The 1972 Act also required those removing or disposing of toxic or dangerous waste to notify the waste disposal authority and the water authority at least three days before doing so, giving details of the composition, quantity, and destination of the waste. The 'notifiable' waste was defined negatively, i.e., all toxic or dangerous waste not specifically excluded by Regulations. The Act thus produced for the first time a substantial amount of information about industrial waste, and indeed was criticised for the amount of paper work involved.

The 1972 Act was repealed in 1981 and the notification system was replaced by the provisions of the Control of Pollution (Special Waste) Regulations 1980 made under Section 17 of the Control of Pollution Act 1974. The introduction of the Regulations caused some controversy because it was argued that the method of defining 'special waste' (an inclusive list and criteria approach - see below) was more restrictive than the 'negative' definition of notifiable waste under the 1972 Act. The government argued that the new Regulations concentrated controls where they were most needed, and that the site licensing system should provide sufficient control over actual disposal of wastes.

The Section 17 Regulations provide for a control system (sometimes said to apply 'from the cradle to the grave') including:

- a requirement that a waste producer notifies the receiving waste disposal authority of the intention to dispose of a consignment of special waste at least three days but not more than one month in advance;
- a consignment note system under which a consignment note travels with the waste and also provides confirmation that any particular consignment of special waste has been disposed of at a site licensed to receive it;
- a register containing a record of the despatch, conveyance and disposal of the special waste by each of the parties handling it;
- a permanent record of the location of disposals of special waste within a landfill or at an underground disposal site;
- a power for the Secretary of State to direct acceptance and disposal of special waste at a particular site or plant.

The Section 17 Regulations define 'special waste' as waste which is a medicinal product or waste containing any of the substances listed in a Schedule to the Regulations in such concentrations that it has:

(i)   the ability to be likely to cause death or serious damage to tissue if a single dose of not more than $5cm^3$ were to be ingested by a child of 20kg bodyweight, or
(ii)   the ability to be likely to cause serious damage to human tissue by inhalation, skin contact or eye contact on exposure to the substance for 15 minutes or less, or
(iii)   a flash point of $21^{\circ}C$ or less.

Aside from (iii), the definition of 'special waste' is therefore essentially by reference to its possible effect on human health rather than on the environment (as when a lorry load is dumped or accidentally spilled so as to pollute water), and this point will be seen to have significance when discussing Directive 78/319 (see Section 8.2). Effects on the environment, particularly water, are an essential part of the site licence conditions but these conditions do not normally extend to waste while being transported (although there is nothing to prevent a waste disposal authority from making conditions about the movement of waste to the site in question).

126

5. Other Legislation

The Health and Safety at Work etc Act 1974 lays responsibilities on employers concerning the safety of workers and this extends to workers handling waste. The Health and Safety Executive, a central Government agency established under the Act, has powers to supervise safety at work.

Under the Alkali Works etc Act 1906, major industrial emitters to air, including all chemical waste incinerators, are registered with and controlled by the Industrial Air Pollution Inspectorate (formerly the Alkali Inspectorate).

The movement of hazardous materials, including waste, is controlled by a whole host of specific Regulations.

The Refuse Disposal (Amenity) Act 1978 places a duty on a local authority to provide sites where residents may deposit bulky household refuse free of charge, and also governs the disposal of abandoned motor cars.

Waste oils and polychlorinated biphenyls (PCBs), which are the subject of individual EEC Directives, are not covered by separate British legislation but are controlled under the general legislation described above.

6. Administration

From this brief outline of the legislation relevant to EEC Directives it follows that waste disposal is very largely a local government function. Central government has reserve powers and has an appellate role exercised, for example, when an applicant for a disposal (or site) licence appeals against conditions imposed by the waste disposal authority, or to resolve a dispute between a water authority and a waste disposal authority. Central government activity is otherwise confined to developing overall policy, promoting research and issuing advice and, of course, negotiating EEC Directives and answering to the Commission for their implementation. Examples of government advice include the series of 'Waste Management Papers' issued by DOE on such topics as waste disposal plans, site licensing, disposing of particularly difficult wastes, and on the definition of 'special wastes'.

In 1981 the House of Lords' Select Committee on Science and Technology carried out a very thorough inquiry into hazardous waste disposal policy (4) and, while concluding that the 1974 Act provides the right framework for the close supervision of hazardous waste disposal and monitoring, made a number of recommendations for strengthening the system, including the formation of a small central 'Hazardous Waste Inspectorate'. The Government accepted this proposal.

An example of central Government involvement in instigating research is the large scale research programme on the 'Behaviour of Hazardous Wastes in Landfill Sites' (5) which considered the effects of the practice, known as 'co-disposal', of mixing hazardous waste together with household waste. This concluded that sensible landfill is realistic and that an ultra-cautious approach to landfill is unjustified, although some substances are not suitable for landfill and each case has to be treated on its merits. A complaint by a local authority about the practice of 'co-disposal' at Pitsea - one of Britain's largest landfill sites receiving toxic waste - led to the Lords' Report mentioned above, but the Lords' Report found co-disposal to be a valid method if well executed.

7. Scotland and Northern Ireland

The legislation covering Scotland and Northern Ireland is not always identical to that for England and Wales but broadly the same provisions apply.

8. Future Developments

The government announced the appointment of a new Chief Inspector of Hazardous Waste on 8 August 1983. Other recommendations of the same Lords' Report which are under consideration by the government and which are particularly relevant to the discussion of Directive 78/319 (see Section 8.2) are that producers of toxic waste should effectively keep records, and that transporters of waste should be licensed. The government is also actively considering tightening controls over imported hazardous waste, a subject which is also covered by a proposed Directive. The Section 17 Regulations concerning special waste are also being reviewed.

References

(1) Dr A Key (Chairman), **Disposal of Solid Toxic Wastes,** Department of the Environment/Scottish Development Department, HMSO, 1970

(2) J Sumner (Chairman), **Refuse Disposal,** Department of the Environment, HMSO, 1971

(3) Eric Ashby, **Reconciling Man with the Environment,** OUP 1978

(4) House of Lords Select Committee on Science and Technology, **Hazardous Waste Disposal,** 1st Report Session 1980-81, HMSO, 1981

(5) **Co-operative Programme of Research on the Behaviour of Hazardous Wastes in Landfill Sites,** HMSO, 1978.

8.1   Waste — Framework Directive

75/442/EEC (OJ L194 25.7.75)   Directive on waste
proposed 10.9.74 - COM(74)1297

Binding dates
    Notification date: 18 July 1975
    Formal compliance: 18 July 1977
    Situation reports: Every three years - first
                                  report due 18 July 1980[*]

Purpose of the Directive

In all Member States waste disposal was regarded as a local or regional problem until the early 1970s. Several Member States then introduced or proposed legislation to provide some kind of national framework for dealing with it and the Directive accordingly seeks to set out a coherent set of measures applicable in all Member States. The Directive is sometimes referred to as a framework Directive, more detailed measures being provided by other Directives, such as those on toxic waste (see Section 8.2) and on polychlorinated biphenyls (PCBs) (see Section 8.3).

Summary of the Directive

A general duty is placed on Member States to take the necessary measures to ensure that waste is disposed of without endangering human health and without harming the environment. 'Disposal' and 'waste' are defined, and certain categories of waste are excluded from the scope of the Directive (e.g., radioactive waste, mining waste, some agricultural wastes, waste waters and gaseous effluents).
The Directive contains four main mandatory elements:
- competent authorities with responsibility for waste are to be appointed;
- waste disposal plans are to be prepared by these competent authorities;
- permits from the competent authorites are to be obtained by installations or undertakings handling waste, and
- the 'polluter pays' principle is to apply.

---

[*]   This is to assume that the first three-year period started with the date for formal compliance - an assumption made by the Commission (see reply to European Parliamentary Question OJ C178 16/7/80). But the Directive is ambiguous and periods normally run from the date of notification. This ambiguity does not arise with the Directive on toxic waste (see Section 8.2) which states that the three-year period starts from the notification date.

In addition the Directive requires Member States to encourage recycling. Situation reports are to be prepared every three years.

(a) Competent Authorities

The competent authorities are to be responsible in a given zone for the planning, organisation, authorisation and supervision of waste disposal operations.

(b) Plans

The plans which are to be drawn up by the competent authorities 'as soon as possible' must cover:
- the type and quantity of waste to be disposed of;
- general technical requirements;
- suitable disposal sites;
- any special arrangements for particular wastes,

and may cover:
- the body empowered to carry out the disposal of waste;
- the estimated costs;
- appropriate measures to encourage rationalisation of the collection, sorting and treatment of waste.

(c) Permits

Permits must be obtained by an installation or undertaking treating, storing or tipping waste on behalf of third parties relating in particular to:
- the type and quantity of waste to be treated;
- general technical requirements;
- precautions to be taken, and
- the information to be made available at the request of the competent authority concerning the origin, destination and treatment of waste and the type and quantity of such waste.

The competent authorites must make periodic inspections to ensure that the conditions of the permit are being fulfilled.

It will be noted that undertakings storing, tipping or treating their own waste do not require permits. However, they must still be subject to supervision by the competent authority. Similarly, undertakings transporting and collecting their own waste or waste on behalf of third parties do not need permits but must be subject to supervision by the competent authority.

(d) 'Polluter Pays' Principle

The cost of disposing of waste is to be borne by the holder who has waste handled, and/or by the previous holders or the producer of the product from which the waste came.

(e) Recycling

Member States are to encourage the prevention, recycling and processing of waste, the extraction of raw materials and possibly energy, and any other process for the re-use of waste. They are to inform the Commission of any draft rules to such effect. In addition they are to inform the Commission of the use of products which might be a source of technical difficulties as regards disposal or might lead to excessive disposal costs.

(f) Situation Reports

Every three years Member States are to draw up a situation report on waste disposal and forward it to the Commission. In its turn the Commission is to report to the Council and the Parliament on the application of the Directive.

Development of the Directive

At the time that the Commission began work on the Directive, a German law of 1972 required regional authorities and private individuals to use special installations for the treatment, storage and removal of waste, these installations having to conform to regional waste disposal plans. The drawing up of waste disposal plans was also an important feature of the British Control of Pollution Act which was then under discussion as a Bill. The French Government also had a preliminary draft law on waste disposal and the recovery and recycling of materials. The Directive therefore had to take account of these three items of existing or proposed legislation.

In Britain the responsible Minister, Denis Howell, claimed, when giving evidence to the House of Commons Scrutiny Committee in 1975, that the:

"Control of Pollution Act...was in fact a model for this Directive. It has the same aims. I think that we can claim that here the EEC has been following our Control of Pollution Act rather than the other way about..."

He went on to say: "May I sum up this Directive by saying that in general we believe that this is a very enlightened and acceptable document".

The European Parliament welcomed the Directive although it suggested a number of minor changes. One of these was that the title should be changed from 'waste disposal' to 'the waste sector' since the Directive dealt with recycling as well as disposal. In the event the briefer title of 'waste' was adopted. The Directive was agreed ten months after being proposed and with very little change, suggesting that no major objections were raised by any country during deliberations in Council.

Formal Compliance in the UK

When the Minister told the Commons' Scrutiny Committee that he welcomed the Directive and that it was based on the Control of Pollution Act, he added one caveat:

"There is the question of timing, which is probably the only part of it which might cause us any slight doubts".

He went on to say that because of 'economic stringencies' there had been delay in bringing the relevant part of the Act into force but that the "Government do not intend that it be delayed for very long". In the event, Section 2 of the Act, which requires waste disposal authorities to prepare waste disposal plans, was delayed longer than originally thought and was not brought into force until 1st July 1978 (The Control of Pollution Act 1974 (Commencement No 11) Order 1977 - SI 1977 No 2164) so that Britain was one year late in implementing a major element of the Directive. This point was conceded in the statement of compliance sent by DOE to the Commission on 5th October 1977. The statement did, however, point out that most disposal authorities in England had already begun preparatory work for the plans on an extra-statutory basis.

A fuller statement of how each Article of the Directive is implemented in Britain was sent to the Commission in March 1982 with the first situation report on waste disposal required by the Directive. This shows that all the main elements of the Directive are now implemented in England, Wales and Scotland largely by the Control of Pollution Act 1974, and in Northern Ireland by the Pollution Control and Local Government (NI) Order 1978, although various other Acts, such as the Town and Country Planning Act 1971, the Local Government Act 1972, and the Health and Safety at Work Act 1974 are also relied upon for certain Articles.

In summary, the position on implementation is as follows: the Local Goverment Act 1972 appointed as waste disposal authorities the county councils in England and district councils in Wales. In Scotland it is the district and island councils that are waste disposal authorities by virtue of the Control of Pollution Act. Section 2 of the Control of Pollution Act requires waste disposal authorities to draw up plans, and Sections 3-11 provide for the licencing of sites to receive waste (i.e., the 'permits' of the Directive).

The Control of Pollution Act in several places goes further than the Directive in that the licensing provisions apply to undertakings disposing of their own waste as well as waste being disposed of for third parties. Furthermore, the Directive says nothing about publishing the waste disposal plans or the need for any consultations during their preparation, both of which are features of the Control of Pollution Act.

It is worth noting that the Directive requires the waste disposal plans to be drawn up 'as soon as possible'. The Control of Pollution Act in contrast contains no words suggesting any such urgency although, as originally enacted, the Secretary of State was empowered "to give to any authority a direction as to the time by which the authority is to perform any duty specified..." (Section 2(7)). No such direction has ever been made but a Circular issued to local authorities in 1978 (DOE Circular 29/78) expressed the hope that substantial progress would have been made with plans within 18 months to two years. The power to make directions about the time by which plans must be produced was subsequently repealed by the Local Government Planning and Land Act 1980 (Schedule 2), but the Secretary of State still has broad reserve powers under Section 97 of the Control of Pollution Act to declare an authority to be in default if it has failed to perform any function and to direct the authority to perform that function.

The DOE never formally notified waste disposal authorities of the existence of the Directive until April 1978 when it issued DOE Circular 29/78 dealing with Directive 78/319 (see Section 8.2). The reason given for this is that there is nothing in the Directive that is not already covered by existing legislation and practice.

Effect on UK Practice

It is most probable that the Minister was correct in saying that the Directive was modelled on the Control of Pollution Act. Certainly the two are broadly similar, with the detailed requirements for plans in the Directive being closer to the British Act of 1974 than to the German Act of 1972. It follows that what is required by the Directive would have been done without its existence and the Directive cannot be expected to have had much practical effect in Britain. One effect, however, has already been noted. Implementation of some sections of the Control of Pollution Act was delayed, and the Directive must have provided pressure for not deferring implementation of Section 2 of the Act concerned with waste disposal plans much longer. There is no knowing how long Section 2 would have been delayed but for the Directive.

Another effect of the Directive may be attributed to the requirement to supply the Commission every three years with a situation report on waste disposal. The first report was due in July 1980 but was not in fact submitted till March 1982. Britain was not alone in being late, and part of the explanation for the delay is that the Commission let it be known that it would issue guidelines for the preparation of the situation reports, but these were not issued until September 1981.

By June 1983 only the Federal Republic of Germany and Luxembourg, in addition to Britain, had submitted situation reports (see reply to European Parliamentary Question OJ C212 8.8.83).

The British situation report contains a quantity of information and statistics about waste all of which was already available to the DOE and did not have to be collected specifically for the situation report. Similar information will now have to be collected every three years, and the Directive therefore has the effect of ensuring that central government cannot now leave information in the hands of local authorities but must continue to be involved with their work.

The first situation report set out the position on the preparation of waste disposal plans. It showed that in March 1982 three plans had been completed, three had been referred to the Secretary of State and more than half the remaining 159 were expected to be ready in draft form by the end of the year. The position at the end of July 1983 was as follows:

	Complete	Draft referred to Secretary of State	Others	Total
England	4	18	24	46
Wales	2	0	35	37
Scotland	3	1	52	56
N. Ireland	4	0	22	26
TOTAL	13	19	133	165

8.2   Toxic Waste

78/319/EEC (OJ L84 31.3.78)   Directive on toxic and
proposed 22.7.76 - COM(76)385   dangerous waste

Binding dates
        Notification date: 22 March 1978
        Formal compliance: 22 March 1980
        Situation reports: Every three years - first
                                          report due 22 March 1981

Purpose of the Directive

An earlier Directive 75/442 (see Section 8.1) laid down a broad
framework of control for both household and toxic wastes involving the
establishment of competent authorities responsible for producing plans and
authorising installations handling waste.   The present Directive lays down
more stringent controls for toxic and dangerous waste within that
framework.

Summary of the Directive

The main provision of the Directive is that toxic and dangerous waste
may be stored, treated and/or deposited only by authorised undertakings, and
that anyone producing or holding such waste without an appropriate permit
must then have it stored, treated or deposited by an undertaking that is so
authorised.   The Directive also makes provision for plans to be made,
records kept, transport controlled, inspections made, and reports produced.
'Toxic and dangerous waste' is defined as:

> "...any waste containing or contaminated by the
> substances or materials listed in the Annex to this
> Directive of such a nature, in such quantities or in such
> concentrations as to constitute a risk to health or the
> environment"

but certain materials are excluded from the scope of the Directive such as
radioactive waste, certain agricultural wastes, explosives and hospital
waste.   The Annex lists 27 toxic or dangerous substances.   'Disposal' of
toxic waste is defined to include "the transformation operations necessary
for its recovery, re-use or recycling".
        The Directive places a general duty on Member States to ensure that
toxic and dangerous waste is disposed of without harming human health or
the environment, and in particular without risk to water, air, soil, plants or
animals.   A general duty is also placed on them to encourage the prevention
and reuse of toxic waste.

134

The Directive makes the following more specific provisions:

(a) Competent Authorities and Plans

The requirement of Directive 75/442 that competent authorities be appointed to authorise and supervise waste disposal and to produce plans is repeated.   This time there is no requirement that these plans be drawn up 'as soon as possible', but an addition to the earlier Directive is that they must be kept up to date and be made public.   Another addition is that the plans must also be forwarded to the Commission, which together with the Member States must arrange for regular comparisons to ensure sufficient coordination.

The plans may include the estimated costs of disposal operations, but must include:
- the type and quantity of waste;
- the methods of disposal;
- specialised treatment centres where necessary;
- suitable disposal sites.

(b) Permits

Establishments storing, treating and/or depositing toxic and dangerous waste must obtain a permit from the competent authority.   (Unlike Directive 75/442 this also applies to establishments handling their own waste).   Undertakings engaged in the carriage of toxic and dangerous waste do not require a permit but "must be controlled by the competent authorities".

The permits may include conditions and obligations.   They may be granted for a specified period.   They must cover:
- the type and quantity of waste;
- the technical requirements;
- the precautions to be taken;
- the disposal site(s);
- the methods of disposal.

(c) Records

Any undertaking which produces, holds and/or disposes of toxic and dangerous waste (but not apparently ones treating such waste) must:
- keep a record of the quantity, nature, physical and chemical characteristics, and origin of such waste, and of the methods and sites used for disposing of it, including the dates of receipt and disposal; and/or
- make this information available to the competent authority on request.

(d) Transport

When toxic and dangerous waste is transported in the course of disposal (which includes transformation operations necessary for recovery, re-use or recycling) it must be accompanied by an identification form containing the following details:
- nature;
- composition;
- volume or mass of the waste;
- name and address of the producer or of the previous

135

holder(s);
- name and address of the next holder or of the final
disposer;
- location of the site of final disposal where known.

(e) Inspection

All undertakings producing, holding or disposing of toxic and dangerous waste must be subject to inspection and supervision by the competent authorities to ensure fulfilment of the provisions adopted under the Directive and the terms of any authorisation.

(f) Separation and Packaging

Member States must take the necessary steps to ensure that:
- toxic and dangerous waste is, when necessary, kept
separate from other matter and residues when being
collected, transported, stored or deposited;
- the packaging of toxic and dangerous waste is appropriately labelled, indicating in particular the nature,
composition and quantity of the waste;
- such toxic and dangerous waste is recorded and identified in respect of each site where it is or has been
deposited.

(g) 'Polluter Pays' Principle

The cost of disposing of toxic and dangerous waste is to be borne by the holder who has waste handled by a waste collector, and/or by the previous holders or the producer of the product from which the waste came. If Member States charge levies on the monies used to cover these costs, the yield may be used for financing control measures relating to toxic and dangerous waste or for financing research pertaining to the elimination of such waste.

(h) Situation Reports

Every three years, and for the first time by 22nd March 1981, Member States are to draw up a situation report on the disposal of toxic and dangerous waste and forward it to the Commission. In its turn the Commission is to report to the Council and the Parliament on the application of the Directive.

(i) Adaptation

Provisions are made for amending the Annex to the Directive in order to adapt it to scientific and technical progress. This adaptation is to be done by a committee, chaired by a representative of the Commission, and able to take decisions by qualified majority.

Development of the Directive

In its memorandum accompanying the proposed Directive the Commission attributed its origins to no particular Member State but explained that several had recently introduced laws or draft laws of varying scope to control toxic wastes.

Some ideas can nevertheless be attributed to particular countries. The Belgian law of 1974 foreshadowed the proposal - subsequently deleted from the Directive before it was agreed - that liability for damage to a third party caused by toxic waste disposed of by an unauthorised undertaking be jointly shared by the original holder of the waste and that undertaking. To the French law of 1975 can probably be attributed the obligation that the holder of toxic waste must surrender it to an authorised establishment. Similar words appear in the Directive, although strictly they are redundant since they are implicit in an authorisation procedure.

A British official, giving evidence to the Lords' Scrutiny Committee, claimed that Britain was a major contributor:

> "The Directive was quite deliberately based on the Control of Pollution Act. The Commission did use it as their main model..."

and perhaps for this reason expressed herself broadly satisfied:

> "I think that this Directive, with which we have been involved from the outset... has been approached in a sensible, logical and scientific manner and I have no grave misgivings about the way the thing has been handled..."

The Directive as proposed differed in several ways from what was finally agreed by including:
- a definition of toxic waste which would have included any waste containing the substances listed in the Annex, with no qualification about quantity or concentration so that trace quantities would also be covered;
- the provision about liability for damage, mentioned above;
- a prohibition on undertakings discriminating on the grounds of the origin of the waste;
- a provision that transporters of toxic waste be authorised.

The Minister responsible, Denis Howell, speaking in the House of Commons' debate said:

> "There is nothing in the Directive which presents us with major difficulties of policy, although we shall have to obtain a few important amendments if we are to avoid administrative difficulties".

He went on to specify four main reservations about the Directive as proposed:
- that recycling should be kept outside its scope on the grounds that toxic waste is no longer waste when it has been identified as suitable for recycling;
- that the control of transport of toxic waste should be outside its scope on the grounds that the transport of dangerous material needs to be controlled whether the material being transported is waste or not;
- that the definition of toxic waste should contain a qualification to ensure that it only applied when the toxic substance was present in such a con-

137

centration that there was a degree of hazard;
- that the technical progress committee should not have excessive powers to amend the Annex.

The government was unsuccessful on the recycling point but seems to have secured some amendments on the other three points, the most important being the qualifications made to the definition of toxic waste. Britain, of course, was not alone - the Dutch government, for instance, took the same view on the authorisation of transporters (according to evidence given to the House of Lords' Scrutiny Committee). Since then the House of Lords' Select Committee on Science and Technology (see Section 8.0) has recommended that transporters be licensed.

An explanation of how the list in the Annex was arrived at was given to the House of Lords' Scrutiny Committee:

> "The list, which represents the distillation of the work that has been done by the scientific expert group the Commission set up, is really a condensation of a much longer list that was drawn up originally and now contains the materials of concern to one or other of the Member States. Problems have been identified in one or other of the Member States with the materials listed,...and although obviously, like all these things, we are perhaps not quite so concerned about some of the things on the list as others, on a scientific and technical basis we are reasonably happy that there are not any materials included here unnecessarily."

Among the points made by the European Parliament was the need for a supplementary proposal as soon as possible "specifying in a uniform manner the levels of concentration of toxic and dangerous substances above which wastes fall within the field of application of the Directive". The laying down of concentrations had been an issue between the Dutch and British governments during negotiations with the Dutch in favour and the British opposed. This conflict was deferred and the Commissioner, Mr Tugendhat, in replying to the debate in the European Parliament, undertook to bring forward a supplementary proposal on concentrations. This proposal has yet to emerge although it has been the subject of discussions.

The European Parliament were successful with their suggestion that asbestos be added to the Annex.

Formal Compliance in the UK

According to the DOE, all Articles in the Directive were formally implemented by the due date of 22nd March 1980 except for the Article concerned with the identification form to accompany waste being transported and the keeping of records. Implementation of that Article had to await the Regulations made under Section 17 of the Control of Pollution Act - the Control of Pollution (Special Waste) Regulations 1980 (SI 1980 No 1709) - which came into force on 16th March 1981, although, as explained below, there is uncertainty as to whether the Article is yet fully complied with. The Directive was drawn to the attention of waste disposal authorities, within a few days of being agreed, by DOE Circular 29/78 dated 5th April 1978, and the Section 17 Regulations were drawn to their attention by DOE Circular 4/81 dated 20th February 1981.

A full statement of how each Article in the Directive is implemented was sent to the Commission in March 1982 with the first situation report on toxic waste disposal required by the Directive. Compliance has largely been achieved in England, Wales and Scotland under the Control of Pollution Act 1974, and in Northern Ireland by the Pollution Control and Local Government (NI) Order 1978, although various other Acts and Regulations have also been relied upon (a total of 28 in all).

In summary, the requirement to appoint competent authorities, to draw up waste disposal plans, and to issue permits is covered by the same legislation that covers the similar requirements of Directive 75/442 (see Section 8.1). The keeping of records for toxic wastes leaving a producer's premises or being disposed of to land is covered by the Section 17 Regulations, as is the requirement of an identification form when toxic waste is being transported. The Article concerned with separation and packaging of toxic waste is covered by a large number of separate Regulations (e.g., concerned with asbestos, corrosive substances, inflammable substances).

One gap in the implementation of the Directive is that there is no British legislation requiring records to be kept of toxic waste **produced** or **stored**, since the Control of Pollution (Special Waste) Regulations 1980 only require records for waste deposited on land (Regulation 14) or before the waste **leaves** the producer's premises (Regulation 4). Article 14(1) of the Directive is however clear that records are to be kept by "any installation, establishment or undertaking which **produces, holds** and/or disposes of toxic and dangerous waste". Under existing British Regulations, if the producer stores (i.e., holds) toxic waste for a long time without disposing of it he need keep no records, and indeed the producer may argue that he is only holding the toxic waste because he does not regard it as waste. If, however, the producer disposes of toxic waste on land within the curtilage of his factory he may be required to have a licence under Section 3 of the Control of Pollution Act and will then have to keep records. The House of Lords' Select Committee on Science and Technology (1) (see Section 8.0) has recommended that all producers of hazardous waste should be registered and should make a quarterly report of waste produced: implementation of this recommendation would then fulfil the requirement of the Directive.

The British Regulations are more stringent than the Directive in some respects. For instance, the Directive places no requirement on the producer of waste to notify the disposal authority in advance that a consignment is coming, and this prenotification provision is indeed unique to Britain.

When the Control of Pollution (Special Waste) Regulations 1980 were laid before Parliament a campaign was launched by the county councils to have them withdrawn and amended, leading to debates in both the House of Lords and Commons. In the Commons a motion to revoke the Regulations was moved unsuccessfully by the Opposition spokesman on the environment, Denis Howell, who, as we have seen, happened to have been the responsible Minister at the time the Directive was being negotiated and agreed. In the debate he alleged that the Regulations were contrary to the Directive, and given the source of the allegation it must be considered seriously.

Mr Howell has not publicly elaborated on his reasons for believing that the Directive is not complied with, but in a personal letter to the author he said it was because the substances controlled during transport by the Regulations are defined as having to be dangerous to human life or health, whereas the Directive also covers risk to the environment.

The point that the Regulations do not cover environmental considerations has been conceded by the DOE in Waste Management Paper No 23 (para 3):

> "The Section 17 controls are not mainly concerned with wider environmental issues such as water pollution, site sterilisation and damage to vegetation, which are matters already dealt with by site licensing, and are covered in other technical memoranda in the Waste Management Paper series".

Thus a load of waste which could pose a risk to water can be moved by lorry without being accompanied by the consignment note (British terminology) or identification form (terminology of the Directive) so long as it is not a 'special waste' defined by reference to danger to human life if ingested (see Section 8.0). As the National Water Council put it in evidence to the House of Lords Select Committee on Science and Technology (1):

> "...special waste is primarily defined by reference to the toxicity to a child of an ingested five cubic centimetres of the material. This is most unsatisfactory from the Council's point of view; for example, waste containing up to 40,000mg/kg mercury might not require notice under these regulations (the Section 17 Regulations) yet a lorry load might contain, say, 300-400 kilogrammes of mercury compounds. Such a quantity would be sufficient to contaminate well over 100 million cubic metres of water beyond the limit of the EEC Directive on Surface Water for Abstraction for Drinking. It is therefore clearly the total toxic content of a load that is critical..."

The Directive (Article 5) says that Member States are to:

> "...take the necessary measures to ensure that toxic and dangerous waste is disposed of without endangering human health and without harming the environment, and in particular: - without risk to water, air, soil, plants or animals"

and (Article 14(2)) that:

> "...when toxic and dangerous waste is transported in the course of disposal it shall be accompanied by an identification form..."

Is 'transport' part of 'disposal'? On this the Directive is quite clear.

Article 1 defines 'disposal' to include 'collection' and 'carriage' as well as tipping, from which it must follow that identification forms are required for waste being transported if there is a risk to the environment as well as to human health. Furthermore, the Directive defines toxic waste as meaning any waste containing the substances in the Annex in **such quantities** or in such concentrations as to constitute a risk to health or the environment. The example given by the National Water Council shows that it is possible for a large quantity of waste to be transported and thus create a risk to the environment without the waste falling within the British definition of 'special waste'. It seems that Mr Howell is right in that Article 14(2) concerning notification forms has not been fully complied with. It remains to be seen whether the Section 17 Regulations will be amended, and if they are not, whether the Commission takes any action. If it does not, the matter could eventually be tested in the Courts[*].

It has to be added that the wording of the Directive has been drafted very widely indeed since any toxic substance, however dilute and however small in quantity, can pose some risks to the environment. Nevertheless it should be possible to include within the definition of 'special waste' not only a reference to concentration but also a reference to the total quantity. This would meet the point made by the National Water Council in a practical way and would go some way to meeting the requirements of legal implementation. DOE officials for their part maintain that wherever the line is drawn some waste will fall outside the scope of the Directive which could have some harmful effects on the environment, and that although the line they have drawn is primarily by reference to human health, it also ensures that waste most harmful to the environment is covered.

Another gap in implementation is that the Special Waste Regulations do not apply to wastes that are to be recycled whereas these are covered by the Directive. Having failed to get the Directive narrowed during negotiations the government has effectively decided to ignore what it must regard as an unnecessary provision. However, recyclable wastes carried in road tankers have to be accompanied by details of the substances carried - under The Dangerous Substances (Conveyance by Road in Road Tankers and Tank Containers) Regulations 1981 - and it is the government's intention to extend the requirements to other types of vehicle.

There are two further gaps in the implementation of the Directive. British legislation does not cover waste produced by the Crown (e.g., the Armed Services) while the Directive makes no exemption for them. This problem has arisen with Directive 76/464 (see Section 7.8) on discharge of dangerous substances to water, and presumably the Commission turns a blind eye. However, it is possible that problems could arise if a third party adversely affected by Crown waste sought to have the Directive enforced in the Courts. DOE Circular 4/81 says that "the Secretary of State believes that the Armed Services and Government Departments will wish to take account of the Provisions of the (Control of Pollution) Act and the new Regulations under Section 17".

---

[*] Thus a waste disposal authority could interpret 'special waste' in accordance with the Directive and more stringently than the Section 17 Regulations. If a resulting dispute reached a British Court, the British Court could then apply, under Article 177 of the Treaty of Rome, to the European Court for a ruling on the interpretation of the Directive.

Another gap in implementation is that the Directive does not exclude all agricultural waste while the Section 17 Regulations do.

Effect on UK Practice

The site licensing provisions of the Control of Pollution Act were brought into force in June 1976 before the Directive was proposed and will not have been influenced by it. The effect of the Directive will therefore largely have been on the form of the Section 17 Regulations made after the Directive was agreed, and the possibility of influence was explicitly stated by an official giving evidence to the House of Lords' Scrutiny Committee in 1977:

> "We are hoping to make regulations...under Section 17...We have deliberately not put firm recommendations to Ministers at this stage because it seemed sensible at the lowest (sic - least?)...to listen to what people had to say in the course of the Brussels' discussions. They are knowledgeable and sensible and if they make good points we want to take them into account. We clearly want the two things (the Directive and the British Regulations) to be in line. We have our own ideas and we know what we do not want and what we would want to resist in the Brussels' discussions, but the two things are really marching in parallel and we have deliberately kept to ourselves a degree of flexibility at this stage."

We have already seen how the Annex to the Directive listing the substances to which the Directive applies was arrived at collectively by the Member States, and the substances listed in the Section 17 Regulations include all of these and some others. There must therefore have been some influence here. As is to be expected, DOE officials play down the overall effect of the Directive on the Section 17 Regulations maintaining that its basic tenets were unchanged, while Commission officials emphasise that the Directive helped to clarify British thinking and point out that the British legislation did not exist even in draft before the Directive.

The Directive requires Member States to forward the waste disposal plans to the Commission which will then, together with the Member States, arrange for regular comparisons. This process has not yet started because so few plans are yet complete (see Section 8.1). When comparison comes to be made it could have a long term effect on British practice as authorities in countries learn from each other.

Other effects of the Directive include the pressure generated to introduce the Section 17 Regulations without excessive delay, and the pressure it must now be creating to implement the House of Lords' recommendation that producers of waste keep records. Without this extra legislation the Directive cannot be fully implemented.

Further Developments

In January 1983 the Commission proposed a Directive concerned with transfrontier shipment of hazardous waste (OJ C53 25.2.83 - COM(82)892).

The proposal involves the competent authority in the country of destination being notified in advance that a shipment of hazardous waste is coming. The waste will also have to be accompanied by a consignment note.

References

(1) House of Lords Select Committee on Science and Technology, **Hazardous Waste Disposal**, First Report, Session 1980-81, HMSO, 1981.

8.3   Disposal of PCBs

76/403/EEC (OJ L108 26.4.76)   Directive on the disposal of
proposed 10.2.75 - COM(75)38   polychlorinated biphenyls and
                                      polychlorinated terphenyls

Binding dates
   Notification date: 9 April 1976
   Formal compliance: 9 April 1978
   Situation reports: Every three years - first
                                      report due 18 July 1980[*]

Purpose of the Directive

Polychlorinated biphenyls (PCBs) are organohalogen compounds which are now used mainly as dielectric fluids, but which were also more widely used before 1973 as hydraulic fluids, heat transfer fluids, lubricants and as plasticisers in such products as paints and carbonless copying paper. PCBs are not believed to occur naturally, but being very resistant to degradation they have been widely detected in the environment, particularly in predatory birds feeding on aquatic organisms. PCBs may have accounted for the spectacular catastrophe among wild birds in the Irish Sea in 1969. It is known that some aquatic organisms such as shrimps may be killed at very low concentrations of PCBs in water. PCBs can be destroyed in high temperature incinerators.

A separate Directive 76/769 (see Section 10.2) restricts the sale and use of PCBs and the present Directive sets out a system of control over the disposal of PCBs within the framework of Directive 75/442 (see Section 8.1).

Summary of the Directive

PCB is defined to include polychlorinated terphenyls and mixtures containing one or both substances. The definition of 'disposal' does not include the words dumping or tipping but refers to the collection and/or destruction of PCB, or transformation operations necessary for regenerating PCB. (There is an ambiguity in the use of the words 'and/or'. If the definition is interpreted to include collection without destruction the purpose of the Directive would be nullified. It must be intended to mean destruction with or without prior collection).

Four duties are placed on Member States:
- to prohibit the uncontrolled discharge, dumping and tipping of PCB and of objects and equipment containing PCB;

---

[*]   This is to assume that the report is due on the same date as the report under Directive 75/442. The Directive is not clear on the point but Article 10 says the report is to be drawn up within the framework of the 75/442 report (see Section 8.1).

- to make compulsory the disposal (i.e., collection and/or destruction, regeneration) of waste PCB and PCB contained in equipment no longer capable of being used;
- to ensure that PCB is disposed of (i.e., collected and/or destroyed, regenerated) without endangering human health and without harming the environment;
- to ensure, as far as possible, the promotion of the regeneration of waste PCB.

In order to carry out these duties the competent authorities are to set up or designate the undertakings authorised to 'dispose of' PCB on their own account or on behalf of third parties. Anyone holding PCB who is not so authorised is to hold it available for 'disposal' by an authorised undertaking. Member States are themselves to lay down the specific provisions with which the holders of PCB and the authorised undertakings must comply. The 'polluter pays' principle is to apply.

Situation reports on the 'disposal' of PCB are to be drawn up every three years within the framework of the report required by Directive 75/442 (see Section 8.1). This may be intended to mean that the two reports are due at the same time. The Commission is to circulate the reports to the other Member States. In its turn, the Commission is to report to the Council and to the Parliament on the application of the Directive.

Development of the Directive

Following a number of incidents including one in Japan where PCB-contaminated rice oil caused injury to humans and death to poultry, the Council of the OECD issued a Decision[*] in February 1973 requiring Member States of the OECD to regulate both the use and disposal of PCBs.

Following that OECD Decision, the French government forwarded to the Commission preliminary draft 'Conditions of the Use of PCBs' which also dealt with PCB disposal, and the Commission decided to propose two separate Directives, one dealing with the use of PCB and the other with its disposal.

In July 1974 a Directive was proposed (Directive 76/769 - see Section 10.2) restricting the sale and use of PCBs to closed circuit electrical equipment (transformers, resistors and inductors), condensers (capacitors) and a few other limited applications. Seven months later the Commission proposed the present Directive.

Neither the House of Commons nor the House of Lords commented on the proposed Directive so there is no publicly available record of the attitude of the British government to the proposal.

The European Parliament welcomed the proposal but suggested that the Commission should report on the application of the Directive to the Parliament and to the Council. This is one of only two amendments (other than drafting amendments) made before the Directive was agreed, the other being the insertion of the duty to promote regeneration of PCBs.

---

[*] An OECD Decision places an obligation on Member States to put it into effect but there is no Court to ensure that effective action is taken as with an EEC Directive. It is significant that notwithstanding the OECD Decision the Community nevertheless felt the need for a Directive.

Formal Compliance in the UK

In December 1978, that is to say some eight months after the due date, the government submitted a statement to the Commission of how it complied with the Directive. This referred to the site licensing provisions of the Control of Pollution Act 1974 as providing the powers to control the disposal of waste generally (the word 'dispose' being used in the usual sense to include tipping and not being restricted to the special sense of the Directive). These site licensing provisions were brought into force in England and Wales in June 1976 and in Scotland in January 1978, i.e., well before the due date. The statement of compliance also referred to the forthcoming Regulations to be made under Section 17 of the Act and to the Deposit of Poisonous Waste Act 1972. Under the 1972 Act any transport of PCB for the purpose of being deposited on land (which included delivery to an incinerator) had to be notified in advance. The 1972 Act was replaced in 1981 by the Section 17 Regulations which provide a more precise definition of toxic waste and more precise control arrangements. Any transport of waste containing at least 1% by weight of PCB, including transport to a high temperature incinerator, now has to be notified in advance and must be accompanied by a consignment note.

In July 1979 the Commission wrote formally to the government asking it to submit observations for its failure fully to implement the Directive, and in October 1979 the government replied that it intended to lay Regulations under Section 17 of the 1974 Act before Parliament by mid-1980.

Despite this letter the Commission issued a Reasoned Opinion in May 1980 to the effect that since it had not been informed of all the provisions adopted to comply with the Directive, it was compelled to assume that the United Kingdom had failed to fulfil its obligations.

In July 1980 the government replied by letter that it was now the hope that the Section 17 Regulations would be laid before Parliament by the end of the month. The letter referred again to the Deposit of Poisonous Waste Act 1972 and stated that it was the government's view (an erroneous view, see below) that it already had the necessary legislation to enable it to fulfil its strict obligations under the Directive.

After some further delay, the Section 17 Regulations were laid before Parliament in November 1980 and came into operation on 16th March 1981. This is not the only Directive which will have created a pressure for the introduction of the Regulations (see also Sections 8.2 and 8.4).

The government sent the Regulations to the Commission in April 1981 in a letter which carefully specified those Articles of the Directive that were implemented by the 1974 Act and the new Regulations made under it. The Article concerned with compulsory 'disposal' was not mentioned.

In March 1982 the DOE submitted a situation report to the Commission, as required by the Directive, containing a further statement of the legislation under which the Directive is implemented. This referred incidentally to the Alkali Act 1906 and to the duty on the Alkali Inspectorate to control high temperature incinerators.

Neither the letter of April 1981 nor the original statement of compliance sent in December 1978, nor the situation report of March 1982, made any reference to measures implementing the duty to make **compulsory** the 'disposal' (i.e., collection and/or destruction, regeneration) of waste PCB. There is at present no British legislation preventing someone holding a quantity of waste PCBs on his premises (e.g., in an old transformer which may begin to leak) until an occupational hazard is posed. On 29th July 1982, however, the Under Secretary, Giles Shaw, announced in Parliament that Regulations would be made requiring that storage of liquid waste be licensed. It remains to be seen whether the proposed Regulations meet the requirements of the Directive, but for the moment there is nothing to compel someone holding an old transformer to have it collected for destruction or regeneration. If, however, the holder has the waste transported he must, under the Section 17 Regulations, pre-notify the recipient and disposal may only take place at a licensed plant or site. The duty in the Directive to make 'disposal' compulsory has therefore only partly been implemented by legislation and if there has been full implementation of this duty it must be by some non-legislative means, although it is hard to see how the word 'compulsory' in the Directive can allow for non-mandatory action. In 1976 the DOE issued a Code of Practice contained in a Waste Management Paper (1) but since this provides nothing which could fulfil the duty, it must be concluded that full compliance has not been achieved.

Another difficulty over compliance arises from ambiguity in the text. It is the practice in Britain, and presumably in other Member States, for small capacitors (e.g., from domestic fluorescent lights) to be deposited with household waste into landfill sites. This is 'controlled tipping' in the language of the Directive and hence permitted since the relevant Article only prohibits 'uncontrolled tipping'. However, another Article also lays a duty on Member States to make compulsory the 'disposal' (i.e., collection and/or destruction, regeneration) of waste PCB contained in equipment no longer capable of being used. This duty, on its own and unqualified by the other prohibition, should result in a prohibition of the practice of tipping even small capacitors on landfill sites. This inconsistency must have been overlooked or ignored when the Directive was being agreed since it leads logically to a meaningless interpretation of the Directive. Thus if the deposit of small capacitors in landfill sites is 'controlled tipping' and hence is permitted by the Directive then, by the same token, there is nothing to prevent a Member State allowing the 'controlled tipping' of large capacitors or even large transformers on landfill sites. This cannot be the intention of the Directive. The conflict between the two prohibitions could be resolved by an amending Directive qualifying the duty to destroy or regenerate PCB-filled equipment to cases where this can reasonably be done, and additionally or alternatively indicating a maximum volume or weight permitted for landfill. (British government officials, however, argue that tipping of small capacitors constitutes 'destruction' since eventually PCBs degenerate. This is an interesting argument but does not overcome the difficulty: if PCB in small capacitors eventually degenerates so will PCB in larger equipment. Yet a purpose of the Directive is to prevent tipping of such equipment).

The existence of the Directive has never been formally drawn to the attention of waste disposal authorities. The Waste Management Paper (1) which was sent to all waste disposal authorities merely said that the EEC would shortly be publishing two Directives relating to PCBs.

Effect on UK Practice

The DOE Waste Management Paper of 1976 described the uses of PCBs, the amount of wastes arising, their toxicity, methods of disposal, and set out

147

a Code of Practice. The DOE plan to revise the Paper.

The major uses of PCBs are now in transformers, and large capacitors. Small capacitors for domestic use are virtually no longer filled with PCB. From 1971 the sole British manufacturer restricted sales to dielectric applications and for research purposes, and Directive 76/769 (see Section 10.2) now makes that mandatory. Production of PCB in Britain ceased in 1977.

Small capacitors were used in fluorescent lights and so are bound to find their way into household and commercial waste. The Code of Practice says that no special precautions need be taken in the disposal of these small capacitors unless there is undue concentration (more than one capacitor per tonne of refuse) at one particular landfill site. The tipping of small capacitors in landfill sites is therefore controlled for the purposes of the Directive by the site licence (or its equivalent for a local authority owned site) and by the normal supervision that takes place at any landfill site, and no change has resulted from the Directive.

The Code of Practice recommends that waste PCBs from transformers and large capacitors be removed for reclamation or incineration. Incineration is to be carried out at over 1,100° C for at least two seconds with a minimum excess oxygen content of three per cent. The situation report states that one firm is licensed for the storage of PCB waste from the refilling of existing electrical equipment, and five high temperature incinerators are licensed for the disposal of PCB waste. These incinerators (four English and Welsh and one Scottish) are all registered under the Alkali Act and are controlled by the Inspectorate. The total quantity of PCB incinerated at these five incinerators in the 20 months from 1980 to August 1981 was 227 tonnes at a cost to the disposer of around £600 per tonne of concentrated PCB waste. Some of this waste PCB was imported – since most Member States have inadequate incinerator capacity. The practice of incineration will not have been affected by the provisions of the Directive.

The Waste Management Paper explained that since 1971 new transformers in Britain containing PCBs had been labelled by the manufacturers. This has been done on a voluntary basis. Some manufacturers have contacted all their customers, even those who bought articles in the 1940s, advising them of the need for adequate disposal. Some retrospective labelling has been carried out on the older equipment still in use but difficulties arise when there are no adequate records. The Waste Management Paper says that identification can be assisted by an examination of the original capital cost and siting of the unit and by the fact that the operating and maintenance procedures for PCB-filled units are different from those filled with hydrocarbon oils.

Despite this advice, instances have been known of PCB filled transformers being sold for scrap without the scrap merchant being notified of the contents. Since 1981 the movement of such transformers to the scrap merchant will have been an offence under the Section 17 Regulations but the holding of an unused transformer is not an offence. If it begins to leak, and thus creates a hazard, an employer will have obligations to his employees under the Health and Safety at Work etc Act 1974.

In a House of Commons' debate on 16th March 1982 the Under Secretary, Giles Shaw, said that there was no complete record of the number of transformers still in use containing PCBs and that the government was trying to find out. He preferred an estimate of around 3,000 to the figure of 20,000 sometimes quoted. He also explained that factory inspectors have written instructions on the hazards of PCBs and the precautions to be observed, and that if plant containing PCBs is found in the course of inspection appropriate advice is given.

Whatever the difficulties in legislating to prevent people unknowingly holding old transformers or selling them for scrap, the fact remains that the Directive places a duty on Member States to make **compulsory** the collection and/or destruction, or regeneration, of PCB contained in equipment no longer capable of being used, and this duty has not been fully complied with. This problem must have arisen in other Member States and it would be extremely helpful if the Commission were to compare legislation on the subject. New British legislation could for instance take the form of a requirement on all owners of transformers which are not marked with their contents to have them examined, and to 'dispose' of any containing PCB which are no longer in use: if such legislation were to be introduced it would of course be one effect of the Directive.

The Waste Management Paper of 1976 reported that one centre in Britain offered a PCB reclamation service (regeneration in the language of the Directive) but this has since closed, and the situation report of 1982 says that there is no regeneration facility in Britain at present. The duty on Member States to promote regeneration is qualified by the words 'as far as possible' and in the absence of facilities regeneration must now be regarded as not possible in Britain.

As with the other waste Directives, the DOE is now obliged to continue to collect information about PCB disposal for the purposes of the three-yearly situation reports. The Commission has yet to draw up its own report consolidating the information gathered from the first national situation reports.

References

(1) Department of the Environment, **Polychlorinated Biphenyl (PCB) Waste,** Waste Management Paper No 6, HMSO, 1976

8.4   Waste Oils

75/439/EEC (OJ L194 25.7.75)   Directive on the disposal of
proposed 20.3.74 - COM(74)334   waste oils

Binding dates
Notification date: 18 June 1975
Formal compliance: 18 June 1977
Final date for permits: 18 June 1979
Situation reports: Every three years - first
                                   report due 18 June 1980*

Purpose of the Directive

A survey before the Directive was proposed showed that in some
Member States as much as 20 to 60 per cent of all waste oils were disposed of
without any control, resulting in a significant proportion of all industrial
pollution. The Directive is designed primarily to deal with this
environmental problem, but it also seeks to prevent waste of resources and
to ensure that different financial arrangements adopted to promote safe
disposal and recycling do not create barriers to the common market.

Summary of the Directive

A general duty is placed on Member States to ensure the safe collection
and disposal of waste oils, and to ensure that they are 'as far as possible'
recycled. Disposal is not defined. The definition of 'waste oils' is not
restricted to lubricating oils but by including the words 'used products' it
excludes wastes from, e.g., oil refineries. The following are to be
prohibited:

- discharge of waste oils to water and drainage systems;
- any deposit and/or discharge harmful to the soil;
- any uncontrolled discharge of residues from
  processing;
- any processing of waste oils causing air pollution
  which exceeds the level prescribed by existing
  provisions.

Where the above aims cannot otherwise be achieved, Member States
are to ensure that one or more undertakings carry out the collection and/or
disposal of waste oils in assigned zones. Holders of waste oils who cannot
comply with the above prohibitions must place the oils at the disposal of
these undertakings.

___

* Assuming the period runs from the date for compliance (see section 8.1).

Indemnities may be granted to these collection and disposal undertakings as a reciprocal concession for the obligations imposed on them. These indemnities must not exceed annual uncovered costs and must not cause any significant distortion to competition or give rise to artificial patterns of trade in the products. The indemnities may be financed by a charge on waste oils or on products which after use are transformed into waste oils. The 'polluter pays' principle is to apply.

Any undertaking which disposes of waste oil must obtain a permit from the competent authority. The permit may be subject to conditions. The undertakings must supply certain information to the competent authority on request and must be periodically inspected.

Holders of certain quantities of waste oils containing impurities in excess of certain percentages must handle and stock them separately. These quantities and percentages are to be fixed by the competent authorities and may differ according to the category of product (Article 8).

Any establishment producing, collecting and/or disposing of more than 500 litres of waste oils per annum (Member States may set a lower limit) must keep a record of the quantity, quality, origin and location of the oils and of their despatch and receipt, including dates of receipt (Article 10).

Every three years Member States must submit a situation report on the disposal of waste oils to the Commission. (Unlike the other waste Directives, there is no obligation on the Commission to submit a consolidated report to the Council or Parliament). In addition, Member States must periodically convey to the Commission their technical expertise, experience gained and results obtained through the application of the measures taken under the Directive. The Commission is to send an overall summary of such information to the Member States.

Development of the Directive

Under a German law of 1968 controlling the disposal of waste oil, a levy on the sale of lubricants is used to cover losses during waste oil disposal operations. This law provided one inspiration for the Directive, but the Commission's work was initiated by a legislative proposal from the Dutch government rather similar to the scheme in Germany, and by French draft legislation. This explains why the Directive preceded the framework Directive on waste (section 8.1). In fact the Directive - agreed at the Council meeting of 7th November 1974 - was the very first to be agreed under the Action Programme on the Environment.

Since the proposed Directive was not considered by either the House of Commons or the House of Lords, there is no parliamentary record of the attitude of the British government at that time, other than the inference that can be drawn from the comment of a British member (James Hill) made during the European Parliament's debate. He said that it was not the British government's intention to take powers to pay subsidies to firms which collect or dispose of waste oils, and pointed out that the proposed Directive made it clear that such subsidies were payable at the discretion of the Member States. The lack of parliamentary scrutiny may also explain how Britain came to accept obligations which it has subsequently not completely fulfilled.

The European Parliament welcomed without reservation the provisions

151

aimed at 'banning the destruction of waste oils' and 'making regeneration of waste oils obligatory', thus giving a much more stringent interpretation to the language of the Directive than it actually bears.

The Economic and Social Committee concentrated largely on the financial arrangements and proposed an alternative scheme which, in their view, applied the 'polluter pays' principle more rigidly.

Before the Directive was agreed it underwent some changes including an increase from 200 to 500 litres per annum of the threshold above which records have to be kept by establishments producing, collecting or disposing of waste oils.

Formal Compliance in the UK

In October 1977, that is to say nearly four months after the due date, the government submitted a statement to the Commission of how it complied with the Directive. This referred to the site licensing provisions of the Control of Pollution Act which had been brought into force in June 1976 and to the Deposit of Poisonous Waste Act 1972. It referred to the DOE's advisory Waste Management Paper No 7 on 'Mineral Waste Oils' (1) dated 1976, and it also referred to the forthcoming Regulations to be made under Section 17 of the Control of Pollution Act. Additionally, the statement referred to various other pieces of legislation controlling the discharge of waste oils to water or soil and controlling air pollution. The reference to the Section 17 Regulations said that these would "control the handling, storage and disposal of waste oils containing certain impurities in significant quantities", a promise which has since been only partially fulfilled. The statement also referred to the Section 17 Regulations in connection both with the duty on establishments handling more than 500 litres per annum to keep records, and with the duty on holders of waste oil containing impurities to handle them separately. These statements indicate that it was then the intention of the government to implement these provisions of the Directive.

The waste disposal authorities were informed of the existence of the Directive by being sent a copy of the Waste Management Paper. It contains a reference to the Directive.

In May 1980 the Commission issued a Reasoned Opinion to the effect that since it had not been informed of all the provisions adopted to comply with the Directive, it was compelled to assume that Britain had failed to fulfil its obligations.

In July 1980 the government replied by letter that it was now the hope that the Section 17 Regulations would be laid before Parliament by the end of the month, but also went on to argue that the requirements for records and separate handling were already covered by the site licensing provisions of the Control of Pollution Act. The letter concluded (erroneously as is now admitted, see below) that they had the necessary legislation to enable them to fulfil their strict obligations under the Directive.

After some further delay, the Section 17 Regulations were laid before Parliament in November 1980, and came into operation on 16th March 1981. They were sent to the Commission in April 1981.

In March 1982 the DOE submitted a situation report to the Commission, as required by the Directive, containing a further statement of how the Directive was implemented. This explained that the discretionary

152

provisions for indemnities to be paid to waste oil collection and disposal undertakings specially authorised on a zonal basis have not been used in Britain:

> "The disposal of waste oil to various outlets is not regulated other than in conformity with legislative measures for the protection of the environment. The functions of collection, reclamation and ultimate disposal of waste oils are exercised by producers and private (and public) undertakings within the market economy system".

All other provisions of the Directive (apart from those requiring separate handling of oil containing impurities, and the keeping of records) including the requirements for permits, were said to be covered by general environmental legislation including the Town and Country Planning Acts, the Alkali Act, the Health and Safety at Work etc Act, and the Control of Pollution Act.

The situation report admitted that the requirement that establishments **producing** and **collecting** waste oils should keep records (Article 10) had not been complied with:

> "Producers are not currently required to maintain records of the quantity, quality, origin and location of the waste oils they generate.
> "Undertakings collecting waste oil are not currently required to maintain records of the quantity, quality, (and) origin of the waste oil other than to meet the requirements of HM Customs and Excise in respect of oil purchased for onward sale and subject to liability for Value Added Tax".

For establishments **disposing** of waste oils the position is different since waste disposal authorities are empowered to specify in the site licence that records be kept of the characteristics and qualities of waste oil and oil-bearing residues handled on site. Additionally, requirements for records apply if the waste oils contain toxic impurities and so become 'special waste' under the Section 17 Regulations.

The situation report also admits failure to comply with another provision of the Directive (Article 8):

> "There is no specific legal requirement for holders of waste oils to handle and store these separately according to the content of impurities'.

The British government has no immediate plans to implement the provisions of Articles 8 and 10.

There is a further difficulty over implementation since the Directive places a prohibition on discharges of waste oils to water and drainage systems. Such an absolute ban - there is no provision for exceptions - must be regarded as impractical since some waste oils are bound to find their way into industrial discharges. This is admitted in the Waste Management Paper:

"At most premises where oil is used, interceptors are provided in the drainage system in order to minimise the discharge of oil to sewers and rivers..." (para 1.9).

"In the past there has tended to be a small chronic contamination of the environment via drainage systems and rivers but the greater care now exercised in the handling of oil products has generally resulted in an improvement of the situation" (para 1.10).

"Where a discharge to a watercourse is inevitable, the requirement 'no visible oil' is often specified: this in effect may mean up to 20ppm depending on the droplet size" (para 2.3.1).

The situation report further confirms this by giving figures of over 100,000 tonnes per annum of waste oils disposed to the environment and commenting that these "include oily wastes deposited at licensed landfills and oil also contained in consented effluents discharged to water systems".

It is clear from these official statements that not only is the prohibition not complied with formally in the sense that there is no legislation banning such discharges, but also that such a ban could anyway not be complied with. The fault here lies in the drafting of the Directive and again raises the problem of outright bans which we have encountered in the case of the groundwater Directive (see Section 7.9). On that occasion the House of Commons adopted a resolution that "This House...cannot accept proposals that require a ban on all types of direct discharge, particularly those found acceptable in the United Kingdom". It is interesting to speculate whether, if the waste oils Directive had been scrutinised by either of the two Houses of Parliament, it would have passed unscathed.

There is a more general difficulty that goes to the very root of the Directive and concerns the duty to ensure that 'as far as possible', 'disposal' is to be carried out by recycling. The Directive, inspired as it was by German legislation, envisaged the possibility of a special regime to deal with the recycling of waste oils. If in Britain a significant amount of oil has not been recycled which could and would have been recycled with a system similar to that in Germany, can the government argue that it has indeed ensured that 'as far as possible' waste oils are being recycled?

The German system has been described in an OECD report of 1981 (2). A charge on both virgin and reprocessed oil provides a fund from which aid is distributed to firms which must agree to collect, within specified zones, all waste oils in quantities exceeding 200 litres, and arrange storage when smaller quantities are involved. The oil recovery industry in Britain, as represented by the Chemical Recovery Assocation, on the other hand believes that the intense competition among a large number of small specialist recovery firms ensures that all recoverable oil in Britain is indeed recovered. The Association would strongly resist the introduction of a system similar to the German system in Britain. A rather more rigid system has recently been introduced in France and is now the subject of litigation on the grounds that authorised collectors have been given a monopoly.

If the claim that all recoverable oil is indeed recovered in Britain is correct then the main obligation of the Directive is complied with, since the indemnity provision of the Directive is an optional one. There is obviously a need for an objective assessment of the merits of the British and German system, not merely for the intrinsic interest of such a comparison but also to be able to judge whether a legal obligation has been fulfilled.

The failure of Britain to implement Articles 8 and 10 (records for producers of waste oils and separate storage according to the impurity content) has yet to be fully explained. One explanation is that the Directive was rushed through immediately after an oil crisis when all Governments were possibly more ready to undertake new obligations. Another is that being the first environmental Directive the British officials concerned were unfamiliar with the procedures and did not fully realise the consequence of a failure to comply with every detailed article. Parliamentary scrutiny could have led to a discussion of the value of the two provisions. Whatever the reasons, this Directive is the only environmental Directive where failure to implement is not only admitted, but also where there is no stated intention of remedying the deficiency. The 1981 Report of the House of Lords' Select Committee on Science and Technology (see Section 8.0) recommended that producers of toxic waste should effectively keep records and the implementation of that recommendation, which is now under consideration by the government, could go some way to fulfilling the deficiency. Despite this admitted deficiency the Commission is turning a blind eye. In reply to a European Parliamentary Question the Commissioner, Mr Narjes, said that Belgium is the only Member State which has not yet fully implemented the Directive (OJ C177 4.7.83).

The Effect on UK Practice

There have been no changes to British practice caused by changes in legislation attributable to the Directive since there have been no such legislative changes. Although the Section 17 Regulations were introduced after the Directive they were not introduced primarily for the purpose of implementing this Directive (see Section 8.2).

In 1977, after the Directive was agreed, the DOE published a Waste Management Paper on 'Mineral Oil Wastes' (1) which included a statement in the foreword that the advice given accorded with the approach established in the Directive. The Paper ended with a Code of Practice dealing with minimising environmental problems and encouraging recovery. There is no advice to establishments handling oils to keep records, nor to stock separately oils containing impurities, although caution is urged when burning contaminated oils. Advice on recycling includes the following:

> "The total of potentially recoverable oil, generated as
> small arisings, is considerable and the collection of this
> oil warrants closer examination: in particular the
> economics of collection could be improved by the
> provision of reception points at Civic Amenity Sites and
> of joint storage facilities for example on industrial
> trading estates. The dissemination of information on the
> available reception (collection) facilities for spent oils in
> local areas is strongly recommended."

The production of the Waste Management Paper may be regarded as one consequence of the Directive.

The situation report submitted to the Commission in March 1982 contains the following figures for Britain (1,000 tons):

	1979	1980
Lubricating oil sales	1031	896
Waste oil generation	533	443
Waste oil collection		
Collected for disposal by commercial undertakings	280	270
Recycling: by type of undertaking		
Recycled in house by generators as fuel/lubricant	160	120
Recycled by commercial undertakings as lubricants or fuel	210	200
	370	320
Recycling: by type of use		
Waste oil to fuel use	280	240
Waste oil reprocessed as lubricants and other oil fractions	90	80
	370	320
Final disposal		
Incineration	20	10
Disposal to the environment	133	113
	153	123

One effect of the Directive is that the DOE will have to produce comparable figures every three years for further situation reports. The Commission is under no obligation to publish a report comparing figures in the Member States, and unless it chooses to do so it will not be easy to tell whether a higher or lower proportion of waste oils is recycled in Britain compared with other countries.

References

(1) Department of the Environment, **Mineral Oil Wastes,** Waste Management Paper No 7, HMSO, 1979

(2) Organisation for Economic Co-operation and Development, **Economic Instruments in Solid Waste Management,** 1981

CHAPTER 9
Air

9.0　Relevant British Legislation

British air pollution policy is marked by a great divide, but to assume that the division lies between industrial emissions on the one hand and domestic emissions on the other, or between 'noxious gas' - as the legislation calls it - and smoke is to come sufficiently close to the mark as to cause confusion. These divisions are important, but not so important for the shaping of British policy as the division of responsibility for controlling emissions between the national inspectorates and local authorities. Thus unlike both water pollution and waste disposal, responsibility for air pollution is only partly a local or regional matter. But even at the national level the task of controlling air pollution has been devolved to administrative agencies: the Industrial Air Pollution Inspectorate in England and Wales (formerly the Alkali Inspectorate) and the Industrial Pollution Inspectorate in Scotland. Indeed, the Secretary of State has rather limited powers over air pollution, and although he has some powers to set emission standards (for grit and dust under the Clean Air Act 1968) and to set product standards for fuels, he has no general powers to set emission standards or air quality standards, to direct industries to use one fuel rather than another even in an emergency, or to set ceilings on total emissions in particular areas or nationally.

A history of the separate development of controls over 'noxious gases' and smoke and of the powers of the Alkali Inspectorate and local authorities has been written by Eric Ashby and Mary Anderson (1), and it is by reference to its origins that British air pollution policy is best understood.

'Scheduled' Processes

The Inspectorate is responsible for 'scheduled' processes giving rise to particularly noxious or offensive emissions. The number of 'scheduled' processes has increased steadily since 1863 when the first Alkali Act was passed, so as to cover today over 60 processes involving over 2,000 plants. The Inspectorate now operates partly under the Alkali etc Works Regulation Act 1906, which consolidated various Acts passed after 1863, and partly under the Health and Safety at Work etc Act 1974 which will eventually replace the 1906 Act completely. Formally the Inspectorate (together with the Factory Inspectorate and various other inspectorates) is now part of the Health and Safety Executive, which was established under the 1974 Act. The 1906 and 1974 Acts allow the Secretary of State by regulation to extend the Schedule in the 1906 Act listing the processes under the Inspectorate's control.

Scheduled processes must be registered annually with the Inspectorate and any changes in the process and ownership must be notified. Registration is not, however, the equivalent of the granting of a licence to emit a certain quantity or quality of gases (similar to the 'consent' given subject to conditions for a discharge to a river), but instead there is a statutory duty on the operator of the process, and on the Inspectorate, to ensure that the process is operated using the "best practicable means for preventing the escape of noxious or offensive gases...and for rendering such gases where discharged harmless and inoffensive". One of the conditions of first registration is that the plant must have such appliances as the Inspectorate considers necessary to comply with the requirements of the Act.

The way the term 'best practicable means' is interpreted is therefore of considerable importance, and in Chapter 2 we have already seen the Inspectorate discussing the term in connection with the removal of sulphur from emissions from power stations.

In practice the Inspectorate discusses the ways of reducing emissions with representatives of the industry concerned and brings to bear its own technical knowledge and knowledge of what has been done abroad. The Inspectorate then publishes the conclusions in 'Notes on Best Practicable Means'. These 'Notes' will describe treatment plant to be used and its maintenance; methods of operation; and also may include a 'presumptive limit' for emissions, i.e., so much of a pollutant per cubic metre of gases emitted from a chimney stack. If the limit is being met then there is normally a presumption that the 'best practicable means' are being used. These 'presumptive limits' are therefore emission standards, but since they are not enshrined in legislation but are set administratively they can be tightened by the Inspectorate as required to keep pace with advances in abatement technology. The 'Notes on Best Practicable Means' including the 'presumptive limits' apply nationally, although inspectors can exercise discretion in modifying them to take into account the circumstances of particular plants and local conditions. Cost is a major factor taken into account. The Chief Alkali Inspector in his 1966 Annual Report explained that:

> "...the expression 'best practicable means' takes into account economics in all its financial implications, and we interpret this not just in the narrow sense of a works dipping into its own pockets, but including the wider effect on the community" (quoted in (2)).

The term 'best practicable means' has been authoritatively discussed most recently in the Chief Inspector's report for 1981 (3). However, it is not abundantly clear from that description or from other literature to what extent the Inspectorate takes into account local environmental conditions in deciding on the 'best practicable means' for a particular plant, although it is the view of the Inspectorate that it should be taken into account and that there should be some variation. The Royal Commission on environmental Pollution in its fifth report (4) explained (para 91) that the District Inspector "has discretion to impose tighter (but not laxer) requirements than the general best practicable means would call for if this is justified by particular local conditions". Since the duty under the Act is first to prevent 'the escape of noxious or offensive gases' whether harm is being caused or not, it can indeed be inferred that the 'presumptive limit' should not be relaxed merely because a particular plant is remote from a centre of population. The position seems to be that laxer standards than the 'presumptive limits' are permitted for existing plant and that for new plant more stringent conditions are sometimes applied, but that less than the 'presumptive limit' is not permitted. The provisions of 'best practicable means' other than the 'presumptive limits' appear to be more open to variation including the height of chimneys. The desirability of having some uniformity across the country was nevertheless explained by one Chief Inspector in the following words:

> "It is to the trade's advantage to have uniformity of application of control measures and it would be unjust to give one works a commercial advantage over another".(5)

The term 'best technical means' or equivalent words are not be found in British legislation, although they are used in other countries. The term 'best technical means' could be expected to differ from 'best practicable means' by taking no account of local circumstances and less account of cost. It cannot presumably take no account of cost, since almost any amount of abatement is theoretically possible but at a price which no-one would be prepared to pay. All such phrases as 'best practicable means' or 'best technical means' can only be understood by a close examination of how they are interpreted and applied, which are bound to be matters of tradition that evolve within an enforcement agency. They are therefore likely to cause considerable problems in Community legislation.

Once a process is scheduled, the Inspectorate is responsible for all emissions from it, including smoke.

Processes not 'Scheduled'

All processes that are not 'scheduled' are the responsibility of local authorities whose powers are exercised by environmental health officers. The Clean Air Act 1956 (amended in 1968) strengthened the powers of local authorities previously contained in the Public Health Act 1936 to control non-scheduled processes. However, the Clean Air Acts only cover combustion processes and emissions of smoke, grit and dust.

The 1956 Act prohibits dark smoke from being emitted from any trade or industrial premises. Any new furnace (other than domestic boilers) must be capable so far as practicable of being operated continously without emitting smoke, and local authorities must be notified of any proposal to install a new furnace. Plants over a certain size must be equipped to the satisfaction of the local authority with plant to arrest the emission of grit and dust, and the height of a new chimney must be approved by the local authority who must be satisfied that it will be high enough to prevent the emissions becoming prejudicial to health or a nuisance (6). The Secretary of State has made Regulations setting limits on the emission of grit and dust from furnaces.

Emissions other than smoke, grit and dust from processes that are not 'scheduled' can only be controlled by the statutory nuisance provisions of the Public Health Act 1936 or the Public Health (Scotland) Act 1897. If a local authority is satisfied that a nuisance exists it must serve on the person responsible a notice requiring him to take whatever steps are necessary to abate the nuisance. This procedure cannot be used to anticipate a nuisance so that control over gases from non-scheduled processes are limited (e.g., the emissions of metals from certain foundries).

The Control of Pollution Act 1974 includes a Part IV dealing with air.

This part does not have the same comprehensive character as the parts on water and waste, but it does extend the powers of local authorities to obtain information about emissions - though these are difficult to use.

Domestic Smoke

Smoke from domestic chimneys is also the responsibility of local authorities. Under the Clean Air Acts local authorities may make smoke control orders prohibiting the emission of smoke from any building in a specified area, although specific buildings may be exempted. In these areas householders who have to change their means of cooking or heating may receive grants. The 'smoke control order' has been the principal instrument of policy to reduce pollution of air by smoke that was such a feature of British towns within even the last 20 years, but it remains a matter for conjecture to what extent the marked improvement has been advanced by smoke control orders and to what extent it is the consequence of a spontaneous change from open fires to other forms of heating. As we will see in Section 9.2, the smoke control order is the principal instrument being used to implement Directive 80/779 setting air quality standards for smoke and sulphur dioxide.

Composition of Fuels

The Control of Pollution Act 1974 also gives the Secretary of State power to make Regulations controlling the sulphur content of oil fuels and the composition of motor fuels including lead in petrol and sulphur in diesel fuel. These have been used to implement Directives (see Sections 9.1 and 9.5).

Vehicle Emissions

Vehicle emisions can be controlled by specifying the construction of the vehicle itself as well as by specifying the composition of the fuel. The Secretary of State for Transport has powers under the Road Traffic Act 1972 to make Regulations on vehicle emissions and, as will be seen in Section 9.5, a whole series of such Regulations has been made to implement various Directives.

Further Developments

The Royal Commission on Environmental Pollution's fifth report (4) dealt with air pollution and made a number of recommendations including the setting of air quality guidelines, although it opposed mandatory air quality standards. By the time the government replied (7) six years later, Directive 80/779 setting mandatory air quality standards (Section 9.2) had already been agreed, so that the niceties of air quality standards versus guidelines did not form a part of the government's response. In his annual report for 1981 (3) the Chief Air Pollution Inspector argued that the integration of 'best practicable means' with the air quality concept was a priority for consideration in the immediate future. In December 1982 the government announced a comprehensive review of air pollution legislation.

References

(1)   Eric Ashby and Mary Anderson, **The Politics of Clean Air,** Clarendon Press, Oxford, 1981.

(2)   J McLaughlin and M J Foster, **The Law and Practice Relating to Pollution Control in the United Kingdom,** Graham and Trotman, 1982.

(3)   Health and Safety Executive, **Industrial Air Pollution 1981,** HMSO, 1982.

(4)   Royal Commission on Environmental Pollution, **Air Pollution Control: An Integrated Approach,** Fifth Report, HMSO, 1976.

(5)   F E Ireland, **Control of Special Industrial Emissions in Britain,** Proceedings of the Second International Clean Air Congress, Academic Press, London and New York, 1971.

(6)   Department of the Environment, **Pollution Control in Britain: How it Works,** Pollution Paper No 9, HMSO, 1976.

(7)   Department of the Environment, **Air Pollution Control: The Government Response to the Fifth Report of the Royal Commission on Environmental Pollution,** Pollution Paper No 18, HMSO, 1982.

9.1 Sulphur Content of Gas Oil

75/716/EEC (OJ L307 27.11.75)
proposed 11.2.74 - COM(74)158

Directive on the approximation of the laws of the Member States relating to the sulphur content of certain liquid fuels

Binding dates
Notification date: 25 November 1975
Formal compliance: 25 August 1976
Limits to be met: 1 October 1976
                                          1 October 1980

Purpose of the Directive

A limit is set on the sulphur content of gas oil both to eliminate barriers to trade resulting from different limits in different countries and also to reduce air pollution by sulphur dioxide.

'Gas oil' is a term of art used to describe certain medium distillates used mostly for domestic heating and cooking and also 'Derv' for diesel engined motor vehicles. Gas oil differs from 'fuel oil' which is a term of art for heavier oil used for industrial heating and in power stations. Gas oil is also sometimes referred to as 'light fuel oil'. A Directive on the sulphur content of fuel oil was proposed but never agreed (see Section 9.2).

Summary of the Directive

Only two grades of gas oil are to be permitted for sale in the Community. Type A, having the lower sulphur content, may be used without restriction, while Type B is only to be used in zones designated by Member States. These zones are to be either where ground level concentrations of atmospheric sulphur dioxide are sufficiently low, or where gas oil accounts for an insignificant proportion of sulphur dioxide pollution. Member States must inform the Commission and the other Member States of the Type B zones they have designated with their reasons.

The sulphur compound content of both types is to be reduced in two stages:

	Type A	Type B
From 1st October 1976	0.5% (by weight)	0.8%
From 1st October 1980 (1985 in Ireland)	0.3%	0.5%

Member States are to ensure sampling of the sulphur content. A reference method for determining the sulphur content is specified.

If, as a result of sudden changes in crude oil supplies, there is a

163

shortage of desulphurisation capacity, a Member State may allow the use of gas oil with more than the specified sulphur content but must inform the Commission. The Commission, after consulting the other Member States, must decide within three months on the duration and details of the derogation.

Gas oil used in power stations and shipping and contained in the tanks of inland waterway vessels or motor vehicles crossing zones or crossing a frontier into the Community is excluded from the Directive.

Development of the Directive

In 1969 the Commission had instituted a General Programme of measures to eliminate technical or non-tariff barriers to trade. As a result of a study of the difficulties encountered by the oil industry in adjusting to the different requirements of different Member States, the Commission incorporated 'petroleum oils used for heating or for the propulsion of motor vehicles' into the General Programme in May 1973. This step preceded the First Action Programme on the Environment of November 1973 which, however, mentioned the General Programme as a possible instrument of environmental policy and, by way of example, referred to a limit on the sulphur content of gas oil. By the time it was formally proposed, the Directive was therefore seen both as an environmental protection measure and as a measure to facilitate trade. From a trade point of view, what matters is that the limits are the same in the different Member States, and the contribution of the Community's environmental policy has been to ensure that the limits are as low as reasonably possible.

A spur to action was provided by information supplied in 1973 by the Dutch, French, Italian and German Governments of proposals for further legislation concerned with fuels, and it may be assumed that the idea of Type A and B gas oils with Type B being restricted to certain zones stems from one or more of these proposals for domestic legislation. The principle is in some respects the same as the smoke control areas of the Clean Air Act 1956.

The Economic and Social Committee and the European Parliament both welcomed the proposal while criticising points of detail. Both agreed with the opinion of the Commission that implementation of the Directive would not entail any appreciable increase in costs for the refining industry nor any significant increase in fuel consumption. The Commissioner, Mr Gundelach, in the Parliament's debate contrasted this with heavy fuel oils for which desulphurisation would create greater problems. He promised to propose a Directive on fuel oil and although he did not specifically mention a proposed Directive on air quality standards for sulphur dioxide (see Section 9.2), an obligation to consider this possibility was placed on the Commission by Article 6 of Directive 75/716.

The Economic and Social Committee made the point that Type A gas oil should be prescribed throughout the Community for use in road and rail transport without the establishment of special zones because of the difficulties of changing fuel and marketing two grades of fuel. This suggestion was not adopted in the Directive but has been adopted in Britain.

The DOE submitted an Explanatory Memorandum (see below) to Parliament but neither the House of Commons nor the House of Lords published a report on the proposal or debated it.

There can have been little argument about the proposed Directive in the Council of Ministers because the Directive was agreed within two years of being proposed and differs only in detail from the proposal.

Formal Compliance in the UK

No new primary legislation was introduced after the Directive was agreed in order to implement it, because Sections 75 to 77 of the Control of Pollution Act 1974 already give the Secretary of State powers to make regulations controlling the content of liquid fuels. These powers, however, had been introduced in anticipation of a Directive, as was explained by the Minister, Baroness Young, during the Committee stage (4th February 1974) in the House of Lords on the Protection of the Environment Bill:

> "...It is perfectly true that one reason why it (the clause) is included is because the Commission of the European Economic Communities are preparing a draft Directive on the sulphur content of gas oil, which is a kind of fuel oil; and, on the assumption that a Directive on those or similar lines will eventually emerge, this clause provides the necessary powers for its implementation in the United Kingdom."

Although the Protection of the Environment Bill never reached the Statute Books because of the resignation of the government in February 1974, the Control of Pollution Act introduced by the new government was very similar to the earlier Bill.

On 8th December 1976, that is three and a half months after the due date for compliance, two Regulations made under the Control of Pollution Act 1974 were laid before Parliament:

SI 1976 No 1988	The Oil Fuel (Sulphur Content of Gas Oil) Regulations 1976, and
SI 1976 No 1989	The Motor Fuel (Sulphur Content of Gas Oil) Regulations 1976

On 10th December a circular letter to local authorities (DOE Circular 105/76) was jointly published by the Departments of the Environment, Transport and the Welsh Office summarising the Directive and explaining that the Regulations had been made to implement it. The circular stated that it had been decided that only the lower sulphur content (Type A) gas oil was to be used on roads and that the rest of the UK was to be regarded as a zone in which the higher sulphur content (Type B) gas oil was to be permitted. The circular stated that Weights and Measures Authorities were to be responsible for enforcing the Motor Fuel Regulations and that the Oil Fuel Regulations were to be enforced in England and Wales by the Alkali Inspectorate and by district councils.

The Commission had earlier asked why the government had not complied with the Directive by the due date. In the letter of reply of 22nd December 1976 the government enclosed the two Regulations and regretted the delay. It seems that this was caused by the lawyers in the DOE being involved with the consequences of that year's drought, but the letter to the Commission explained that no adverse consequences had resulted because the sulphur content of the relevant fuels was already below the permitted levels.

In March 1977 the Commission asked for an explanation of the designation of the zones which the Directive required Member States to provide it with. The government explained in reply that in the UK ground level concentrations of atmospheric sulphur dioxide were sufficiently low to permit the general use of Type B gas oil apart from the road system where concentrations were higher. For this reason, the road system had been made a zone for Type A only (an exception being made for the Orkney and Shetland Islands because of the low volume of traffic there). This letter of explanation was then sent to all other Member States as required by the Directive.

It is not clear whether such an extraordinarily shaped zone – the whole of the UK minus the road system – was ever anticipated by the Commission in drafting the Directive. The desirability of allowing only low sulphur content fuel for motor vehicles had been set out in the report of the Economic and Social Committee and the simpler way to have introduced this possibility into the Directive would have been to provide for restrictions on Type B gas oil by use as well as by geographical zone.

The Motor Fuel Regulations extend to Northern Ireland but the Oil Fuel Regulations do not. Separate Regulations were therefore made for Northern Ireland for oil fuel under the Pollution Control and Local Government (Northern Ireland) Order 1978 but these did not come into operation until 5th March 1979, i.e., two and a half years after the due date.

The Effect on UK Practice

According to an Explanatory Memorandum submitted by the DOE to the House of Commons in December 1974 gas oil, including 'Derv', then represented about 20 per cent of the total inland market for oil fuels. The Memorandum explained that the sulphur content of Derv, which represented 5 per cent of the total, was already 0.3 per cent while that of the rest of the gas oil was then about 0.8 per cent. This suggests that there was no difficulty in meeting the standards set by the Directive from 1st October 1976. (A British Standard 2869 had previously specified non-mandatory requirements for petroleum fuels for diesel engines with a sulphur content limit of 0.5 per cent, but notwithstanding this standard the majority of oil companies were supplying diesel with less). The Explanatory Memorandum further explained that as North Sea oil has a sulphur content of about 0.2 per cent, its use in Britain would lessen the demand for desulphurisation of gas oil obtained from Middle East crude. The Directive was therefore "likely to have relatively small effects in the United Kingdom in terms of desulphurisation costs to the industry". The Explanatory Memorandum went on to say that the use of low sulphur content fuels should secure some small environmental improvement, although this was difficult to quantify. Since Middle East crude continues to be refined in Britain the Directive's second stage reduction to 0.5 per cent will have had some effects on the amount of desulphurisation required in Britain.

In Britain a large proportion of domestic heating is by North Sea gas, and cooking is mostly by gas or electricity. Gas oil is used in Britain to some extent for central heating and is also used as a starter fuel for generating plant which normally runs on fuel oil. In some other Member States gas oil is much more widely used for domestic heating and cooking and has been the source of much sulphur dioxide pollution in towns. The Directive can be expected to have had a more substantial effect in those countries particularly if they use Middle East crude.

It should be noted that the government has not justified its decision to designate the whole of the UK - except the road system - for Type B gas oil by arguing that gas oil accounts for only an insignificant proportion of atmospheric pollution. Instead it has argued that ground level concentrations of sulphur dioxide are sufficiently low (except on roads) and this argument should be judged in the light of the information gathered for the purposes of the Directive on air quality standards for smoke and sulphur dioxide (see Section 9.2). Nothing in the Directive prevents the existing zones being changed at a later date; for example to include all areas at risk of not meeting the standards set out in the air quality Directive.

9.2   Smoke and Sulphur Dioxide in Air

80/779/EEC (OJ L229 30.8.80)
proposed 25.2.76-COM(76)48

Directive on air quality limit
values and guide values for
sulphur dioxide and suspended
particulates

Binding dates

Notification date:	17 July 1980
Formal compliance:	17 July 1982
Limit values to be met, if possible:	1 April 1983
Improvement plans to be submitted to Commission where limit values not met:	1 October 1982
Limit values must be met:	1 April 1993

Purpose of the Directive

Although air quality guidelines had previously been set in some Member States, and had been set mandatorily in the Federal Republic of Germany, the Directive is the first piece of Community-wide legislation to lay down mandatory air quality standards.   These standards relate to SO_2 and smoke and are intended to protect human health and the environment, but the Directive foresees Member States setting more stringent standards in zones needing special environmental protection.

Summary of the Directive

An Annex I sets limit values for the ground level concentration of sulphur dioxide and suspended particulates (smoke) which must be met throughout Member States during specified periods, as follows:

Reference Period	Limit values ($\mu g/m^3$)	
	Smoke	**Sulphur dioxide**
Year (Median of daily values)	80	If smoke less than 40: 120 If smoke more than 40: 80
Winter (Median of daily values 1st October-31st March)	130	If smoke less than 60: 180 If smoke more than 60: 130
Year (peak) (98 percentile of daily values)	250	If smoke less than 150: 350 If smoke more than 150: 250

The table contains all the information in Annex I but in a more easily comprehensible form. It is taken from DOE Circular 11/81. Figure 2 (below) and associated discussion helps to explain the table.

The limit values are given in microgrammes per cubic metre using a prescribed measuring method for SO_2 and an OECD method of measurement for smoke - the 'black smoke' method - which differs from the method usually used in Britain. The Directive allows another method - the gravimetric method - to be used also, in which case different limit values apply.

The limit values should be met by 1st April 1983, but if that seems unlikely in certain zones the Commission is to be informed and plans for the progressive improvement of those zones are to be submitted to the Commission by 1st October 1982. The limit values must, at the latest, be met by 1st April 1993.

A general duty is also laid on Member States to endeavour to move towards more stringent guide values set out in an Annex II. These guide values can also be used as reference points for the establishment of specific schemes in two types of zone which Member States may designate:

- zones where the Member State considers it necessary to prevent a foreseeable increase in pollution in the wake of urban or industrial development (Article 4(1))
- special environmental protection zones (Article 4(2))

What is known as the 'standstill principle' is also enunciated: air quality is not to be allowed to deteriorate significantly even in areas where pollution is well below the limit values as a consequence of applying the measures taken under the Directive. However, a minute of a Council meeting records a declaration of both Council and Commission that this is not to be interpreted as prohibiting the siting in such areas of new plants that may be sources of smoke or sulphur dioxide[*].

Member States must establish monitoring stations designed to supply data necessary for the application of the Directive, in particular in zones where the limit values are likely to be approached or exceeded.

Member States fixing values in border regions must consult one another and the Commission may attend these consultations.

Once a year Member States must inform the Commission of instances when limit values have been exceeded, together with the reasons and the measures which have been taken to avoid recurrences.

Each year the Commission must publish a summary report of the application of the Directive.

Development of the Directive

Following agreement on the sulphur content of gas oil Directive (section 9.1) the Commission proposed two more Directives on sulphur dioxide which came to be considered together. Initially the British government was opposed to both proposals, but then changed its attitude to

---

[*]   Council minutes are not usually published unless the Council so decides but the essence of this declaration is given in DOE Circular 11/81.

one of general support for the air quality proposal while maintaining its opposition to the proposed Directive on the sulphur content of fuel oil - COM(75)681. A DOE witness before the Lords' Scrutiny Committee put it like this (introducing incidentally a note of scientific nationalism):

> "These two Directives...are very closely related. Our view... is that they are of very unequal weight and indeed of unequal merit. The (air quality) Directive is medically based and does seem to us to be sensible. We might clearly want to argue about the phraseology in the Directive, but since it is based upon the World Health Organisation Report 506, which was very largely written by Professor Lawther on the basis of UK material we do not wish to oppose that Directive fundamentally. The fuel oil Directive is quite another matter..."

The fuel oil proposal would have required Member States to designate 'special protection zones' wherever specified pollution levels were exceeded. Oil burning installations inside these zones would then be required to use low-sulphur fuel oil, although plants with tall stacks could be exempted. In addition, large oil burning installations, wherever sited, would be required to maintain a stock of low-sulphur oil to which they would have to switch when high levels of pollution had been recorded for 24 hours.

The fuel oil proposal was an attempt by the Commission to prevent distortion to competition following similar national legislation proposed in the Netherlands, but the proposal effectively died in early 1978 when only four Member States were found to support it even in principle. The British government was opposed on the grounds that the cost to industry would have produced little environmental benefit, since a switch to low sulphur fuel oil would have to be made even if coal was the major cause of the pollution. The government took the view that the air quality proposal effectively achieved the same desired end but left Member States free to use the most appropriate means. A fear not far below the surface was that agreement on a fuel oil Directive would be followed by a proposal for a coal Directive which could involve considerably greater costs for Britain. There is no reason to suppose that the fuel oil proposal was intended as a stalking horse for the air quality proposal but it came close to being just that at least in Britain.

Opposition in principle to the air quality proposal came from the French government, which felt that the proposed standards were at once too strict (some French industrial zones did not meet the limit values) and not strict enough (most rural areas had better air quality and the limit values would then be seen as a licence to pollute). These points were met by amending the proposal to include:

- the derogation provision allowing time (till 1993) for meeting the values, and
- provision for Member States at their own discretion to set more stringent values.

The European Parliament welcomed the proposal but in one of its detailed points of criticism revealed a lack of understanding of what is meant

170

by an environmental quality standard. The Parliament's Resolution called for an amendment requiring Member States to ensure that their national legislation made provision "for the imposition of fines on undertakings which do not comply with the norms". This Resolution failed to take into account the difficulty of separating quantitatively the effects of the different sources of pollution, a problem inherent in any mandatory quality standard. In London, for example, failure to meet a quality standard is as likely as not to be the result of innumerable domestic fires or road traffic. An individual householder can be fined for producing dark smoke by burning raw coal in a smoke control area designated under the Clean Air Act, as can an industrialist, but except in the case of a very large emitter it is hard to see how proof can be established that a particular installation has been responsible for breaking an air quality standard covering a large area. Therefore although there is a distinction between a mandatory air quality standard and a mere guideline it is not so sharp a distinction as between a mandatory emission standard and a guideline: whereas a mandatory emission standard can be legally enforced, this is not so easy with a mandatory air quality standard.

The House of Lords' Scrutiny Committee considered the fuel oil and air quality proposals together and perhaps for that reason gave less attention to the air quality proposal than it deserved. Although they heard evidence from Professor Lawther (from whose epidemiological work the limit values are said to have been largely derived), from the DOE, from British Petroleum, from the Central Electricity Generating Board and from the National Society for Clean Air, their report did not express any definite view on the proposal as a whole. The report made detailed suggestions for improvement - with the implication that the Committee were not totally opposed to it; on the other hand, the report included in an Annex, without comment, an excerpt from the Fifth Report of the Royal Commission on Environmental Pollution (1) which had dealt with the same subject six months earlier (the Scrutiny Committee and Royal Commission had overlapping memberships) saying "we are also opposed to the imposition of air quality standards". The final paragraph of the Committee's report asked the government to present an account of any significant changes which might be agreed, implying that the Committee might return to the subject, but despite a letter from the DOE some 17 months later, the Committee did not do so, nor did the House debate the report.

The consequence was that a significant turning point in British air pollution policy was allowed to pass largely unremarked in Parliament. It is true that in the Commons' debate (18th May 1977) the Minister, Denis Howell, drew attention to what he called matters of principle, but no-one in the Commons' debate, apart from the Minister, showed any realisation that to introduce mandatory air quality standards was a departure from current British practice and worthy of comment. Since some members of the Royal Commission sat in the House of Lords, it is hard to believe that if a debate had been held in the Lords some explanation would not have been forthcoming of the apparent conflict between the Directive and the opposition of the Royal Commission to "the imposition of air quality standards". The Royal Commission had instead recommended guidelines but there can be no doubt that the Directive does indeed impose standards which have to be met by a certain date - with the Commission and the Court of Justice ready to ensure compliance. The words that the Minister, Denis

Howell, used in the Commons' debate did not conceal the point, nor it must be said, did they draw particular attention to the change of policy. He said:

"There are matters of principle which I must draw to the attention of the House. The use of air quality standards to be achieved by a stated time represents a new departure for us. But there are no legal penalties involved for individuals. It is left to us to determine how we must meet the required standard..."

In addition to the changes made to satisfy the French objections some changes to the limit values were also made in response to British pressure. The German government insisted on being able to continue using the gravimetric method of measurement rather than that proposed by the Commission and as a result the Directive allows either to be used despite the fact that the two methods are hard to compare.

Technical Issues

Some important technical criticisms of the proposal for the Directive were never answered publicly, at least in Britain, before it was agreed and have never been answered since by the Commission or by the British government.

The limit values set by the Directive are for the two pollutants (smoke and SO_2) considered together. If one is low, more is allowed of the other. The Fifth Report of the Royal Commission (1) gave some tentative support to this kind of trade-off between the two pollutants:

"Moreover, some pollutants have a combined effect which is much more serious than that of each by itself and cannot sensibly be considered apart. The classic example is smoke and sulphur dioxide. Together they can affect health at concentrations which used to be common in British cities. However, now that in many urban areas smoke has reached low levels the acceptable levels of SO_2 less damaging by itself, are probably much higher." (para 171)

Professor Lawther roundly contradicted this when giving evidence to the Lords' Scrutiny Committee. Referring to the Commission's proposal and its authors, he said:

"There is another failure in the documents, a fundamental error, which I think is the only serious fundamental error; that is, they still have not got the message which we have given them repeatedly and that is that there is no evidence of synergism between sulphur dioxide and smoke. They have always confused the idea that sulphur dioxide acting with smoke gives an effect greater than either acting singly. They seem incapable of getting hold of the idea that the only reason why we bracket smoke and sulphur dioxide is that in the epidemiological work they exist together. This has led to an absurdity in the latter part of the document in which they say that they suggest criteria for smoke and sulphur dioxide, but then say if, in certain situations, the sulphur dioxide is low, then that allows us to have more smoke, and the reverse: that if smoke is low, we can tolerate more sulphur dioxide. This ridiculous suggestion implies that we know which is the villain and that I suppose implies further that they are equal in effect. We have repeatedly told them that all we can say is that in the most sensitive methods available, the epidemiological surveillance of very susceptible people, then the things occur together and we are not able yet to separate them."

This damaging criticism was left unanswered, though it must be said that there is no evidence that synergism does not take place.

To understand the way in which the two pollutants are traded off against each other in the Directive it helps to consider the limits in the graphical form shown below, where the SO_2 concentration and smoke concentration at various notional sites are plotted against each other[*].

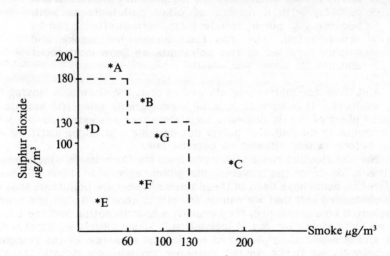

Figure 2: Graphical presentation of winter mean limit values

The dashed line represents the winter mean limit values set by the Directive by way of example. Notional sites A, B and C would be in breach of the values, while sites D, E and F would not. Site G might be said to be at risk of exceeding the limits given the variability of pollution from year to year.

It is immediately apparent that the step form of the dashed line must be arbitrary. Rather than having a step form - which is an inevitable con-

---

* Taken, with permission of the author, from a paper by P Evans of the DOE.(2)

173

sequence of having smoke value 'trigger points' (40, 60 and 150) with different SO_2 limit values associated with them - one could as easily have postulated an equally arbitrary curved line which could not then so easily be represented in the tabular form adopted in the Directive.

Lord Ashby, when the DOE gave evidence to the Lords' Scrutiny Committee, pointed to the arbitrary nature of these 'trigger points':

> "I would be very surprised, I was not present when Professor Lawther spoke, if he was happy about the splitting down into more than 40 micrograms or less than 40. Anyone who has done science knows you cannot do this. This is just nonsense. I would hope you would not accept this list and put up the best defence you can against it and get something much simpler like the original WHO one."

Dr Reed of the DOE (now the head of the Industrial Air Pollution Inspectorate) replied:

> "...I do not think there is any evidence to say that the smoke and SO_2 act together synergistically. All one knows is that when these are together in combination and probably with a number of other pollutants as well, because you cannot isolate them, certain effects can be demonstrated. One has then picked out smoke and sulphur together as two pollutants we know most about and can do something about.'

And there the matter was allowed to rest, the discussion moving on to other subjects. It is hard to imagine a comparable scientific assault on a proposed piece of purely domestic legislation that was establishing a wholly new principle in air pollution policy not drawing a stronger justification in public before it was allowed to become law.

The justification could have come from the Commission which proposed the limits, or from the governments which agreed to them.[*] Such a justification could have been in these terms: "these are pollutants that need to be controlled and that we can do something about. Rough and ready as the selected boundaries are, they provide a spur to action and are the best that we can propose by way of legislation." Such a reply would at least be frank and is much to be preferred to the bald assertion of the responsible Commissioner, Mr Burke, in the European Parliament's debate (11 March 1977) that the Commission had produced proposals "with an incontrovertible scientific basis".

Formal Compliance in the UK

Although the Directive represents a turning point in British air pollution policy, it is not the immediate intention of the government to

---

[*] The parliamentary record in countries other than Britain has not been studied. It is possible that a justification was attempted by some other government.

introduce any new legislation to implement it despite the absence of legislation either setting air quality standards or empowering a Minister to set such standards. This was the view set out in an explanatory memorandum that the DOE submitted to Parliament in 1976, and seven years later it remains the view:

> "It is thought that if the Council adopted this Directive it could be implemented in the UK without further legislation."

In July 1982 the government wrote formally to the Commission enclosing a memorandum listing the legislation and other measures that, in the government's view, fulfilled the formal requirements of the Directive. This included:

Clean Air Acts 1956 and 1968
Alkali etc. Works Regulation Act 1906
Control of Pollution Act 1974
Pollution Control and Local Government (Northern Ireland) Order 1978

together with various Regulations made under these laws and various government circulars.

The Clean Air Acts give local authorities power to control domestic and industrial smoke and empower the Secretary of State to direct local authorities to submit smoke control programmes and carry them out. The Alkali Act empowers the Inspectorate to control emissions from registered chemical and industrial processes. The Control of Pollution Act empowers the Secretary of State to control the composition of motor fuel and the sulphur content of oil fuel, and also empowers local authorities to obtain information about air pollution.

One Act which could have been, but was not, mentioned is the Road Traffic Act 1972 which empowers the Secretary of State for Transport to regulate the construction of vehicles to avoid smoke and other emissions and gives powers for authorised examiners to check vehicles. Since smoke from vehicles, particularly from diesel engines, is now responsible for a significant proportion of smoke emissions in some larger cities, including London, it could be that strict enforcement of the vehicle smoke emissions will prove to be an important means of achieving the limits of the Directive. The ability of Member States individually to set more stringent emission limits to smoke from vehicles is however constrained by the Directives on vehicle emissions (see Section 9.6).

It follows from this array of different powers in different hands that achieving the objective of the Directive is largely a task of co-ordination so that the appropriate powers are used by the appropriate authority, when and where required. Monitoring thus plays an important part. In its memorandum to the Commission the government explained that:

> "...the UK has had an extensive network of monitoring stations for smoke and sulphur dioxide for many years and measurements will continue in all areas where there is a possibility of approaching or exceeding the limit values. Measurements are carried out by the local authorities but

the measurements are supervised and the results received
and analysed centrally by the Warren Spring Laboratory
(Department of Industry). Powers exist to require
measurements to be taken wherever necessary."

Although the Secretary of State can issue guidelines and can ask the
appropriate authorities to try to ensure that the mandatory air quality
standards are met (and in the case of smoke control has the power of
direction), the question nevertheless must be asked whether the existing
powers are sufficient to comply with standards that are mandatory.

The difference between a guideline and a mandatory standard is the
existence of some kind of sanction, and the sanction in this case is that the
government is answerable for achieving the limit values to the Commission,
and the Commission can in the extreme have recourse to the European Court
for a declaration that the Directive must be implemented.

In a letter to the Commission dated 15 February 1983 (see below) the
DOE listed certain areas that would not comply with the standards by April
1983, but went on to say that the extension of smoke control areas would
ensure that the requirements of the Directive would be met by 1993 at the
latest.   In the absence of evidence to the contrary it is hard to see how the
Commission can question this opinion, and if the standards can be achieved
then it must follow that no new legislation is required.   It would of course
be possible for Parliament to enshrine the limit values of the Directive in
domestic legislation or to give to the Secretary of State general powers to
set air quality standards to cover both the present Directive and the lead in
air Directive (see Section 9.5) - and indeed any other Directives that may
come to be agreed on air quality standards.   Whether or not such a change is
desirable, it cannot be regarded as essential for compliance with the main
part of the Directive.

The Directive also requires Member States to endeavour to move
towards more stringent guide values set out in Annex II and to fix values for
smoke and sulphur dioxide lower than the limit values in two kinds of zone
(Article 4(1) and 4(2)) if the Member State considers they are in need of
such protection.   Since the Secretary of State at present has no powers to
set such mandatory limits he would have to ask Parliament to provide him
with them if use is to be made of Article 4.   The DOE has stated in a
Circular 11/81 drawing the attention of local authorities to the Directive
that "the government does not see any areas in which it would be either
desirable or economically feasible for it to set up either type of zone" and so
would presumably argue that the absence of the necessary powers does not
prevent it from complying with the Directive in law, since even if it had the
powers it would not use them.   Article 4 serves to underline the desirability
of new legislation, but does not make it essential.

The obligation to endeavour to move towards more stringent guide
values can clearly be achieved without the power to set mandatory
standards.   DOE Circular 11/81 has merely asked local authorities to note
this objective and, where pollution is below the mandatory standards, to
consider whether any further progress towards the guide values is desirable
and economically feasible.

It should also be noted that the government has no powers to require
any factory or other major user to burn a particular fuel, e.g., gas instead of
oil or coal, should this ever be necessary to achieve the limit values.

Further legislation along these lines would give to the government additional powers to implement the Directive should it ever prove necessary.

The Effect on UK Practice

The DOE issued Circular 11/81 on 27th March 1981 drawing the attention of local authorities to the Directive and setting out action "thought likely to be necessary to implement the Directive". The Circular listed 71 district councils in England and Wales containing sites where it was thought that the limit values of the Directive might be exceeded - mostly because of insufficient coverage by smoke control orders under the Clean Air Acts. In addition districts in Scotland and Northern Ireland were also identified. These local authorities were asked to:

> "...order their priorities within the general restraint on public expenditure so as to complete any necessary extension of smoke control by 1983. Where this is not possible, authorities should aim to complete any necessary programme as soon as possible after that date and at the latest by 1993".

In addition the Circular said that the government would allocate its financial contribution to local authorities for smoke control by reference to areas exceeding the limit values.

The Circular asked local authorities who considered that SO_2 alone might be a problem to contact the DOE but only one did so and then decided that the standards were indeed met.

In February 1983 the DOE wrote to the Commission listing 21 district councils in England, four in Scotland and three in Northern Ireland (but none in Wales) which, on the basis of analysis of monitoring results over the years, contained areas which would not comply with the limit values by April 1983. An extra district was added in England in August 1983. In all cases the cause was smoke alone and the smoke was said to arise primarily from domestic coal burning. The discrepancy in number between the 71 Districts in England and Wales said to be at risk in 1981 and the 22 for the whole of Great Britain communicated to the Commission is partly explained by the original list being over cautious, partly by the introduction of smoke control in some districts, and partly by the improvement in air quality that is taking place as householders spontaneously switch from coal to other fuels such as North Sea gas.

The DOE letter to the Commission said it was the government's intention to ensure that additional smoke control programmes would be introduced so as to ensure that the limits would be met by 1993 at the latest. This letter constituted, in the government's view, the "plans for the progressive improvement of the quality of air in those zones" required by the Directive, but it is understood that the Commission will be asking for rather fuller plans.

From what has happened so far it follows that the major effect of the Directive will be to provide an impetus and a strategic framework for the completion of smoke control that began with the 1956 Act. Indeed, the effect has already been felt in compelling the identification of areas likely

177

to exceed the limits and the pressure this has already generated for the introduction of smoke control. There may well not be any effect on sulphur dioxide control except as a result of controlling the burning of coal primarily to reduce smoke.

Some tricky issues may yet arise in implementing the Directive. If, for instance, a local authority, perhaps a mining area where domestic coal burning is encouraged by free allowances of coal for miners, does not of its own volition introduce smoke control in time because it has higher priorities for spending its money, central government will then have to direct the local authority to do so under the powers contained in the Clean Air Act of 1968. Those powers have never previously been used - which does not mean they have not been having a persuasive effect - and central government prefers not to have to resort to compulsion since to do so is to breach the principle of devolved responsibility that we have discussed in Chapter 2. In the discussions that will ensue, the local authority may well argue that on the one hand it is being told to cut back on expenditure while, on the other hand, it is being directed to adopt a policy that entails increased expenditure.

It is because responsibility lies primarily with the local authority that the government may well have difficulty in submitting the precise plans for improvement that the Commission would prefer to have, and the Commission will need to recognise the importance of not upsetting the delicate balance between central and local government.

Another effect of the Directive has been on monitoring. The National Survey of Smoke and Sulphur Dioxide has been in operation since 1961. Initially there were some 500 monitoring sites, increasing to about 1200 by 1966 and providing the most comprehensive survey in the world. The monitoring is carried out largely by local authorities but is co-ordinated by the Warren Spring Laboratory which falls under the Department of Industry. It so happened that this survey was in the process of being reviewed when the Directive was agreed. The long term plan is to reduce the network to about 150 sites (3) but Circular 11/81 said that the adequacy of existing monitoring stations was being considered in relation to the requirements of the Directive. As a result around 400 sites are being maintained for the time being where areas are at risk of breaching the standards in the Directive. The number of sites will be progressively reduced as the areas at risk diminish, but without the Directive these 400 sites would not all have been maintained.

One possible effect of the Directive is the influence it could have on town and country planning. An attempt by Cheshire County Council to include air quality standards in a structure plan was struck out by the Secretary of State in 1978 at a time when there were no national air quality standards and no policy on the subject. Now that the Directive exists it is possible that the arguments would come out differently. Circular 11/81 went so far as to advise local authorities with areas exceeding the limit values to take into account the need to attain the limit values when preparing or reviewing structure plans or local plans.

Transboundary Air Pollution

The effect of the Directive on long range transboundary air pollution - the only form of relevance to Britain - is problematic. This is because the Directive is concerned with ground level concentrations and not with the total quantity of smoke or sulphur dioxide emitted. Nevertheless a connection is sometimes assumed because following agreement on the Directive, a Council Resolution was adopted on 15th July 1980 (OJ C222 30.8.80) in the following terms:

"Taking due account of the facts and problems involved, the Member States will endeavour, in accordance with the objective of Council Directive 80/779/EEC of 15th July 1980 on air quality limit values and guide values for sulphur dioxide and suspended particulates to limit and as far as possible gradually reduce and prevent trans-boundary air pollution by sulphur dioxide and suspended particulates".

Action under the Directive should to some extent reduce total emissions which should in turn reduce long range movements. On the other hand, if to achieve the ground level limits, more sulphur dioxide were to be emitted at a high level this could increase long range pollution, although this point has been partly disputed by the government-appointed Commission on Energy and the Environment. Its report on 'Coal and the Environment' (4) said (para 17.52):

"There appears to be some misunderstanding about the contribution made by tall stacks to long range air pollution, namely that large emitters using tall stacks greatly enhance the transport of sulphur dioxide for long distances. This is not so: the long distance transport of sulphur dioxide is almost independent of chimney height. The main effect of tall stacks is to delay the time and distance before the plume returns to the ground and thus reduce the ground path for sulphur dioxide absorption by some 10 kilometres. In exceptional weather, however, it appears possible that plumes can be isolated above an inversion layer and carried relatively rapidly for some hundreds of kilometres."

In June 1981 by a Council Decision (OJ L171/11 27.6.81) the European Community concluded the Convention on long range transboundary air pollution to which the UK had already adhered. That Convention came into force on 16th March 1983 and any action by Britain to reduce transboundary air pollution is, for the time being at least, as likely to be the result of that Convention as of the Council Resolution. Although the government has argued that total emissions of SO_2 have fallen by 20% during the last decade, total British emissions of SO_2 nevertheless remain the highest of the Member States. The first hint of positive British action on long range SO_2 pollution is contained in the 1981 report (5) of the Alkali and Clean Air Inspectorate (para 198):

"The powers of the Inspectorate stem from legislation intended to protect the population and environment of England and Wales and it is unlikely that action could be taken under the legislation in order solely to protect the

179

environment in other countries. However, the first duty of the Inspectorate is to prevent emissions to air where it is practicable to do so, irrespective of whether damage is caused. In the UK, there are currently no proposals for new fossil fuel generating plants, but if and when they come forward, the scope for preventing or reducing the emissions of SO_2 will need to be considered positively in the light of experience now being gained in other countries".

As we discussed in Chapter 2, this is an example of the development of policy by a government agency, without reference to Ministers, within the existing legal framework. It is hard to imagine a more discreet way of making a policy statement of such importance as the introduction of flue gas desulphurisation.

Further Developments

In April 1983, following a request from the German government which had become increasingly concerned about the effects of air pollution on forests and had announced a policy of reducing German emissions, the Commission proposed a framework Directive (OJ C139 27.5.83 - COM(80)173) to control emissions to air from stationary plants. It is proposed that specified plants will have to be authorised and that emission standard limit values will be fixed at Community level in subsequent Directives. The need to reduce air pollution to protect forests featured on the agenda of the Summit meeting - the meeting of the heads of State or government of the Community - held in Stuttgart in June 1983 which implies considerable political pressure for Community action.

References

(1) Royal Commission on Environmental Pollution, Fifth Report, **Air Pollution Control: An Integrated Approach,** HMSO, 1976.

(2) P Evans, **The EC Directive on Smoke and Sulphur Dioxide: The Future for Smoke Control,** 47th Annual Conference of the National Society for Clean Air, 1980.

(3) A W C Keddie, F P Williams and B D Gooriah (Warren Spring Laboratory), **Monitoring - Where Next?,** National Society for Clean Air Workshop, 1981.

(4) Commission on Energy and the Environment, **Coal and the Environment,** HMSO, 1981.

(5) Health and Safety Executive, **Industrial Air Pollution 1981,** HMSO, 1982.

9.3   Lead in Petrol

78/611/EEC (OJ L197 22.7.78)
proposed 5.12.73 - COM(73)2050

Directive on the approximation of
the laws of the Member States
concerning the lead content of
petrol

Binding dates
  Notification date: 5 July 1978
  Formal compliance: 5 January 1980
  Limits to be met: 1 January 1981

Purpose of the Directive

Lead is added to petrol as one way of increasing its octane rating so
that it can be used in high compression ratio engines in motor cars.   The
Directive limits the lead content of petrol for two reasons: to eliminate
barriers to trade in petrol and motor cars resulting from different limits in
different countries, and to reduce air pollution by lead.

Summary of the Directive

From 1st January 1981 the maximum permitted lead content of petrol
sold within the Community is set at 0.40 grams per litre.   Member States may
set an upper limit between 0.40g/l and 0.15g/l but cannot insist on less than
0.15g/l.   (In other words the Directive does not prohibit the sale of lead
free petrol but no Member State may ban lead in petrol).

A derogation of five years is provided for Ireland with the possibility
of a further five year extension.   (Ireland is not now taking advantage of
this provision).

Member States are to ensure that reducing the lead content does not
cause a significant increase in the quantities of other pollutants or a
deterioration in the quality (e.g., octane rating) of petrol.   A reference
method for the measurement of the lead content is specified.

Member States are to supply the Commission, at its request, with
information on the effects of implementing the Directive; developments in
lead emission reducing systems; development of the concentrations of lead in
the urban atmosphere and their effects on health; and the effects on energy
policy of reducing lead emissions.   Once this information has been asked for
the Commission must then report to the Council and the European Parliament
on the information obtained, and must make suitable proposals for taking it
into account in order to develop further Community policy on the lead
content of petrol.

If, as a result of a sudden change in the supply of crude oil, it becomes
difficult for a Member State to apply the limit, the Commission must be
informed and a higher limit may be set for four months.   This period may be
extended by a qualified majority vote in the Council on a proposal from the
Commission.

Development of the Directive

The development of this Directive shows that in favourable circumstances a determined Member State can pull the rest of the Community along behind it so that higher environmental standards are achieved throughout the Community more quickly than if the Member States had proceeded at their own pace.

From 1st January 1972 the lead content of petrol sold in the Federal Republic of Germany was restricted to 0.40g/l and it was the knowledge that Germany was proposing to make this reduction that stimulated the Commission into proposing a Directive requiring a limit of 0.40g/l by 1st January 1976.

In 1971 the Commission, learning of the German government's plans, established two committees to study the health and technical aspects of lead pollution from motor vehicles, and the work of these committees is summarised in the explanatory memorandum accompanying the proposal for a Directive issued in December 1973. The memorandum includes a table showing that permitted lead levels then differed considerably in the different Member States, some having limits up to 0.84g/l and some having no limits at all. The memorandum concluded that although there was no immediate danger for public health, it was desirable to prevent an increase of air pollution by lead and hence to limit lead because of the increase in car use. The other reasons were to prevent technical barriers to trade.

The German government, in addition to reducing lead to 0.40g/l in 1972, also announced its intention of making a second stage reduction from 1st January 1976 to 0.15g/l. A level of 0.15g/l seems to have been chosen because it is near the lowest level usable in existing petrol engines without special adaptations. The Commission proposed a rather less severe second stage reduction with a limit of 0.15g/l from 1st January 1978 for regular grade petrol but leaving the limit for premium grade at 0.40g/l. The lead content of intermediate grades would be limited to an equivalent blending of regular and premium grades.

Shortly after the Directive was proposed and during discussions in the House of Lords (4th February 1974) on the Protection of the Environment Bill the Minister, Baroness Young, referred to the proposed Directive and said:

"I should perhaps make it quite clear that this Directive is supported by us. I hope I can assure the noble Baroness, Lady White, who asked whether we took a lead in these matters, that in fact we have taken a leading part in the drafting of the European Community Directive on lead in petrol. The standards set in this draft are largely the outcome of British initiative. The noble Baroness is of course quite right in saying that the Federal Republic of Germany has asked for more stringent measures..."

In the debate in the European Parliament (10th November 1975) the rapporteur of the Environment Committee said that the proposed second stage reduction (to 0.15g/l for regular grade petrol) had "met with insurmountable opposition in the Committee" because it would have involved the industry in substantial investment as well as increasing petrol consumption. "Since", he went on, "these objections could not be refuted, the committee preferrred to require the Commission to postpone the introduction of the second stage". The limit of 0.40g/l was however approved by the Committee. Spokesmen for four political groups in the Parliament supported the Committee's resolution but James Spicer, speaking for the European Conservative Group (the British Conservatives) explained that his group would be voting against the proposal largely because of the costs entailed and the absence of proof that there was any harm to health from lead in petrol.

The Commissioner, Mr Gundelach, in defending the Commission's proposal referred to the studies that had been done and said:

> "...our proposals are built to the best of our or anyone
> else's ability on the probabilities presented by these
> studies - I say 'probabilities' because nothing beyond that
> exists, neither here nor a few hundred kilometres away in
> the Federal Republic of Germany."

He explained that the Commission was not convinced that it was necessary to go as far as the German government was proposing, but pointed out that the delay in obtaining an opinion from the Parliament meant that it would not now be possible to obtain a Council decision on the proposal before the second stage reduction took effect in Germany on 1st January 1976. All the subsequent discussion in the Council was therefore coloured by an existing German limit of 0.15g/l. The Directive finally agreed in 1978 therefore had to allow Member States to introduce a national limit of 0.15g/l but its main provision was an upper limit of 0.40g/l. The provision in the Directive to prevent a limit less than 0.15g/l which is not to be found in the original proposal was put in at the suggestion of the British government among others, presumably to ensure that no barriers to trade in motor cars would be created by any one Member State insisting on lead free petrol. As a result, the Directive has lost some of its claim to be an environmental protection measure.

The House of Commons debated the proposal on 4th March and 5th April 1976 and resolved:

> "that this House.....accepts the principle of reducing the
> maximum lead content of petrol to 0.40 grams per
> litre.....and, whilst recognising that this will have an
> adverse effect on the United Kingdom balance of
> payments, nevertheless calls on Her Majesty's Govern-
> ment to achieve this aim by staged reductions."

Given that the limit in Britain at the time of the debate was 0.55g/l and that the government had announced three years before that it intended to reduce the limit to 0.45g/l (see below) the debate was surprisingly heated, with the one and a half hours allotted for the debate on 4th March proving insufficient so that the debate had to be continued on 5th April. Several speakers argued that expenditure should not be incurred in the absence of proof of medical ill-effects, and many who supported the motion acknowledged that the medical evidence was not conclusive.

The Minister, Denis Howell, explained that the government had already decided in 1972 that air lead levels should not increase above the 1971 levels (see below) and that given current trends in petrol consumption a reduction to 0.40g/l would have to be made by 1981. This therefore was the government's policy so far as the timing of the Directive was concerned, and it seems unlikely to be a coincidence that it is this same date that appears in the Directive - a date five years later than that originally proposed. Notwithstanding the comments made two years earlier by Baroness Young that the government supported the proposed Directive the British government succeeded in slowing down its introduction, though it is probable that other countries were also anxious not to be compelled to move too fast.

The facts as seen by the British government at the time the Directive was proposed emerge from the report of an inter-Departmental working party published in 1974 under the title of 'Lead in the Environment and its Significance to Man'.(1) This helps to explain the levels set in the Directive:

> "The cost of achieving a reduction of lead in petrol to a maximum of 0.45g/l as was previously planned for the end of 1975, has been estimated to require a capital investment of £28 million (1974 costs) and an additional 4.6 million tons of crude oil to maintain 1974 levels of petrol manufacture. There would be substantial additional costs in reducing the lead content of petrol further and these have to be balanced against the costs of alternative courses of action. A limit of 0.40g/l has been identified by the oil industry as a critical point below which the cost of producing petrol of high octane rating (necessary for most of today's cars) rises rapidly as the lead content is reduced. This is because more severe refining processes, resulting in less petrol from each barrel of crude oil, are required to maintain a satisfactory octane rating in the absence of acceptable substitutes for lead alkyls. The possibility of replacing one pollutant which has not, as yet, been shown to cause actual harm at present levels, by another or others, possibly more dangerous, cannot be ignored here. In addition, difficult engineering problems such as excessive wear of valve gear and inadequate combustion in high-compression engines, arise at concentrations below 0.15g/l. These result in reduced performance and higher fuel consumption. Here, the probability of exacerbating possible fuel shortage and of raising emissions of other pollutants also present in vehicle fumes cannot be overlooked. Even if reductions in both fuel quality and vehicle performance were accepted, if all petrol was required to be lead-free, capital expenditure on modifications to refineries would reach about £250 million (1971 costs), about a quarter of the total present investment. This cost would be borne ultimately by the consumer. At the same time, the yield of petrol from a

given quantity of crude oil would be reduced by about 10 per cent."

Formal Compliance in the UK

No new primary legislation had to be introduced following agreement on the Directive because Section 75 of the Control of Pollution Act 1974 already gives the Secretary of State powers to control the composition of motor fuel for the purpose of limiting or reducing air pollution. We have already seen (see Section 9.1) how the power to control the sulphur content of fuel oil was introduced in order to enable that Directive to be implemented, and it is the same Section of the Act that confers power to control the lead content of petrol. Although the prospect of the lead in petrol Directive may have been an additional reason for the power it was not given as such during parliamentary discussion. Before the power took effect the lead content of petrol had been reduced by voluntary agreement with the oil companies and it is possible that the government would have continued to rely on voluntary agreements in the absence of the Directive. On the other hand, the government may have wanted to introduce legislation even had there been no Directive on the grounds that voluntary agreement might have become more difficult at lower lead levels. Section 75 of the Act cannot therefore with certainty be attributed to both this Directive as well as to the sulphur in gas oil Directive (Section 5.2.1).

The following Regulations concerning lead have been made under Section 75 of the Act but only the 1979 Regulations were made specifically to implement the Directive:

SI 1976 No 1866	The Motor Fuel (Lead Content of Petrol) Regulations 1976
SI 1979 No 1	The Motor Fuel (Lead Content of Petrol) (Amendment) Regulations 1979
SI 1981 No 1523	The Motor Fuel (Lead Content of Petrol) Regulations 1981

The Effect on UK Practice

In 1971 the government received advice from its Chief Medical Officer that air lead levels should not be allowed to increase above the levels then prevailing and accordingly in 1972 the government announced a three-stage reduction as follows:

1st Reduction	1.1.73	from 0.84g/l	to 0.64
2nd Reduction (postponed to Nov '74)	1.1.74		to 0.55
3rd Reduction (postponed and modified)	1.1.76		to 0.4

The first two reductions were agreed voluntarily with the petroleum industry but the next reduction, when it eventually came to be made in two stages in 1976 and 1978, was done by means of Regulations. A fifth reduction has been made, and a sixth will be brought into force, both by means of Regulations:

3rd Reduction	30.11.76	to 0.50
4th Reduction	1.1.78	to 0.45
5th Reduction	1.1.81	to 0.40
6th Reduction	31.12.85	to 0.15

The second reduction was postponed because of the oil crisis of 1973, and in December 1974 - that is after the Directive had been proposed - the Secretary of State for Energy announced that no further reductions would be made pending a review of the economic and medical implications. This review had been completed by the time of the debate in March 1976 and as a result the third and fourth reductions were made. The fifth reduction was made specifically to implement the Directive. Even if the Directive did not bring forward the date of the reduction to 0.40g/l, it will have ensured that there could be no postponement in the event, say, of a falling off of traffic. While it was still a proposal, the Directive must also have focussed the government's mind on the earliest acceptable date for moving to 0.40g/l, and must have provided pressure for an early date.

A 'Working Party on Lead in Petrol' (WOPLIP) set up in 1978 by the Department of Transport to assess the feasibility and costs of various options for reducing lead emissions reported in 1979 (2). Another working party was also set up in 1978 by the Department of Health and Social Security under the Chairmanship of Professor Lawther to consider the health effects of environmental lead pollution, and reported in 1980 (3). In May 1981, in response to the Lawther working party's recommendation that emissions of lead to the air from traffic and other sources should be progressively reduced, and possibly also in response to new evidence and subsequent criticisms of the working party's conclusions, the government announced a further reduction to 0.15g/l to take effect from 31st December 1985. The figure of 0.15g/l may well have been influenced by being the lowest allowed in the Directive - although as explained above there are technical reasons for the choice of 0.15 g/l. But had the government wished to introduce lead-free petrol it could have said so, and could have announced that it was intending to raise the matter in the Council with the intention of seeking an amending Directive. The Directive indeed provides a procedure for doing this: the Commission may ask Member States for information about developments on lead concentrations in air and their effects on health and **must** then make proposals for taking such data into account in order to develop further Community policy on the lead content of petrol.

In April 1983 the Royal Commission on Environmental Pollution recommended (4) that the government should initiate negotiations immediately with the Commission and other Member States with a view to securing the removal of the minimum limit contained in the Directive. The objective of these negotiations would be that from the earliest practicable date all new petrol-engined vehicles sold in the UK should be required to run on unleaded petrol. The government - possibly as a result of a public campaign - immediately accepted this recommendation. Other countries, including the Federal Republic of Germany, have supported the idea of an amending Directive.

In conclusion it can be said that the Directive has been consistent with government policy that existed before the Directive was proposed and that continued until April 1983. Its practical effect will have been to ensure no departure from that policy. The Directive will have made the new policy of unleaded petrol more difficult to achieve, but if British pressure leads to an amending Directive requiring unleaded petrol throughout the Community it will be to repeat the story of the origins of the Directive, a story of one Member State taking the initiative to force the pace in others. In the unlikely event of the Directive not being amended, the feelings of frustration will be considerable and the government may well regret that it insisted on having a lower limit of 0.15g/l inserted into the Directive.

References

(1) Department of the Environment, Pollution Paper No 2, **Lead in the Environment and its Significance to Man,** HMSO, 1974.

(2) Working Party on Lead in Petrol (WOPLIP), Department of Transport, **Lead in Petrol: An Assessment of the Feasibility and Costs of Further Action to Limit Lead Emissions from Vehicles,** 1979.

(3) Professor P.J.Lawther (Chairman), **Lead and Health: the Report of a DHSS Working Party on Lead in the Environment,** HMSO, 1980.

(4) Royal Commission on Environmental Pollution Ninth Report, **Lead in the Environment,** HMSO, 1983.

9.4 Screening for Lead

77/312/EEC (OJ L105 28.4.77)
proposed 16.4.75 - COM(75)166

Directive on biological
screening of the population for
lead

Binding dates
Notification date: 31 March 1977
Formal compliance: 31 March 1978
Screening to be concluded: 31 March 1982 (? – see below)

Purpose of the Directive

Lead can reach individuals by many pathways (e.g., air, water, food, pica) and to judge the significance of any one source it is necessary to know the total body burden of lead. The purpose of the Directive is to provide a much more comprehensive and accurate picture than previously existed of blood lead levels in the population as a whole and among critical groups. (The Directive is placed here with the air pollution Directives so that it can sit between the section on lead in petrol (9.3) and the section on lead in air (9.5) with which it was associated in its origins.)

Summary of the Directive

Member States are to undertake two screening campaigns, co-ordinated across the Community, and separated by an interval of two years. This is to be done by sampling the blood of volunteers to determine blood lead levels, though ALAD* measurement may be used as a supplementary test. The whole procedure is to be concluded within four years but it is unclear whether this period is intended to run from the date of the notification of the Directive, or from the start of the first campaign, or from the date for legal compliance. (If the period is supposed to have started with the notification date then it will have been over-run).

During each campaign 50 or more persons per million inhabitants per Member State are to be sampled. Samples in the second campaign need not be taken from the same individuals as in the first campaign. During each campaign, sampling is to be carried out on the following three groups:

(1) groups of at least 100 persons in urban areas with more than 500,000 inhabitants;
(2) groups of at least 100 persons, in so far as this is feasible, chosen from among people exposed to significant sources of lead pollution;
(3) critical groups determined by the competent authorities in the Member States.

---

* ALAD, i.e., enzymatic activity of delta-aminolevulinic acid dehydrates, is used as an indicator of the presence of lead.

In assessing the results of the screening, the following reference levels are to be used:

- a maximum of 20µg of lead per 100ml of blood for 50% of each group;
- a maximum of 30µg of lead per 100ml of blood for 90% of each group;
- a maximum of 35µg of lead per 100ml of blood for 98% of each group.

Where these reference levels are exceeded, the validity of the results must be checked, and the Member States must then take action to trace the sources responsible and, at their discretion, to take all 'appropriate measures'. The Commission is to be notified of these measures and of the factors presumed to have led to the reference levels being exceeded.

To ensure comparability of results, the Member States are to inform the Commission of the laboratories taking part in the screening programme and the methods of analysis used. The Commission, together with the Member States, is to organise inter-comparison programmes.

A designated competent national authority must provide the Commission with the relevant information about each campaign in agreed form. Complete anonymity of persons sampled is to be preserved. Twice a year the Commission is to convene a meeting of representatives of governments to ensure comparability of the screening programmes and to exchange results.

The Commission is to draw up a collated annual report which is to be forwarded to the Member States, Council and Parliament. At the end of the programme the Commission is to draw up a general report to form the basis for any further proposals.

Development of the Directive

Proposals for two separate Directives were communicated to the Council together in the same document - COM(75)166 - and in their early stages were considered together. One of these proposals - concerned with air quality standards of lead - was not agreed until 1982 (see Section 9.5).

The other proposal was amended to become the biological screening Directive, but in its original form it would have set biological **standards** for lead (which would have had more of a mandatory character than the reference levels of the screening Directive) and would also have required a new screening campaign every two years. The standards would have been mandatory in the sense that if they were exceeded (a) Member States would have had to identify the abnormal sources of exposure and (b) notify the Commission of them. Then within two months (c) the Commission would have had to issue an opinion, after which (d) the Member States would have had to take suitable measures and (e) inform the Commission of these.

The European Parliament welcomed the proposal for mandatory standards in general terms but considered it essential that samples be taken only from volunteers - a point left unclear in the proposal. It also felt that 35µg per 100ml could prove too stringent. The Economic and Social Committee reiterated this point by saying that it might prove impossible for 100 per cent of the population to have blood lead levels below 35µg per 100ml and suggested a figure of 98 per cent instead - a suggestion that came to be adopted even for the reference levels of the screening Directive.

The British government's view was expressed by the Minister, Denis Howell, in the Commons' debate (4th March 1976) and more fully by the Minister, Baroness Stedman, in the Lords' debate (1st April 1976):

"The Commission's proposals on biological standards for lead in blood and air quality standards for lead go, in our view, too far...The scientific evidence, despite the effort put in over a number of years, is still not such that we can advance to the point where we should lay down, in legislation, precise standards. Such a step would imply in law that every individual exceeding the blood lead limit and everybody in an area in which the air quality standard was exceeded would be in danger. We would not dissent from the view that the sort of figures for the standards proposed are reasonably reliable indicators of where investigation of the sources of lead should be initiated and action taken. We are, however, opposed to the rigidity and overemphasis on particular figures which would be consequent on enshrining them in legislation and which would carry with them the absolute obligation that they should not be exceeded".

The debate in the Lords had followed a report from the Lords' Scrutiny Committee which had criticised the proposal for biological standards as being a wasteful deployment of money and skilled manpower. The Committee agreed that high priority should be given to research on the effects of intermediate lead levels but did not feel that emergency Community legislation along the lines set out was justified. This opinion was largely based on the evidence of Sir Richard Doll, the epidemiologist, who said that the monitoring proposed was worth doing once, but was hardly worth doing every two years:

"...I really do not know what the frequency distribution of blood lead levels throughout the country is. I think it would help our thinking a lot if we had some really firm figures for the country as a whole and for special areas, but I see no reason to suppose there is any change from one year to another. Repeat it again in ten years' time, yes".

Sir Richard Doll had begun his evidence by saying that:

"...together with many people, I am disturbed by the fact that blood levels of lead in this country are getting - or perhaps I should say are, rather than are getting - uncomfortably close to what is generally recognised as a toxic level. They are closer to a toxic level than blood levels of any other element or toxic substance..."

He went on to refer to the figures proposed:

"My understanding is that the sort of figures which are

190

given here would be perfectly reasonable figures to aim at but that at the present moment we would find considerable embarrassment in applying them. Maybe it would be good that we should be embarrassed but we should find considerable embarrassment because there would be many areas of the country where these figures might be exceeded."

In the debate the Minister, Baroness Stedman, welcomed the support for the government's views expressed by the Lords' Scrutiny Committee and said:

"We have good reason to believe that a number of other Member States share our views on the Directive and we look forward to arriving at an agreed form of Community document which will meet the real needs of the Community in this matter."

In the form finally agreed mandatory biological standards were abandoned as was the commitment to regular screening. What remained was a substantially different Directive concerned with only two screening campaigns designed to collect information but using certain reference levels: if these were exceeded it would be for the Member States themselves to decide on what measures to take and it would not be for the Commission to express an opinion.

Formal Compliance in the UK

The life of this Directive is limited in time. This is in contrast with most other Directives which continue indefinitely until an amending Directive is issued by the Council on a proposal from the Commission.

The Directive only makes two formal, as opposed to practical, requirements:

- Member States are to designate a competent authority (Article 9);
- Member States shall take the necessary measures to enable the procedure laid down by this Directive to enter into force within 12 months following its notification and shall immediately inform the Commission thereof (Article 12).

The government fulfilled the Article 9 requirement by creating an ad hoc 'Steering Group of Implementation of the Directive on Biological Screening of the Population for Lead', but apparently never informed the Commission in writing of the 'necessary measures' under Article 12, nor was the Commission apparently concerned by this omission. In fact, no new legislation was introduced and the government relied on the Public Health Act 1936, Section 91 of which places a duty on local authorities to inspect their districts from time to time for the detection of statutory nuisances. Section 92 includes among statutory nuisances 'dust or effluvia' caused by any trade if they are 'prejudicial to the health of, or a nuisance to, the inhabitants of the neighbourhood'. The government has no powers to compel local authorities to conduct the screening required by the Directive and the local authorities taking part in the two campaigns did so of their own volition. Two local authorities which took part in the first campaign presumably satisfied themselves that there was no nuisance in their areas and consequently felt unable to participate in the second campaign.

Local authorities also have powers under the Control of Pollution Act 1974 (Section 79) to undertake research on air pollution.

None of the people sampled in the first group (i.e., people in urban areas with more than 500,000 inhabitants) were children because, as was explained in evidence to the Lords' Scrutiny Committee, a blood sample taken from a child, even with the parents' consent, could constitute an assault unless it was taken for the benefit of the child. To take a sample for the benefit of the public generally is a different matter, and only where the child is exposed to significant sources of lead pollution can it be argued that the sampling is also for the child's benefit.

The Effect on UK Practice

As the main purpose of the Directive has been to provide information rather than immediately to change practice that is how it should primarily be judged. The work done by the Commission in preparing the Directive involved a survey by R L Zielhuis (1,2) of all available literature reporting blood levels and this enabled him to propose the reference values set out in the Directive. Before the Zielhuis literature survey there was no coherent view of either the normal or the safe distribution of blood lead levels in the population as a whole. The final results of the screening campaign throughout Europe have not yet been analysed and published but it is already clear that some deficiencies in the reference levels have been revealed and that there is now a better data base for proposing new reference levels.

Reports of the two British campaigns carried out in the spring of 1979 and 1981 have been published (3,4) and have been summarised by M J Quinn (5), a DOE official, from which the following description has largely been taken with the author's permission.

The screening in Britain was co-ordinated by the DOE in co-operation with the Department of Health and Social Security, the Welsh Office and the Scottish Home and Health Department. No surveys were undertaken in Northern Ireland. Sampling was carried out by the local authority with advice from its Medical Officer of Environmental Health, or by the Area Health Authority.

In the 1979 campaign there were 39 surveys in Britain in which nearly 5,000 samples were collected. Two thousand randomly selected adults took part in the inner and outer areas of Birmingham, Leeds, Liverpool, London, Manchester and Sheffield; there was one city-wide survey in Glasgow. Two thousand children, either children of leadworkers or living near a leadworks, were sampled in nine locations. Three hundred adults and 500 children living near major roads were sampled in London and Leeds. In Glasgow, in addition to the random surveys of adults, blood concentrations of mothers and their three month old infants were measured as part of a study of dietary intakes of lead. These infants were the only ones in Britain forming a 'critical group' (see Summary of Directive). There were no random samples of children for the legal reason given above.

In the 1981 campaign there were 35 surveys in which about 3,500 people took part. As the results of the 1979 campaign had shown that the blood lead concentrations in the random surveys of adults were generally well below the reference levels, the emphasis was placed upon specific sources of exposure and groups were selected of people either living in predominantly older housing, or near major roads. About 1,700 adults were sampled in the same major cities as before, plus Bristol. The surveys of children exposed to leadworks were repeated, except at three places where it was generally agreed that the position was satisfactory. In addition, there was a survey of mothers with young children at Ayr in Scotland where the water was known to dissolve lead from pipes, and a survey of Bangladeshi infants in the London Borough of Tower Hamlets.

In 1979 33 of the 39 groups studied met all three reference levels generally by comfortable margins. All groups met the 20µg/100ml reference level; only the group of infants in Glasgow breached the second reference level of 30µg/100ml, and six groups exceeded the upper reference level of 35µg/100ml including all three surveys in Glasgow and children of leadworkers at Chester or living near the leadworks. When the results of the 1979 campaign became known the water authority in Glasgow increased the lime dosing of the water supply to reduce its acidity and substantial reductions of lead concentrations in water have been achieved. In Chester the leadworks has closed.

In 1981 three of the 35 surveys did not meet the reference levels. The group of mothers of young children in Ayr exposed to high levels of lead in water, was the only survey in the whole of the British campaign which breached all three reference levels. As a result, for a time a lead-free supply of drinking water was provided for young children, and the acidity of the water supply has been reduced. The randomly selected adults living near the Archway Road in Islington, while otherwise showing fairly typical results for inner city areas, nevertheless revealed three men exceeding the 35µg/100ml level. Two were found to have been stripping old lead paint and the third had been burning cables containing lead.

All groups where breaches of the reference levels were found in the 1979 campaign were sampled again in 1981 and met the reference levels.

Blood lead levels were already being measured in more than 25 different places in Britain before the Directive was agreed, but these were all population groups at risk. Without the Directive, samples would probably not have been taken from the first group mentioned in the Directive (people in urban areas with more than 500,000 population) and so a broader picture of blood lead levels in the population at large has now been provided. The Directive has also ensured that screening in Britain is now carried out in a more co-ordinated way, both in time and in the methods used. In addition to its main aim of producing information it is also evident from what has been said above that the Directive has also resulted in some practical action.

The expenditure incurred by local authorities and central government is estimated at not much more than £60,000 for the first campaign and £50,000 for the second campaign. This represents actual payments and not the salaries of officials.

A summary of the results of the first screening campaign in all Member States was published by the Commission in March 1981 (6) and is discussed in the paper by Quinn (5). Blood lead levels in Britain were about in the middle of the range of other countries, with those in Italy and Belgium being generally higher and those in Germany, Denmark and the Netherlands being generally lower. A summary report of the second campaign has yet to be published. (It should be noted that the Directive requires the Commission to publish annual reports - it has not done so).

A circular letter sent to the local authorities in September 1982 (DOE Circular 22/82) noted that a Department of Health and Social Security working party had reported in 1980 (7) that there was no convincing evidence of adverse health effects at blood lead levels below 35µg/100ml, and noted that less than one per cent of the groups sampled as a result of the screening carried out under the Directive were over this level even though the groups were deliberately sampled to over-represent those exposed to high levels of lead.   However, the Circular went on to say that as a result of more recent scientific work the Department of Health and Social Security is now recommending that where a person - particularly a child - is confirmed as having a level over 25µg/100ml his or her environment should be investigated for sources of lead. The Circular said that it is now government policy (i) to tackle local environmental 'hot spots' where exposure to one source or several is likely to give rise to blood lead levels over 25µg/100ml and (ii) to seek to reduce exposure generally as far as is reasonably practicable.

The report of the 1981 campaign shows that a small number of people in most groups studied had blood lead levels exceeding 25µg/100ml - in Ayr 32% exceeded this level.

References

(1) R L Zielhuis, **Biological Quality Guide for Inorganic Lead,** International Archives. Arbeitsured, Vol 32, pp 103-207, 1974.

(2) R L Zielhuis, **Dose-response Relationships for Inorganic Lead,** International Archives of Occupational Health. Vol 35, pp 1-18 and 19-35, Issue 1.

(3) Department of the Environment, CDEP, **European Community Screening Programme for Lead: United Kingdom Results for 1979-80,** Pollution Report No 10, 1981.

(4) Department of the Environment, CDEP, **European Community Screening Programme for Lead: United Kingdom Results for 1981,** Pollution Report No 18, 1983.

(5) M.J.Quinn, **The Findings of the EC Blood Lead Survey,** Paper given to the 49th Annual Conference of the National Society for Clean Air, October 1982.

(6) Commission of the European Communities, **Progress Report on the Implementation of the Directive 77/312 - COM(81)88,** March 1981.

(7) Professor P.J.Lawther (Chairman), **Lead and Health: the Report of a DHSS Working Party on Lead in the Environment,** HMSO, 1980.

9.5   Lead in Air

82/884/EEC (OJ L378 31.12.82)
proposed 16.4.75 - COM(75)166

Directive on a limit value for
lead in the air

Binding dates

Notification date:	9 December 1982
Formal compliance:	9 December 1984
Report to Commission if limits exceeded:	annually from 1 July 1985[*]
Commission to publish report:	annually from 9 December 1986[*]
Commission to be informed of places likely to exceed limits and of improvement plans:	9 December 1986
Limit values should be met:	9 December 1987
Plans must ensure limits achieved by:	9 December 1989

Purpose of the Directive

Breathing air containing lead contributes to the body burden of lead, and in order to protect human health an air quality standard is laid down.

Summary of the Directive

The concentration of lead in the air is not to exceed two micrograms per cubic metre, expressed as an annual average mean concentration, as from December 1987. This limit value does not apply to occupational exposure (e.g., inside factories). Member States may set more stringent values.

Where a Member State considers that the limit value may be exceeded in December 1986 it must inform the Commission, and must by December 1986 send the Commission plans for the progressive improvement of the quality of the air in those places. These plans, drawn up on the basis of information as to the nature, origin and development of the pollution, must describe the measures already taken or envisaged and the procedures implemented or planned. (The difference between a 'measure' and a 'procedure' is not explained). The objective must be to bring air in those places within the

---

[*]   There is ambiguity about these dates because although the Directive sometimes refers to the date of notification, which is clear enough, it sometimes refers to the date of 'implementation' which could mean the date of formal compliance (December 1984) or the date by which the limit is to be met (December 1987). Here it is assumed that that date of formal compliance is intended. In Article 3(2) a date of four years after 'notification' is given and in Article 3(3) a date of two years after 'implementation': they turn out to be the same date (December 1986).

limit as soon as possible and at the latest by December 1989.

Sampling stations are to be installed and operated at places where individuals may be exposed continually for a long period and where there is a possibility that the limit value will not be observed.   Member States are to supply the Commission, at its request, with information on the sampling sites and sampling and analysis procedure.   An Annex sets out how to choose the sampling method, and also a reference method of analysis.   If Member States use some other method of analysis they must prove to the Commission beforehand that it will produce equivalent results.

Annually from 1st July 1985 Member States must inform the Commission of the places where the limit has been exceeded in the previous year and of the concentrations recorded.   Within a further year they must notify the Commission of the measures taken to avoid recurrence.

Annually the Commission is to publish a summary report on the application of the Directive.

Measures taken as a result of the Directive are not to bring about a significant reduction in the quality of the air where the level of lead is low compared to the limit.

The usual Committee is established for the adaptation to scientific and technical progress of the sampling method and the reference method of analysis.

Development of the Directive

More than six years elapsed between the Directive being proposed and being agreed, largely because it was blocked by Britain, although other Member States were not enthusiastic for it either.   The proposal was made at the same time as a proposed Directive on biological standards for lead (see Section 9.4) and, as a result, the air quality proposal was rather neglected in parliamentary discussion.   Thus, although the House of Commons held a debate (5th April 1976) to take note of the two proposed Directives as well as the proposed lead in petrol Directive (see Section 9.3) no-one mentioned the proposed air quality standard.   In a House of Lords' debate (1 April 1976), however, the Minister (Baroness Stedman) made clear the government's opposition to both proposals:

"The Commission's proposals on biological standards for lead in blood and air quality standards for lead go, in our view, too far...The scientific evidence, despite the effort put in over a number of years, is still not such that we can advance to the point where we should lay down, in legislation, precise standards.   Such a step would imply in law that every individual exceeding the blood lead limit and everybody in an area in which the air quality standard was exceeded would be in danger.   We would not dissent from the view that the sort of figures for the standards proposed are reasonably reliable indicators of where investigation of the sources of lead should be initiated and action taken.   We are, however, opposed to the rigidity and overemphasis on particular figures which would be consequent on enshrining them in legislation and

196

which would carry with them the absolute obligation that they should not be exceeded. Until we know more, therefore, we should prefer something less rigid in the form of guidelines, or possibly quality objectives. These would set targets to be achieved which, in the light of further evidence, may be further modified or possibly adopted as standards..."

The proposed biological standard was turned into a screening campaign, as we have seen, and the air quality standard was deferred. In 1978 the government established a working party to consider the health effects of environmental lead pollution under the Chairmanship of Professor Lawther. The report (1) was published in 1980 and effectively provided the further evidence that the Minister had said was necessary. It recommended an air quality standard for lead of two micrograms per cubic metre. On 11th May 1981 the Minister, Tom King, announced in the Commons that the government agreed with this standard which was the same as that in the proposed Directive, and on 30th June 1981 at a press conference at the start of the British Presidency of the Council, he announced that he hoped to reactivate the proposed Directive.

As originally proposed the Directive would have had two standards:

- an annual mean of $2\mu g/m^3$ in urban residential areas and areas exposed to atmospheric lead other than motor vehicle traffic, and
- a monthly median of $8\mu g/m^3$ in areas particularly exposed to motor vehicle traffic.

A specific proposal about roadside sampling stations being between 1 and 2 metres from the kerb and between 1.5 and 2 metres above the ground was heavily criticised in the House of Lords' Scrutiny Committee's report as producing results unrepresentative of air actually breathed in, and this argument must have prevailed since the Directive as agreed instead requires that "sampling stations are installed and operated at places where individuals may be exposed continually for a long period..." In the case of roadside locations this presumably means where people live rather than pavements where they may walk for only brief periods each day. The monthly limit of $8\mu g/m^3$ was dropped.

Formal Compliance in the UK

Until the government informs the Commission, which it must do by December 1984, one can only speculate on how the Directive will be complied with formally, since there is as yet no legislation which sets air quality standards or authorises the Minister to set them. This point has been discussed in connection with air quality standards for smoke and SO_2 (see Section 9.2).

Emissions from lead smelters are controlled under the Alkali Act and emissions of lead from vehicles are controlled by standards applied to the lead content of petrol. As we have seen (Section 9.3), a decision has already been made that the mandatory lead content of petrol should be 0.15g/l, which is the lowest permitted by Directive 78/611, and there are

197

moves to have the Directive amended.

Effect on UK Practice

It is premature to say what will be the effect on practice, but some arrangement will have to be made between the DOE and the local authorities who carry out monitoring to ensure that this is done in conformity with the Directive. Arrangements will also have to be made to ensure that appropriate action is taken if levels are found to be above $2\mu g/m^3$. DoE Circular 22/82 issued to local authorities on 7 September 1982 said that the decision to reduce the lead content of petrol to 0.15g/l should bring about a proportionate reduction in lead in air near main roads and enable the $2\mu g/m^3$ standard recommended in the Lawther Report to be achieved virtually everywhere. It added that breaches of this standard in places where people are exposed for long periods, even close to main roads, are rare even at present.

In anticipation of the obligation arising from the Directive and to discover what evidence about possible breaches of the standard existed, the Institution of Environmental Health Officers sent a questionnaire to local authority environmental health officers asking whether, by December 1982, any surveys showed that the $2\mu g/m^3$ standard had been exceeded at any time. Of the responding authorities 19 said Yes and 182 said No. It is difficult to draw conclusions from this rather preliminary survey since information is not given about the way, and where, the samples were taken. One effect of the Directive will be to formalise this kind of survey.

References

(1) Prof P J Lawther (chairman), **Lead and Health: The Report of a DHSS Working Party on Lead in the Environment,** HMSO, 1980.

9.6   Pollution from Motor Vehicles

For the reasons given below, the following six Directives have not altered British policy and practice, and are therefore listed here for reference and with only a brief discussion.

Positive Ignition Engines (i.e., petrol engines)

1) 70/220/EEC (OJ L76 6.4.70)   Directive on the approximation
   proposed 1969 - COM(69)939   of the laws of the Member States
                                      relating to measures to be taken
                                      against air pollution by gas from
                                      positive ignition engines of motor
                                      vehicles
2) 74/290/EEC (OJ L159 15.6.74)   (adaptation)
3) 77/102/EEC (OJ L32 3.2.77)   (adaptation)
4) 78/665/EEC (OJ L223 14.8.78)   (adaptation)

Diesel Engines

5) 72/306/EEC (0J L190 20.8.72)   Directive on the approximation
   proposed 1971 - COM(71)1484   of the laws of the Member States
                                      relating to the measures to be taken
                                      against the emission of pollutants
                                      from diesel engines for use in
                                      vehicles

Diesel Engines for Tractors

6) 77/537/EEC (OJ L220 29.8.77)   Directive on the approximation
   proposed 1975 - COM(75)621   of the laws of the Member States
                                      relating to the measures to be taken
                                      against the emission of pollutants
                                      from diesel engines for use in
                                      wheeled agricultural or forestry
                                      tractors

Purpose of the Directives

Air pollution from vehicles can be regulated either by specifying the composition of the fuel or by specifying the construction of the vehicle itself. Two Directives respectively regulate the content of sulphur and lead in fuels (see Sections 9.1 and 9.3) and the six Directives listed above regulate the characteristics of the vehicle. The parent Directive under each of the three above headings was introduced primarily to prevent the Member States creating barriers to trade by setting more stringent standards than those specified, but some of the Directives have subsequently been amended to permit more stringent standards.

Summary of the Directives

The Directives are of the kind known as 'optional' or as providing 'optional harmonisation'*, that is to say, Member States are not obliged to make mandatory the standards in the Directives but they may not refuse national or EEC type approval of a vehicle on grounds relating to air pollution if the requirements of the Directive are met. ('Type approval' shows that a vehicle type conforms with certain standards of design and construction).

70/220 set limit values for emissions of carbon monoxide (CO) and unburnt hydrocarbons (HC) from petrol engined vehicles other than tractors and public works vehicles. 74/290 reduced these limits. 77/102 added limits for nitrogen oxides (NO_x). 78/665 reduces the limits for all three pollutants.

72/306 sets limits on the opacity of emissions from diesel engined vehicles except tractors and public works vehicles. 77/537 sets limits on the opacity of emissions from diesel engined tractors.

Development of the Directives

The United Nations Economic Commission for Europe (ECE) has a Working Group to develop regulations on emissions to air from motor vehicle engines which can then be observed by all countries in Europe. An ECE regulation is not binding but any amendment can only be made by unanimity between those countries that have adopted the original regulation. The Directives have so far all followed ECE regulations and, in order to prevent barriers to trade, ensure that Member States do not set more stringent limits than those laid down in the ECE regulations.

Formal Compliance in the UK

Quantitative limits on vehicle emissions were first set in Britain in 1973 under the Road Traffic Act 1972 by the Motor Vehicles (Construction and Use) Regulations 1973 (SI 1973 No 1347). These made mandatory the standards of Directive 70/220. The following Construction and Use Regulations made mandatory the standards of the subsequent Directives:

SI 1975   No 641   -   Directive 74/290 (petrol engines)
SI 1977   No 1401   -   Directive 77/102 ("   "   )
SI 1980   No 139   -   Directive 78/665 ("   "   )
SI 1974   No 64   -   Directive 72/306 (diesel engines)
SI 1979   No 843   -   Directive 77/357 (tractors)

Since the Directives are of the 'optional' kind, there is no obligation to set limits equal to those in the Directives and any delay in doing so would not constitute a breach of the Directives.

---

*   See Section 12.1 for a discussion of further Directives of the 'optional' kind

Effect on UK Practice

The main purpose of the Directives is to prevent Member States setting more stringent limits than those specified. When setting its standards Britain has been guided by the ECE regulations which, in each case, preceded the Directive so that the Directives themselves have not provided the occasion for a decision to change the standards in Britain. However, once having agreed a Directive, Britain has not been able to adopt the more stringent standards of the next ECE regulations until they are agreed in an amending Directive. The Directives therefore could have an effect if for some reason in the future there was to be some delay between an ECE regulation and an equivalent Directive.

Further Developments

On 5th April 1982 the Commission proposed an amending Directive[*] - COM(82)170 (OJ C181 19.7.82) - also based on an ECE regulation. This would permit, when compared with the standards of Directive 78/665, a 23% reduction in carbon monoxide emissions and a reduction of 20-30% in emissions of hydrocarbons and nitrogen oxides. The proposal also provides for limits to be imposed on emissions of these pollutants from diesel engines. (These standards have been made optional in Britain by Construction and Use Regulations SI 1982 No 1480).

The standards proposed will not require the use of catalytic converters such as are now in use in USA and Japan, but yet further proposed reductions foreshadowed in the Third Action Programme are under consideration which could well require their use. Conventional catalytic converters do not function properly with leaded petrol and if such devices are to be used, then either Directive 78/611 (see Section 9.3) will have to be amended to allow lead-free petrol to be made obligatory, or lead tolerant catalysts will have to be developed. A Commission working group known as 'ERGA' (Evolution of Regulations, Global Approach - Air Pollution) is considering these issues.

---

[*] This amending Directive was agreed by the Council on 16th June 1983 (OJ L197 20.7.83).

CHAPTER 10
Chemicals

10.0   Relevant British Legislation

There are at least three quite separate Acts of Parliament administered by three separate government departments controlling the manufacture or use or sale of chemical substances. These are the Health and Safety at Work etc Act 1974 (HSWA) concerned primarily but not exclusively with the workplace; the Control of Pollution Act 1974 (COPA) concerned with effects on the environment; and the Consumer Safety Act 1978 concerned with protection of the consumer. Since chemical substances are both so numerous and so widespread in their applications there are also likely to be many other items of legislation controlling particular subject areas not considered here (e.g., pharmaceuticals, the transport of substances).

Although the HSWA and COPA were enacted in the same year they had different origins. Nevertheless there was a common concern among those involved with issues of safety at work and those involved with the environment that new chemicals were a potential source of danger unless effectively controlled. Thus the Royal Commission on Environmental Pollution's second report (1) of 1972 referred to the impact of new products on the environment as one of three topics that had frequently arisen during their enquiries following their first report, and in the same year the Robens Report (2) dealing with safety and health at work recommended (para 484) that:

> "...there should be comprehensive powers of control over
> toxic   substances allied to a general statutory obligation
> on manufacturers to ensure adequate safety testing of
> new substances before marketing them for industrial use.
> Anyone marketing a new chemical or other potentially
> harmful substance for industrial or commercial use should
> be required to supply basic information to the Authority
> for   consideration by a standing Advisory Committee on
> Toxic Substances".

Manufacture and Use of Chemicals

The HSWA accordingly places a duty on any person manufacturing, importing or supplying any substance for use at work to ensure (a) that the substance is safe, (b) to have the substance tested as may be necessary and (c) to ensure adequate information about such tests. Regulations supplementing these general duties and defining a workable system were made in 1982 to implement Directive 79/831, known as the 'Sixth Amendment' (Section 10.1).

COPA contains powers to prohibit or restrict the importation and use of injurious substances, and the Consumer Safety Act contains wide powers to ensure that goods are safe and to prohibit goods that are not safe.

Major Accidents Involving Chemicals

HSWA also places a general duty on employers to secure the health, safety and welfare of persons at work and to provide for the protection of the public from work activities. Regulations supplementing these general duties are to be made for the purposes of implementing Directive 82/501 (Section 10.3) on major accident hazards including fires, explosions and massive emissions of dangerous substances when an activity gets out of control.

Pesticides

There is extensive Community legislation covering pesticides (Section 10.5), while in Britain they are largely controlled by the non-statutory Pesticides Safety Precautions Scheme formally agreed between the government and the agrochemical industry.

References

(1) Royal Commission on Environmental Pollution, **Three Issues in Industrial Pollution,** Second Report, HMSO, 1972

(2) Lord Robens (Chairman), **Safety and Health at Work,** HMSO, 1972.

10.1   Preventing Risks by Testing

79/831/EEC (OJ L259 15.10.79)
proposed 8.9.76 - COM(76)433

Directive amending for the sixth
time Directive 67/548/EEC on the
approximation of the laws,
regulations and administrative
provisions relating to the
classification, packaging and
labelling of dangerous substances*

Binding dates
  Notification date: 19 September 1979
  Formal compliance: 18 September 1981
  All dangerous substances
    to be appropriately packaged
    and labelled before marketing: 18 September 1983

Purpose of the Directive

The 'Sixth Amendment' is a significant departure from its parent
Directive 67/548 and the first five amendments.* The earlier Directives
are fairly described by their titles and set out a procedure for classifying
dangerous substances according to the degree of hazard and the nature of
the risks entailed, as well as provisions for packaging and labelling.   Their

---

*   The parent Directive has been 'amended' six times by Council Directives
and the Annexes have been 'adapted' four times by Commission Directives (and once by a Council Directive following Greek accession):

Coun	67/548	L196	16.08.67				
"	69/81	L 68	19.03.69	1st Amendment	–	Annex I amended	
"	70/189	L 59	14.03.70	2nd	"	–	Time limits changed
"	71/144	L 74	29.03.71	3rd	"	–	" " "
"	73/146	L167	25.06.73	4th	"	–	Annexes I-IV rep-laced, Annex V add-ed, articles amended
"	75/409	L183	14.07.75	5th	"	–	Articles amended
Comm	76/907	L360	30.12.76	1st Adaptation	–	Annexes I, III & IV replaced	
"	79/370	L 88	7.04.79	2nd	"	–	Annexes amended
Coun	79/831	L259	15.10.79	**6th Amendment**	–	Articles amended, Annexes VI to IX added	
"	80/1189	L366	31.12.80	Greek language	Annexes I to IV added		
Comm	81/957	L351	7.12.81	3rd Adaptation	–	Annex I amended	
"	82/232	L106	21.04.82	4th	"	–	Annex I amended
"	83/467	L257	16.09.83	5th	"	–	Annexes I-IV, VI amended or replaced

purpose is to protect man, particularly in the workplace. The Sixth Amendment goes much further by adding a new classification of 'dangerous for the environment' and, more importantly, a scheme of prior notification involving tests for potential hazards before a substance is marketed. Not only does the scheme seek to anticipate effects on man and the environment but it also serves the purpose of the common market in chemicals by ensuring a unified system throughout the Community. Restrictions on the use of chemicals are covered by a separate series of Directives (see Section 10.2).

Summary of the Directive

The whole of the substantive parts of the parent Directive 67/548 and the first five amending Directives are replaced by the sixth amending Directive 79/831 with the exception of the formal articles concerned with the introduction of national laws, regulations and administrative provisions. This means that the parent and the first five amendments remain formally in existence but need not be referred to in order to understand the present scope of the legislation.

The parent Directive had four Annexes, the fourth amendment added Annex V, and the Sixth Amendment replaced Annex V by new Annexes V to IX. The Annexes have been subsequently adapted and their current state is to be found in Commission Directives 76/907, 79/370, 81/957, 82/232 and 83/467 as well as in the Sixth Amendment itself.

The Sixth Amendment repeats in an expanded form the provisions of the parent Directive dealing with classification, packaging and labelling of dangerous substances but adds a procedure for testing and notification of new chemicals. Notification is now a prerequisite for the classification procedure. Packaging and labelling follow from notification and classification.

Certain substances are excluded from the scope of the Directive including medicinal products, narcotics, radioactive substances, foodstuffs and feedingstuffs, and waste covered by Directives 75/442 and 78/319 (see Sections 8.1 and 8.2).

(a) Notification

The Member States are to ensure that before being placed on the market substances are notified to the competent authority of the Member State in which the substance is first manufactured or imported, but exceptions are made for categories of substances "which shall be considered as having been notified within the meaning of this Directive". These include: most polymers, substances marketed for research and analysis purposes if they are placed on the market to determine their properties in accordance with the Directive, substances placed on the market for research and analysis under certain specified conditions, and any substances placed on the market in quantities of less than one tonne per year per manufacturer provided the manufacturer announces their identity, labelling, date and quantity to the appropriate competent authority and complies with conditions which may be imposed. Furthermore, a general exception from notification is made for substances already on the market before 18th September 1981. The Commission is to prepare an inventory of such substances and until the inventory is in existence (see below) in effect the manufacturer's declaration and evidence that a substance was already on the market by 18th September 1981 will suffice: thereafter the inventory will be the last word.

At least 45 days prior to marketing the manufacturer must provide the competent authority with the following information as part of the notification:

- a technical dossier containing the information and the results of tests and studies defined in Annex VII or justification for their omission (known as the 'base set');
- a declaration concerning the unfavourable effects of the substance in terms of the various uses envisaged;
- the proposed classification and labelling;
- proposals for recommended precautions for safe use.

Manufacturers may acquire the right to use data submitted by others in prior notifications but they cannot be freed from their obligations to provide the technical dossier unless the substance falls outside the scope of the Directive or was originally notified 10 years previously. They must still provide a basic notification including information on proposed use and production. Finally, notifiers remain responsible for informing the competent authority about changes in annual or total quantities placed on the market, new knowledge about the substance, new uses, or any change in properties due to a change in composition.

(b) Testing
The testing requirements linked to notification are laid down in Annexes VII and VIII. Annex VII defines the 'base set' of information required with every notification (which are essentially identical to the Minimum Pre-Market Set of Data sufficient for an initial hazard assessment set out in an OECD Council Decision of December 1982). Annex VIII defines two further levels or steps (hence the term step sequence testing). The first additional level (Level 1) beyond the base set must be considered once 100 tonnes per year or 500 tonnes in all of a substance have been marketed, but competent authorities may already require these tests at one tenth this amount. 'Level 2' is reached when 1,000 tonnes per year are marketed (or 5,000 tonnes total) and then a further programme of tests must be drawn up by the competent authority as set out. These tests concern primarily long term health and environmental effects (e.g., toxicity to aquatic species) and their predictive ability and cost increase with each level.

(c) Role of Competent Authority
Member States are to appoint the competent authority responsible for receiving the notification and examining its conformity with the Directive, in particular the findings on any risks, classification and labelling, and recommended precautions. The competent authority may ask for further information, carry out sampling or take measures relating to safe use of a substance pending the introduction of Community measures (this is a reference to Directive 76/769 - see Section 10.2).

Following notification the Commission must be sent a copy of the dossier or a summary together with any relevant comments - but if a summary is sent the Commission and the other competent authorities nevertheless have assured access to the dossier as well as to any further information obtained. The Commission must then forward this information to the other Member States. The competent authority of any Member State may consult the authority which received the original notification or the Commission on specific details and suggest further tests.

(d) The Inventory (EINECS) and the List of Notified Substances

The Directive requires the Commission to draw up an inventory of substances that were on the Community market before 18th September 1981. A Commission Decision of 11th May 1981 (OJ L167 24.6.81) explains how the inventory, known as EINECS (European Inventory of Existing Commercial Chemical Substances), is to be drawn up. It is composed of a core inventory known as ECOIN (European Core Inventory) drawn up by the Commission from the data at its disposal - published in May 1982 - and a list of substances made the subject of subsequent declarations by the chemical manufacturers and communicated to the Commission by the Member States. These declarations were to have been made by 31st December 1982 - they numbered over 130,000. The procedure for making these declarations was set out in an explanatory document published by the Commission entitled 'Reports for the EINECS inventory'. EINECS will be published but not before the end of 1985.

In addition to the inventory (EINECS) of substances on the market before 18th September 1981 the Commission is to keep a list of all new substances notified under the Directive as well as a list of those that that are classified as dangerous under various categories (see below). The Directive thus requires three lists.

(e) Confidentiality

The notifier may indicate the information he "considers to be commercially sensitive and disclosure of which might harm him industrially or commercially" and must provide adequate justification, but it is the competent authority that decides on its own responsibility that the information is to be treated as confidential. Certain items including the name of the substance and the interpretation of tests may not be claimed as confidential under any circumstances.

(f) Classification

The Directive sets out 14 danger categories including the category 'dangerous for the environment' (which did not appear in the parent Directive). Annex V (which has yet to be agreed and which will be based on an OECD Council Decision) will set down the procedure for determining the physico-chemical properties and toxicity and eco-toxicity of the substances. The general principles of the classification requirements are set out in Annex VI. Annex I contains the list of dangerous substances under their classification categories to which new substances will be added as they are classified following notification.

(g) Packaging and Labelling

Member States must ensure that substances are not placed on the market unless they are packaged and labelled according to the quite specific requirements laid down in the Directive. A novel feature of the Sixth

Amendment is that all dangerous substances and not just those on Annex I are to be subject to the packaging and labelling requirements as from 18th September 1983.

(h) Committee for Adaptation

A committee is established with power to adapt to technical progress the Directives concerning the elimination of technical barriers to trade in dangerous substances and preparations (including those concerned with restrictions on marketing and use - see Sections 10.2 and 10.5). It may take decisions by qualified majority. Annex VI (Part I) and the essential Annexes VII and VIII are excluded from this procedure.

(i) Access to the Market

Member States may not introduce their own notification scheme or otherwise impede access to their market for reasons of classification, packaging or labelling of a substance complying with the Directive unless it has 'detailed evidence' that a substance constitutes a hazard to man and the environment, in which case they may take provisional measures. (The provisions for Community restrictions are set out in Directive 76/769 - see Section 10.2). In other words, notification in one Member State provides assured access to the entire Community market after 45 days.

Development of the Directive

The first Action Programme on the Environment of 1973 specifically charged the Commission "to investigate the measures still required to harmonise and strengthen control by public authorities over chemicals before they are marketed". This had become an issue in several Member States and in the United States, and indeed the development of the Directive would have been quite different if it had not been for the legislative activity in the USA and international discussions within OECD.

In Britain, the concept of an 'early warning system' was put forward in 1972 both in the Robens Report on Health and Safety at Work (1) and by the Royal Commission on Environmental Pollution. The Royal Commission included the impact of new products on the environment in their Second Report (2) as one of three topics which had 'frequently arisen' during the Commission's enquiries following their First Report and which it believed 'need to be aired in public'. The Royal Commission already identified scale of production and projected use as two key criteria for pinpointing substances requiring testing as well as the need to provide exceptions for 'laboratory curiosities'. The origin of the public debate in Britain thus coincided with the drafting process of the Community's first Action Programme in late 1972.

For several years some confusion appears to have reigned, both in Britain and in the Community, about the most appropriate point of departure: in Britain, a control scheme for new chemicals was seen as a responsibility of the Health and Safety Executive (HSE) - provision for it was made in the Health and Safety at Work etc Act 1974 - but was also being developed within DOE. Within the Commission, debate centred on whether to amend yet again the existing Directive 67/548 on packaging and labelling (arising out of the internal market harmonisation policies) or to develop an entirely new draft. At times, two independent draft proposals appear to have existed prepared by different departments with a power struggle between them.

In November 1974 the OECD adopted a Recommendation on the Assessment of the Potential Environmental Effects of Chemicals, and the preparation of this Recommendation and subsequent work on it provided a forum for technical discussion involving representatives from the USA and Canada as well as all Member States, with the lead for Britain being taken by DOE.

In June 1975 draft French legislation on a scheme of pre-market testing for new chemicals (which had existed for some months) was communicated to the Commission under the information agreement and served to provide impetus and focus to these discussions. The fact that this draft law was notified by the French environmental authorities to the Commission's environment service may have helped ultimately to strike a distribution of roles rather more favourable to environmental concerns than might otherwise have been achieved in the Community and in several Member States, including Britain.

A working group was established by the Commission and this had the immediate effect of linking discussions which were going on in several Member States at a time when these had reached tentative conclusions only in France. From this time on there was formal liaison in Britain between the HSE and DOE. Development of the Sixth Amendment can thus be considered as an example of the ideal situation where an issue requiring Community action can be taken up at Community level before sometimes conflicting legal constraints have been created in several Member States. Clearly the absence of any prior legislation on pre-market testing of chemicals was an important factor in facilitating agreement on a very complex and potentially divisive topic. On the basis of the French communication and the consultations in the working group, the Commission was able to prepare a proposal for a Directive within just 15 months. In 1976 the Toxic Substances Control Act was passed in the USA but the full effect of this began to emerge only in 1977 following publication of implementation rules by the US Environmental Protection Agency (EPA). Thereafter the US legislation became an increasingly important factor in the negotiations in Brussels, mainly as a precedent for some of the problems that arose during negotiations and as an argument for strengthening environmental aspects of the Directive.

The basic structure of the Directive as adopted can already be discerned in the proposal. But if one considers the very numerous changes of detail including the requirement for an inventory of existing substances, the ultimately adopted Directive must be considered as having been fundamentally changed.

The Economic and Social Committee was favourably inclined to the proposal. The European Parliament was concerned only about a technical issue of labelling and wanted to see the use of national languages on labels an absolute requirement. Neither point was taken up in Council.

The House of Commons debated the proposal rather summarily (11th July 1977) because it was linked with four proposals dealing with pesticides. A junior Minister from the Ministry of Agriculture simply outlined the proposal and expressed concern about maintaining confidentiality of commercially valuable information and the provision (subsequently deleted) to control the use of substances by majority voting. The opposition generally welcomed the proposal but speakers expressed concern about the need to avoid excessive bureaucracy and costs to industry.

The House of Lords' Scrutiny Committee published its report on 26th April 1977 and a debate took place on 15th November 1977. The report and most of the subsequent debate were concerned primarily with the labelling provisions and their relationship to UN schemes for labelling in transport, and with the general practicability of testing. The Lords' report recognised the need for some further limitation of the testing requirement beyond that provided in the draft for 'research, development or analysis' but had doubts about tonnage limits. Only the reply of the Minister, Lord Wallace, to the debate placed what were to be the central issues of the following two years clearly on the table: the definition of appropriate exclusions, and control of use. In the first instance, the difficulties of both an approach through categories ('research', 'development', 'analysis') and of volume were recognised, with British preference indicated for a tonnage cut-off. The ultimately adopted scheme involving both categorical and tonnage cut-offs therefore appears to have been a solution to these difficulties developed at Community level. The British point of view that use should not be controlled under the Sixth Amendment but under the existing Directive on the control of marketing and use of dangerous substances (see Section 10.2) ultimately prevailed in Council - but apparently only at the very last minute. Not mentioned at all in the Lords' debate was the issue of step sequence testing which was to prove vital in allaying some of industry's fears. Apparently this aspect was new within the British context, even though it is accurate to say, as several speakers emphasised in the House of Lords, that the thrust of the draft was entirely in keeping with British discussions on the issue.

In general, it must be said that both the Economic and Social Committee and the European Parliament failed to appreciate the significance of the draft Directive or even to reflect what were to become the major issues of subsequent concern. In Britain only the House of Lords gave substantial attention to the draft, and even so only covered part of the major problems.

In May 1977 the Health and Safety Commission (HSC) published a discussion document 'Proposed scheme for notification of the toxic properties of substances'(3). A comparison made in 1981 by HSC (4) of this 1977 discussion document with the Directive gives a clear indication of the impact in the following years of Community deliberations on the British position. Seven points of difference were noted:

(a) The Directive requires the notification at least 45 days before the substance is placed on the market, whereas the HSC favoured a period of 30 days.

(b) The Directive requires the announcement of a limited amount of information (mainly related to identity particulars and the quantity produced) in respect of new substances placed on the market in quantities of less than one tonne per annum. The HSC proposals made no provision for such substances on the grounds that it was important to concentrate available scarce resources on substances where the quantity produced suggested a potentially greater degree of hazard.

(c) The Directive excludes from the full testing and notification procedure substances which are subject to similar testing and notification requirements under existing Directives. The HSC proposals were designed to include such substances even though they were subject to notification under existing UK schemes, e.g., pharmaceuticals, pesticides and food additives, because those schemes related only to the areas of specific use.

(d) The Directive does not require the notification of isolated intermediate compounds as was envisaged in the HSC scheme.

(e) A more specific provision is made in the Directive than proposed by HSC for the carrying out of further tests and the provision of additional information (step sequence testing).

(f) The Directive requires an inventory of existing substances unlike the HSC proposal.

(g) The Directive extends to the protection of the natural environment whereas the HSC proposals were designed principally to assess the potential of a substance to cause harm to people both in the workplace and outside where they may be affected by the work activity.

The Directive as finally adopted reflects very long, detailed and complex consideration in the Council working group. The nature of changes incorporated, sometimes involving subtle shifts from Article to Article, are a clear indication of the difficulties which were encountered. It is consequently one of the most difficult of Directives to understand.

A particular contribution made by Britain was the 'base set' of information that has to be submitted with every notification of the proposal to market a new substance. The Robens Report (1) had recommended in 1972 that 'basic information' should be notified and the HSE then developed what this should include. These ideas - later published in outline in the 1977 discussion document (3) - were incorporated with some modification by the Commission into the proposed Directive.

The most important change after the Directive was proposed was the introduction of step sequence testing at the initiative of the German government which was being prodded by its chemical industry. In actual fact, no public allusion to step sequence testing - let alone any text setting out its principles and provisions - can be found in any official document prior to publication of the Directive in the Official Journal. But quite apart from this major omission, by late 1977 it was already increasingly evident that the Directive as finally adopted would differ significantly from the proposal, making the Sixth Amendment one of the most obvious cases where lack of intermediate public information makes the Community legislative process so difficult to reconstruct.

Formal Compliance in the UK

The provisions dealing with the notification of new substances have been implemented separately from those dealing with classification, packaging and labelling.

(a) Notification

The Health and Safety at Work etc Act 1974 places a duty on any person who manufactures, imports or supplies any substance for use at work (a) to ensure that the substance is safe and without risks to health when properly used, (b) to have the substance tested as may be necessary, and (c) to ensure adequate information about such tests and about conditions of use. In addition the Act empowers inspectors to serve 'improvement notices' and 'prohibition notices' to secure enforcement of those general duties. These general provisions, which do not extend to protection of the environment, have been supplemented by the Notification of New Substances Regulations 1982 (SI 1982 No 1496) made under both the Health and Safety at Work etc Act 1974 and the European Communities Act 1972. Separate Regulations will be made for Northern Ireland.

The Regulations came into operation on 26th November 1982, i.e., over one year after the date set in the Directive, and the Commission was formally sent a copy in January 1983 together with copies of a guidance booklet (5) that had been issued and four Approved Codes of Practice relating to test methods and procedures. The failure to implement the Directive on time was a result of a dispute between the Health and Safety Commission (HSC) and the chemical industry (see below). In February 1981 the HSC had proposed draft Regulations (4) which would have gone further than the Directive in some respects but these were resisted by the industry. In the event the views of industry prevailed and the draft Regulations had to be modified.

The competent authority for the purposes of the Directive is the Health and Safety Executive (HSE) and the DOE acting jointly (the Scottish Development Department and Welsh Office have agreed that the DOE will act on their behalf), and the Regulations require manufacturers to supply information about new substances to the HSE who in turn must forward the information to the DOE. It is because the Regulations give the DOE powers to require information about environmental effects of substances which are outside the powers conferred on HSE by the Health and Safety at Work etc Act that they have also had to be made under the European Communities Act 1972.

On 17th September 1981 (i.e., the day before the Directive came into effect) the HSC issued a press statement describing the administrative arrangements that would apply pending the Regulations. Manufacturers and importers intending to market new substances were invited to submit notifications as set out in the Directive and these would be accepted as having been made under the Regulations when they took effect.

The four Approved Codes of Practice sent to the Commission deal with the principles of good laboratory practice and methods for determining toxicity, eco-toxicity and physico-chemical properties. They are issued by HSE and are largely based on methods agreed within OECD.

Because of the complexity of both the Directive and the Regulations no view is here expressed on whether the Regulations adequately implement the Directive.

(b) Classification, Packaging and Labelling

The following Regulations, also made both under the European Communities Act 1972 and the Health and Safety at Work etc Act 1974, are concerned with classification, packaging and labelling:

SI 1978   No 209   The Packaging and Labelling of Dangerous
                                Substances Regulations 1978

SI 1981   No 792   (Amendment) 1981

SI 1983   No 17   (Amendment) 1983

SI No 209 implemented Directive 67/548 as amended the first five times and as adapted the first time by Directive 76/907. SI No 792 implemented the second adaptation made by Directive 79/370. SI No 17 implemented the third and fourth adaptations made respectively by Directive 81/957 and Directive 82/232.

Britain must have been in breach of the parent Directive and its various amendments until the 1978 Regulations were made, and the 1981 Regulations were also late in implementing Directive 79/370 so that the Commission issued a 'Reasoned Opinion' to the effect that there was a failure to implement. The explanation appears to be a desire to await the further adaptation that after delay became Directive 81/957 and that introduced significant changes to Directive 79/370. This is a recurring problem when a Directive is being continually amended, because implementation then becomes an attempt to hit a moving target. With the 1983 Regulations the packaging and labelling requirements of nearly 1,000 chemicals are now specified. Further Regulations will complete the implementation of the packaging and labelling requirements of the Sixth Amendment itself which extends to all substances whether on Annex I or not, but this cannot properly be done until Annex V is agreed.

Separate Regulations are being prepared for Northern Ireland.

Effect on UK Practice

This Directive is possibly the most important of all the environmental Directives agreed so far. The subject matter is important. The costs incurred for industry could be about £40,000 for fully testing one new substance with an estimate of 400 new substances to be notified in the Community each year. The administrative arrangements necessary for making the system workable are extensive and require trained manpower in both the public and private sectors. Novel relationships between the competent authorities in the Member States have been established. Above all, the Directive is a significant attempt to make concrete the principle enunciated in the first Action Programme that prevention is better than cure. A yet further aspect of the Directive is that it has enabled the Community to speak with one voice in discussions within the OECD and with the United States and other countries and has strengthened its position in ensuring that the operation of the US Toxic Substances Control Act does not create obstacles to the European chemical industry. The Sixth Amendment and the US Act have similar goals and eventually some arrangement may be reached to ensure that chemicals notified in USA can be marketed in Europe and vice versa. The ability of the Commission – which can speak for a larger market than that of the USA – to enter into discussions with the USA has been greatly enhanced by the Directive and it is unlikely that each European country on its own could do so as effectively. On 30 May 1978 the Council authorised the Commission to negotiate with the USA, and in 1981 the Commission reported on the state of these negotiations – COM(81)69.

These discussions were still continuing in 1983 (see Bull. EC 7/8 - 1983).

The effect of the Directive on Britain is therefore extremely difficult to assess because it must take into account all these disparate and uncertain matters.

It is evident that had there been no Directive some comparable system for pre-notification would have been introduced in Britain. We have already noted above some of the differences between the system proposed by the HSC in 1977 with that of the Directive, but it would be a mistake to assume that what was proposed in Britain in 1977 would necessarily have been adopted in precisely that form, so a comparison is not particularly helpful in establishing the effect of the Directive even on the detailed form of the British procedure.

One effect of the Directive is similar to an effect of the Seveso Directive (see Section 10.3). There is nothing in either Directive to prevent Member States including more substances within the scope of national regulations than are required by the respective Directives. The scheme proposed by HSC in 1977 involved notification of 'isolated' intermediate compounds, that is to say compounds which are not to be marketed but which are produced or are used to arrive at the marketable product. Some intermediate compounds are transitory compounds produced in a reaction while others are stored and transported and may require labelling (referred to as isolated intermediate compounds). Given the emphasis of the Health and Safety at Work etc Act it was natural that the British proposals would seek to ensure that intermediate compounds that could affect the workforce would be brought within the scheme, but because of the bias of the Directive toward substances placed on the market, and the problems of definition, intermediate compounds were left out of the Directive. Nevertheless the HSC in the draft Regulations issued for consultation in 1981 proposed to go further than the Directive by bringing such intermediate compounds within the scope of the Regulations. This was resisted by the chemical industry represented by the Chemical Industries Association (CIA) on the grounds that these were already controlled by industry and assessed by the Factory Inspectorate so that the proposals "would substitute an efficient and cost-effective means of direct discussion with the enforcing authorities by a cumbersome bureaucratic mechanism for centralising information"(6). The CIA argued - as they did with the Seveso Directive - that the proposed Regulations should not impose greater burdens on British industry than the Directive placed on its competitors. The CIA view prevailed, thus ensuring that in this field Community legislation is coming to set both the maximum as well as the minimum standard for domestic legislation.

A further important effect of the Directive has already been noted. The British scheme proposed in 1977 would have been made under the Health and Safety at Work etc Act and would not have been concerned with effects on the environment. Because the Directive was proposed by the Commission as an environmental Directive and specifically refers to environmental effects which are beyond the responsibilities of the HSE, the DOE has had to be involved and the HSE and DOE jointly act as the competent authority. Without the Directive a liaison in quite this form would not have been achieved. HSE and DOE were both involved in negotiating the Directive and continue to be involved jointly in the further discussions that are still proceeding.

The HSE has established a new Inspectorate (7) to ensure that test data for notifications has been generated in accordance with the principles of good laboratory practice agreed within OECD.

Finally there is the effect on classification and packaging that can be easily overlooked in concentrating on notification. Britain had no provisions similar to those in the parent Directive and the early amendments, and although a comparable system could well have been introduced and indeed is provided for in the Health and Safety at Work etc Act, the Directive has ensured that this has happened and has prescribed the form.

The full effects of the Directive will not be felt for some time. By June 1983 only a very few substances had been notified by Britain to the Commission and none had been received by the HSE/DOE via the Commission from the competent authorities in other Member States. Many matters still have to be resolved such as the information that will appear on the Commission's list of notified substances, how the competent authorities will handle the provisions for confidentiality and step sequence testing, and how the information in the notification is to be interpreted. The competent authorities from the different Member States meet regularly with the Commission to review the working of the Directive, and their developing relations may yet be creating something entirely new: a Community 'agent', indeed, that in Chapter 3 we said hardly existed in the environmental field. The HSE guidance booklet (5) has gone so far as to say that "a notification made to the (British) competent authority is made to the European Community as a whole, the competent authority in effect acting on behalf of the Community".

References

(1) Lord Robens (Chairman), **Safety and Health at Work,** HMSO 1972.

(2) Royal Commission on Environmental Pollution, **Second Report: Three Issues in Industrial Pollution,** HMSO 1972.

(3) Health and Safety Commission, **Discussion Document: Proposed Scheme for the Notification of the Toxic Properties of Substances,** HMSO 1977.

(4) Health and Safety Commission, **Consultative Document: Notification of New Substances: Draft Regulations and Approved Codes of Practice,** HMSO 1981.

(5) Health and Safety Executive, **A Guide to the Notification of New Substances Regulations 1982,** HMSO 1982.

(6) Chemical Industries Association, **Notification of New Substances: Vol 1 Comments and Recommendations on the Regulations,** 1981.

(7) Health and Safety Executive, **Establishment of a Good Laboratory Practice Compliance Programme,** 1983.

10.2 Restrictions on Marketing and Use

1) 76/769/EEC (OJ L262 27.9.76)   Directive relating to restrictions
   proposed 25.7.74-COM(74)1189   on the marketing and use
   and 29.4.75-COM(75)186   of certain dangerous substances
                                   and preparations

2) 79/663/EEC (OJ L197 3.8.79)   (First Amendment)
   proposed 2.3.79-COM(79)84
   and 19.3.79-COM(79)123

3) 82/806/EEC (OJ L339 1.12.82)   (Second Amendment)
   proposed 10.10.80-COM(80)570

4) 82/828/EEC (OJ L350 10.12.82)   (Third Amendment)
   proposed 11.1.80-COM(79)792

5) 83/264/EEC (OJ L147 6.6.83)   (Fourth Amendment)
   proposed 1981 - COM(81)573

Binding dates

Formal compliance	76/769:	3 February 1978	
"	"	79/663:	26 July 1980
"	"	82/806:	25 November 1983
"	"	82/828:	10 December 1982 (where appropriate)
"	"	83/264:	19 November 1984

PCT to be phased out as a
tooling compound: 31 December 1984

Purpose of the Directives

Certain other Directives restrict the use of specific substances in specific products, e.g., lead in petrol (Section 9.3), sulphur in gas oil (Section 9.1). Another Directive (Section 10.1) requires new substances to be tested and notified to the authorities before being marketed and then appropriately packaged and labelled. The first of the present series of Directives goes further by creating a general framework for bans or restrictions on the marketing and use of dangerous substances. Restrictions are set out in an Annex and subsequent Directives have extended the Annex. A separate Directive restricts the marketing and use of pesticides (see Section 10.5).

Summary of the Directives

76/769 - Member States are to take all necessary measures to ensure that the dangerous substances and preparations listed in an Annex are only placed on the market or used subject to the conditions specified in the Annex. The restrictions do not apply to marketing or use for the purposes of research and development or analysis. The Directive does not apply to:

- the carriage of dangerous substances;
- substances exported to non-member countries;
- substances in transit and subject to customs inspection.

The Annex lists polychlorinated biphenyls and terphenyls (PCBs, PCTs) and monomer vinyl chloride. PCBs and PCTs may only be used in closed system electrical equipment, large condensers and for certain other specified applications. Monomer vinyl chloride may not be used as an aerosol propellant.

79/663 adds to the Annex of 76/769. Trichloroethylene, tetrachloro-ethylene and carbon tetrachloride may not be used in ornamental objects intended to produce light or colour effects by means of different phases, for example in ornamental lamps and ashtrays. (The substances are defined by reference to Directive 67/548 – see Section 10.1). Tris (2,3 – dibromopropyl) phosphate, commonly known as Tris and used as a fire retardant, is not to be used in textile articles intended to come into contact with the skin.

82/806 adds benzene to the Annex and bans its use in toys where the concentration of benzene is in excess of 5 mg/kg of the weight of the toy.

82/828 relaxes the Annex of 76/769 by allowing PCTs to be used until 31st December 1984 in reusable thermoplastic tooling compounds in the manufacture or maintenance of certain products including: gas turbines; nuclear reactors; ship and aircraft frames; semi-conductor devices; and high-precision lenses.

83/264 adds to the Annex two substances used as fire retardants and three used in sneezing powers and in novelties, jokes and hoaxes.

Development of the Directives

Although the parent Directive sets out a general scheme for restrictions on marketing and use of products, its origin is to be found in a draft French law introduced to implement the decision by the Council of the Organisation for Economic Co-operation and Development (OECD) restricting one particular group of substances – PCBs (described more fully in Section 8.3). The Commission, however, saw the need for a general measure on the grounds that some Member States were already restricting some substances and that Community measures were needed to prevent barriers to trade – the Commission's explanatory memorandum, for example, quotes a British restriction on benzene in toys as the origin of directive 82/806. The Commission had originally envisaged the Directive establishing a Committee empowered to add other substances by qualified majority vote but this was resisted by Britain, and doubtless other Member Staes, and in the event extra substances have to be added to the Annex by the Council in separate Directives.

There was some discussion whether the power to restrict marketing and use should form part of the Directives requiring notification and testing of substances before marketing (see Section 10.1), but the power has been kept separate although the two groups of Directives are clearly linked.

Directive 82/828 which relaxes the restriction on PCTs for certain applications for a certain period seems to have arisen because it was found in Britain that PCTs were in use despite the restrictions of Directive 76/769. The deadline for eliminating use of PCTs is intended to stimulate research for a substitute material.

Formal Compliance in the UK

Section 100 of the Control of Pollution Act 1974 gives the Secretary of State powers to make regulations prohibiting or restricting the import, use in connection with trade, or supply for any purpose, of certain substances for the purpose of preventing damage to man or the environment. The Consumer Safety Act 1978 also gives the Secretary of State wide powers to ensure that goods are safe and to make orders prohibiting goods that are not safe.

The Control of Pollution (Supply and Use of Injurious Substances) Regulations 1980 (SI 1980 No 638) made under the Control of Pollution Act restrict the use of PCBs and PCTs in the manner specified in Directive 76/769 as amended by Directive 82/828. The Regulations came into operation some two and a half years after the date for compliance with Directive 76/769 but 18 months before Directive 82/828 was even agreed. The reason for not immediately complying with Directive 76/769 was the discovery that there was no readily available substitute for PCTs for the purposes exempted by Directive 82/828. Until Directive 82/828 was agreed Britain was therefore technically in breach of Directive 76/769 although there was a voluntary restriction on its use.

The Dangerous Substances and Preparations (Safety) Regulations 1980 (SI 1980 No 136) made under the Consumer Safety Act 1978 implement Directive 76/769 as respects vinyl chloride monomer (chloroethylene) in aerosols, and also implement Directive 79/663 for ornamental objects and Tris in certain textile products.

The Novelties (Safety) Regulations 1980 (SI 1980 No 958) preceded Directive 82/806 and deal with the only novelty containing benzene then on the British market. New Regulations are being drafted to implement the Directive and will then cover any toys containing benzene.

Effect on UK Practice

The two Directives dealing with PCBs can have had little effect in Britain because according to a DOE Waste Management Paper (1) the sole British manufacturer had since 1971 voluntarily operated a more stringent restriction than that now made mandatory by the Directives. That this cannot have been entirely the case is illustrated by the need to relax Directive 76/769 to allow the use of PCT in tooling compounds.

There had been no ban on vinyl chloride monomer in aerosols in Britain before Directive 76/769 but it was not in use in Britain. There had also been no ban on the use of the substances listed in Directive 79/663 in ornamental objects before that Directive. The Directive arose as a result of accidental deaths in other Member States, and a precautionary measure taken in one Member State has now resulted in precautionary measures in all. The Community ban on Tris-treated nightwear was in fact prompted by a British ban made under the Consumer Safety Act by the Nightwear (Safety) Order 1978 which has since been superseded by SI 1980 No 136.

The major effect of this series of Directives is to provide a mechanism whereby precautionary measures adopted in one Member State are quickly and uniformly applied across the Community. It is also foreseen that the Annexes will be extended to take account of hazards notified to the authorities under Directive 79/831 (see Section 10.1).

Further Developments

A fifth amending Directive 83/478 to extend the Annex to cover asbestos was agreed by the Council in June 1983 but not published until September (OJ L263 24.9.83).

References

(1) Department of the Environment, **Polychlorinated Biphenyl (PCB) Waste,** Waste Management Paper No 6, HMSO, 1976.

10.3 Major Accident Hazards

82/501/EEC (OJ L230 5.8.82)   Directive on the major accident
proposed 16.7.79 - COM(79)384   hazards of certain industrial
                                 activities

Binding dates
Notification date: 8 July 1982
Formal compliance: 8 January 1984
Initial declarations for
  existing industrial activities: 8 January 1985
Annexes I,II,III to be reviewed: 8 January 1986
Commission to publish report: 8 July 1987
Supplementary declarations for
  existing industrial activities
  (unless waiver granted):   8 July 1989

Purpose of the Directive

The risks for man and the environment arising from any industrial activity are of two kinds: routine risks in normal operating conditions, and exceptional risks such as fires, explosions and massive emissions of dangerous substances when an activity gets out of control. The Directive is concerned with the second kind of risk and requires measures to be taken to prevent major accidents and to limit the consequences of those that do occur. These measures include notifying the authorities of dangerous substances used in industrial activities and preparing hazard surveys and emergency plans.

The Directive is often called the 'Seveso' or 'post-Seveso Directive' since it was the notorious accident in Italy in 1976 that prompted the Community to legislate.

Summary of the Directive

The Directive can be thought of as in two parts: a general or framework part and a specific part.

(a) Framework Part

Industrial activity is defined firstly by reference to a list of process installations (Annex I) involving dangerous substances and including transport and associated storage within the establishment, and secondly to include isolated storage as set out in an Annex II. Dangerous substances are defined as substances fulfilling the criteria set out in an Annex IV. Various activities are excluded from the Directive, e.g., nuclear installations, munitions manufacture, mining and military installations.

A general duty is placed on Member States to adopt provisions necessary to ensure that the person in charge of industrial activities (as defined) is obliged to take all measures necessary to prevent major accidents and to limit their consequences for man and the environment.

Member States must ensure that all manufacturers are required to prove to the competent authority at any time that they have identified major accident hazards, have adopted the appropriate safety measures, and have provided people working on the site with information, training and equipment in order to ensure their safety.

(b) Specific Part

(1) **Notification:** Manufacturers must notify the competent authorities if an industrial activity involves the dangerous substances listed in an Annex III in certain quantities, or if the dangerous substances listed in an Annex II are stored in certain quantities. The notification is to contain information (which the Directive specifies in some detail) relating to:

- the substances in Annexes II and III including the data specified in an Annex V;
- the installations including a description of where the hazards could arise and the measures to prevent and control them (known as a 'hazard survey' or 'safety case' in Britain);
- possible major accident hazard situations including on-site emergency plans ('off-site' emergency plans are to be prepared by the competent authority - see below).

For new installations the notification must reach the competent authority a reasonable length of time before the industrial activity commences. New activities are to include any modification to an existing activity likely to have important implications for major accident hazards. The notification is to be updated periodically to take account of new technical knowledge.

When an industrial activity is modified, the manufacturer must revise the accident prevention measures and must inform the competent authority in advance if it affects the notification.

For the purposes of notification a manufacturer with a group of installations close together must aggregate the quantities of a substance listed in Annex II or III.

(2) **Existing Industrial Activities:** Extra time is allowed for submitting the notification relating to existing activities, but by 8th January 1985 manufacturers must have submitted in a **declaration** to the competent authority a part of the notification, including information about the types of industrial activity and of the substances involved. A **supplementary declaration** completing the notification and containing a hazard survey and 'on-site' emergency plans must be provided by 8th July 1989 unless this requirement is waived by the Member State. In the event of a waiver the supplementary declaration must be submitted if requested by the competent authority.

(3) **Duties of Competent Authority:** Member States must appoint the competent authorities who are to receive the notification and examine the

223

information provided, and who are to ensure that an emergency plan is drawn up for action outside the establishment housing a notified industrial activity (i.e., an 'off-site' emergency plan in contrast with the 'on-site' emergency plan which has to be prepared by the manufacturer as part of the notification).

The competent authority must if necessary request supplementary information and must ascertain that the manufacturer takes the most appropriate measures to prevent accidents and to limit the consequences. It must also organise inspections.

(4) Persons outside Installations: Member States must ensure that persons liable to be affected by a major accident at a notified industrial activity are informed of the safety measures and of the correct behaviour to adopt in the case of an accident. Member States must also make available to other Member States concerned, as a basis for all necessary consultation within the framework of their bilateral relations, the same information as that which is disseminated to their own nationals.

(5) Action following Accident: As soon as a major accident occurs the manufacturer must:

- inform the competent authority;
- provide the authority with information on the circumstances of the accident, the dangerous substances involved, the data available for assessing the effects, and the emergency measures taken;
- inform the authority of the steps envisaged to alleviate the medium and long term effects of the accident and to prevent recurrence.

The competent authorities must ensure that any emergency and medium and long term measures which may prove necessary are taken, and must collect where possible the information necessary for a full analysis of the accident.

Member States must inform the Commission as soon as possible of major accidents and must provide the details set out in an Annex VI.

(6) Community Information System: Member States must inform the Commission of the organisation with relevant information on major accidents able to advise the competent authorities of other Member States.

Member States may notify the Commission of any substance which in their view should be added to Annexes II and III and of any measures they may have taken concerning such substances. The Commission must forward this to the other Member States.

The Commission must maintain at the disposal of the Member States a register containing a summary of major accidents including an analysis of the causes, experience gained and measures taken.

Restrictions are placed on the use of information obtained by the competent authorities and the Commission, some of which may not be used for any purpose other than that for which it was requested. This is not to preclude publication by the Commission of general statistical data.

The Member States and the Commission are to exchange information on experience of preventing and limiting major accidents. By July 1987 the Commission must send to the Council and the Parliament a report on the working of the Directive based on this exchange of information.

(7) Review and Amendment: By 8th January 1986 the Council is to review Annexes I, II and III. A procedure for adapting Annex V to technical progress is laid down.

(8) More Stringent Measures: The Directive allows Member States to apply more stringent measures than those in the Directive.

Development of the Directive

The Directive was proposed in response to pressure from the European Parliament following a disaster in 1976 when toxic dust - dioxin - escaped from a factory at Seveso near Milan in Italy and spread over the surrounding countryside. Other major accidents at Flixborough, UK (1974), Beek, Netherlands (1975) and Velbert, FRG (1979) underlined the need for special measures. The Commission's explanatory memorandum accompanying the proposal recorded that the Netherlands, UK and Italy had all informed the Commission of proposed legislation in the field and the Directive was therefore also an attempt to ensure comparable procedures in all Member States.

Within six months of the Directive being first discussed in the Council machinery the broad outlines of a draft had been generally approved by the Member States except for the issue of transfrontier responsibilities. The proposals on this point were not acceptable to France and took a further 18 months to resolve.

The Department of Employment submitted two explanatory memoranda to Parliament, the first on 8th October 1979 and the second, on 18th June 1980, accompanied by an Appendix giving the latest available version of the text of the proposal then to have emerged from the Council machinery - one of the rare occasions when such a document has been rendered public. Between the dates of these two memoranda the proposal had changed in a number of respects and was to change again.

In Britain the Health and Safety at Work etc Act 1974 had been enacted just before the Flixborough explosion in which 28 people were killed. This Act established the Health and Safety Commission (HSC) with broad responsibilities. Following the Flixborough explosion in 1974 the HSC set up an Advisory Committee on Major Hazards. The Committee published a first report (1) in September 1976 recommending legislation similar to the Directive in providing both for notification of installations handling dangerous substances and for the preparation of hazard surveys. These were published in 1978 in a consultative document (2) as draft Hazardous Installations (Notification and Survey) Regulations. A second report (3) of the Committee was published in 1979 just before the Directive was proposed. In a debate in the House of Commons (23rd June 1980) the Minister, Patrick Mayhew, said that the government had from the outset supported the principle of the Directive and went on to say:

> "The European Commission's proposal has adopted some
> features of our own proposed regulations, which is
> satisfactory. There are however considerable difficul-

ties involved in any attempt to produce a Directive which is satisfactory to all Member States. Many countries do not possess such broadly based legislation as our own Health and Safety at Work etc Act 1974. Under that Act, all employers are already required to conduct their operations with full regard for the safety of workers and the public. This foundation of general obligations readily permits the introduction of additional requirements, which can be concentrated on activities which present exceptional risks to public safety."

The Scrutiny Committee of the House of Lords had earlier published a report criticising the Commission's original proposal for trying to apply across a wide and uncertain spectrum the stringent controls appropriate for the most hazardous installations. It recommended that the Directive be limited in its scope and made more precise in its drafting to specify exactly those areas where Member States should focus their efforts. In this it should, said the report, be brought closer to the regulations proposed by the Health and Safety Commission.

To some extent this happened. The Minister explained in the Commons' debate how the framework part of the Directive had been restricted in two ways: the obligation on manufacturers to draw up a safety report had been curtailed and changed to a requirement to demonstrate to the competent authority that provision had been made for identifying major accident hazards and the appropriate measures taken. Secondly, 'industrial activity' was more precisely defined by references to Annexes.

The more specific part of the Directive had also been changed. All the dangerous substances to which the notification requirement applied were listed and quantified in Annexes - somewhat longer than the proposed British list although applying to fewer substances in isolated storage than under the proposed British Regulations. The notification scheme was also simplified, and the degree of reporting was made comparable with the level required for a hazard survey under the proposed British Regulations.

The Minister summed up the changes:

"There is no doubt that implementation of the original draft Directive would have greatly increased the commitment of resources by both industry and the HSE. Under the revised proposals this increase in commitment will be far less than originally expected and the more selective nature of the proposals should make for greater uniformity of enforcement by Member States".

The Minister also explained that the government was troubled by the use of the word environment and believed that the Directive should be confined to substances directly affecting man. As will be seen below, the retention of the word environment may well come to have a considerable effect on British administration.

A significant change to the Directive made after the House of Commons' debate, at the insistence of the German government, gives to Member States the right to waive the requirement that manufacturers must submit a hazard survey for existing plant.

Another significant change to the original proposal is that manufacturers do not have to inform people working at the installation and people outside of potential **risks,** but only of safety measures and of the behaviour to adopt in the event of an accident.

The original proposal made no mention of the transfrontier responsibilities of the Member States, and it seems that the provision to be found in the version submitted to the House of Commons in June 1980 was inserted at the insistence of the Benelux countries. In that version the provision read as follows:

> "Where a Member State considers that there is a major accident hazard due to an industrial activity carried out within its territory and notified in accordance with this Directive, affecting persons and/or the environment in one or more Member States, it shall forward to the latter all appropriate information.
>
> "The Member States concerned shall consult on the measures required to prevent major accidents and to limit their effects on man and the environment."

A new article in broadly similar terms was published by the Commission as a formal amendment to the original proposal five months later – COM(80)747 – in response to the Resolution of the European Parliament (OJ C175 14.7.80). It is possible that without the pressure of the Parliament the proposed article would not have survived at all since it was not acceptable to the French government. The formula eventually agreed after a long delay requires information to be made available between Member States 'within the framework of their bilateral relations' and means that the Commission does not have the same right to insist on implementation as it would have had otherwise. It also means that other Member States have no rights at all.

Formal Compliance in the UK

Until the government sends its letter of compliance to the Commission (due by 8th January 1984) one can only speculate as to how the Directive will formally be complied with.

The Health and Safety at Work etc Act 1974 places a general duty on employers to secure the health, safety and welfare of persons at work and provides for the protection of the public from work activities. It also provides, in cases to be prescribed, that an employer is obliged to give prescribed information both to his employees and to other persons whose health or safety may be affected. The Act is not concerned with the protection of the environment.

The Act established the Health and Safety Commission (HSC), consisting of seven to ten persons (representing employers, employees, and local authorities) and the Health and Safety Executive (HSE) to exercise certain of the HSC's functions. The HSC has the power to propose regulations to the Secretary of State and the duty to consult certain bodies before proposing them.

We have already seen how in 1978, before the Directive was formally

227

proposed, the HSC had issued a consultative document (2) with draft Hazardous Installations (Notification and Survey) Regulations. These would have required information to be supplied about activities involving significant quantities of hazardous substances and also the preparation of hazard surveys where more substantial quantities were involved.[*] The consultation process was complete and draft Regulations were ready to be laid before Parliament in January 1980 when a decision was taken not to proceed before the Directive was agreed. This was because the Regulations were not entirely consistent with it. Negotiations over the Directive were so prolonged because of the dispute over the transfrontier provisions that in September 1981 a decision was taken to proceed independently of the Directive with Regulations restricted to information about activities involving hazardous substances but omitting the need for the hazard survey. These were the Notification of Installations Handling Hazardous Substances Regulations 1982 (SI 1982 No 1357) made under the Health and Safety at Work Act. One of the pressures for their introduction was a proposal to amend planning legislation so that a manufacturer would require specific planning permission before changing an existing process to one using hazardous substances in excess of a certain quantity. The Regulations now provide a definition of the substances and quantities for planning purposes. The proposal to amend planning legislation stemmed from the reports of the Advisory Committee on Major Hazards (1,3) and are not required to implement the Directive.

Since these Regulations (SI 1982 No 1357) list fewer substances than the Directive they do not fully implement that part of the Directive requiring the supply of information about substances.

In September 1983 the HSE issued a consultation document with draft Regulations designed fully to implement the Directive but to go no further. The intention is that these should then be laid before Parliament early in 1984 and should come into operation shortly thereafter, although probably a little after the due date of 8th January. These Regulations will:

- extend the requirements about information relating to substances to all the substances listed in the Directive at the specified quantities;
- make hazard surveys mandatory (no waivers are to be given beyond 8th July 1989);
- require on-site emergency plans;
- place a duty on local authorities to prepare 'off-site' emergency plans;
- require appropriate information to be provided to the public.

Whereas the HSE will be the competent authority to receive and check the 'notifications', the county councils will be appointed competent authorities for the purpose of preparing 'off-site' emergency plans, for the reason that they already prepare emergency plans in connection with other matters. Although there is no legislation specifically giving any central government department or Minister power to compel a county council to prepare the kind of emergency plan envisaged by the Directive, county coun-

---

[*] In the British Regulations the word 'notification' is limited to information about installations handling specified hazardous substances. It is not used to cover hazard surveys and emergency plans as it is in the language of the Directive.

cils do already have appropriate staff and in 1975 received central government advice in Home Office Circular ES7/75 on 'Major accidents and natural disasters' (also issued by the DOE as DOE Circular 80/75). To implement the Directive fully the county councils will have to have a duty placed on them to prepare emergency plans rather than doing so in response to advice, and this duty will be placed on them under the European Communities Act 1972.

The Directive requires manufacturers - under the supervision of the competent authorities - to limit the consequences of any major accident on the environment as well as man. Since under the Health and Safety at Work Act the responsibility of the HSE extends only to effects on man, it will be necessary for the duty and the power to consider environmental effects to be placed on the HSE. This significant extension of the powers of the HSE will be done under the European Communities Act 1972.

Effect on UK Practice

The effect of the Directive so far in Britain has been:

- to delay the introduction of the Regulations requiring notification and hazard surveys;
- to require fewer hazard surveys than previously intended;
- to require a duty to be placed on local authorities to prepare 'off-site' emergency plans relating to specified installations;
- to require information to be made available to the public relating to specified installations;
- to require the powers and duties of the HSE to be extended to embrace effects on the environment as well as on man.

In the absence of the Directive the draft Hazardous Installations (Notification and Survey) Regulations should have come into effect some time in 1980 and hazard surveys would by now have been mandatory. The Regulations that are now expected early in 1984 will not only be later in date but are likely to contain a later date by which hazard surveys have to be prepared for existing plant than originally envisaged. This delay is because the Directive sets a final date of 8th July 1989 for hazard surveys and industry has been able to argue that it should not be pressed harder than the Directive presses its competitors abroad.

The whole delay cannot however be attributed to the Directive although the Directive will have provided the occasion for the delay. Thus it will be over a year after the Directive was adopted (June 1982) before the issuing by HSC of a consultative document with draft Regulations, and this time will have been taken up with negotiations within government departments about the form of the regulations needed to implement the Directive and within the HSC on whether or not they should go further than the Directive as originally intended in 1978. During the four years between the original draft Regulations and agreement on the Directive the economic climate had deteriorated so that it became that much more difficult to resist the arguments of industrialists that they should go no further than required by the Directive.

The reason the Directive will require fewer hazard surveys than the

Regulations proposed in 1979 is that these Regulations would have covered more installations storing hazardous substances. It is true that the Directive lists more substances than the proposed Regulations so that some extra installations will be covered, but many of the substances listed are not used in Britain. It is the intention of the HSE that further regulations will eventually require hazard surveys for storage installations not covered by the Directive.

The procedural requirements of the Directive are not signficantly different from what would have been required in Britain in the absence of the Directive except for the duty to be placed on county Councils to prepare 'off-site' emergency plans, the duty to inform the public, and the duty on the HSE to consider environmental effects. The 'off-site' emergency plans will now have to be prepared for all the specified activities, and not all might have been covered under the non-mandatory arrangements that have prevailed hitherto and that would have continued in the absence of the Directive. In this respect the Directive will have strengthened the British system.

The charge is sometimes made - more often in countries other than in Britain - that Community legislation is the lowest common denominator of that in all Member States. The discussion of the environmental Directives in this study gives no support to this charge, but the Seveso Directive is one instance where proposed British legislation has been weakened by the delay occasioned by the Directive. It is an irony that the reason for the delay - the inability of the French government to accept the earlier transfrontier provisions - concerned a matter of little concern to Britain.

The very same Directive that will have weakened one aspect of proposed British legislation will also have stretched the duties of the HSE to include consideration of the environment. If a Royal Commission, say, or the DOE had recommended that the duties of the HSE be extended in this way, it is highly unlikely that a change would have been made, in the absence of some evident disaster, before very many years had passed. Community legislation is not constrained by the parliamentary timetable and the inertia entailed, but is subject instead to the pressure to reach agreement in the Council. The result is that Member States will sometimes find themselves having to accept changes, which may well be beneficial, which would not have occurred under purely national procedures.

References

(1) Health and Safety Commission, **Advisory Committee on Major Hazards: First Report,** HMSO, 1976.

(2) Health and Safety Commission, **Consultative Document - Hazardous Installations (Notification and Survey) Regulations 1978,** HMSO, 1978.

(3) Health and Safety Commission, **Advisory Committee on Major Hazards: Second Report,** HMSO, 1979.

10.4   Chlorofluorocarbons

80/372/EEC (OJ L90 3.4.80)
proposed 1979-COM(79)242

Decision concerning chlorofluorocarbons in the environment

82/795/EEC (OJ L329 25.11.82)
proposed 8.10.81-COM(81)558

Decision on the consolidation of
precautionary measures concerning
chlorofluorocarbons in the
environment

Binding dates
Notification date - 80/372:   31 March 1980
Notification date - 82/795:   19 November 1982
30% reduction in aerosol use
compared with 1976:   31 December 1981

Purpose of the Decisions

Chlorofluorocarbons (CFCs) are relatively non-toxic and non-
flammable gases used as propellants in aerosol spray cans, in refrigeration
and air conditioning plants, as solvents, and in the manufacture of
polyurethane foam. Some research suggests that the release of CFCs could
result in the destruction of ozone in the stratosphere thus increasing
ultraviolet radiation reaching the earth. If this is so, it could result in an
increase in the incidence of skin cancer and could also affect vegetation and
eco-systems, e.g., oceanic plankton which forms a fundamental part of the
food chain. As a precautionary measure the Decisions seek to limit the
production of CFCs and reduce their use in aerosols which, in Europe,
accounts for about 65% of production.

Summary of the Decisions

Decision 80/372 places a duty on Member States to take all appropriate
measures to ensure that industry situated in their territories does not
increase production capacity of two types of CFCs known as F-11 and F-12.
In addition, Member States were to ensure that by 31st December 1981
industry situated in their territories achieved a 30% reduction in the use of
CFCs in aerosol cans as compared with 1976 levels.

The measures taken were to be re-examined in 1980 in the light of the
scientific and economic data available and Member States were to provide
the Commission with the results of any study or research available to them.
The Council was to adopt such further measures as were necessary by 30th
June 1981.

Decision 82/795 was the result of this re-examination. It repeats the
obligation of Decision 80/372 not to increase production capacity but adds a
definition of production capacity and a reference figure of Community CFC

231

production (480,000 tonnes per year of F-11 and F-12 by the ten producers in the Community at March 1980).

Member States are to facilitate the periodic collection by the Commission of statistical information, and are to co-operate with the Commission in action aimed at reducing CFC losses and developing the best practicable technologies in order to limit emissions in the synthetic foam, refrigeration and solvent sectors.

There is to be a further re-examination not later than 30th June 1983 and the Council is to adopt such further measures as may be necessary not later than 31st December 1983 (see below).

Development of the First Decision

The hypothesis was first advanced in 1974 that the release of CFCs could result in depletion of the ozone layer. Theoretical studies then suggested that the continual release of CFCs at 1973 rates would result in ozone destruction until a steady state would eventually be reached in more than 50 years' time with a predicted reduction of between 6% and 18% (1). Scientific work continues and although the reduction predicted has tended to decrease, the hypothesis cannot immediately be disproved since the calculated reductions to date are very close to or less than the limit of detection.

In October 1976 the USA began to place a ban on non-essential uses of CFCs as aerosol propellants - the ban becoming fully effective in 1979. In August 1977 the Commission proposed a Recommendation, and in May 1978 the Council adopted it as a Resolution (C133 7.6.78) calling for a limitation on production. This was then followed by an intergovernmental meeting held in Munich in December 1978 which recommended precautionary measures to reduce global releases of CFCs.

It was thus against a background of international concern that a proposal for a Decision was made in 1979. There was a heated debate in the European Parliament since the report of its Committee on the Environment, Public Health and Consumer Protection had argued for a reduction of 50% - instead of the 30% proposed by the Commission - in aerosol use by December 1981 and a total ban (except for essential medical purposes) by December 1983. In the result the Parliament endorsed the Commission's proposal and turned down the more stringent proposals of its own Committee.

The House of Commons' Scrutiny Committee noted that in Britain an agreement not to increase production of CFCs already existed and that their use in aerosols was already declining. It also recorded that British industry appeared generally to accept the proposal while maintaining that the scientific evidence was not sufficient to justify large changes. The DoE in an explanatory memorandum to the Scrutiny Committee said that before agreement could be reached on the proposal they needed to be satisfied that any scheme for reporting data should preserve the commercial confidentiality of manufacturers. This may explain the deletion from the proposal of a requirement that Member States should supply the Commission with data on aerosol use. (To overcome this difficulty an arrangement has now been made - see COM(81)261 below.)

The Decision also differed from the proposal in being restricted to the two types of CFCs known as F-11 and F-12.

Development of the Second Decision

Between the first and second Decisions the Commission submitted a total of five communications to the Council: two in fulfilment of the obligation to re-examine the measures taken in the light of the scientific and economic data available, one proposing the second Decision, one proposing that the Commission should participate in the negotiations for a global convention on protection of the ozone layer, and a further one reporting progress.

The first communication - COM(80)339 (16.6.80) - reviewed the scientific work carried out in the USA and UK and concluded that uncertainty still remained. It also reported a 6.8% drop in Community production of CFCs between 1976 and 1979, a 22.8% drop in sales for aerosols, but a 32.3% increase for foam plastic. The UK was reported to be the largest producer in the Community of aerosol units, having actually increased output between 1975 and 1978. In 1974 68% of UK aerosol units were filled with CFCs and 30% with hydrocarbons. The Communication also reviewed CFC substitution and pointed to the substantial capital investment entailed in converting to hydrocarbons because of the extensive safety precautions required. It also concluded that a reduction in aerosol use much beyond 30% would be likely to cause socio-economic problems because of existing overcapacity in the industry.

The second communication - COM(81)261 (26.5.81) - made four recommendations for action at Community level:

(a) maintaining and consolidating the precautionary measures of the first Decision;
(b) an improvement in the collection of scientific, technical and economic data;
(c) engagement in projects together with the industry concerned designed to decrease CFC emission in other sectors than aerosol filling;
(d) measures at an international level.

The communication revealed that there were about 400 commercial concerns engaged in filling aerosol cans in the Community with 70 of these accounting for 80% of all fillings. Half of these locations were not equipped to handle flammable propellants and 80% of these were not suitable for conversion.

To improve the collection of statistics on CFC production and use the Commission proposed to formalise a system under which producers supplied data to an independent auditor (a UK firm of chartered accountants) who aggregated them while keeping confidential the figures for individual producers.

The third communication - COM(81)558 (8.10.81) - proposed the second Decision and recorded that the Council meeting of 11th June 1981 had endorsed the four recommendations of COM(81)261. The fourth communication - COM(81)734 (30.11.81) - proposed a Council Decision authorising the Commission to participate in the negotiations for a global convention on the protection of the ozone layer being drafted under the auspices of UNEP (United Nations' Environment Programme).

The fifth communication - COM(82)307 (7.6.82) - was a general progress report. The scientific uncertainties were said to remain and no change in the precautionary policy was recommended. It recorded that total Community CFC production between 1976 and 1981 was down 8.1% and that the 30% target reduction in CFCs in aerosols has been achieved for the Community as a whole - though without giving percentage reductions for individual Member States. It noted a significant increase in use of CFC in sectors other than aerosol fillings. It outlined an action programme in the sectors of refrigeration, foam plastics and solvents. It also recorded that on 19.1.82 the Council had authorised the Commission to participate on behalf of the Community in the negotiations on the global convention.

The second Decision differed from the proposal by omitting a requirement that Member States should ensure that industries did not increase CFC use for aerosols above the 1981 levels. Press reports (2) have suggested that this deletion was made because it would have penalised those industries that had cut back most.

Formal Compliance in the UK

Unlike most Directives a Decision does not require Member States to report to the Commission on the laws or other measures used to implement it formally.

The CFC Decisions leave to Member States how the duties placed on them are to be carried out and in Britain (as in most Member States apparently) the targets have been reached by voluntary agreement with the industry.

Effect on UK Practice

Since hydrocarbons are cheaper than CFCs there are commercial reasons for aerosol manufacturers to use the cheaper propellant, but pulling in the other direction is the better spray produced by CFCs and the reduced risk of fire which entails less expensive safety equipment in the factory. Even before the possible threat to the ozone layer was considered, hydrocarbons were widely used in aerosols particularly for water based household products, with CFCs being used for alcohol based cosmetic, medical and industrial products. Some manufacturers blended CFCs with hydrocarbons.

The world-wide concern about the ozone layer - which the EEC Decisions reflected - prompted manufacturers to look at alternatives to safeguard their operations and many of the larger manufacturers then invested in the safety equipment required for hydrocarbons. In some cases this investment has paid off already. By and large the medium sized and smaller manufacturers did not make the switch.

The result was that the 30% reduction of the Decisions was achieved, but it is difficult to say that the reduction was achieved because of the Decisions. The Decisions reflected the scientific concern, and simultaneous concern in the industry about the possibility of compulsion had already stimulated the industry to take certain measures. In fact there is reason to believe that the figure of 30% was chosen because it was known that it could be achieved without creating too much difficulty for the industry. Nevertheless the Community legislation was a formalised

234

response to the scientific concern and provided a definite percentage reduction and a date by which it had to be achieved. It made action obligatory and has prevented any backsliding.

The economic recession has depressed consumer demand so that in 1983 the market has been fairly steady. If because of an economic upturn or for any other reason sales of aerosols were to increase significantly, then the likely way that the Decision would have to be adhered to would be for the smaller manufacturers who are still using CFCs to switch to hydrocarbons. This may cause some of them difficulties. As with any overall limit questions of equity arise in allocating quotas.

The Decisions provide the first example in Britain of a limit on the total emission of a particular substance achieved, in this instance, by a limit on total production. A limit to the total emissions of lead from motor car exhausts had been agreed earlier in Britain (see Section 9.3), but that did not cover other sources of air pollution by lead.

Further Developments

On 31st May 1983 the Commission submitted a communication to the Council - COM(83)284 - which reexamined the position and recommended no change in policy. This was accepted by the Council in June 1983. The communication reported that the UNEP Co-ordinating Committee on the Ozone Layer (CCOL) had estimated eventual reductions in the ozone column attributable to CFC 11 and 12 of about 3 to 5% (compared to 5 to 10% the previous CCOL report). Use in aerosols in the Community was 37% below the level of 1976 and production had declined. The communication discussed various codes of practice for preventing escape of CFCs when used for refrigeration, solvents, and rigid and flexible foam plastics. It was expected that the relevant trade associations would provide the Commission with written acceptance of the codes.

References

(1) Department of the Environment, **Chlorofluorocarbons and their Effect on Stratospheric Ozone,** Pollution Paper No 15, HMSO 1979.

(2) Environmental Data Services Ltd (ENDS) Report No 95, December 1982.

10.5 Pesticides and Plant Protection Products

Pesticides and other plant protection products are covered by the following three groups of Directives which are listed for completeness and without a full discussion*. In addition pesticides are incidentally covered by several other Directives dealing with, e.g., water pollution and waste disposal. Pesticides are mainly controlled in Britain by the non-statutory Pesticides Safety Precautions Scheme formally agreed between the British government and the agrochemical industry, and it is under this Scheme that the following Directives are largely implemented. The Pesticides Safety Precautions Scheme may have to be reviewed following a letter of intent dated 23rd February 1983 from the Commission to the British Agrochemical Association saying that their code of practice - which forms an important part of the Scheme - infringes Article 85 of the Treaty of Rome concerned with the rules of competition. A European Parliamentary Question (OJ C218 23.8.82) revealed that the Scheme itself was being considered by the Commission in the light of Articles 30 and 36 of the Treaty.

1) 76/895/EEC (OJ L340 19.12.76)	Directive relating to the fixing of maximum levels for pesticide residues in and on fruit and vegetables
80/428/EEC (OJ L102 19.4.80)	(Amendment)
81/36/EEC (OJ L46 19.2.81)	(Amendment)
82/528/EEC (OJ L234 9.8.82)	(Amendment)
2) 78/631/EEC (OJ L206 29.7.78)	Directive on the approximation of the laws of the Member States relating to the classification, packaging and labelling of dangerous preparations (pesticides)
81/187/EEC (OJ L77 2.4.81)	(Amendment)
3) 79/117/EEC (OJ L33 8.2.79)	Directive prohibiting the placing on the market and use of plant protection products containing certain active substances
83/131/EEC (OJ L91 9.4.83)	(Amendment)

---

* The effect of the Directives will form part of a study of British pesticide policy being undertaken by David Gilbert of the Centre for Environmental Technology, Imperial College, who has supplied the summary of the Directives included here.

Summary of the Directives

1. 76/895 – Pesticide Residues

Maximum residue limits are laid down for particular pesticides for certain specified fruit and vegetables.   Member States may not prohibit the marketing of fruit and vegetables on the grounds that they contain pesticides if these do not exceed the specified limits.   (Residue limits do not have to be enforced.   In Britain they are not enforced, but the recommendations for the use of pesticides, and the harvesting intervals, of the Pesticides Safety Precautions Scheme are designed to ensure that residue levels do not create a risk to human health.   Food quality in Britain is controlled under the Food and Drugs Act 1955).

2. 78/631 – Classification, Packaging and Labelling

Pesticides in the form in which they are supplied to the user are to be classified as 'very toxic', 'toxic', or 'harmful'.   Packaging and labelling requirements are specified.   Pesticides are not to be marketed unless they comply with the Directive.   Member States may not prohibit the marketing of pesticides on the grounds of classification, packaging and labelling if they satisfy the requirements of the Directive.   The Directive refers to Directive 67/548 now amended by 79/831 (see Section 10.1).

3. 79/117 – Prohibition on Use

Member States are to ensure that plant protection products (including products intended to destroy undesired plants) containing the substances listed in an Annex may not be marketed or used.   The Annex lists five mercury compounds and eight persistent organochlorine compounds (DDT, aldrin, dieldrin, endrin, chlordane, HCH, heptachlor, hexachlorobenzene).   However, by way of derogation, Member States may permit the use of the products in certain cases specified in the Annex, but in such cases they must inform the other Member States and the Commission.

No exceptions are made from the ban on chlordane in the Directive, but in reply to a European Parliamentary Question (OJ C225 3.8.82) the Commissioner explained that preparations containing chlordane used for the control of earthworms responsible for depositing casts on the surface of high quality turf are not plant protection products within the meaning of the Directive.   They are presumably protecting 'grass' meaning a lawn and not 'grass' meaning a plant.

In June 1982 the Commission issued a communication to the Council (OJ C170 8.7.82) which concluded that on the basis of existing scientific evidence a Community-wide ban on the marketing and use of 2,4,5-T herbicides in the context of Directive 79/117 would not be justified.   The Commission recommended instead various precautionary measures.

237

CHAPTER 11
Wildlife and Countryside

11.0   Relevant British Legislation

Whereas the Community has made a significant entry into the field of protecting fauna with the Directive on birds (Section 11.1) and Regulation on whales (Section 11.2), its only connection with the protection of flora is as a consequence of its involvement with certain international Conventions (Section 11.3).   There is also no legislation forming part of the Community's environmental policy concerned with landscape or countryside protection, although Directive 75/268 on farming in less favoured areas (Section 11.4) which forms part of the agricultural policy does include countryside protection among its objectives.   This description therefore covers only a small part of British legislation on the subject.

The first Act protecting certain species of birds was passed in 1869 and the number of species protected has been extended several times, most recently in the Wildlife and Countryside Act 1981 which has consolidated much previous legislation.   The 1981 Act protects certain animals in addition to birds, but also protects species of flora and provides powers to protect habitats.   The relevant aspects of this comprehensive Act are described in connection with the birds Directive (Section 11.1).

In Britain, unlike some other European countries, a distinction is made in the machinery of government administration between the protection of nature and the protection of landscape.   Nature protection is the responsibility of the Nature Conservancy Council (NCC) which was formed under the Nature Conservancy Council Act 1973 out of the former Nature Conservancy.   The powers of the NCC to declare national nature reserves are contained in the National Parks and Access to the Countryside Act 1949 which also made it possible to declare Sites of Special Scientific Interest (SSSIs) for the purpose of drawing attention to land of "special interest by virtue of its flora, fauna, or geological or physiological features..."   The powers to designate SSSIs are now contained in the Wildlife and Countryside Act 1981 and it is the NCC that carries out this function.

The control of international trade in endangered species is now consolidated in the Endangered Species (Import and Export) Act 1976.   This requires a licence for the import and export of almost all wild flora and fauna, and although it does not itself ban any trade it is possible for the licensing authority (which is the Department of the Environment) to withhold licences and thus achieve the same effect.

The government agency responsible for landscape beauty and amenity is the Countryside Commission (CC), which became a corporate body in 1982 under the Wildlife and Countryside Act 1981.   The CC was created under the Countryside Act 1968 to replace the former National Parks Commission. Among its other functions the CC designates national parks and areas of outstanding natural beauty.

Although most agricultural developments are outside the controls available to local authorities under the Town and Country Planning Act 1971, these controls nevertheless have a role in protecting habitats and landscape from certain forms of development.

11.1   Birds and their Habitats

79/409/EEC (OJ L103 25.4.79)	Directive on the conservation
proposed 20.12.1976-COM(76)676	of wild birds

Binding dates
Notification date: 6 April 1979
Formal compliance: 6 April 1981
First annual report on
   derogations relating to
   capture and killing: 6 April 1982*
First three-yearly report: 6 April 1984

Purpose of the Directive

The Directive arose out of public disquiet at the annual slaughter of migratory birds that was common in southern Europe, but goes further in providing a general system of protection for all species of wild birds found in Europe. Not only does it seek to control the hunting and killing of wild birds and to protect their eggs and nests, but it also requires the provision of a sufficient diversity and area of habitats so as to maintain the population of all species. Some species found in Europe are said to be in danger of extinction and the populations of others have been falling.

Summary of the Directive

(1) General Obligations

A general duty is placed on Member States to maintain the population of all "species of naturally occurring birds in the wild state" in the European territory "at a level which corresponds in particular to ecological, scientific and cultural requirements, while taking account of economic and recreational requirements".

Member States are to preserve, maintain or re-establish a sufficient diversity and area of habitats for birds. This is to be done primarily by creating protected areas, managing habitats both inside and outside protected areas, and re-establishing destroyed biotopes and creating new ones.

Member States are to lay down a general system of protection for all species of wild birds, although exceptions are made for hunting and for certain other reasons. In particular the following are prohibited:

- deliberate killing or capture by any method;
- deliberate destruction of, or damage to, their nests and eggs or removal of nests;

---

*   This is to assume that the first year starts with the date for compliance rather than the notification date. The Directive is unclear.

- taking eggs in the wild and keeping them even if empty;
- deliberate disturbance particularly during breeding and rearing;
- keeping birds whose hunting and capture is prohibited.

(2) Special Measures Concerning Habitats

Annex I lists 74 particularly vulnerable species which are to be the subject of special conservation measures concerning their habitat in order to ensure their survival and reproduction in their area of distribution. Member States are to classify the most suitable territories (both land and sea) as special protection areas for the conservation of these species. Similar measures are to be taken for regularly occurring migratory species not listed in Annex I. Particular attention is to be paid to the protection of wetlands.

Member States are to send the Commission information about the measures they have taken so that the Commission can ensure that these form a coherent whole.

Member States are to strive generally to avoid pollution or deterioration of habitats, but in respect of the special protection areas they are to take appropriate steps to avoid pollution or deterioration of habitats or any disturbances affecting the birds in so far as these are significant to the objectives set out for habitat protection.

(3) Hunting and Killing

The 72 species listed in **Annex II** may be hunted under national legislation, but Member States are to ensure that hunting does not jeopardise conservation efforts.

Annex II is in two parts. The 24 species in Annex II/1 may be hunted anywhere, but the 48 species in Annex II/2 may be hunted only in the Member States indicated in the Annex.

Member States are to ensure that hunting complies with the principles of wise use and ecologically balanced control of the species concerned. In particular, Member States are to ensure that birds are not hunted during the rearing season nor during the various stages of reproduction. Migratory birds are in addition not to be hunted during their return to their rearing grounds.

Member States are to send the Commission all relevant information on the practical application of their hunting regulations.

The methods of killing birds listed in **Annex IV(a)** are to be prohibited. These include snares, explosives, nets, use of blind or mutilated live birds as decoys, and semi-automatic or automatic weapons with a magazine capable of using more than two rounds of ammunition. **Annex IV(b)** prohibits hunting from aircraft, motor vehicles and boats driven at more than five kilometres per hour (an exception to the speed limit can apply in the open sea for safety reasons).

Member States may derogate from the prohibitions on killing or capture, where there is no other satisfactory solution, for the following reasons:

- in the interest of public health and safety;
- in the interest of air safety;
- to prevent serious damage to crops, livestock, forests, fisheries and water;
- for the protection of flora and fauna;
- for the purposes of research and teaching;

242

- for repopulation or reintroduction;
- to permit, under strictly supervised conditions and on a selective basis, the capture, keeping or other judicious use of certain birds in small numbers.

An annual report of these derogations must be submitted to the Commission which must ensure that they are compatible with the Directive. Derogations must specify: the species; the authorised methods for killing or capture; the time and place; the conditions of risk; the authority empowered to declare that the conditions obtain and to decide what methods may be used, within what limits and by whom; and the controls.

(4) Restriction on Sale

Sale of the species included in Annex I (including the transport, keeping, or offering, for sale) is to be prohibited. This prohibition is to extend to live or dead birds and to any recognisable parts or derivatives of such birds. Sale of the seven species of birds listed in **Annex III/1** is not prohibited provided the birds have been legally killed or captured or otherwise legally acquired. A further 10 species listed in **Annex III/2** may also be exempted from this prohibition by Member States who must first consult the Commission. If the Commission believes that sale of any of these species will result in it being endangered the Commission is to forward a reasoned recommendation to the Member State. If the Commission believes there is no such risk it must say so. The Commission's recommendation is to be published in the Official Journal.

A further nine species listed in **Annex III/3** are to be the subject of further studies by the Commission with a view to inclusion in Annex III/2. The Commission's report was due by 6th December 1980.

(5) Other Provisions

Every three years Member States are to forward a report on the implementation of national provisions taken to comply with the Directive. In its turn, the Commission is to prepare a composite report and the part of the draft report covering information supplied by a Member State is to be verified by the authorities in that Member State. The final version of the report is to be sent to the Member States but it does not have to be sent to the Parliament and thus made public.

Member States are to encourage research and any work required as a basis for protection and management of birds. Particular attention is to be paid to research on the subjects listed in **Annex V**. The Commission is to co-ordinate research.

Member States are to see that the introduction of species of bird which do not occur naturally does not prejudice the local flora and fauna. They are to consult the Commission.

Member States may introduce stricter protective measures than those provided for under the Directive.

A committee is established for adapting Annexes I and V to technical and scientific progress.

The Resolution

On the same day that the Directive was adopted (2nd April 1979) the Council also passed a Resolution (OJ C103 25.4.79) calling upon the Member

States to notify the Commission within two years of (a) the special protection areas which they had classified under the Directive, (b) the wetlands which they had designated or intended to designate as wetlands of international importance, and (c) any other areas classified according to national legislation for bird protection. The Commission was to draw up a list of these areas and keep it up to date. The Resolution noted the Commission's intention of submitting proposals regarding the criteria for determining the special protection areas.

Development of the Directive

The Directive stemmed from the public disquiet at the annual slaughter of migratory birds that has been customary in southern Europe and northern Africa. As early as 1971 questions were being asked in the European Parliament (OJ C119 26.11.71) with suggestions for Community legislation, and this disquiet was reflected in the first Action Programme on the Environment of 1973: "Hundreds of millions of migratory birds and songbirds are captured and killed in Europe every year provoking worldwide protests against the countries which allow the trapping of birds".

The Action Programme proposed a study with a view to possible harmonization of national regulations on the protection of animal species and migratory birds in particular. The Programme promised action by the end of 1974.

In the autumn of 1974 the European Parliament received a petition (No 8/74) from national and international animal protection organisations under the title 'Save the Migratory Birds'. This called for an international conference to investigate the problem at a bicontinental (European-African) level and recommended a halt to the hunting of birds until the results of the conference were known. This petition resulted in the adoption of a resolution by the Parliament on 21st February 1975 calling in particular for a general prohibition on the trapping of wild birds with nets but also recommending the preservation of certain species and the creation of suitable breeding grounds.

On 9th February 1976 - already over a year behind the date set in the Action Programme - the Commission replied to an oral question in the Parliament explaining the guidelines which the draft Directive was to follow: there was to be a general system for the protection of wild birds comprising the prohibition of killing and trapping and of trade in birds both dead and alive, followed by exceptions (e.g., for game birds).

An early draft of a proposed Directive dated 12th May 1976 became public and was attached to another petition (No 10/76) presented to the Parliament in August 1976. This draft was criticised in a debate (15th October 1976) for allowing hunting of certain species (certain larks, thrushes and finches) - a point that was to cause trouble later - and in reply a Commissioner explained that the published draft was only one document of many and that no definite position had been taken. He stressed the complexity of the problem and that the emotive atmosphere surrounding it obliged the Commission to be scrupulously careful in preparing its proposals.

Meanwhile the Commission had conducted studies and consulted experts and its proposed Directive eventually published in December 1976 turned out to be much more comprehensive than the Parliament had ever suggested.

The Parliament debated it on 14th June - one day before the Council was due to discuss the proposal - but it took a further 18 months for important points of detail and a major point of conflict to be resolved. This conflict was the desire of Italy and France to allow hunting of the skylark (Alauda arvensis) and the ortolan bunting, and before agreement could be secured the Council had to insert the skylark into Annex II/2 - but not the ortolan bunting.

Both the Economic and Social Committee and the European Parliament welcomed the Directive. Not all their proposed amendments were reflected in the final Directive.

In Britain the Directive was not considered in the House of Lords but was the subject of two reports from the Scrutiny Committee of the House of Commons leading to a debate.

In preparing its first report the Commons' Scrutiny Committee took evidence from the DOE, from organisations representing shooting interests, landowners, the Nature Conservancy Council and the Royal Society for the Protection of Birds (RSPB). The RSPB claimed that the Directive was based to a large extent on British legislation (in the drafting of which they had had a hand in the 1920s although it was not enacted until 1954) and indeed it follows the British pattern of providing general protection for all wild birds, providing extra protection for some, and allowing the killing of others.

The first report of the Scrutiny Committee noted that all organisations consulted were generally in favour of the Directive but said that several matters needed further consideration, including the needs of game bird management, the restriction on the sale of dead birds, provision for falconry, and the control of birds for airfield clearance. It drew attention to the undesirability of attempting to impose uniform conditions of bird protection throughout the Community.

In the second report the Scrutiny Committee noted that most of these points had been met by promised amendments. It noted that the DOE held that uniform conditions of bird conservation throughout Europe would be of great benefit, but that the derogation procedure had been amended to allow Member States autonomy to take action in the interests of public health and safety, aircraft safety and agricultural pest control.

In the Commons' debate (17th November 1977) the Minister, Kenneth Marks, explained that the government had consistently expressed strong support for the principles of the Directive, while seeking a number of detailed changes in its provisions. He was able to report that having consulted a wide range of interests the government had been able to reach agreement on the amendments that should be sought. He outlined the amendments under discussion and reported that the Directive was likely to emerge in a form even closer to present British legislation, so that few amendments would be required to the Protection of Birds Acts.

Although the Minister only made the point guardedly other MPs took the opportunity to claim national credit. Peter Mills said:

> "I think too that as we in Britain look at the draft
> Directive we can congratulate ourselves as a nation,
> because most of the Directive follows closely the general
> framework of the United Kingdom legislation on the
> protection of birds....I only wish that other countries - I
> mention Italy as one, and the southern Mediterranean
> area - had the same concern that we have had over the

years. I think that we can pat ourselves on the back for
our legislation and for the fact that it is a pattern for the
Community."

Peter Hardy made a similar point, touching simultaneously on the question of
habitat protection:

"I am not always enthusiastic about many of the
Directives that we have to consider, but I do believe that
this one is especially welcome. That is because it is
relevant to the interests of many and is broadly similar to
our own legislation. It may - perhaps rightly - put a
little more stress on habitat than our own legislation, but
by and large it is acceptable. I am delighted that it will
not require anything but minor amendment to our own
legislation."

Concern about habitat protection had been raised in the Scrutiny
Committee when DOE officials gave oral evidence but did not feature in the
Scrutiny Committee's report. The Chairman, Peter Mills, put it like this in a
question:

"Could we turn to the important point about the
maintenance of habitats. The agriculturalists and
landowners say there is going to be further interference
in their use of agricultural land. What is the
Department's view on this and what is the possibility of
compensation?"

In reply the responsible DOE official played down the concern:

"I do not see the Directive making a great deal of
difference in this respect for this reason....We do it
through the work of the Nature Conservancy Council
which has national nature reserves, sites of special
scientific interest, and through the work of voluntary
bodies such as the RSPB, the Wildfowl Trust and the
WAGBI. They all have nature reserves, so that they are
in the business of protecting habitats already. We would
not see this Directive as imposing any greater obligation
in the UK than we are already doing."

On being pressed further he continued:

"Clearly the debate has to go on between agricultural and
conservation interests as to how one marries the needs of
agriculture with the needs of conservation. What I am
saying is that I do not think there is anything in this
Directive which tilts the balance. I think as far as this
Directive is concerned, what we are doing already in
terms of the protection of habitats would more than meet
the requirements of what is in here. We shall certainly,

though, want to continue to have the debate with the agricultural and other interests as to where the balance should be struck as between nature conservation and certain farming practices."

The Commons' debate hardly touched on habitat protection - which was to cause such dissension during the passage of the Wildlife and Countryside Act 1981 - but otherwise many incisive points were made. Neville Sandelson put his finger on a key aspect of Community environmental policy:

"I stress the extent to which the Directive shows how the Community is often able to achieve internal advances that are beyond the internal capability of individual Governments. No amount of pressure over many years on particular Member States which have been the principal offenders in permitting the indiscriminate slaughter of migratory birds has had any real effect. In spite of the efforts of all the bodies in this country - the Royal Society for the Protection of Birds and others - which have done so much valuable work in bringing these appalling circumstances to public and international attention, there has been very little effect before the Community itself stepped in. We have the culmination now in this very welcome draft Directive."

The Minister, Kenneth Marks, took this point one step further by recognising the ability of the Community to influence policy not only within Member States but outside the Community too:

"Of course it is desirable to extend the principles beyond the limits of the EEC. We are already involved in discussion in the Council of Europe and with the International Union for the Conservation of Nature about further conventions on this subject. We hope that Spain will take part in the conventions. However, these are some way off, and we cannot yet be sure how effective they will be.

"I am convinced that it is right to start at the Community level. Then we can use the Directive as the basis for these wider discussions, as our own Acts have been used as the basis for this Directive".

Formal Compliance in the UK

Notwithstanding the influence of the Protection of Birds Acts 1954-67 on the form of the Directive, some changes in legislation were necessary both in respect of habitat protection and relating to protection of birds themselves. These were made in the Wildlife and Countryside Act 1981 which received the Royal Assent more than six months after the date for formal compliance with the Directive (April 1981). In fact the sections

247

dealing with bird protection did not come into effect until September 1982 when the Protection of Birds Acts were repealed. Britain was not alone in being late and the Bulletin of the European Communities No 10-1981 records that the Commission had initiated infringement proceedings against the Federal Republic of Germany, Netherlands, Belgium, France, Italy and the UK. The proceedings against the UK were not proceeded with once it appeared that legislation was being introduced.

It is possible that the government would have introduced an Act dealing with countryside matters and wildlife habitats had there been no Directive if for no other reason than to implement the obligations of the Berne and Bonn Conventions (see Section 11.3), but the Directive ensured that existing bird protection legislation had to be amended. The RSPB were seeking to have the existing Acts amended and the Directive provided the opportunity. In fact rather few changes concerned with protection of species can be directly attributed to the Directive although these include (i) controls on taxidermy, (ii) a reduction in the number of species regarded as pests which may be killed at all times under licence, (iii) greater controls on the sale of dead birds, (iv) greater controls on the possession of eggs and birds and (v) the ban on killing using repeating shotguns, although these were probably not much used in Britain. The more significant changes brought about by the Act relevant to bird protection concern habitats, and Section 29 of the Act specifically refers to compliance with international obligations as a reason for the making of nature conservation orders. This can be taken as a reference to the Berne and Bonn Conventions (see Section 11.3) and Ramsar Convention of 1971 concerned with wetlands, as well as to the Directive. The combination of all these international obligations seems to have convinced the government that it would be best to have statutory powers for habitat protection and Section 29 cannot be attributed entirely to the Directive. Indeed a view held within government during negotiation on the Directive was that no extra powers for habitat protection were necessary.

On 31st August 1982, i.e., over one year late, the DOE wrote to the Commission in accordance with the Council Resolution of 2nd April 1979 notifying it of the steps taken to classify special protection areas under the Directive. This letter explained the types of protected area in Britain (national, local and voluntary nature reserves and sites of special scientific interest - SSSIs) and the power of the Secretary of State to make nature conservation orders. It also referred to the relevant legislation:

National Parks and Access to the Countryside Act 1949
Countryside Act 1968
Countryside (Scotland) Act 1967
Wildlife and Countryside Act 1981.

The letter explained that the government was now notifying as special protection areas those nature reserves which were safeguarded from development to the greatest extent by being owned by the Nature Conservancy Council. Seven areas were listed. The letter also explained that although a good number of the 4,000 SSSIs had been designated because of their importance to birds, not all were sufficiently safeguarded to meet the requirements of special protection areas. The government had earlier informed the Commission of 19 wetlands of international importance which

248

were covered by the Ramsar Convention but these are not classified as special protection areas for the purposes of the Directive. The Nature Conservancy Council (NCC) has drawn up a list - in fact based on a list prepared by RSPB - of more than 180 sites satisfying scientific criteria which enable them to be regarded as internationally important as regards birds, and it is apparently the intention of the government to classify at least some of these as special protection areas under the Directive. (The RSPB regard the seven sites classified so far as quite inadequate).

On 13th December 1982 the government sent the Commission a statement of how it believed each Article of the Directive was complied with. The habitat protection measures were those already submitted to the Commission, as described above, in accordance with the Council Resolution. All other Articles were said to be covered by the Wildlife and Countryside Act which extends to Scotland as well as England and Wales. An Order in Council for Northern Ireland should in due course cover the same subject matter.

The British legislation appears generally to fulfil the obligations of the Directive with doubt about its adequacy in only the two respects discussed below: the habitat protection measures and the derogations from prohibitions on killing or capture. On these points much will turn on how the British legislation is applied in practice.

The obligations as to habitat protection in the Directive are very general but certain principles are laid down: special conservation measures are to be taken to ensure the survival of the species in Annex I taking certain factors into account, and Member States "must classify in particular the most suitable territories in number and size as special protection areas for the conservation of these species". The British legislation to implement the obligation is complicated and for its effectiveness relies upon the goodwill of the landowning and farming community, their willingness to enter into management agreements with the NCC, and the amount of money made available to the NCC.

Although the Secretary of State is given the new power by Section 29 of the Wildlife and Countryside Act to make nature conservation orders in respect of land and to specify operations which may cause damage, the NCC is not furnished with the power to prohibit such operations, but must first offer to enter a management agreement which may entitle the owner to compensation. The NCC has the ultimate power of compulsory purchase - a power which it has had since 1949 and has only used twice. Both management agreements and compulsory purchase cost money and the NCC's funds are limited. Thus, although the Act in theory provides adequate legal powers to implement the obligations in the Directive - since the NCC could compulsorily purchase many sites if it had the resources - much will turn on how the powers are actually used.

The issue over the power to derogate from the prohibitions on killing and capture is also complicated. The Directive is clear about what the derogations must specify and the purposes for which they may be given, while Section 16(5) of the Wildlife and Countryside Act enables 'general' as well as 'specific' licences to be given to people to kill birds. Such general licences could be, for example, to control grey geese in all of central and eastern Scotland and could allow licence holders to permit others to kill for sporting purposes. This point was raised in a European Parliamentary Question (OJ C168 8.7.81) and in reply the Commissioner, referring to the Bill as amended after debate in the House of Lords, expressed the Commission's opinion that clause 16 (now Section 16) was wider than the Directive permits but went on to say that much would depend on the way the powers of licencing under the Bill are in fact exercised. Government officials have discussed this point with Commission officials and it has been agreed that the annual report on derogations that the government has to submit to the Commission would be the evidence on which the Commission would judge implementation of the Directive.

In May 1982 the DOE submitted the first annual report on derogations in three parts. The first part covered the period between the coming into force of the Directive and the Wildlife and Countryside Act. The second part was a statement on how the new licensing provisions were to be operated. The third part dealt with Northern Ireland. It may be some little time before there is enough experience for the Commission to satisfy itself that the licences conform with the derogation provisions.

There are three detailed points about the derogations that require comment because all were raised during discussion of the proposed Directive in the House of Commons. Section 4(2) of the Wildlife and Countryside Act specifically allows for 'mercy killing', i.e., killing a bird so seriously disabled that there is no chance of its recovering, but there is no comparable provision in the Directive. The Berne Convention (see Section 11.3) similarly does not provide for mercy killing but when this was raised by British government officials during negotiations it was generally agreed that mercy killing went without saying. It may therefore be assumed that the Commission and everyone else will overlook this inconsistency between the Act and the Directive.

Falconry may be licensed under Section 16(1) of the Act but is not mentioned as such in the Directive. Derogations for falconry (both the keeping of the falcons and the killing of their prey) appear to fall within the wording of Article 9(c):

"to permit, under strictly supervised conditions and on a selective basis, the capture, keeping or other judicious use of certain birds in small numbers".

Finally, the taking of gulls' eggs for human consumption and their sale is allowed for by Section 16(2) of the Act although not specifically mentioned in the Directive. It is justified by the government as being a derogation under Article 9(a) and 9(c) from the prohibition on the taking of eggs. Article 9(a) allows derogations 'for the purpose of protecting flora and fauna' and the taking of eggs is one way of keeping down the population of gulls that may otherwise displace other birds. The selling of the eggs is regarded as 'judicious use' under Article 9(c) quoted above – though it should be noted that the Directive speaks of the judicious use of birds and not their eggs and also talks of small numbers.

Effect on UK Practice

It is generally recognised that Britain had amongst the most far reaching bird protection legislation of any European country before the Directive was agreed. Public opinion and that of the farming and landowning community has also in the past been generally favourable to bird protection so it would be surprising indeed if the Directive were to make any significant difference to British practice. If there were to be any effects one would expect them to be small. Nevertheless, one effect can already be discerned and in the long term the Directive could significantly affect habitat protection.

The discernible effect concerns the licences that may be given under Section 16 of the Act to kill or take birds. As we have seen, these licences may be 'general' or 'specific' although the Minister, Hector Munro, in the Committee stage of the Wildlife and Countryside Bill (2nd June 1981) tried to play down fears about 'general' licences:

> "I want to say this loud and clear. Many people have been concerned that there will be blanket licences for doing this and that. That will not be the case..."

The possibility of 'general' licences would nevertheless remain were it not for the check provided by Article 9 of the Directive which requires an annual report to the Commission on derogations.

The RSPB claim, for example, to have evidence that barnacle geese are being shot on the island of Islay in Scotland under licence from the Department of Agriculture and Fisheries in Scotland so as not 'to prevent serious damage to crops' and 'where there is no other satisfactory solution' but for sporting purposes. In the absence of the Directive the RSPB would have made representations to the relevant government departments and will continue to do so. But they can now not only refer to the provisions of the Act but also to the provisions of the Directive. They can and do make representations to the Commission too. What used to be a discussion between two parties now becomes a discussion between three, and the Commission has a duty under Article 155 of the Treaty to ensure that "the measures taken by the institutions (e.g., a Directive issued by the Council) are applied".

Possibly the more important and long term effect of the Directive will concern habitat protection. We have seen that the Act provides some powers for habitat protection but that much will turn on how these are used. There had been much heated discussion in Britain during the passage of the Wildlife and Countryside Bill on whether the powers would be adequate and this continues. Only time will tell whether the government's policy of reliance on essentially voluntary rather than statutory action will work, and whether the provisions for compensation to farmers to forego certain profitable agriculture practices which may be damaging to nature conservation are realistic. The Act lacks general principles about bird and habitat protection comparable to those in the Directive, so that if persons concerned with bird protection feel that habitats are being lost to an unacceptable extent they are likely to rely on the general obligations enunciated in the Directive in preference to the Act in arguments with government. If they feel that the government is not honouring the obligation it entered into in agreeing the Directive they will doubtless not hesitate to involve the Commission too. Thus pressure to strengthen the existing statutory provisions for habitat protection - which already exists - may well develop a Community dimension.

Finally, the Directive may have long term effects on the Common

Agricultural Policy. If it can be demonstrated that measures under that policy to increase productivity (as required by Article 39 of the Treaty) are having the effect of destroying habitats which Member States have an obligation to protect under the Directive, then an extra element will be injected into policy discussions. The Commission which previously would have been pursuing one policy will find itself with conflicting policies resulting in internal conflicts. Outsiders may only be able ever to guess what form they may take.

11.2 Whales

Reg 348/81 (OJ L39 12.2.81)
Proposed 25.4.80–COM(80)150

Council Regulation on common rules for imports of whales or other cetacean products

Reg 3786/81 (OJ L377 13.12.81)

Commission Regulation laying down provisions for the implementation of the common rules for imports of whales or other cetacean products

Binding dates
Commission to be informed of
competent authorities: 1 July 1981
Ban takes effect: 1 January 1982

Purpose of the Regulations

The objective of conserving whales is to be advanced by a ban on the import into the Community of certain cetacean products. Cetaceans include whales, porpoises and dolphins. The preamble to the Regulation does not attempt to justify the ban on the grounds that all species of whales are threatened with extinction and, whatever the legal justification, the ban is a response to the repugnance felt by many at the killing of whales.

Summary of Regulation 348/81

From 1st January 1982 the products listed in an Annex can be imported into the Community only upon production of an import licence. Licences may be issued only for such purposes as scientific research and no licence is to be issued for commercial purposes.

The Annex lists a number of cetacean products (e.g., meat, bones, fats, oil, spermaceti but not ambergris*); leather treated with oil from cetaceans; and also articles of leather or furskins treated with oil from cetaceans (e.g., handbags and shoes). The Annex in fact includes about 95% of all secondary whale products, but excludes for instance cosmetics and lubricating oils containing small quantities of whale products.

Member States must notify the Commission of the competent authorities who are to issue licences and the Commission is to inform the other States.

A Committee on Cetacean Products is set up with a Commission representative as Chairman and is to give opinions on the application of the Regulation. The Commission has power to make implementing Regulations if the Committee, acting on a qualified majority, agrees. The Commission

---

* Ambergris used commercially is not obtained generally from killed whales but is gathered from beaches.

also has power to make implementing Regulations on its own, despite an adverse opinion of the Committee, after having submitted the proposal to the Council and in the event of the Council failing to agree within three months. One implementing Commission Regulation No 3786/81 has been issued prescribing the form of the import licence and making minor exceptions from the need for a licence (e.g., personal luggage of travellers).

At the earliest opportunity the Commission is to submit a report to the Council on whether the list of products in the Annex should be extended. The Council can extend the list acting on a qualified majority. Pending such a decision, Member States may themselves ban products not in the Annex. (In reply to a European Parliamentary Question - OJ C218 23.8.82 - the Commission stated that a study had been carried out but that the Committee on Cetacean Products had advised that extension of the Annex should be considered at a later stage after the Regulation had been in operation for longer.)

Development of the Regulation

The Action Programmes made no reference to an import ban on whale products and the origin of the Regulation is to be found in a British initiative of October 1979. The Regulation shows that the Community can move very quickly: the Regulation was formally proposed in April 1980, agreed in principle in June, formally agreed in December and the ban came into effect one year later.

A United Kingdom ban on the import of products from baleen whales had been in existence since 1973 but the ban did not extend to sperm whale oil used for treating leather and for certain other purposes. As a result of a national campaign in Britain against the killing of whales whether threatened with extinction or not, the Conservative party, during the election campaign of May 1979, promised to press for a moratorium on commercial whaling for a limited period if it were to be elected, and Michael Heseltine, soon to be Secretary of State for the Environment, had made a speech before the election calling for a European ban on the import of products from endangered species, in particular sperm whale oil and whale meat. In July 1979 the International Whaling Commission narrowly failed to ban all commercial whaling but agreed to ban commercial whaling by factory ships, except for minke whales. Although this decision reduced the number of sperm whales killed it would not have completely cut the supply of sperm whale oil and because of its election pledge the government was pressed to take action. In the event it decided to press for a ban at Community level for three reasons: there was doubt whether a unilateral ban would be consistent* with the provisions of the Treaty of Rome on the free movement of goods*; a unilateral ban would have put British leather manufacturers at a commercial disadvantage in comparison with their continental competitors; and a Community ban would be more effective in the objective of protecting whales. (It should be noted that the uncertainty about the legality of a unilateral ban also applied to the existing ban on the products of baleen

---

* A common organisation of the market in oils and fats is established by EEC Regulation No 1917/80 (OJ L186 19.7.80) (which amended earlier Regulations).

254

whales. That ban was introduced at about the time that Britain joined the Community and perhaps for the reason that it did not extend to products of the same commercial importance as sperm whale oil had not been criticised by the Commission.)

In October 1979 the Secretary of State for the Environment, Michael Heseltine, accordingly wrote to the President of the Commission, Roy Jenkins, asking for a Community ban on the primary products of all whales and, as a result, the Commission proposed a Regulation embodying a ban in April 1980. This proposed ban went further than the British request by including leather treated with oil from cetaceans, though it did not include leather products.

The European Parliament in November 1980 adopted a lengthy resolution which welcomed the proposal to limit imports of whale products but wanted the limit extended to cover all products that could be shown to derive from cetaceans. The Parliament's resolution also ranged much more widely than an import ban and requested the Commission among other matters to put forward a ban on commercial whaling in European waters.

The House of Commons' Scrutiny Committee in a report dated 25th June 1980 noted the concern of the British Leather Federation that the proposed Regulation would permit the free import into the Community of leather products treated with whale oil while British manufacturers would suffer the disadvantage of not being allowed to import either treated leather or whale oil. The Committee noted that consideration was being given to the inclusion of leather products treated with whale oil in the list of restricted products, and this inclusion was in fact formally made in a proposal from the Commission - COM(80)788 - in November 1980.

On 8th December 1980 the House of Commons debated the Commission's proposal on a motion that welcomed 'the Government's initiative for this Regulation'. In the debate the Minister, Marcus Fox, explained that agreement in principle had been secured for the Regulation at the Council meeting on 30th June, but that there had been prolonged debate on three issues: the legal basis for the ban; whether Member States could go beyond the Regulation; and the list of products to be covered by the ban. Two of these issues had been resolved and the only outstanding point was the legal basis: should the Regulation be based on Article 113 of the Treaty concerned with commercial policy or Article 235 giving the Council general powers? Pressed in the debate, the Minister named Denmark and Germany as the two countries holding out for Article 235 while all other Member States supported the use of Article 113. In the event, Danish and German arguments prevailed.

The Government was congratulated on all sides during the debate on its initiative and one MP said of the Regulation:

> "There is no doubt that it will be welcomed by thousands,
> if not millions, in this country who have campaigned for a
> long time".

The principal criticism made by some Members of Parliament was that the Regulation did not ban all products, but the Minister explained that 95% of secondary products would be covered, and that to cover the next 5% would multiply by a far greater percentage the number of checks that would have to be made. To enforce a complete ban was said to be difficult, if not impossible.

There is nothing in the Regulations to prevent manufacturers using up existing stocks of sperm whale oil and this possibility made the ban more acceptable to some Member States. It may be a few years before existing stocks are all used.

Formal Compliance in the UK

Community Regulations are directly applicable law and so no legislation is required to implement the whale Regulations in Britain. However, the previous ban on the import of baleen whale products had been enforced under the Endangered Species (Import and Export) Act 1976 and the new ban is being enforced under an Order made under the Act (SI 1982 No 1230). The Commission has been notified that the competent authority that is to issue licences in Britain under the Regulation is the Department of the Environment, Wildlife Conservation Licensing Section, Tollgate House, Bristol. HM Customs and Excise are the enforcement agency.

Effect on UK Practice

Although the Regulation covers most primary and secondary whale products, import of these into Britain was already largely banned with the exception of sperm whale oil. The effect of the Regulation in Britain can therefore be considered in terms of this one product but its effect will have been larger in those Member States which did not already have as extensive a ban.

Use of sperm whale oil had already been falling in Britain as a result of the cuts in the allowable catch by the International Whaling Commission and the leather industry was also under considerable pressure from environmentalists not to use sperm whale oil. As a result the industry had developed alternatives to sperm whale oil and no great difficulty was encountered in finally phasing out its use by the date specified. The Regulation therefore effectively came at the end of a process of change that had been going on for several years.

The Regulation will have ensured that the British leather industry is not at the disadvantage in comparison with its continental competitors that it would have been in the event of a unilateral ban. This is because leather treated with sperm whale oil is, in the opinion of some, superior to that treated with the alternatives available.

Some organisations that campaigned against the killing of whales had criticised the government's decision to seek a Community ban rather than to proceed unilaterally. Their grounds would probably have been, if they were expressed, that Community action would take longer and would be less certain. In the event a Community ban was secured and has denied whale products to a market of 250 million people as opposed to one of 55 million.

256

11.3 International Conventions on Fauna and Flora

The Community is involved with the four international Conventions listed below concerned with fauna and flora. (In addition the Community is involved with the Protocol to the Barcelona Convention concerning Mediterranean specially protected areas but that does not affect Britain though it may affect Gibraltar).

Britain is a signatory to all four Conventions. It has ratified three of them and intends to ratify the Bonn Convention too. Community accession to these Conventions should not therefore place additional obligations on Britain, nor should it affect action in Britain and by British nationals, although it may well affect the British position over future negotiations leading to any modification of the Conventions since the Member States will presumably act collectively and the Commission will be involved.

The Community has concluded the Bonn and Berne Conventions and the Convention on conservation of Antarctic marine living resources by means of the Decisions listed below (the whole question of Community accession to international conventions is complicated by the extent to which the Community has competence in the fields covered by the convention in question. Thus the Community has competence in the field of bird protection by virtue of the birds Directive (Section 11.1) but does not have competence in the field of protection of wild plants – both are covered by the Berne Convention). The Washington Convention (known as CITES) has only recently been amended in such a way as to allow the Community to accede, but the amendment does not become effective until a number of signatory countries have ratified the amendment, and this may take several years. The Council has meanwhile issued a Regulation which obliges all the Member States to implement the Convention whether or not they have ratified it. Since this Regulation does not in general go further than the Endangered Species (Import and Export) Act 1976 its effects in Britain are likely to be of a detailed kind. For these reasons the three Decisions and one Regulation are listed here for reference and without a full discussion.

1. Convention on the conservation of Antarctic marine living resources

81/691/EEC (OJ L252 5.9.81) proposed 1980 — Decision on the conclusion of the Convention of Antarctic marine living resources

The Convention was drawn up in May 1980 and seeks to control the harvesting of marine living resources in the Antarctic, particularly krill.

2. Berne Convention

82/72/EEC (OJ L38 10.2.82) proposed 17.7.79 – COM(79)414 — Decision concerning the conclusion of the Convention on the conservation of European wildlife and natural habitats

The Convention - drawn up by the Council of Europe in September 1979 - seeks to conserve wild flora and fauna and their natural habitats, particularly endangered species, especially when conservation requires the co-operation of several states. These obligations are being fulfilled in Britain under the Wildlife and Countryside Act 1981.

3. Bonn Convention

82/461/EEC (OJ L210 19.7.82)
proposed 18.4.80 - COM(80)187

Decision on the conclusion of the Convention on the conservation of migratory species of wild animals

The underlying principle of this Convention, drawn up in June 1979, is that states within whose borders there are threatened populations of migratory species should take concerted action to ensure appropriate conservation and management. Britain is a signatory but has not yet ratified the convention. The government believes the obligations can be fulfilled using existing legislation.

4. Washington Convention (CITES)

Reg 3626/82 (OJ L384 13.12.82)
proposed 21.7.80 - COM(80)413

Regulation on the implementation in the Community of the Convention on international trade in endangered species of wild flora and fauna

The Convention, drawn up in March 1973, institutes a system of licensing for the trade in endangered species and prohibits trade in some species. The Regulation does the same but goes rather further, e.g., in banning trade in certain species which the Convention does not ban. The Regulation formally came into force on 31st December 1981 and its provisions become effective on 1st January 1984. It is directly applicable law but, as with the whale Regulation (see Section 11.2), Britain will implement it using the Endangered Species (Import and Export) Act 1976.
The Act requires licensing for the import and export of almost all wild fauna and flora and although it does not ban any trade it is possible for the licensing authority (the Department of the Environment, Wildlife Conservation Licensing Section, Tollgate House, Bristol) to decide to withhold licences. When it does so it informs those involved in the the trade, and the public is informed by means of publications including a booklet called 'Essential Information for Travellers' issued with passports by the Passport Office.
The Regulation may have some effects on administration in Britain since it empowers the Commission to prescribe the form of various documents (OJ L344 7.12.83). Although current British practice is at least as stringent as the requirements of the Regulation, and in some respects more so, the Regulation ensures that this must remain the case. The major effect of the Regulation will be to compel those Member States that had not ratified the Convention to implement it. One justification for the Regulation was that unequal implementation by different Member States would upset the operation of the common market, but the Regulation does allow Member States to maintain or take stricter measures than those set out in the Regulation.

11.4 Countryside Protection in Agriculturally Less Favoured Areas

75/268/EEC (OJ L128 19.5.75) proposed 1973 - COM(73)202	Directive on mountain and hill farming and farming in certain less favoured areas
76/400/EEC (OJ L108 26.4.76)	(Amendment)
80/666/EEC (OJ L180 14.7.80)	(Amendment)
82/786/EEC (OJ L327 24.11.82)	(Amendment)

In addition to these four Directives a separate Directive for each Member State was issued in 1975 listing the less favoured areas falling within the meaning of Directive 75/268. The one relevant to the UK is Directive 75/276 (OJ L128 19.5.75) but the areas listed were adjusted in Directive 76/685 (OJ L231 21.8.76) and again in Directive 82/656 (OJ L277 29.9.82).

Binding dates

Notification date (75/268):	30 April 1975
Formal compliance (75/268):	30 April 1976
Aids may be introduced:	1 October 1974
Financial contributions from Community:	During 1975 and thereafter

Purpose of the Directives

These Directives are often thought of as environmental measures but this is not strictly correct. Their purpose is stated as "the continuation of farming thereby maintaining a minimum population level or conserving the countryside" in certain agriculturally less favoured areas. This is to be achieved by selective financial incentives.

A reply by the Commission to a European Parliamentary Question (OJ C287 4.11.82) explained:

"...that Directive 75/268 may not be used to encourage conservation per se but is to be used for the encouragement of farming which, in turn, will (sic) have a positive effect on the conservation of the countryside. This does not interfere with the Member States' right to introduce additional schemes for aid for conservation".

The use of the word 'will' is perhaps overconfident and 'may' would have been more appropriate.

The Directives are tied in part to an earlier Directive 72/159 (OJ L96 23.4.72) concerned with the modernisation of farms. Together they form part of the common measures within the meaning of Council Regulation No 729/70 (OJ L94 28.4.70) on the financing of the common agricultural policy.

Thus, although the Directives exist optionally for environmental purposes they are formally part of the agricultural policy.

The first Action Programme on the Environment of 1973 noted the interconnection between environmental and agricultural policy by mentioning that a Directive on this subject had been proposed and affirming that the Commission would increase:

> "...its campaign in the future for the protection of the natural environment and particularly within the framework of the agricultural policy".

The need to integrate environmental policy with other Community policies has since been given new emphasis in the third Action Programme on the Environment.

A full assessment of the effect of these Directives can only be undertaken within the context of an assessment of agricultural policy which is not a part of the present study (see Chapter 3). The Directives are therefore merely listed here for reference but with little discussion.

Summary of the Directives

Member States are authorised to introduce a special system of aids for specified less favoured areas in order to ensure the continuation of farming thereby maintaining a minimum population level or conserving the countryside. The areas are to be proposed by the Member States but have to be agreed by the Council. In practice this has been done in a series of separate Directives. The areas are to fall into one of three categories (all must have adequate infrastructures, e.g., access roads to farms, electricity and drinking water):

- **mountain areas** handicapped, because of high altitude, by a short growing season, or at a lower altitude by steep slopes, or by a combination of the two (Article 3(3));

- **less favoured areas in danger of depopulation:** these are areas, regional in character, where the conservation of the countryside is necessary and which exhibit all the following three disadvantages: infertility, poor economic situation and a low or dwindling population dependent on agriculture (Article 3(4));

- **other less favoured areas affected by specific handicaps:** these may be small areas in which farming must be continued in order to conserve the countryside and in order to preserve tourist potential or in order to protect the coastline. (According to the Commission, the specific handicaps referred to must arise principally from permanent natural conditions which are unfavourable for farming[*]. This appears to mean that the

---

[*] Reply to European Parliamentary Question No 819/82, C 287 - 4.11. 82. This reply also stated that small areas under Article 3(5) had been included in the Community list of less favoured areas in Germany, Greece, France, Italy, Luxembourg and Netherlands.

handicaps cannot have been artificially imposed by, e.g., conservation legislation). The total extent of such areas in any Member State is not to exceed 2.5% of the area of the State (Article 3(5)).

A map has been published in the Official Journal (OJ L128 19.5.75) showing all the areas throughout the Community initially listed. The areas in the UK initially listed all fell within the category of less favoured areas "in danger of depopulation and where the conservation of the countryside is necessary" (Article 3(4)), but in 1982 the Scilly Isles were added under Article 3(5) and are thus designated as "areas in which farming must be continued in order to conserve the countryside...or to protect the coastline". No areas in the UK have been listed as mountain areas (Article 3(3)). The proportion of the area in the UK in agricultural use that is listed is 42.4%.
The special system of aids fall under four headings and Member States are free to choose which to apply:

(a) Compensatory allowances
Annual allowances to compensate for permanent natural handicaps may be paid in the form of headage payments for beef cattle, sheep and goats at rates decided by the individual Member States but subject to a maximum and minimum of 97 and 15 ECU per livestock unit (one cow equals one unit, one sheep or goat 0.15 units). Payments may only be made to farmers using at least two hectares. Cows whose milk is intended for marketing may be eligible for payments in limited circumstances. In certain circumstances, allowances may also be paid per hectare.

(b) Investment aids to farms suitable for development
Farms holding development plans approved under the terms of Directive 72/159 may receive an interest rate subsidy of up to 7% instead of the 5% elsewhere. In addition, farms which concentrate on beef or sheep meat production may receive a guidance premium at a rate one third higher than that paid elsewhere. Investment in tourist and craft industries on farms may be aided. More relaxed conditions of eligibility are applied to farmers seeking a development plan.

(c) Investment aids to farms ineligible for development plans
National investment aids may be given so long as they are not more favourable than those given under development plans approved under Directive 72/159.

(d) Aids for joint investment schemes
Aids may be given for joint investment schemes for fodder production, and for improvement schemes for pasture and hill grazing land which is farmed jointly.

Member States may receive 25% reimbursement (more in parts of Italy, Ireland and Greece) from the Guidance Section of the European Agricultural Guidance and Guarantee Fund on compensatory allowances and investment aids given to development plan farmers.

Effect on the UK

Since in Britain all the areas, with the exception of the Scilly Isles, have been designated under Article 3(4) they have been identified by the government and the Community as areas 'where the conservation of the countryside is necessary'. The Directive therefore embodies a policy statement of considerable importance for a very large proportion (42%) of land in agricultural use in Britain since no comparable statement about conserving the countryside had previously been made. It is by no means certain that the implications of this have been understood either by the relevant Ministries or by environmental bodies concerned with countryside protection.

In evidence given to the House of Commons' Select Committee on Agriculture (1) the Ministry of Agriculture, Fisheries and Food said that the Directives had provided a means of continuing special aids to the hills and uplands, and also that the UK had been the major beneficiary of Community money. Two reports from the House of Lords' Select Committee on the European Communities (2,3) have discussed the Directives. A report published by the Council for National Parks (4) is critical both of the Directives and of the UK farm support system for less favoured areas which it regards as a "parody of the EEC Directive under which it is supposed to operate, and through which it obtains a quarter of its finance". A report by the Arkleton Trust (5) compares the operation of the Directives in six Member States including Britain.

References

(1) House of Commons, **Agriculture Committee, 1st Report,** Session 1981–82, HMSO.

(2) House of Lords, Select Committee on the European Communities, 27th Report, Session 1979-80, **Policies for Rural Areas in the European Community,** HMSO.

(3) House of Lords, Select Committee on the European Communities, 2nd Report, Session 1982-83, **Socio-structural Policy,** HMSO.

(4) Malcolm MacEwan and Geoffrey Sinclair, **New Life for the Hills,** Council for National Parks, 1983.

(5) The Arkleton Trust, **Schemes of Assistance to Farmers in Less Favoured Areas of the EEC,** 1982.

CHAPTER 12
Noise

12.0   Relevant British Legislation

Legislation to control noise in the environment generally - often known as neighbourhood noise - is contained in Part III of the Control of Pollution Act 1974, which replaced and extended the Noise Abatement Act 1960. Before the 1960 Act neighbourhood noise was not a matter for the public authorities but could only be controlled by the courts following a common law action for nuisance.

Since all the existing Directives concerned with noise set standards for noise from specific mobile sources - vehicles, aircraft and construction plant - British legislation on neighbourhood noise is not described here.

Vehicles

Noise standards for cars, lorries, buses, motor cycles and tractors are now all laid down in Regulations made under the Road Traffic Act 1972, although the first such Regulations setting quantitative limits were set in the 1968 Motor Vehicles (Construction and Use) Regulations and came into effect in 1970.   Enforcement in service is a police responsibility.

The Road Traffic Act 1974 provides for the operation of a compulsory national type approval scheme under which the manufacturer, before marketing a new type of vehicle, has to produce a sample production vehicle for testing by the Department of Transport.   The vehicle has to comply with all relevant safety and environmental standards including noise, and the manufacturer has to demonstrate that he has adequate quality assurance procedures.   He then has to certify that every vehicle sold conforms to an approved type and random checks are made to establish that this is so.

National type approval for cars was introduced by Regulations in 1976 and is now governed by the Motor Vehicles (Type Aproval) (Great Britain) Regulations 1981 (SI 1981 No 1619).   National type approval for lorries was introduced in 1982 by the Motor Vehicles (Type Approval) (Great Britain) Regulations 1981 (SI 1981 No 1340).   There is no type approval in Britain for motor cycles, and although there is limited type approval for tractors it does not extend to external noise.

Aircraft

The Civil Aviation Act 1949 (as amended by the Civil Aviation Act 1968) provides for the prohibition of any aircraft landing or taking off in Britain unless it has a noise certificate and is complying with the certificate's requirements. The scheme is based on international agreements drawn up within the International Civil Aviation Organisation (ICAO).   The current order made under the Act is the Air Navigation (Noise Certification) Order 1979 and this contains in its Schedules the noise emission standards prescribed by ICAO although the Civil Aviation Authority is empowered to relax prohibitions.   Any exemptions made are listed in the Authority's Official Record.

Construction Plant

Two sections of the Control of Pollution Act 1974 deal specifically with noise from construction plant. Section 60 empowers local authorities to specify the plant that may or may not be used on a construction site, the hours when works may be carried out and the noise levels which may be emitted from the premises. Section 68 creates the power to make Regulations requiring the use of devices or arrangements for reducing the noise caused by plant or machinery, or for limiting the noise of construction plant when in use. The wording of this section – which has not yet been used – is a little unclear and may not cover construction plant as manufactured (as opposed to when in use), a fact which may cause difficulties when implementing certain Directives (see Section 12.4).

References

Department of the Environment, **Pollution Control in Great Britain: How it Works,** Pollution Paper No 9, HMSO 1976.

12.1 Noise from Cars, Buses and Lorries

The noise of four-wheeled vehicles (other than tractors) is regulated by two Council Directives and two Commission Directives:

1) 70/157/EEC (OJ L42 23.2.70)
   proposed 11.7.68 - COM(68)529

   Council Directive relating to the permissible sound level and the exhaust systems of motor vehicles

2) 73/350/EEC (OJ L321 22.11.73)

   Commission Directive adapting 70/157 to technical progress

3) 77/212/EEC (OJ L66 12.3.77)
   proposed 24.7.74 - COM(11)75

   Council Directive amending 70/157

4) 81/334/EEC (OJ L131 18.5.81)

   Commission Directive adapting 70/157 to technical progress

Binding dates

Formal compliance - 81/334	1 January 1982
EEC type approval may only be granted if limits of 77/212 are met. Limits may be made mandatory:	1 October 1982
EEC type approval may only be granted if limits of 77/212 met using measuring system of 81/334:	1 October 1984
Measuring method of 81/334 may be made mandatory:	1 October 1985

Purpose of the Directives

Vehicle noise is generally recognised as the biggest single source of noise nuisance. Directive 70/157 preceded the first Action Programme on the Environment and sought to ensure that noise limits introduced by individual Member States did not create barriers to trade. It was also introduced as part of an EEC 'type approval' procedure set out in Directive 79/156 which was agreed at the same time but which is not yet in operation. ('Type approval' shows that a vehicle type conforms with certain standards of design and construction). Directive 77/212 lowered the noise limits for environmental reasons and Directive 81/334 introduced a new measuring method which has the effect of further lowering the noise limits although it does not change the numerical limits. These Directives are of the kind known as 'optional' or as providing 'optional harmonisation', which means that Member States are not bound to set limits equal to those in the Directive but may not erect trade barriers by setting more stringent limits.

Summary of the Directives

Directive 70/157 defines 'vehicles' to mean four-wheeled road vehicles having a maximum design speed greater than 25 kph but excluding agricultural tractors and public works vehicles. An Annex lists seven categories of cars, buses and lorries and sets a noise limit against each. A noise measuring method is specified covering both the conditions of measurement and the vehicle operating conditions. The Annex also sets out requirements for exhaust systems (silencers).

No Member State may prohibit the sale or use of a vehicle or may refuse to grant EEC type approval or national type approval of a vehicle on grounds relating to the permissible sound level or the exhaust system if these satisfy the requirements in the Annex. The Directive thus prevents Member States from setting more stringent noise limits than those specified. (If one Member State chooses to adopt national limits equal to the limits in the Directive, then manufacturers from other countries interested in selling in that market will be induced to meet the limits of the Directive. It can therefore have a powerful persuasive effect.)

The Directive has a provision allowing the Annex to be adapted by the Commission to take account of technical progress but not so as to make changes to the noise limits set against each category of vehicle. That power is reserved to the Council.

Directive 73/350 expands the requirements in the parent Directive relating to silencers.

Directive 77/212 amends the Annex to 70/157 and reduces the noise limits in dB(A) as follows:

	77/212	**(70/157)**
Cars	80	(82)
Goods vehicles		
Less than 3.5 tonnes	81	(84)
Over 3.5 tonnes	86	(89)
Over 12 tonnes and 200HP	88	(91)
Buses		
Less than 3.5 tonnes	81	(84)
More than 3.5 tonnes	82	(89)
Over 3.5 tonnes and 200HP	85	(91)

Directive 77/212 introduces various transitional arrangements which have become irrelevant with the passage of time. It specifies that from 1st October 1982 Member States may no longer issue an EEC type approval certificate and may refuse a national type approval certificate for any type of vehicle that does not satisfy the requirements of the Directive. It also allows Member States from 1st October 1982 to prohibit the initial entry into service of vehicles that do not satisfy the requirements of the Directives.

Directive 81/334 introduces a new test procedure to reflect the increased range of gears now commonly used. It requires tests using more than one gear rather than one gear only as previously. It also contains

267

provisions to permit replacement silencers for passenger cars and light commercial vehicles to be type approved. From 1st October 1984 type approval may only be granted if the limits of Directive 77/212 are met using the new test method, and from 1st October 1985 Member States may prohibit the entry into service of vehicles that have not been tested by the new method.

Development of the Directives

The parent Directive 70/157 was agreed before Britain joined the Community and was the earliest Community legislation concerned with noise. It was closely modelled on the United Nations Economic Commission for Europe's non-mandatory Regulation 9. The explanatory memorandum accompanying the proposal for Directive 77/212 records that on 20th June 1973 and 5th September 1973 the governments of France and the United Kingdom respectively had informed the Commission of their interest in a substantial reduction of the limits set in 70/157. The explanatory memorandum set out a short-term programme aiming at an initial reduction of the existing limits - which resulted in Directive 77/212 - and a longer-term programme to find a new method of noise measurement which would more accurately reflect the actual conditions in which vehicles are used in urban traffic - which resulted in Directive 81/334. It took two and a half years for Directive 77/212 to be adopted and much earlier dates were proposed than were agreed - for example according to the proposed Directive Member States would have been able to make the limits mandatory from October 1976 rather than October 1982, a difference of six years.

When Directive 77/212 was agreed the Council made a declaration that:

> "...efforts should be made to achieve a noise level of
> around 80dB(A) for all categories of vehicles by 1985.
> The levels decided on will have to take into account what
> is technically and economically feasible at the time.
> Moreover, they will have to be established sufficiently
> early to give manufacturers an adequate transition period
> in which to improve their products".

This declaration therefore intended, not that a new Directive should be agreed by 1985, but that a new Directive would have to be agreed in sufficient time for vehicles meeting the limits to be on the road by 1985. It became clear by 1981 that this target would not be met (see reply to a European Parliamentary Question, OJ No C240 18.9.81), and failure to meet the target has been confirmed by a Directive proposed in 1983 (see below).

Formal Compliance in the UK

Motor vehicle noise was first controlled in Britain in 1970 by the 1968 Motor Vehicles (Construction and Use) Regulations made under the Road Traffic Act. On accession to the Community in 1973 Britain became subject to Directive 70/157 which prescribed slightly different limits: 2dB(A) more

268

stringent for cars and 2dB(A) more relaxed for buses and lorries. Since the Directive is 'optional' it was not necessary to tighten the British limits for cars but in order to prevent a barrier to trade the limit for buses and lorries had to be relaxed. This was done by the Motor Vehicles (Construction and Use) Regulations 1973 (SI 1973 No 1347) made under the Road Traffic Act 1972.

In 1980 new Regulations - the Motor Vehicles (Construction and Use) Regulations (Amendment) (No 6) 1980 (SI 1980 No 1166) - were made to apply the limits of Directive 77/212 for vehicles covered by the Directive and manufactured on or after 1st April 1983 and first used on or after 1st October 1983.

New Regulations will be needed to make mandatory the measuring methods set out in Directive 81/334, but meanwhile the Motor Vehicles (Construction and Use) (Amendment) (No 5) Regulations 1982 (SI 1982 No 1422) make them optional.

National type approval for cars was introduced by the Motor Vehicles (Type Approval) (Great Britain) Regulations 1976 (SI 1976 No 937) made under the Road Traffic Act 1974 and this set the limits of Directive 70/157, i.e., 82dB(A) for cars. This was amended by Motor Vehicles (Type Approval) (Great Britain) Regulations 1981 (SI 1981 No 1619) to introduce the limits of Directive 77/212.

National type approval for lorries was introduced on 1st October 1982 by the Motor Vehicles (Type Approval) (Great Britain) Regulations 1981 (SI 1981 No 1340) and sets the same limits as the Directives.

Effect on UK Practice

When Britain joined the Community in 1973 British noise limits for lorries and buses were more stringent than elsewhere in Europe. The first practical effect of Directive 70/157 was therefore a relaxation of the noise limits for buses and lorries from 89dB(A) to the 91dB(A) specified. Unlike the bulk of the other environmental Directives, the noise Directives, reflecting their origins as measures to prevent barriers to trade, prevent Member States from setting more stringent standards than those specified. The British government had in fact been ready just before accession to the Community to reduce noise levels still further and in December 1970 had issued a draft consultation document proposing further reductions. These had to be abandoned upon accession but the frustrated intentions nevertheless created the pressure that led to the British request to the Commission in September 1973 for a substantial noise reduction which led in turn to Directive 77/212. However, any claim that Community legislation has continued as a brake on British efforts to reduce vehicle noise cannot easily be sustained since the British motor industry was not in a position to lower noise levels for all vehicles to meet the limits of Directive 77/212 at the earliest date allowed by the Directive (October 1982), so that these limits were only made obligatory in Britain for new vehicles manufactured after 1st April 1983 and first used from 1st October 1983. This point is explained in a memorandum submitted by the Department of Transport for a House of Lords' report reviewing Community noise policy (1).

The net result of the Directives is that noise limits for new vehicles in dB(A) have been reduced in Britain as follows (the figures in brackets are those in a proposed Directive - see below):

	1970	1983	(1988/9) (proposed)
Cars	84	80	(77)
Heaviest buses	89	85	(83)
Heaviest lorries	89	88	(84)

There has thus been an overall reduction of 4dB(A) for cars and buses in 13 years but only a 1dB(A) reduction for lorries. A further effective reduction for some new vehicles of 2 or 3 dB(A) will be made in 1984 when the testing method of Directive 81/334 is introduced in Britain although the numerical limits will not change. More substantial reductions must await the new Directive proposed in 1983 (see below).

The question whether Britain would have set more stringent limits after the early 1970s if it had not been for Community legislation is difficult to answer. The vehicle market is international and it is difficult for a vehicle manufacturing country interested in the export market to set significantly more stringent limits than its competitors if this entails a cost penalty. Nevertheless, there has been considerable pressure in Britain for a reduction in lorry noise, and as a result of public pressure an experimental quiet heavy vehicle (QHV) was developed in government research laboratories during the 1970s (2) which meets the 1977 target of 80dB(A) using the then test procedure. The Commission admitted, in reply to a European Parliamentary Question in 1980 (OJ C236 15.9.80), that in no other Member State was there a prototype of the heaviest category of lorry that also met the target. Given the opposition there has been in the British Parliament to an increase in lorry weights for environmental reasons it is quite possible that the government would have been forced to insist on some tighter noise limits for lorries if Community legislation did not preclude this, even if not down to 80dB(A).

A Department of Transport official put it like this in giving evidence to the House of Lords (1):

"In the early 1970s we had gone out to consultation about more stringent noise levels with the idea of introducing these in 1974 and our entry into the Community did in fact slow that. However I think it must be seen against our longer-term goals, and you probably know that the various Ministers have made known that we are trying to get heavy lorries to around 80 decibels...and I think it is open to debate whether our membership of the Community will have moved that target further away. My own personal view is that for that goal it is not retarding it...".

Further Developments

In June 1983 the Commission proposed a new Directive amending the noise limits (OJ C200 27.7.83 and COM(83)392). Three of the proposed limits are shown in the table above. If the Directive is agreed the limits for cars would be introduced from October 1988 and for the heaviest buses and lorries from October 1989. The draft Directive also proposes that the Council should decide on a further review of possible new measures by the end of 1990. The target of 80dB(A) for all vehicles by 1985 has slipped into the future.

References

(1) House of Lords, Select Committee on the European Communities, **Noise in the Environment,** 13th Report, Session 1981-82, HMSO, 1982.

(2) P M Nelson and M C P Underwood, **Operational Performance of the TRRL Quiet Heavy Vehicle,** Transport and Road Research Laboratory, Supplementary Report 746, 1982.

12.2 Motorcycle Noise

78/1015/EEC (OJ L349 13.12.78)
proposed 12.12.75 - COM(75)634

Directive on the permissible
sound level and exhaust system of
motorcycles

Binding dates
Notification date:
Formal compliance:
Limits not to take effect
  until:
Council to decide on further
  reduction in limits:

27 November 1978
1 October 1980

27 May 1981

31 December 1984

Purpose of the Directive

Noise limits for motocycles are set both for environmental reasons and
to prevent national limits creating barriers to trade.   Like the vehicle noise
Directives (see Section 12.1) the present Directive is of the 'optional' kind.

Summary of the Directive

An Annex sets out a measuring method and sets the following noise
limits (mopeds, i.e., motorcycles under 55cc, are not covered):

Cubic capacity (cc) of motorcycle	db(A)
Less than 80	78
80-125	80
125-350	83
350-500	85
Over 500	86

Member States may not refuse national type approval or refuse sale or
use of motorcycles which have been officially tested in accordance with the
Directive and meet the above limits.

Before 31st December 1984 the Council, on a proposal from the
Commission, is to decide on a reduction in the noise limits.   The preamble to
the Directive says that "in the case of more powerful motorcycles an
endeavour should be made to lower the noise limits to around 80dB(A) by
1985" and "that these levels should be fixed in good time so as to give
manufacturers a sufficient period to improve their products".   Other
amendments to adapt the Annexes to technical progress may be made by the
Committee set up under Directive 70/156 (see Section 12.1).

Development of the Directive

In January 1974 the French Government notified the Commission that it
intended to introduce national legislation on motorcycle noise and this led to

272

a proposal for a Directive in 1975. It took over three years for the Directive to be agreed which suggests some resistance from Member States.

Formal Compliance in the UK

The Motor Vehicles (Construction and Use) (Amendment) (No 6) Regulations 1980 (SI 1980 No 1166) made under the Road Traffic Act 1972 specifically refers to Directive 78/1015 and to the test method and noise limits set out in the Directive. The noise limits are to be met by motorcycles manufactured on or after 1st October 1982 and first used on or after 1st April 1983. There is no type approval procedure for motorcycles in Britain.

Effect on UK Practice

Noise limits for motorcycles were first set in Britain in 1970 by the Motor Vehicles (Construction and Use) Regulations 1968. These set limits of 77dB(A) for mopeds (less than 50cc); 82dB(A) for motorcycles between 50 and 125cc; and 86dB(A) for motorcycles of over 125cc. These noise limits remained unchanged until modified by the 1980 Regulations mentioned above which introduced the noise limits and measuring method of the Directive.

The Directive has therefore had no effect on the numerical noise levels of the most powerful motorcycles (over 500cc) but the testing method under the Directive differs from that in the previous Construction and Use Regulations so that in practice there has been a 3dB(A) reduction in noise levels. For the less powerful categories of motorcycle the numerical noise limits have in all cases been reduced.

In a memorandum to the House of Lords for its review of Community noise policy (1) the Department of Transport noted that:

> "...there have been statements in the motorcycling press that some manufacturers will be unable to meet the new limits but the Department of Transport have been assured by the manufacturers that they will be able to comply with the Regulations."

Although the point cannot be proved, it seems probable that in the absence of the Directive the limits set in 1970 would have been lowered by now so that whether the Directive has had a positive or negative effect cannot be established. Again, it must be remembered that the market for motorcycles is international and action on noise by one country alone is extremely difficult even in the absence of a Directive. Since the Directive is of the 'optional' kind there was no obligation on the United Kingdom to reduce its limits to meet those in the Directive and the reasons for doing so will have been mainly environmental, but also so that the rather small British motorcycle industry has to meet the same limits for the home market as for export.

References

(1) House of Lords, Select Committee on the European Communities, **Noise in the Environment**, 13th Report, Session 1981-82, HMSO.

12.3 Tractor Noise

1) 74/151/EEC (OJ L84 28.3.74)
   proposed in April 1966

   Directive relating to certain parts and characteristics of wheeled agricultural or forestry tractors

2) 77/311/EEC (OJ L105 28.4.77)
   proposed 15.3.74 - COM(74)316

   Directive relating to the driver perceived noise level of wheeled agricultural or forestry tractors

Binding dates
  Notification date (74/151):   7 March 1974
  Formal compliance (74/151):   7 September 1975

Purpose of the Directives

Directive 74/151 is concerned with preventing the creation of barriers to trade in tractors. It was introduced as part of an EEC type approval procedure for tractors set out in a separate Directive 74/150 which is not yet in operation. It relates to a number of technical characteristics, such as maximum weight, in addition to noise levels and silencers. Directive 77/311 sets standards, also as part of the EEC type approval procedure of Directive 74/150, to protect the hearing of agricultural workers driving tractors. As such it is not concerned with environmental protection and will not be further described here. Both Directives are of the 'optional' kind (see Section 12.1).

Summary of Directive 74/151

The Directive is restricted to two-axle agricultural or forestry tractors having pneumatic tyres and a maximum design speed of between 6 and 25 kph.
No Member State may prohibit the sale or use of tractors or may refuse to grant EEC type approval or national type approval if these satisfy the requirements set out in the Annexes on grounds relating to:

- maximum laden weight;
- the location of rear registration plates;
- fuel tanks;
- ballast weight;
- audible warning devices;
- noise levels and exhaust system (silencer).

Provision is made for adapting the Annexes to technical progress with the exception of the noise limits. The Annexes relate to the various technical requirements listed above and only Annex VI is concerned with noise limits and a method of measuring noise. The noise limits in dB(A) are as follows:

Unladen weight greater than 1.5 tonnes	89
Unladen weight less than 1.5 tonnes	85

Development of the Directive

The Directive was proposed well before Britain joined the Community.

Formal Compliance in the UK

The Motor Vehicles (Construction and Use) (Amendment) (No 6) Regulations 1980 (SI 1980 No 1166) made under the Road Traffic Act 1972 specifically refer to Directive 74/151 and require the test method set out in the Directive to be used in achieving certain noise limits. These noise limits are not the same as those in the Directive. Thus there is no requirement for tractors with an unladen weight of less than 1.5 tonnes to meet a noise limit of 85dB(A). Instead there is a limit of 89dB(A) for tractors less than 90hp and 92dB(A) for tractors greater than 90hp. These are to apply for tractors made after 1st October 1982 and first used after 1st April 1983. Since the Directive is of the 'optional' kind it is nevertheless complied with in law. There is limited national type approval of tractors in Britain but it does not extend to external noise.

Effect on UK Practice

The Directive has not had any effect in reducing tractor noise limits in Britain as it is of the 'optional' kind.

Noise limits for tractors were first set in Britain in 1970 by the Motor Vehicles (Construction and Use) Regulations 1968. These set limits of 89dB(A) for the vehicle as constructed but noise levels when the vehicle was in use on a road could be 3dB(A) more, i.e., 92dB(A). These noise limits remained unchanged until modified by Regulations made in 1980. When, in October 1979, the Department of Transport issued these Regulations in draft to introduce the measuring method of the Directive it received representations from tractor manufacturers that 92dB(A) rather than 89dB(A) should be allowed for tractors fitted with engines of more than 90 hp. According to a memorandum submitted by the Department to a House of Lords' Committee (1), these tractors are made in relatively small numbers and are used almost entirely off the road and because of the use to which they are put the fitting of engine shields to reduce noise was considered impracticable. It seems possible that these tractors were not meeting the previous limits.

References

(1) House of Lords, Select Committee on the European Communities, **Noise in the Environment,** 13th Report, Session 1981-82, HMSO.

12.4 Construction Plant Noise

1) 79/113/EEC (OJ L33 8.2.79)　　　Directive relating to the
   proposed 20.12.74 - COM(74)2195　determination of the noise
   　　　　　　　　　　　　　　　　　　emission of construction plant
   　　　　　　　　　　　　　　　　　　and equipment

2) 81/1051/EEC (OJ L376 30.12.81)　(Directive amending 79/113)
   proposed 1979 - COM(79)573

Binding dates
　Notification date (79/113):　　　22 December 1978
　Formal complaince (79/113):　　 22 June 1980
　Notification date (81/1051):　　14 December 1981
　Formal compliance (81/1051):　 14 June 1983

Purpose of the Directives

　　Construction plant noise is to be regulated by a whole array of
Directives intended partly to prevent the creation of barriers to trade but
also intended to reduce noise levels.　A framework Directive will set out an
approval, verification and certification procedure and a series of daughter
Directives will then deal with individual types of plant (e.g., compressors,
bulldozers, tower cranes, current generators, pneumatic concrete breakers -
see Appendix 2).　Directive 79/113 and the amending Directive 81/1051 are
the only ones so far adopted and relate, respectively, to methods of
measuring noise radiated away from the machines and at the operator's
position.

Summary of the Directives

　　Annex I to Directive 79/113 lays down methods to be used for testing
the noise radiated from the items of plant forming the subject of daughter
Directives unless a daughter Directive lays down different or supplementary
provisions.
　　Directive 79/113 is amended by Directive 81/1051 by adding an Annex
II that sets out a method for testing the noise emitted to the operator's
position.
　　A committee on the adaptation to technical progress of the Directives
on construction plant noise is established.

Development of the Directives

　　The first Action Programme on the Environment of 1973 proposed
legislation to reduce noise from construction plant but by then the
Community had already decided to legislate in the field in order to prevent

the creation of trade barriers.

According to a memorandum submitted in March 1982 by the Department of Industry for a House of Lords' review of Community noise policy (1), the terms of a framework Directive concerning the approval, verification and certification procedure have been agreed but formal adoption by the Council has been held up pending resolution of what is referred to as the 'third country' question. Proposals have also been made for a number of daughter Directives but agreement on the noise levels has not yet been reached in all cases.

There are two aspects to the 'third country' question. First, since the Directives would allow a manufacturer to obtain Community-wide type approval or certification in any Member State and thereby free him to sell the product in all Member States, and since it is argued that in certain fields not every Member State has the expertise and facilities to test all equipment, a manufacturer outside the Community may choose a 'weak' Member State in which to have his product approved and so gain entry to the whole Community market. Secondly, certain Member States believe that if a third country is given access to the Community market there should be some reciprocal agreement by which access is given to the market of that third country. The 'third country' question illustrates how matters quite unrelated to environmental policy may hold up agreement on environmental measures.

Formal Compliance in the UK

Directive 79/113 has not been formally complied with in Britain despite the period for doing so having elapsed, and strictly therefore Britain is in breach of the Directive. This failure is defensible since the Directive is ineffective until the framework Directive and at least one daughter Directive have been agreed. The government's intention appears to be to wait for that to happen before complying with the Directives - whether this be by invoking Section 2(2) of the European Communities Act 1972 or Section 68 of the Control of Pollution Act 1974 or in any other way that may be appropriate. This delay has been justified by events since Directive 81/1051 amends Directive 79/113 and if Regulations had been made implementing the earlier Directive they would themselves by now have had to be amended.

Section 60 of the Control of Pollution Act empowers local authorities to specify the plant that may or may not be used on a construction site, the hours when works may be carried out, and the noise levels which may be emitted from the premises. This provision formed a part of the Protection of the Environment Bill introduced into Parliament in November 1973 and which, after a change of government in 1974, provided a model for the Bill that became the Control of Pollution Act 1974. The original Bill had no provision for the making of Regulations setting noise limits on items of construction plant and this provision, which is now to be found in Section 68 of the Control of Pollution Act, may well have been added so as to be able to implement the Directives that were then being developed by the Commission. The Parliamentary record is silent as to the reasons for the introduction of the clause that became Section 68 but it is perfectly plausible that, like the clause dealing with the constituents of motor fuels (see Sections 9.1 and 9.3)

277

it was introduced at least in part in an attempt to anticipate Community legislation. There is nevertheless some difficulty with Section 68 since it only empowers the Secretary of State to make regulations requiring the use of silencers on plant or machinery, or for limiting the noise of construction plant when in use. It is not completely clear whether this covers the plant as manufactured and whether it can therefore be relied upon to implement the Directives.

Effect on UK Practice

Until at least one daughter Directive is agreed there can be no effect on practice except to the extent that manufacturers modify their plant in the knowledge that they will eventually have to meet certain noise limits. However, the noise limits of the daughter Directives have all yet to be settled.

References

(1) House of Lords, Select Committee on the European Communities, **Noise in the Environment,** 13th Report, Session 1981-82, HMSO.

12.5 Aircraft Noise

1) 80/51/EEC (OJ L18 24.1.80)   Directive on the limitation of
   proposed 20.4.76 - COM(76)157   noise emissions from subsonic
                                    aircraft

2) 83/206/EEC (OJ L117 4.5.83)   (amendment)
   proposed 15.9.81 - COM(81)512

Binding dates

Notification date (80/51):	21 December 1979
Notification date (83/206)	26 April 1983
Formal compliance (80/51):	21 June 1980
Formal compliance (83/206):	26 April 1984
Ban on use of non-noise certificated subsonic jets on registers of Member States:	1 January 1987
Ban on use of aircraft registered outside the Community and not meeting standards:	1 January 1988

Purpose of the Directives

The Directives ensure that Member States implement the noise standards for subsonic aircraft which have been agreed, but without mandatory force, within the International Civil Aviation Organisation (ICAO). They also implement certain recommendations of the European Civil Aviation Conference (ECAC) concerning non-noise certificated aircraft. The Directives differ from the other noise Directives by not precluding the imposition of stricter measures by Member States (see Sections 12.1 to 12.4).

Summary of the Directives

The two Directives taken together require Member States to ensure that the relevant categories of civil aircraft registered in their territories are not used unless certificated in accordance with certain chapters of Volume 1 of Annex 16/5 to the Convention on International Civil Aviation. (Annex 16 only covers certain categories of aircraft).

Subject to certain exemptions Member States are also to ensure that from January 1980 all civil subsonic jet aeroplanes newly registered in their territories that use aerodromes situated in any Member State are certificated in accordance with requirements at least equal to the applicable standards of Volume 1 of Annex 16/5. From June 1980 the same rule applied to propeller driven aeroplanes weighing not more than 5,700 kg but a Member State may make exceptions if the aeroplanes operate only in their territory or in that of consenting States.

279

Each Member State is to ensure that as from 1st January 1987 civil subsonic jet aeroplanes registered in its territory may not be used unless granted noise certification in accordance with requirements at least equal to those in Part II, Chapter 2 of Volume 1 of Annex 16/5. Temporary exceptions may be made in specific circumstances.

As from 1st January 1988 Member States are not to permit the operation of civil subsonic jet aeroplanes which are registered outside the Member States and which do not comply with the noise standards of Part II, Chapter 2 of Volume 1 of Annex 16/5. Temporary exceptions may be made in specific circumstances.

Development of the Directives

The first international standards for aircraft noise were adopted by ICAO in 1971 and have been revised on several occasions since. ICAO's Recommendations are not legally binding on its 144 Member States but most of the major aircraft manufacturing countries base their national regulations upon ICAO's work.

The first mention of Community action on aircraft noise is to be found not in the first Action Programme on the Environment of 1973 (although the preamble to Directive 80/51 claims erroneously that there is such a mention) but in a written reply in 1973 (No 654/73) by the Council to a European Parliamentary Question. Given that there were discrepancies between Member States in the implementation of the ICAO standards the Commission decided that the best approach for the Community was not to lay down its own standards but to ensure that the existing standards were applied consistently across the Community.

In the original proposal for a Directive an 'EEC noise limitation certificate' would have been introduced but this idea was abandoned. The proposal was also changed by the introduction in mandatory form of recommendations emanating from the European Civil Aviation Organisation (ECAC) concerning non-noise certificated aircraft.

In the House of Commons considerable concern was expressed that acceptance of the Directive might lead to an extension of Community competence into the field of aviation. It was envisaged that the Commission might want to represent the Member States at international meetings such as those of ICAO. However, any fears in the mind of the government were overcome and in a debate (19th June 1979) the Minister, Norman Tebbit, expressed himself satisfied that "the extension of the Community's authority which the Directive will produce is justified by the extra powers that it will bring to enable us to limit the noise of aircraft from other Member States".

The House of Lords (1) considered the proposal for the amending Directive as a natural extension of the parent Directive and supported its adoption. It brought the parent Directive up to date by incoporating new standards agreed by ICAO in 1979 and also introduced a ban on foreign registered aircraft that do not meet specified standards by 1st January 1988.

Formal Compliance in the UK

The Air Navigation (Noise Certification) Order 1979 (SI 1979 No 930) made under Section 19 of the Civil Aviation Act 1968 came into operation on

1st August 1979. This Order, which replaces earlier Orders, contains in its Schedules the noise emission standards prescribed by ICAO in Annex 16 (1978 Edition). The Order prohibits the use of all aircraft which do not conform to the prescribed international standards, including some categories which are not yet covered by Annex 16, but the scope of the prohibition is then relaxed by the use of exempting powers given to the Civil Aviation Authority by the Secretary of State for Trade under Article 16 of the Order. Exemption is given to all aircraft outside the categories defined in ICAO Annex 16. These exemptions are listed in the Authority's Official Record. The end result is that British legislation gives full effect to the provisions of Directive 80/51 and whilst the Civil Aviation Authority have delegated powers of exemption these can only be used after consultation with the Secretary of State. A further Order will be introduced to take account of Directive 83/206.

Effect on UK Practice

Directive 80/51 has had no effect on British registered aircraft since the ICAO recommendations and those of ECAC were already applied in Britain. The main effect of the Directive will be to compel those Member States that were not already applying the standards to do so eventually. This was explained in evidence given by the Department of Trade to a House of Lords' Select Committee for its review of Community noise policy (1). Giving evidence in April 1982, an official said that Italy, Luxembourg and Greece did not have legislation on the subject two years after the due date. To the extent that aircraft registered abroad, which have the right to land in Britain, now have to conform to the standards there will have been a slight improvement to the environment in Britain. The ban from 1988 of aircraft registered outside Member States unless they meet certain standards should also have a beneficial effect.

Further Developments

In October 1981 the Commission proposed a Directive limiting helicopter noise (OJ C275 27.10.81 - COM(81)554).

References

(1) House of Lords, Select Committee on the European Communities, **Noise in the Environment,** 13th Report, Session 1981-1982, HMSO.

PART THREE

CHAPTER 13
Effect on British Legislation

The full extent of Community legislation in the environmental field has been set out in Part Two of this book, and the list is a long one. It may therefore come as a surprise to find how little new primary legislation has so far had to be introduced in Britain in order to implement Directives, and that considerably fewer items of secondary legislation have been introduced than there are Directives. By primary legislation is meant an Act of Parliament while secondary, or subordinate, legislation includes Regulations which Ministers are empowered to make under primary legislation. Although secondary legislation is frequently of an administrative or technical nature it will sometimes introduce provisions every bit as important as those to be found in primary legislation.

The only two Acts of Parliament shown in Part Two to have been influenced by existing or proposed Community environmental legisation are the Control of Pollution Act 1974 and the Wildlife and Countryside Act 1981. Nevertheless some Regulations made under the European Communities Act 1972 can also be regarded as performing the function of primary legislation, and in addition a number of Regulations have been made under existing Acts. Community environmental legislation has also created pressure for bringing into force parts of Acts which were already on the statute book, and for the introduction of some new legislation.

European Communities Act 1972

The European Communities Act 1972 (ECA) contains powers in Section 2(2) for Ministers to make Regulations in order to implement any obligation arising out of Community membership. Government departments nevertheless prefer to rely on the powers in existing legislation wherever possible and usually resort to the ECA only when no other powers are available. Resort to the ECA is therefore the equivalent of introducing new primary legislation although in its form it is secondary legislation. Where ECA has had to be relied upon it can therefore be regarded as an indication that existing legislation has been inadequate for the new subject matter introduced by a Directive. In the environmental field the ECA had by mid-1983 been resorted to only twice: the first occasion provided by the detergent Directives (Section 7.1), and the second by the 'Sixth Amendment' and the other Directives dealing with the notification and classification of chemicals (Section 10.1). A third occasion now being contemplated is provided by the so-called Seveso Directive dealing with major accident hazards from industrial activities (Section 10.3).

The detergent Directives could in fact have been implemented by Regulations made under section 100 of the Control of Pollution Act 1974 (COPA), and it seems probable that COPA was not used because provision had already been made before COPA existed for the ECA to be used - see the

European Communities (Designation) Order 1972 (SI 1972 No 1811).

The reason why the ECA has had to be relied upon to implement the 'Sixth Amendment' is that the Health and Safety at Work etc Act 1974 (HSWA) does not confer powers on the Health and Safety Executive to require information about environmental effects of chemical substances as opposed to their effects on man. The Regulations implementing the Directives have accordingly been made under both ECA and HSWA.

The greater part of the Seveso Directive can be implemented under HSWA, but it also requires some measures for which there is no authority in HSWA. The duty being placed on local authorities to prepare emergency plans relating to specified installations and the duty requiring the Health and Safety Executive to consider environmental effects of accidents will be fulfilled by Regultions made under ECA.

Although the changes brought about to British legislation by the detergent Directives may appear to have a rather technical character, they represent a policy change away from reliance on voluntary agreements between government and industry to reliance on legislatively prescribed standards. The changes brought about by the 'Sixth Amendment' and the Seveso Directive have had the effect of stretching the duties of the Health and Safety Executive and of ensuring collaboration between the Health and Safety Executive and the Department of the Environment. These are changes of some significance.

The Control of Pollution Act 1974

The great bulk of COPA owes nothing to the Community's environmental policy and would have been enacted in the same form even if Britain had not acceded to the Community. This can be demonstrated by referring to the various national reports that resulted in the introduction in November 1973 of the precursor of COPA - the Protection of the Environment Bill. These reports include the Jeger report on water pollution (see Chapter 5) and the Key and Sumner reports on waste (see Section 8.0), as well as reports of the Royal Commission on Environmental Pollution. The fact that the Bill preceded agreement on the first Action Proramme on the Environment by a few days is of no significance in this respect since the contents of the Action Programme had been well known much earlier.

There are, however, one or two sections of COPA which were definitely introduced in anticipation of Community legislation or which may have been so introduced. Section 76, which enables the Secretary of State to make Regulations controlling the sulphur content of oil fuel, was admitted in a debate in the House of Lords to have been introduced in anticipation of a Directive (see Section 9.1), and it seems quite probable that the same is true of Section 75 concerned with the composition and content of motor fuel which has been relied upon to implement both the Directive on the sulphur content of gas oil (including diesel fuel) (Section 9.1), and the Directive on the lead content of petrol (Section 9.3). Section 68, concerned with the use of silencers on plant or machinery, may also have been introduced in order to implement Directives on the noise of construction plant (see Section 12.4).

The Sections on air pollution provide another example of a shift away from reliance on voluntary agreements between industry and government towards mandatory standards.

The Wildlife and Countryside Act 1981

It is possible that the government would have introduced a Bill into Parliament dealing with wildlife and countryside matters without the prospect of the Directive on birds (Section 11.1), and indeed the Wildlife and Countryside Act 1981 contains material going well beyond the field covered by the Directive. Nevertheless the Directive will have required some amendments to existing Acts protecting bird species, and will therefore have been one factor in the decision to introduce new legislation. Some of the rather few changes concerned with the protection of species of birds that can be attributed to the Directive are mentioned in Section 11.1. The more significant change brought about by the Act in relation to birds concerns their habitats, and Section 29 refers to compliance with international obligations as a reason for the power to make nature conservation orders. This can be taken as a reference to the Berne and Bonn Conventions (see Section 11.3) and to the Ramsar Convention concerned with wetlands, as well as to the Directive. The combination of all these international obligations seems to have convinced the government that it would be best to have stronger powers for habitat protection.

Regulations Made Under Existing Acts

A number of Regulations to implement Directives made either under the ECA or HSWA or COPA have already been mentioned above. In addition, several Regulations have been made under other Acts in order to implement the noise Directives (see Sections 12.1 to 12.5) and the Directives dealing with vehicle emissions (see Section 9.6). Since some of these Directives are of the 'optional' kind (that is to say Member States are not obliged to adopt the standards but may not adopt more stringent standards), not all the Regulations have had to be made. Nevertheless, given the decision to set standards in Britain, the Directives will have ensured that the Regulations have a particular content.

Regulations have also been made under COPA concerned with the transport of hazardous waste (see Section 8.2), and although some Regulations would undoubtedly have been made even in the absence of the Directive (in order to replace the Deposit of Poisonous Waste Act 1972) the Directive will have influenced their form and content.

Several Regulations have also been made under COPA and the Consumer Safety Act 1978 in order to restrict the marketing and use of certain dangerous substances (see Section 10.2). Some of these Regulations would not have been made in the absence of Directives.

Finally, there is a Regulation made under the Endangered Species (Import and Export) Act 1976 banning trade in whale products (see Section 11.2) which would not have been made in that form in the absence of a Community Regulation. (Strictly the British Regulations are redundant, since a Community Regulation is directly applicable law).

Pressure for Legislation

Community legislation, as well as being responsible wholly or in part for the primary and secondary legislation mentioned above, is also creating

287

pressure for the bringing into force of parts of Acts which were already on the statute book but lying dormant, for the making of new Regulations under existing Acts, and for the introduction of some new legislation. Some of these pressures emerge in the next Chapter on compliance with Directives, but even where compliance is not in issue the need may have been revealed to bring British legislation up to date by incorporating aspects of Community legislation. The power for the Secretary of State to specify air quality standards is one such area (Section 9.1) and it is hard to imagine the review of air pollution legislation that the government has announced ignoring this possibility. The field of pesticides is another where new legislation may be necessary (Section 10.5).

CHAPTER 14

Formal Compliance with Directives

Community Directives place obligations on Member States, the fulfilment of which is referred to as compliance or implementation - the words being used synonymously. In Chapter 6 we drew a distinction between formal and practical compliance, and in this Chapter we consider only formal compliance and the extent to which there has been any shortfall in the case of the environmental Directives.

With the occasional exception, a Directive will set a period of time (usually two years) within which Member States must bring into force the laws, regulations or administrative provisions necessary to comply with the Directive. The only exception in the environmental field is Directive 76/464 on the discharge of dangerous substances to water (Section 7.8), where the omission of a deadline for formal compliance may have been an oversight resulting from its having started life as a proposal for a Decision.

Member States will frequently miss the compliance date but, as explained in Chapter 6, failure of formal compliance does not necessarily imply a failure in complying with the practical obligations in the Directive, and therefore not all failures are equally culpable. It also sometimes happens that the greater part of a Directive will be fully complied with while some relatively minor part may be delayed. A mere catalogue of failures therefore runs the risk of giving a misleading impression by not distinguishing partial from total failure and not indicating whether the failure is one of substance or merely procedural. It is also not very informative in the absence of a comparison with other countries. A delay in formal compliance, even if only in part, will nevertheless create a pressure on the government to introduce the necessary legislation or administrative measures needed for full compliance, and is therefore an indicator that the Directive has or is having an effect on the government's behaviour, that is to say on national policy. It is primarily in the quest for these indicators rather than in order to pass judgement that the extent of formal compliance is reviewed here. Where there are failures they are summarised and a fuller discussion is to be found in the appropriate section of Part Two, which also describes some other lapses in compliance not noted in this review.

The missing of a date may fall only into the category of a procedural failure rather than a failure of substance, despite the fact that the Commission may have taken the first formal step that could lead to a case before the European Court. This step consists of issuing a 'Reasoned Opinion' to the effect that compliance is incomplete. The following are examples of such procedural failures:

- Detergents (Section 7.1). The British Regulations were nearly four years late, but detergents in Britain already met the standards required.

- Sampling surface water (Section 7.3). The DOE was six months late in formally appointing the water authorities as the competent authorities by means of a circular letter. However it was self-evident who was to be responsible.

- Sulphur in gas oil (Section 9.1). The British Regulations were three and a half months late but the standards were already met.

- Restrictions on marketing and use of PCB (Section 10.2). The British Regulations were two and a half years late because no alternative material was available for a use that was to have been banned and the Directive was to be amended accordingly. However the other uses were already the subject of a voluntary ban.

- Noise from construction plant (Section 12.4). No Regulations have yet been made. However, the Directive in question is inoperative until other Directives are agreed.

A number of other failures are arguably more blameworthy, such as:

- Bathing water (Section 7.7). The water authorities were not appointed as the competent authorities until two years after the date for compliance, and were only given advice on how to interpret that part of the Directive dealing with 'a large number of bathers' a few weeks before the bathing season (even now full compliance is in doubt - see below).

- Waste (Section 8.1). The section of the Control of Pollution Act requiring the preparation of waste disposal plans was brought into force one year after the due date.

- Preventing risks by testing - the 'Sixth Amendment' (Section 10.1). The British Regulations were one year late because of a dispute between the chemical industry and the Health and Safety Commission.

- Birds and their habitats (Section 11.1). The Wildlife and Countryside Act 1981 received the Royal Assent six months after the due date, and the part dealing with bird protection was brought into force seventeen months after the due date. However, the bulk of the Directive was implemented under previously existing legislation.

In nearly all the cases noted above, formal compliance was merely delayed and has now been assured. In the case of the seven Directives discussed below, compliance was still incomplete as of October 1983, although it is the government's intention to make good the deficiency. These Directives all concern water and in all cases compliance is incomplete because Part II of the COPA, and in particular Section 32 concerned with controlling discharges, is not in force. Four Directives are concerned with water quality objectives:

- Surface water for drinking (Section 7.2)
- Water standards for freshwater fish (Section 7.5)
- Shellfish waters (Section 7.6)
- Bathing water (Section 7.7)

Although water authorities have identified or designated the relevant waters for the above four Directives and are able to control most discharges to ensure that the specified quality objectives are met, there are some discharges that are not yet controlled. This means that either control over the waters is not complete or that the choice of waters for designation may have been distorted.

In the case of the Directives on surface water for drinking and freshwater fish it is control over discharges to lakes that is required, and in the case of the Directives on shellfish waters and bathing waters it is control over discharges to coastal waters and estuaries that is required.

The following three water Directives specify that there should be controls over certain discharges:

- dangerous substances in water (Section 7.8)
- groundwater (Section 7.9)
- titanium dioxide (Section 7.11)

The Directive on dangerous substances requires all discharges to water that contain certain substances to be authorised, and although discharges to rivers and to some estuaries are presently controlled, discharges to coastal waters and some other estuaries are not. The discharge from one plant manufacturing titanium dioxide is not yet the subject of a consent and some discharges to land which might reach groundwater are not presently controlled.

The government has announced its intention of bringing into force by 1985 those Sections of COPA that will enable discharges to estuaries, coastal waters, lakes and groundwater to be controlled. In order to keep down costs the government is nevertheless exempting from control all discharges except those that might affect waters subject to Directives. These 'exceptions from exemptions' are listed in the Control of Pollution (Exemption of Certain Discharges from Control) Order 1983 (SI 1983 No 1182) which carries an explanatory memorandum specifically referring to six of the above Directives as providing the reason for the exceptions. Parliament presumably intended that Ministers would fairly promptly have brought into force the Sections of the Act concerned with controlling previously uncontrolled discharges. The delay of many years followed by the complicated stratagem of bringing into force the relevant Sections but then exempting discharges (as the Act allows), while excepting from the exemptions those that need to be controlled to ensure compliance with Directives, demonstrates that it is the Directives that have forced the pace and defined the extent of advance.

That, however, is not the end of the matter. Even when Section 32 of COPA is in force doubt will still remain as to whether there is complete compliance with the Directives concerned with water quality objectives. This is the result of a judgement of the European Court and is discussed in Appendix 3. The uncertainty created by this judgement can either be resolved by the Court or by the introduction of a new Act empowering the Secretary of State and the water authorities to specify mandatory water quality standards.

Finally, there are the following three Directives which are not completely complied with but where the government's intention to make good the deficiency is uncertain:

- toxic waste (Section 8.2)
- disposal of PCBs (Section 8.3)
- waste oils (Section 8.4)

All three Directives rely in part on Regulations made under Section 17 of COPA - the Control of Pollution (Special Waste) Regulations 1980 - for compliance, and all three exerted pressure for the introduction of the Regulations. Though late, the Regulations have nevertheless not ensured complete compliance.

The toxic waste Directive specifies, among the many other requirements which are fully complied with, that 'identification forms' shall accompany waste when it is transported in the course of disposal. Disposal includes recycling. This obligation is not completely discharged in Britain by the Special Waste Regulations, since they do not require consignment notes for waste that is to be recycled. There is also no legislation in Britain that says that records must be kept of toxic waste **produced** or **stored** as required by the Directive, although a House of Lords report has recommended this (see Section 8.2). The definition of toxic waste in the Special Waste Regulations is also narrower than that in the Directive in not covering all waste constituting a risk to the environment. These difficult points are discussed more fully in Section 8.2.

The PCB Directive makes compulsory the disposal (i.e., collection and/or destruction, regeneration) of waste PCB, while there is nothing in British legislation preventing anyone holding a quantity of waste PCB on his premises.

The waste oil Directive has two Articles that have not been complied with. There is no British legislation requiring establishments **producing** and **collecting** waste oil to keep records of the quantity, quality, origin and location of the oil, nor requiring holders of waste oil to handle and store these separately according to the content of impurities

Three broad conclusions can be drawn from this review of British compliance with a very large number of environmental Directives. First, it is not uncommon for there to be some delay with formal compliance, and while any such failure is always regrettable, in some of the cases noted above there have been understandable reasons and the consequences have not been significant. Although the Commission frequently issues 'Reasoned Opinions' in order to apply pressure, Britain, unlike some other Member States, has yet to be brought before the European Court for failure to implement an environmental Directive. This suggests that the Commission is circumspect in deciding the cases it takes to the Court. The Commission is rather less circumspect in issuing Reasoned Opinions, since in several cases discussed in Part Two an exchange of letters or even a telephone call could have resolved a relatively minor point that may not have been clear from the government's compliance letter. For their part not all compliance letters have been as complete as could have been desired and the fact that they are now publicly accessible may ensure an improvement in quality in future.

Secondly, a number of the failures to comply has been the consequence of the delay in bringing into force Part II of COPA dealing with water. This delay has been a matter of considerable criticism in Britain and might well have continued if Community Directives had not forced the government to act. It was always possible that the Commission would start proceedings

before the European Court and a surprise to some that it did not do so. Compliance with the water Directives should nevertheless soon be more secure.

Thirdly, there is a continuing failure to comply with parts of three waste Directives. Since compliance with these is far from complete in other countries it is unlikely that the Commission would single out Britain in any action before the Court. This is not to say that the British government should not be considering how to make good the deficiencies if it is to maintain its reputation for not entering into obligations without the intention of honouring them. This would probably involve new secondary legislation.

If the question of compliance is approached with an emphasis on success rather than failure, the position appears rather positive. When Section 32 of COPA is in force, only three Directives out of a very large number will not be fully complied with, and even these are complied with in large measure. Given that rather little new primary legislation has had to be introduced, the conclusion must be that existing British legislation has been remarkably broad and adaptable.

293

CHAPTER 15

Effect on British Policy and Practice

The limited effect of the Community's environmental policy on British legislation belies the extent of its effect on British policy and practice. The broad and unspecific character of so much British legislation, together with the related tradition of devolved responsibility, ensures that there is scope for considerable change in policy without the need for corresponding change in legislation. The introduction of river quality objectives in 1978, for example, was a change of policy carried out by the water authorities, with the approval of the government, but without any amendment of the relevant legislation. Even when the Control of Pollution Act is fully in force there will still be no obligation on water authorities to specify river quality objectives or powers enabling the Secretary of State to do so if the authorities default. In Chapters 2 and 5 we attributed this quite significant policy change to the pressure of Community environmental policy.

A change in national legislation is therefore only one possible effect of Community environmental legislation, and indeed a number of other kinds of effect can be identified:

- it goes without saying that the ultimate purpose of the Community's environmental policy is to protect and improve the environment and some such effects must have taken place even though they may be difficult to demonstrate;

- Community policy affects the behaviour of industrialists and regulatory agencies;

- it can ensure that more information is made available (1);

- as well as the content of legislation, it can affect its style;

- it can prevent national backsliding, including the repeal of existing national legislation even if it has not been responsible for that legislation;

- it can limit the discretion available to regulatory agencies with consequences for the tradition of devolved responsibility discussed in Chapter 2;

- it can provide a dialogue with other countries so that experience from outside can be absorbed and conversely British experience can be imparted;

- more pointedly, it can provide the means for an individual Member State to initiate Community legislation and so directly influence policy in other Member States and indeed beyond;

- finally, it can stretch national policy by providing a yardstick against which it can be measured. Although the converse also applies, and Community policy can be measured against the yardsticks of national policies, the mandatory character of Community policy ensures that the comparison with the Community yardstick is not made out of mere idle curiosity.

It follows that individual items of Community legislation, and the corpus of law that collectively they constitute, can produce results not immediately self-evident from the face of the legislative documents themselves. This point needs repeating since it is not often enough recognised even within the Commission itself, perhaps because knowledge of the interaction of national and Community policies is still so limited. It is almost as if the desire for explicitness that is so characteristic of Community policy is carried over when considering the effects of that policy. The result is that many of the most interesting and long term effects of Community policy can easily be overlooked.

In a national context the danger of taking legislation at its face value is well understood. There are many examples of national legislation failing to produce the intended results and being quickly amended or allowed to lie fallow. It also sometimes happens that what was thought of as a minor piece of legislation has effects that are not anticipated and that grow with importance over time. There is no reason to suppose that Community legislation is not also subject to this same general rule, but with the difference that ten Member States are involved and that the legislation has been shaped by forces quite different from those that shape national legislation. A Community Directive that results in a change in one Member State may have little effect in another, and just because in this book some Directives have been found significant in Britain it does not follow that they would be equally significant in another country. In assessing the overall effect in the Community of its environmental policy no short cuts are therefore possible, and the only sure approach must be Directive by Directive and country by country. Attempts by the Commission to take stock of progress made with the Environment Action Programmes (2,3) are valuable in listing the legislation adopted and in describing the difficulties encountered, but they have hitherto lacked the critical assessment that can only come from a knowledge of the way national policies are implemented in practice in all Member States and how this has changed as a result of Community policy. Although the most recent such report from the Commission (3) recognises the importance of implementation and devotes some four paragraphs to the subject, it confines comment to what in this book we have called formal compliance and which is only a small part of the whole. Assessment of the Community-wide effects of the Community's environmental policy is therefore a task which is only just beginning.

Each section of Part Two of this book has recorded certain effects of Directives in Britain - sometimes of a quite minor kind but some of importance. This chapter does not attempt a complete summary but merely draws conclusions, first under the chapter headings of Part Two and then more generally.

Water

The clarification and formalisation of the concept of environmental quality objectives has been the principal effect on Britain of the Directives

295

on water. There is an apparent paradox in this statement, since British insistence on quality objectives as opposed to limit values has been such a well publicised feature of Community discussions of water pollution policy. The resolution of this paradox resides in separating two things. The British insistence that the Directive on discharging dangerous substances to water (Section 7.8) had to accommodate the British practice of not setting national limit values is one. The fact that the same Directive and some others made the setting of explicit quality objectives mandatory for the first time in Britain is the other.

The same Directive and the discussion of its daughter Directives has also forced both the DOE and the water authorities to pay much more attention than formerly to the dangerous substances in Lists I and II of the Directive. One example of this is the research undertaken at the Water Research Centre that has resulted in proposed water quality objectives for a limited number of List II substances.

The detergent Directives (Section 7.1), as already noted in Chapter 13, represent a change away from reliance on voluntary agreements between government and industry to reliance on legislatively prescribed standards.

The Directives on bathing water (Section 7.7) and shellfish water (Section 7.6) forced the water authorities to consider the quality of coastal waters several years before they would have been required to do so by the Control of Pollution Act 1974. The bathing water Directive in particular has provided a yardstick for the design of new sewage outfalls and has thereby influenced decisions even where no bathing waters have been identified under the Directive. Several Directives have caused water authorities to monitor the presence of certain substances in water which were not previously monitored.

In Chapter 14 we have already recorded the role of the Directives in ensuring the bringing into force of the Control of Pollution Act.

Waste

The waste Directives have had less effect in Britain than the water Directives, in part because the framework Directive (Section 8.1) was largely modelled on Part I of the Control of Pollution Act. One influence, whose full extent is however hard to establish, is the form of the British Regulations concerned with the identification form that must accompany hazardous wastes when being transported (Section 8.2). In Chapter 14 we noted that three of the waste Directives were not fully complied with and it is possible that further changes will have to be made in British legislation if full compliance is to be achieved. These include controls over hazardous wastes being transported for the purpose of recycling, and the keeping of records of hazardous wastes produced and stored.

Air

Just as the water Directives forced Britain to adopt explicit water quality standards or objectives, so the air Directives have caused Britain to adopt air quality standards, initially for smoke and sulphur dioxide and then for lead (Sections 9.1, 9.5). As with the water Directives, these air quality standards have not involved changes to British legislation.

The Royal Commission on Environmental Pollution had in 1976 rejected the idea of air quality standards although it proposed the not too different idea of guidelines. But given that it took six years for the government to reply to the Royal Commission's report, there must be considerable doubt whether the idea of air quality guidelines or standards would have been introduced even now in the absence of Community pressure. One can assume that without a Directive there would have been a long period of discussion on the appropriate level of the guidelines, and whatever the criticisms of the quality standards set by the Directive the figures presented forced the issue. The smoke and sulphur dioxide Directive can therefore be claimed as a turning point in British air pollution policy. Its more practical effect has been to provide an impetus and a strategic framework for the completion of smoke control that began with the Clean Air Act 1956. Another practical effect has been to maintain in place a more extensive monitoring network than there would have been otherwise. The Directive setting an air quality standard for lead (Section 9.5) will likewise require formalised arrangements for monitoring.

The lead in petrol Directive (Section 9.3) in all probability did not bring forward the date when lead in petrol was reduced to 0.4 grams/litre, but the proposal for the Directive must have concentrated the government's mind on the earliest acceptable date and prevented it being put off. The Directive now provides an added reason why Britain cannot unilaterally make unleaded petrol compulsory, and an amendment of the Directive to allow this is now under consideration as a result of a British initiative. It is one of the ironies of Community legislation that it was Britain that caused the Directive to be such that unleaded petrol cannot yet be made obligatory.

The Directive establishing a screening campaign for blood lead levels in the population (Section 9.4) has resulted in better information than would have existed otherwise in Britain and has provided a comparison with other countries. The seemingly innocuous activity of collecting information has had the further effect of feeding the debate on lead in petrol.

Chemicals

The Directive known as the 'Sixth Amendment' (Section 10.1), instituting a scheme of prior notification involving tests for potential hazards before a new substance is marketed, is a major piece of legislation by any standards. Arguably it is the most important environmental Directive agreed so far, not least because it embodies the idea of prevention being better than cure. Although a similar scheme was foreshadowed in the Health and Safety at Work etc Act 1974, it is at least open to doubt whether a truly workable national scheme could have been developed in isolation given the international character of the chemical industry. The most significant effect of the Directive for Britain lies not in the various differences from whatever national scheme might have been devised in the absence of the Directive, but in the way the Directive has created a common position among the Member States and enabled them to speak collectively in wider discussions such as those within the OECD or with the USA. Given that chemicals are traded so widely, internationally agreed arrangements for testing before marketing are essential if they are to be truly workable and are not to impede trade.   Britain, and other European countries, could never have achieved so much influence in these discussions acting alone.

Other effects include the cooperation between DOE and the Health and Safety Executive that results from them jointly being the competent authority for the purposes of the Directive.   This is a result of the Directive seeking to anticipate effects on the environment as well as on man.   Had there been only a national scheme it would have excluded effects that were solely environmental and there would have been no such collaboration. Another form of cooperation resulting from the Directive is that between the competent authorities in all the Member States.   As the Health and Safety Executive put it, "a notification made to the (British) competent authority is made to the European Community as a whole, the competent authority in effect acting on behalf of the Community".   This suggests that we may yet be seeing the creation of a Community 'agent' that in Chapter 3 was said hardly to exist in the environmental field.

The main effect of the Directives on restricting the marketing and use of certain dangerous substances (Section 10.2) has been to create a mechanism whereby precautionary measures adopted in one Member State are quickly and uniformly applied across the Community.

The Seveso Directive on major accident hazards (Section 10.3) has weakened and delayed the introduction of some British measures but has in other respects stretched British measures beyond what was originally intended.   A duty is now to be placed on local authorities requiring them to prepare 'off-site' emergency plans relating to specified installations, and the public will have to be given information about these installations.   In addition the powers and duties of the Health and Safety Executive are being extended to embrace effects on the environment as well as on man.   A feature that the Seveso Directive shares with the Sixth Amendment is that both have come to define not just the minimum legislation for Britain but also the maximum.   The Health and Safety Executive had proposed procedures in some respects more stringent than both Directives, but industry was able to argue successfully that they should be compelled to go no further than the Directives require.

The Decisions on chlorofluorocarbons (Section 10.4) may have encouraged some of the larger manufacturers of aerosol cans to switch to hydrocarbons, but in policy terms the more interesting aspect is the setting of a ceiling on total production of a given substance for environmental reasons.   This is the first time this has happened in Britain.

Wildlife

Although the birds Directive (Section 11.1) has made some small changes to British legislation and to current practice, one of its major effects is likely to lie in the future and another to lie beyond Britain. Unlike existing British legislation, the Directive lays down general principles about bird and habitat protection and these are likely to be relied on increasingly if agricultural pressures continue to threaten bird habitats. The same debates between agricultural and conservation interests will take place, but the conservation interests now have the backing of principles enshrined in Community legislation with the Commission ready to ensure that the obligations set out in the Directive are honoured.   One can only speculate on the possible long term consequences for agricultural policy. That is for the future. For the present the major policy effect can be described as the moral pressure of northern Europe on southern Europe to adopt its standards and values. Without the channel provided by the Community this pressure would have been as ineffective today as it has been in the past.

The whale Regulation (Section 11.2) is another example of the general point that when dealing with a subject not confined by national frontiers, national legislation is inadequate. Quite simply, a Community-wide ban has been more effective than would have been a national ban. Since the Regulation resulted from a British initiative it can quite properly be seen as an example of Britain successfully pursuing a domestic policy abroad.

Noise

The vehicle noise Directives (Sections 12.1 to 12.3) are of the 'optional' kind and have so far had little positively beneficial environmental effects in Britain. Indeed they may have retarded a reduction in lorry noise for a few years and may yet do so in the future.

* * * * *

This review has shown significant effects in Britain in all six fields in which there has been Community environmental legislation, and noise is the only one in which the effect has not on balance been positive. Many of these effects are quite specific to the subject matter of the legislation, but in addition several broader effects emerge.

First, the Community has stimulated discussion in important policy areas and has helped government towards the point of decision. Even though water quality objectives and air quality guidelines had been talked about in Britain, the Community has both established them as principles enshrined in legislation and has ensured that they are articulated in a workable manner. There are still matters to resolve, including the handling of the discharges of particularly dangerous substances to water - the so called List I - and, in the field of air, in integrating the concept of air quality standards with the obligation to use 'best practicable means'. Appendix 4 puts forward some proposals for resolving the water problem. Both the testing of new chemical substances and the handling of major accident hazards were under consideration in Britain, but Community involvement has resulted in significant extensions of what would have otherwise been British schemes. Community policy has thus brought Britain into contact with a larger range of tools for pollution control and has led to refinement in its use of existing tools. The lack of consistency in Britain between the environmental quality objective approach in the water pollution field and the nationally fixed emission standard approach embodied in the Industrial Air Pollution Inspectorate's interpretation of 'best practicable means' has been thrown into relief and will ultimately have to be resolved.

Secondly, the Community has modified the style of policy making. The Community's near inability to make policy except by legislation (see Chapter 3) has meant that British policy has become more explicit by the very act of incorporating Directives. These Directives often include what in Britain would be regarded as administrative matters, i.e., they specify numerical standards but also often enunciate guiding principles so that these are now also more clearly a feature of British environmental policy. They are to be found in the birds Directive, in the air quality standards Directives, and in the water Directives. They have never been wholly absent in Britain and the general duties to be found in the Health and Safety at Work etc Act 1974 are examples. Nevertheless, when held against the yardstick of Community policy the previous absence of guiding principles in Britain has been noticeable.

Thirdly, the institutional arrangements for administering environmental policy have been changed. The reliance on voluntary agreements and guidelines which previously prevailed with detergents, PCBs, the composition of fuels, and with drinking water has shifted to reliance on legislatively prescribed standards. The Health and Safety Executive is having its powers extended to consider environmental matters and a new collaborative arrangement is being established between it and DOE. Pollution control has also become more of a central government function with less discretion being allowed to the regulatory agencies. Thus local authorities now have to take account of national air quality standards when designating smoke control areas, as will the Industrial Air Pollution Inspectorate when determining 'best practicable means'; water authorities now have to conform to certain standards laid down in water Directives and have to submit reports to central government; local authorities will have to prepare 'off-site' emergency plans near hazardous installations; the Health and Safety Executive is now constrained by the views of 'competent authorities' in other countries when considering new chemicals. This transfer of power away from local authorities and regulatory agencies towards central government and the Commission can be regarded as a consequence of the process noted in Chapter 1 of environmental problems being first perceived as local issues, then national ones and now international ones.

Fourthly, Community policy-making has injected a greater sense of urgency into British environmental policy-making. Over the past few years there have been substantial cuts in staff at DOE dealing with environmental matters, and the lengths of time it has taken to reply to reports of the Royal Commission on Environmental Pollution is just one reflection of this. The difficulty of finding parliamentary time for new legislation and the lack of will to do so further inhibits initiative. Action at Community level, on the other hand, is formally set in motion by proposals transmitted by the Commission to the Council. The Commission has consistently shown enthusiasm in proposing legislation and the Council has shared this enthusiasm by the pace at which it has adopted proposals. British Ministers in Council have played their part, but their ability to initiate rather than respond is being jeopardised by the pace of policy-making at home.

Fifthly, there have been three examples of Britain relinquishing to the Community its power of determining not just the minimum required of legislation but also the maximum. With both the 'Sixth Amendment' and the Seveso Directive, initial British plans to go further than the Directive were abandoned. The water part of the Control of Pollution Act is also being implemented only to the extent necessary to comply with Directives. This relinquishing of control has been brought about by pressure from industrial interests and is not one for which the Community can be blamed. It is a tendency which is yet reversible, but if it is not reversed the Community will emerge more strongly as the source that defines the full scope of environmental legislation in Britain.

Finally and most positively, Britain has been provided with a larger canvas on which to paint its own picture of what policies ought to be. Examples of British influence are described in the next chapter, and of these both the whale Regulation and the birds Directive are subjects for which national measures are not enough. Although the Community is no more logical a geographical unit to handle these issues, its very size, the fact that it represents an economic unit of considerable power, and above all that it is able to legislate, means it can set the agenda for other international gatherings. The 'Sixth Amendment' on the testing of chemicals is possibly the most important example of the general point that the position adopted within the Community can set the pattern for the adoption of comparable schemes in other countries. By pursuing policies within the Community, not only can Britain make some of its own policies more effective but can also extend its ability to influence others even outside the Community.

References

(1) N Haigh and G Weber, **A List of Comparative Reports on the Quality of the Environment in Member States Required under EEC Directives and Decisions**, Institute for European Environmental Policy, 1981

(2) Commission of the European Communities, **Progress Made with the Environment Action Programme and Assessment of the Work done to Implement It**, COM(80)222, Brussels, May 1980

(3) Commission of the European Communities, **Ten Years of Community Environment Policy 1973-1983**, Brussels, November 1983.

CHAPTER 16

The British Contribution

One-way influence between two parties hardly establishes a relationship that both will value, and the same must hold when the parties are a Member State and the Community. Because Community policy is embodied in items of legislation it has been possible to assess the influence of the Community on Britain with some degree of confidence simply by comparing the position in Britain before and after each item. The influence in the opposite direction is nothing like so easily measurable. There are so many other sources of influence to disentangle - the other Member States, the European Parliament, national Parliaments, outside pressure groups - and in any event the sources are so diffuse and not to be located in any neatly identifiable document that any assessment must be highly speculative.

Three broadly distinct phases of influence can nevertheless be identified. An item of existing or proposed national legislation, or possibly just an idea in a Member State, can spark the Commission into initiating Community legislation or giving shape to something coming into consideration. Secondly, once a proposal is being developed, the individual Member States will influence it both when it is still in draft, and again when it has been formally transmitted to the Council and is being discussed in the Council working groups and by Ministers themselves. Finally, the seriousness with which a Member State then implements Community legislation both formally and in practice must also constitute an important influence. Although implementation is not often thought of in this way, the ultimate test of any legislation must lie in its application, and if enough Member States studiously neglect an area of Community policy then it is bound to atrophy. Although the Commission has the duty to ensure that measures adopted under the Treaty are applied, and the power of bringing Member States before the European Court, it cannot expect to get anywhere in the face of sufficiently widespread obstinacy or indifference.

The occasions when British legislation or some other initiative has shaped Community legislation are fewer than might have been expected of a country with such a well established environmental policy. The Directive on waste (Section 8.1) is one clear example of the Community following British legislation, and the whale Regulation (Section 11.2) stems from an initiative of a British Minister. Although it was the Seveso disaster of 1976 that stimulated the Commission into proposing legislation on major accident hazards (Section 10.3), the Health and Safety Executive had already recommended British legislation before the disaster and went on to publish a draft before the Commission proposed theirs. Certain ideas were also developing in Britain on the testing of chemicals before the Commission proposed the Directive known as the 'Sixth Amendment' (Section 10.1). Britain made major contributions to both these Directives, but so did a number of other countries. Some of the Community restrictions on marketing and use of chemicals (Section 10.2) followed British restrictions, and it was in part a British initiative - the French were also involved - that led to the lowering of the noise levels in the vehicle noise Directive of 1977 (Section 12.1). The bird Directive (Section 11.1) owed much to British legislation, although it was agitation in other countries that provided the initial impulse for it.

This list is not an insignificant one - and there may be other examples of British influence at an early stage - but certainly none of the water and air pollution Directives owe their origins to British legislation. This is a surprising fact given British experience in these fields, and the very length of that experience may provide the explanation. The breadth of British air and water pollution legislation, coupled with the discretion allowed to administrative agencies to carry out duties so broadly defined, makes it unsuitable as a model for Community legislation with its precise and explicit character. To exaggerate only slightly, numbers are not to be found in British air and water legislation, nor are obligations to draw up improvement plans with deadlines. The incremental character of British policy on water and air makes it look unsystematic when viewed from outside and unappealing to the Commission draftsman. In contrast, the waste part of the Control of Pollution Act, for the very reason that it was so original, is much more coherent and lent itself to being turned into Community legislation. In no other country was there anything so comprehensive. Novelty, clarity, and a measure of detail are the characteristics of national legislation that will render it likely to influence the Community, and the style of British legislation therefore largely disqualifies it.

In modifying proposed Community legislation, Britain has exerted much more influence and in the process has created problems for itself and for the Community which have not always been adequately understood. The problem may be stated as the conflict between practicability and perfection, and was expressed in the following words in connection with one of the water Directives by the then Chairman of the National Water Council (see Section 7.5):

> "The fact is that the Commission are here proposing standards of perfection, which is what they have done before. I have had the pleasure of meeting the officials concerned and I know that this is their policy; they think that the right thing to do is to establish standards of perfection although, quite obviously, in practice it is simply impossible to conform to them. So we do make a stringent criticism of these standards as being higher than is normal in practice for rivers in which fish live and thrive".

Almost the first reaction of British officials when faced with any proposed Community legislation is to ask whether it is practical and what effect will it have in Britain. These questions are essential, but depending on how they are approached Britain can present itself as more or less communautaire. The idea that to criticise a Commission proposal is in some sense to show disrespect for the European idea can be dismissed at once, since it amounts to little less than saying that the Community is so fragile that it has to settle for the second best. But the manner in which the criticism is couched is very important and it has on occasion been couched ineptly. Detailed and constructive criticism of legislation can indeed

303

appear to be very negative, and is certainly a less glamorous task than initiating legislation. It is a task that nevertheless has to be performed and that will be seen to be of increasing importance as the rush to adopt new Directives matures into a concentration on the practical implementation of what has already been agreed. By all accounts - and since meetings take place behind closed doors it is difficult for outsiders to be sure - the refining of proposals is a field in which the British have played a prominent part, with British officals coming well briefed to meetings and making an effort to relate what is proposed to what is possible rather than just to what is desirable on paper. Certainly the public record bears out the British insistence that Community legislation should be practicable, and many instances of numbers being changed on British insistence and procedures made more flexible have been recorded in Part Two of this book.

With certain Directives there has been significant British influence in the sense that Britain refused to agree them unless radical changes were made. The Directive dealing with discharges to water of dangerous substances (Section 7.8) is the best known, and the incorporation of an alternative to limit values set centrally at Community level is a British 'contribution' to Community policy, though not one that the other Member States and the Commission ever welcomed. The significant change to the titanium dioxide Directive (Section 7.11) was also insisted upon by Britain. This painful period of disagreement and the resulting compromises have slowed down the adoption of subsequent daughter Directives dealing with individual dangerous substances, and for this Britain undoubtedly carries the blame in the eyes of the Commission and other Member States. On the other hand, since real issues of policy are at stake which cannot be hidden, the conflict could yet stimulate the necessary thought which will eventually result in a less one-dimensional and more robust water pollution policy in the Community. One of the lessons that can be drawn from the history of British water pollution policy, as outlined in Chapter 5, is that the subject is sufficiently complicated for there to be no one simple solution. Community policy which does not recognise this is bound to be unsuccessful. Some suggestions in this field are made in Appendix 4.

The modifications to Commission proposals made within the Council and its working groups are made behind closed doors, but a public element is nevertheless provided by the European Parliament, and also by national parliaments. While the Committees that prepare the European Parliament's draft resolutions do their work in private, the debates of the Parliament are public affairs. Although several national parliaments also make a practice of considering Commission proposals, nowhere is this done so systematically, so openly, and so thoroughly as in Britain. The key feature of the scrutiny procedures adopted, particularly by the House of Lords' Select Committee on the European Communities, is the public questioning of witnesses including government officials. The style is one of short questions and answers rather than long speeches, with the result that significant points of difficulty from various viewpoints are pursued and quickly pinned down. The fact that both oral and written evidence is usually published with a House of Lords' report gives it a value considerably greater than the conclusions alone, since the process is revealed and public discussion of issues helps to clarify them. The House of Lords' reports have a reputation in the Commission and in other countries, partly because of their qualities and partly because there is nothing like them. Despite their national frame of reference, they must be regarded as an important contribution to the process of Community policy-making. The Commons also consider Community proposals, but with notable exceptions the reports are more summary.

One point that has frequently been expressed in Britain, not least in parliamentary reports, has been the lack of adequate scientific and economic considerations in the preparation of Directives. This continuing insistence on rigour is no doubt expressed in other countries, but certainly can be said to constitute a British contribution.

Implementation - the final possibility for influence that we have identified - has been the theme of this book, but without a comparison with other countries only provisional comments can be made about the extent to which Britain has shown its commitment to the Community by taking its legislation seriously. Unlike several Member States, Britain has not been taken before the Court over formal compliance, despite partial failures of compliance with some waste Directives and also with some water Directives as a result of the long delay in bringing into force part of the Control of Pollution Act (see Chapter 14). That delay can fairly be regarded as showing a certain lack of commitment. Although practical compliance has occasionally been lukewarm, as in the case of the bathing water Directive (Section 7.7), all Directives have been given attention by the appropriate authorities. There is no case comparable to the German decision for the time being to designate no shellfish waters (Section 7.6) and thus to render a Directive totally inoperative in that country while formally complying with it. Even the waste oil Directive (Section 8.4) - probably the most neglected in Britain - has been implemented in part. There is no case where Britain has been significantly later than many other Member States in submitting reports to the Commission, and in the case of the waste Directives it has been among the first to do so.

CHAPTER 17
Prospects

The evidence to substantiate the assertion with which we opened this book is now complete. Whether, when seen from a national viewpoint, the benefits have been worth the pains is a matter for judgement, but it is beyond dispute that membership of the Community has come to change the way an important part of British environmental policy is now thought about, is enunciated, and ultimately is even put into practice. Ten years after embarking on its environmental policy, the Community is hardly in a confident condition, so that attempts to look forward are as uncertain as they ever have been. Environmental policy will not of itself restore the Community to health, but it does provide a persuasive argument why the Community needs to ensure that its remarkable machinery remains effective. At the same time it provides the Community with a quality in rather short supply. Environmental policy has demonstrated the Community's ability to adapt to new found concerns and to tackle problems of considerable and continuing public interest in all Member States that cannot be tackled at the level of the nation state alone. It has demonstrated that the Community is capable of being very much more than a forum for the arbitration of conflicting economic interests and has forced it to open itself to a larger range of interest groups. Many more people now understand better how the Community works as a result of their interest in the environment and environmental policy.

It must now be the case that environmental policy is assured of a place within the Commission - something which could not have been said with confidence a few years ago - and the Member States by their interest have ensured that this is so. Community environmental policy, then, is a fact of life, and for Britain there are two prospects. There is a continuing need to assimilate what has already been established - the acquis communautaire - and to contribute and consider new proposals. The Community for its part will continue to introduce new legislation but will also have to develop in two directions, one of which has been well recognised while the other hardly at all. These can be sumarised by the catch phrases 'integration' and 'implementation'. Together with 'assimilation' and 'new proposals', these provide headings under which to order thoughts about the future.

Assimilation

In the Chapter on chemicals we saw British policy and Community policy being formed virtually simultaneously so that the problem of accommodating Community ideas within a pre-existing national system has hardly arisen. This does not mean that problems of adaptation will not arise but there is no long history to impede the process. It is different with water and air, and to some extent waste. In the field of water, for example, the British government has hardly begun to recognise that the compromise agreement reached over discharges of dangerous substances must be viewed as provisional. It was only by unanimous voting that the compromise was agreed and continues to be held in place, and unanimous voting may well disappear as the Community develops. The Directive in which the compromise is embodied is also flawed by inconsistencies and hardly provides a solid basis for Community policy in this field (see Appendix 4). Mere prudence, if nothing else, suggests that the British government and British industry should be attempting to stimulate discussion in the Community to find a more lasting solution. The retreat behind the argument that the British 'line' represents time-honoured British practice cannot be regarded as the last word even if it were to be correct, and Chapter 5 has shown how far from the case that is. It is quite possible that there will have to be movement in this field despite recent agreement on a first batch of daughter Directives.

The reconciliation of air quality standards with the policy of uniform emission standards implicit in 'best practicable means' has already been recognised as a task by the Industrial Air Pollution Inspectorate and is implicit in the government's declared intention of reviewing air pollution legislation. The fact that there is now considerable pressure for new Community legislation in the air pollution field only reinforces the need for a more coherent British air pollution policy.

Integration

When agreeing the third Action Programme on the Environment the Council made a declaration that the integration of the environmental dimension into other policies must be regarded as of high priority. This simple sounding statement represents a considerable challenge for the Directorate-General for the Environment. Up till now its proposals have hardly touched the other Directorates-General of the Commission, whatever problems they may have caused in the Member States. The new departure entailed in this declaration means that environmental policy will cease to be a fairly self-contained activity within the Commission and the Directorate-General for the Environment will have to involve itself much more in the work of the others. This may well be seen as interference by those responsible for, say, agriculture, transport and energy policy, and anyone with experience of bureaucracies knows what that entails. The Directorate-General for the Environment is no doubt glad to have the backing of the Council for a task that has caused difficulties in all countries - backing that it will continue to need as conflicts develop. A Community environmental policy which does not have much to say about the Common Agricultural Policy is bound ultimately to be regarded as of secondary significance.

Implementation

The fact that national and Community policies, though distinct, cannot now be considered separately has been a theme of this book. When discussing only one country these interconnections can be handled with some ease or this book would not have been possible. When discussing the whole

Community, on the other hand, it becomes so difficult that it is hardly attempted. The result is the flatness that characterises descriptions of Community policy. An explanation of the words in a legal text needs to be related to what practitioners do, and to be expressed in the language of those who do it, before they acquire life; without that they remain mere words and, in the case of Community legislation, words that are disconcertingly different from those used in any country for the reason that they have to have the same meaning in all. The difficulty in bringing Community policy to life is the difficulty in understanding what happens in several countries simultaneously and ensures that the attempt is hardly made. Because the attempt is not made there is a strong temptation to believe that the words in the text represent some kind of reality. To break out of this condition will need many more published studies showing how national and Community policies interlink, and more comparisons of how Directives are actually implemented in practice in all the Member States. This can be done by governments, by the Commission, or by bodies independent of both. For this to be possible there will have to be access to compliance notices. It will also require greater direct communication between practitioners in different countries, a process that national governments and the Commission can facilitate without necessarily themselves acting as channels for that communication.

New Proposals

Some proposals already on the table will extend the Community's environmental policy significantly. One requires an environmental assessment to be made before approval is granted for certain development projects, and another would formalise the provisions of Community finance for the environment (1). The British government's early opposition to the environmental assessment proposal on the grounds that existing British town and country planning procedures were adequate is a text book example of an inability to rise above a purely national viewpoint (2). Fortunately that view was modified, but not till Britain had largely lost its claim to having something substantial to contribute. Britain, which has in its public inquiry procedures the means for assessing environmental effects as good or better than any in Europe (3), failed to see that the proposed Directive would go some way to bringing practices in other countries up to its own standards. The British reaction to the proposal for Community finance for the environment has been much more positive - perhaps surprisingly given the government's general position on the financing of the Community.

To speculate on what new proposals may come forward over the next ten years lies outside the scope of this book, but one development points to the importance now being attached to the Community. The motive force for the bulk of the legislation agreed so far has come from the Commission, even if the ideas originated in one or other Member State. Now several proposals are being developed at the instigation of Member States themselves. The Commission has, for example, been invited to come forward with proposals for unleaded petrol by Britain, strongly supported by some other countries, and the proposed notification scheme for transfrontier shipment of hazardous waste was pressed for by several countries including Britain (4). Most important of all has been a German initiative on air pollution which in

1983 brought environmental matters to a meeting of Heads of State and Government for the first time since 1972. Having for a long time offered passive resistance to international efforts to control transfrontier air pollution as a means of combatting acid rain, the Federal Republic of Germany has suddenly taken a lead on the issue following the discovery of extensive damage to its forests. The consequent proposals that the Commission is now developing for substantial reductions in air pollution could yet move the Community's environmental policy onto a new plane. They will also vividly demonstrate the link between environmental policy and resources policy (in this case between air pollution and forestry) which is a theme of the third Action Programme on the Environment. The environmental issues at stake here are important, but as the problems of apportioning the substantial costs between the Member States are extremely tricky (5) solutions are unlikely to come quickly. If a Community environmental policy had not been put into place over the last ten years it would have been necessary to do so now just to handle this issue alone.

References

(1) Caren Levy, **Towards a European Community Environment Fund,** Institute for European Environmental Policy, 1983

(2) Nigel Haigh, **The EEC Directive on Environmental Assessment of Development Projects,** Journal of Planning and Environment Law, September 1983

(3) Richard Macrory and Martine Lafontaine, **Public Inquiry and Enquête Publique,** Environmental Data Services Ltd, 1982

(4) House of Lords Select Committee on the European Communities, **Transfrontier Shipment of Hazardous Waste,** Ninth Report, Session 1983-84, HMSO, 1983

(5) Konrad von Moltke, **Further Initiatives in Air Pollution Control in the European Communities,** Institute for European Environmental Policy, 1983.

APPENDIX 1

Terminology in the Directives

Different words are sometimes used to describe the same tool for pollution control, and sometimes the same words are used to describe different tools. In an attempt to clarify the terminology, the First Action Programme included an Annex of definitions, and it is thoroughly to be regretted that Directives have sometimes departed from these agreed definitions.

Among the terms defined in that Annex are 'quality objectives' and 'environmental quality standards' and a distinction is drawn between them.

The '**quality objective**' of an environment is defined as referring to "the set of requirements which must be fulfilled at a given time now or in the future, by a given environment or part thereof". '**Environmental quality standards**' are defined as standards "which, with legally binding force, prescribe the levels of pollution or nuisance not to be exceeded in a given environment or part thereof".

The definition of 'quality objective' does not say it is legally binding: it appears to be something to be striven towards and eventually attained and that is the sense in which the River Quality Objectives set by the British water authorities are understood. 'Environmental quality standards', on the other hand, are, under the Community's definition, legally binding. They are not goals which despite the best of intentions we may fail to achieve: the law can be invoked if they are not respected.

Unfortunately, the distinction has not been adhered to. Directive 76/464 (Section 7.8) refers to 'quality objectives' when 'quality standards' are intended. In the daughter Directive on mercury (see Section 7.10) the words 'quality objective' are also used and from the context are intended to be regarded as legally binding, so that the words 'quality standard' should have been used. A certain amount of caution is therefore needed when using the terms. When British water authorities talk about setting consent conditions for discharges so as to meet River Quality Objectives (RQOs), they may not mean quite the same thing as the daughter Directives of Directive 76/464 which requires emission standards to be set by reference to quality objectives.

Yet further meanings have been given to the two terms, which are not necessarily inconsistent with the First Action Programme's definitions. Environmental Quality Objectives (EQOs) are sometimes thought of as statements in words of the uses to which an environment is to be put, e.g., to support salmon or for drinking water supply. Environmental Quality Standards (EQS) can then be expressed numerically (e.g., so many parts per million of specified pollutants in water, sediments or fish flesh) such that the EQO is achieved.

Although the term '**emission standards**' is defined in the First Action Programme as "levels for pollutants or nuisances not to be exceeded in emissions from fixed installations", the term has been used in subsequent Directives in conjunction with the term '**limit values**', which is nowhere defined in the First Action Programme. Both terms are sometimes used together, e.g., Directive 76/464 talks about "limit values which the emission standards must not exceed" which is comprehensible enough, but sometimes 'limit values' is used alone, e.g., 'A proposal for a Council Direcive on the limit values applicable to discharges of mercury...' (Section 7.10) where the words 'emission standards' are implied. The term 'uniform emission standards' is never used in the Action Programmes or Directives.

The usage now seems to be that 'emission standards' are what are set by the authorities in the Member States and must never exceed the 'limit values' set by the Council in Directives (if the limit value approach is being followed). To use the term 'uniform emission standards' to describe the pollution control tool found in Community Directives is therefore incorrect since even where a 'limit value' has been set it is always open to Member States (or water authorities within them) to set emission standards more stringent than the 'limit values'. In other words, 'limit values' do not require 'emission standards' to be uniform but only set an outer bound which they may not exceed.

The term 'limit value' is also sometimes used to set an outer bound for a 'quality standard', e.g., Council Directive 80/779 (Section 9.2) 'on air quality limit values and guide values for sulphur dioxide and suspended particulates'.

Sometimes the term **'emission standard'** is contrasted with **'immission standard'**, the latter meaning the quality standard of the environment receiving the emission. 'Immission standard', though clear enough when written, can cause confusion when spoken. It is rarely used in English although it is used in German. It is not used in either the English or the German text of the Directives.

It must be remembered that the Community is sovereign in its use of language and the United Kingdom has no special say in how Directives are expressed in English, just as Italy has no special say in the use of Italian. If this were otherwise, the Community would have an impossible task in reconciling the special meanings that words may have acquired in particular circumstances or institutions of different countries (e.g., the term 'best practicable means' translated into French would not necessarily carry the same meaning to a Frenchman as in English it does to the Industrial Air Pollution Inspectorate). Hence it is normal for words to have different meanings in Community documents from purely national documents. There is, however, no reason why words cannot be used consistently throughout closely connected items of Community legislation.

APPENDIX 2

Community Legislation not Described in Part Two and Proposals Awaiting Decision

A. LEGISLATION AGREED (1.11.83)

1.	Cadmium discharges	Directive	83/513	L291	24.10.83
2.	Marketing and use of asbestos	"	83/478	L263	24.09.83
3.	Import of seal skins	"	82/129	L91	9.04.83
4.	Protecting workers from asbestos	"	83/477	L263	24.09.83
5.	Protecting workers from lead	"	82/605	L247	23.08.82
6.	Protecting workers from exposure to chemical, physical and biological agents	"	80/1107	L327	3.12.80
7.	Paints, varnishes, inks, glues - classification, packaging and labelling	"	77/728	L303	28.11.77
	Amendment	"	83/265	L147	6.06.83
8.	Solvents - classification, packaging and labelling	"	73/173	L187	1.07.73
	Amendment	"	80/781	L229	30.08.80
	Amendment	"	82/473	L213	21.07.82
9.	Protection from radiation	76/579/Euratom		L187	12.07.76
	Amendment	80/836/ "		L246	17.09.80
10.	Exchange of information on air pollution (sulphur, suspended particulates, metals, NO_x, CO, ozone) (supersedes Decision 75/441, L194, 25.07.75)	Decision	82/459	L210	19.07.82
11.	Information system on pollution by oil discharged at sea	"	81/971	L355	10.12.81
12.	Exchange of information on the quality of surface water	"	77/795	L334	24.12.77

This list of environmental legislation excludes any dealing with international conventions and with purely administrative decisions such as those appointing advisory committees or authorising research programmes. Directives concerned with food law harmonisation, animal feedingstuffs, fertilisers, and materials and articles intended to come into contact with foodstuffs have also been excluded.

B. PROPOSALS AWAITING DECISION BY THE COUNCIL (1.11.83)

Water

1.	Pollution from wood pulp mills	COM(74)2256	C99	2.05.75
2.	Discharges of aldrin, dieldrin and endrin	COM(79)243	C146	12.06.79
3.	Mercury discharges (sources other than the chlor-alkali industry)	COM(82)838	C20	25.01.83
4.	Titanium dioxide waste	COM(83)189	C138	26.05.83
5.	Discharges of lindane	COM(83)422	C215	11.08.83
6.	Oil spills at sea		C273	12.10.83

Waste

1.	Dumping at sea	COM(75)688	C40	20.02.76
2.	Beverage containers	COM(81)187	C204	13.08.81
3.	Sewage sludge in agriculture	COM(82)527	C264	8.10.82
4.	Transfrontier shipment of hazardous waste	COM(82)892	C53	25.02.83

Air

1.	Air pollution from industrial plants	COM(83)173	C134	27.05.83
2.	Air quality standards for nitrogen dioxide		C258	27.09.83

Wildlife and Countryside

1.	Forestry measures	COM(74)170	C44	19.04.74
2.	" "	COM(78)621		
3.	Forest fires and acid rain	COM(83)375	C187	13.07.83
4.	Endangered species (CITES)		C272	11.10.83

Noise

1.	Construction plant and equipment (framework Directive)	COM(74)2195	C82	14.04.75
Proposed daughter Directives:				
1.1	Concrete breakers and jackhammers	COM(74)2195	C82	14.04.75
1.2	Generators for power supply	COM(75)558	C54	8.03.76